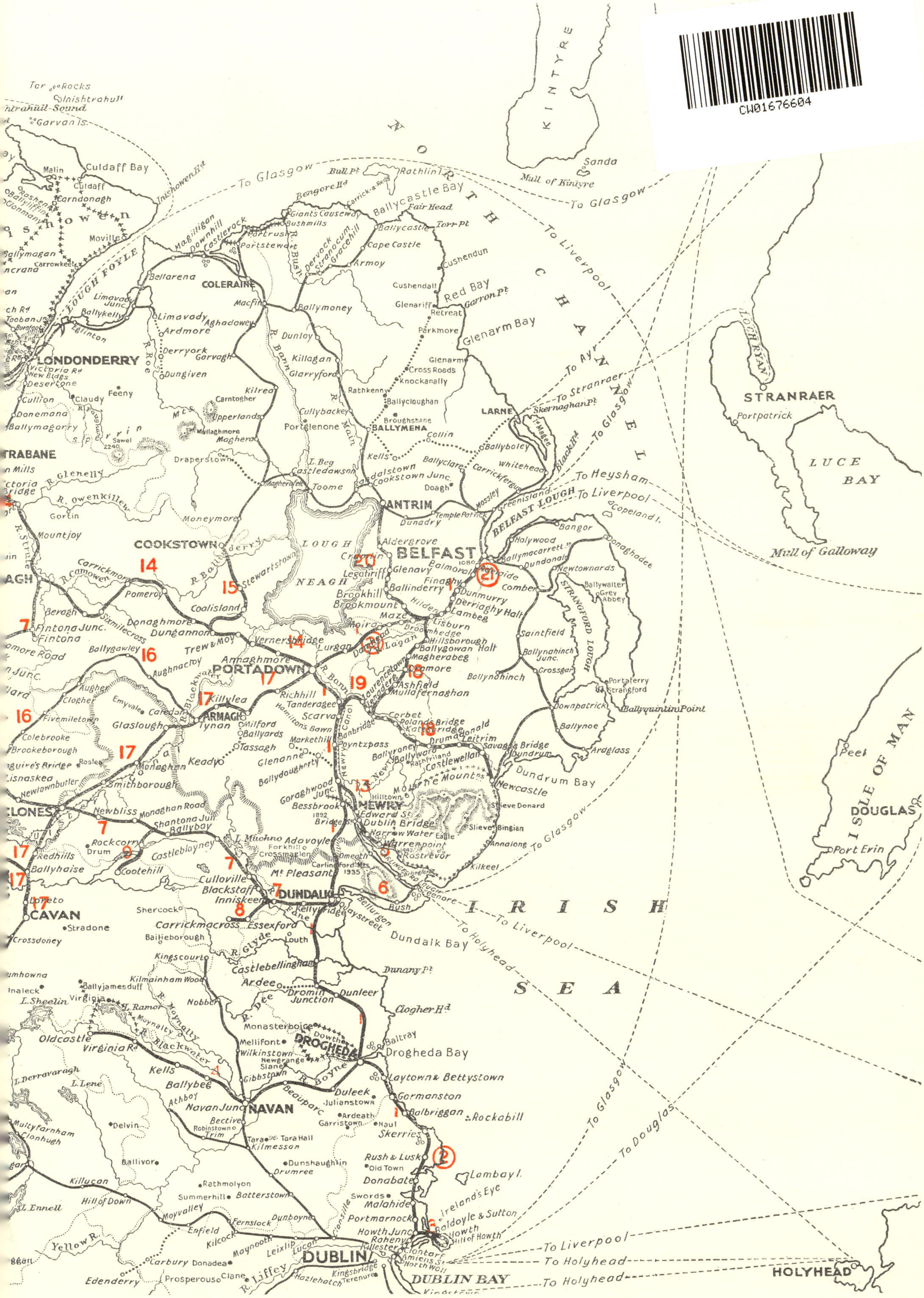

NORTH CHANNEL
IRISH SEA
KINTYRE
Sanda
Mull of Kintyre
To Glasgow
To Liverpool
To Ayr
To Stranraer
To Heysham
To Holyhead
To Douglas
LOCH RYAN
STRANRAER
Portpatrick
LUCE BAY
Mull of Galloway
ISLE OF MAN
Peel
DOUGLAS
Port Erin
HOLYHEAD
Tor Rocks
Inishtrahull
Garvan Is.
Malin
Culdaff Bay
Culdaff
Carndonagh
Inishowen Hd
Moville
Buncrana
LOUGH FOYLE
Rathlin I.
Bull Pt
Bengore Hd
Ballycastle Bay
Fair Head
Torr Pt
Giants Causeway
Bushmills
Portrush
Portstewart
Castlerock
Downhill
Magilligan
Bellarena
COLERAINE
Ballycastle
Cape Castle
Armoy
Cushendun
Cushendall
Red Bay
Garron Pt
Glenariff
Retreat
Parkmore
Glenarm Bay
Glenarm
Cross Roads
Knockanally
Ballymoney
Macfin
Aghadowey
Dunloy
Killagan
Glarryford
Limavady
Limavady Junc.
Ballykelly
Eglinton
Ardmore
Derryork
Dungiven
Garvagh
Kilrea
LONDONDERRY
Victoria Rd
New Bldgs
Desertone
Cullion
Claudy
Feeny
Donemana
Ballymagorry
Carntogher
Upperlands
Sawel 2240
Maghera
Cullybackey
Portglenone
Rathkenny
Ballycloughan
Broughshane
BALLYMENA
Kells
Collin
LARNE
Ballyboley
Ballyclare
Whitehead
Carrickfergus
Greenisland
Mossley
BELFAST LOUGH
Copeland I.
Bangor
Holywood
Donaghadee
STRABANE
R. Glenelly
R. Owenkillew
Gortin
Mountjoy
Draperstown
Magherafelt
L. Beg
Castledawson
Toome
Randalstown
Cookstown Junc.
Doagh
ANTRIM
Templepatrick
Dunadry
Moneymore
COOKSTOWN
Stewartstown
Coalisland
Pomeroy
Carrickmore
Aldergrove
LOUGH NEAGH
Crumlin
Glenavy
Ballinderry
BELFAST
Balmoral
Finaghy
Dunmurry
Derriaghy Halt
Lambeg
Knockagh
Ballymacarrett Jn
Dundonald
Comber
Newtownards
Ballywalter
Greyabbey
STRANGFORD LOUGH
Saintfield
Ballynahinch Junc.
Ballynahinch
Crossgar
Portaferry
Strangford
Ballyquintin Point
Downpatrick
Ballynoe
Ardglass
Brookhill
Brookmount
Hilden
Maze
Moira
Lisburn
Broomhedge
Hillsborough
Ballygowan Halt
Magherabeg
Dromore
Ashfield
Mullafernaghan
Lurgan
R. Lagan
Fintona Junc.
Fintona
Sixmilecross
Beragh
Donaghmore
Dungannon
Trew & Moy
Vernersbridge
Ballygawley
Aughnacloy
Annaghmore
PORTADOWN
Richhill
Tanderagee
Scarva
Killylea
ARMAGH
Tynan
Caledon
Emyvale
Glaslough
Fivemiletown
Colebrooke
Brookeborough
Maguire's Bridge
Lisnaskea
Newtownbutler
Rosslea
Monaghan
Smithborough
Keady
Milford
Ballyards
Tassagh
Glenanne
Markethill
Poyntzpass
Banbridge
Corbet
Katesbridge
Drumadonald
Leitrim
Savage Bridge
Dundrum
Dundrum Bay
Newcastle
Castlewellan
Ballyroney
Ballyward
Rathfriland
Mourne Mountains
Slieve Donard
Slieve Bingian
Annalong
Kilkeel
Hilltown
NEWRY
Edward St
Dublin Bridge
Bessbrook
Goraghwood Junc.
Ballydougherty
CLONES
Newbliss
Monaghan Road
Shantona Jun
Ballybay
Rockcorry
Drum
Redhills
Ballyhaise
Castleblayney
Cootehill
Culloville
Blackstaff
Inniskeen
Crossmaglen
Forkhill
Adavoyle
Mt Pleasant
Narrow Water
Warrenpoint
Rostrevor
Omeath
Carlingford Mts 1935
Greenore
Bush
DUNDALK
Kellybridge
Haystreet
Bellurgan
Dundalk Bay
Loreto
CAVAN
Stradone
Crossdoney
Shercock
Carrickmacross
Essexford
Bailieborough
R. Glyde
Louth
Kingscourt
Castlebellingham
Dunany Pt
Ballyjamesduff
Kilmainham Wood
Virginia
L. Sheelin
L. Ramor
Nobber
Ardee
Dromin Junction
Dunleer
Clogher Hd
Oldcastle
Virginia Rd
R. Blackwater
Monasterboice
Mellifont
Wilkinstown
Dowth
Newgrange
Slane
DROGHEDA
Baltray
Drogheda Bay
L. Derravaragh
L. Lene
Kells
Ballybeg
Athboy
Navan Junc.
NAVAN
Gibbstown
R. Boyne
Beauparc
Duleek
Julianstown
Laytown & Bettystown
Gormanston
Balbriggan
Rockabill
Bective
Robinstown
Trim
Ardeath
Garristown
Naul
Skerries
Delvin
Multyfarnham
Clonhugh
Tara
Tara Hall
Kilmessan
Rush & Lusk
Old Town
Lambay I.
Ballivor
Dunshaughlin
Drumree
Donabate
Killucan
Rathmolyon
Hill of Down
Summerhill
Batterstown
Swords
Malahide
Ireland's Eye
L. Ennell
Moyvalley
Fernslock
Dunboyne
Portmarnock
Baldoyle & Sutton
Enfield
Kilcock
Maynooth
Howth Junc.
Howth
Hill of Howth
Raheny
Yellow R.
Leixlip
Lucan
Killester
Clontarf
Carbury
Donadea
DUBLIN
Amiens St
North Wall
Edenderry
Prosperous
Clane
R. Liffey
Kingsbridge
Hazlehatch
Terenure
DUBLIN BAY

Great Northern Railway of Ireland Road Motor Services 1925-1958

by

Sam Simpson

ISBN 978 1 90530409 7

Preserved AEC Regent III fleet No. 438 photographed at Howth demense.

Front cover
There were only three places in the world where double-deck buses operated across land frontiers requiring customs examination and two of these were in Ireland, one of which was a GNR service. AEC Regent No. 438 (ZH 3937), which is now preserved by the National Transport Museum of Ireland at Howth, is seen here at Carrickarnan on the route between Dundalk and Newry *(MC)*

Rear cover
GNR Gardner No. 390 is also preserved and is seen here at Broadstone immediately after restoration. (MC)

The crest of the Great Northern Railway underwent a subtle change after 1953 when the word 'Board' was substituted for the word 'Ireland'. The final garter style is seen here. *(SS)*

A History of the

Great Northern Railway of Ireland Road Motor Services 1925-1958

. . . a Mysterious &

Enigmatic tale . . .

Venture *publications*

Contents

Introduction

The Road Motor Services of the Great Northern Railway of Ireland, to bestow upon it the full title of this uniquely well managed department of the Railway, was the model to which all other railways in Ireland aspired when it came to operating buses and lorries. The attention to detail in every facet of its operations was legendary. GNR activities were made all the more problematical due to the inter-territorial nature of its operations on both sides of the border. The setbacks suffered by the company were considerable down through the years, yet there was one abiding strength which kept things going – that of the people, the greatest asset the company had. I recall travelling on many former GNR vehicles in CIE days such as Gardners, AEC Regal IIIs and IVs as well as the Regent double-deckers. Most of my travels on these ex-GNR vehicles were in counties Louth Monaghan and Cavan as a boy whilst at school in Armagh in the 'sixties and early 'seventies. People such as George Howden, Dick Meredith, Joe Mackle, Bobby Pelissier, Albert Switzer, Johnny Owens and James Lockhart, to name but a few, stand out as the great men of vision who gave this company an enviable reputation and kept it alive for so long despite great adversity.

The doyen of Irish transport enthusiasts Michael Corcoran writing in Buses Illustrated magazine over 35 years ago described the GNR in the following terms:–

'At an ever-quickening rate the seemingly immutable institutions and permanent at the time when one's world was young disappear and few transport enthusiasts can have regretted the trend as much as those of us in Ireland who saw the extinction of the Great Northern Railway (Ireland).

Regarded by many railway people as the living epitome of the best in pre-1914 railway operation, extant into the second half of the twentieth century, the undertaking was no less magnetic to the student of buses. This was the mysterious and enigmatic company whose 160 strong fleet of blue and cream vehicles were varied almost to the point of unit distinctiveness, yet uniformly elegant.'

The many former employees to whom I have spoken with over the past few years have echoed this description of the Great Northern time and time again. It was for me a personal privilege to meet the men and women of the GNR in the course of my research. It was always my intention to write this volume some ten years ago when there were more former GNR employees still alive with whom I could obtain first hand accounts of significant events. Unfortunately this was not possible. I found a window of opportunity during 1998 to start serious research and started this process in Ireland during March of that year. During my research I met with many wonderful people in all parts of the former GNR territory even those who were never employees of the company; all fondly recalled the blue and cream buses. Those I met recounted friendly staff immaculate buses both inside and out and the family atmosphere that pervaded every facet of the company's operations.

Everyone that I met who worked on the GNR spoke in very affectionate terms about their time with the company. They talked about times of high morale a family atmosphere, where everybody knew each other on first name terms, irrespective of rank or status. On a couple of occasions whilst in conversation with past GNR men emotion got the better of them when they were recalling those halcyon days. It was with a tear in their eye that they recounted just how it used to be. A big thanks to all the people who have helped and encouraged me with this enterprise. Particular thanks go to Michael Corcoran, founding President of the Transport Museum Society of Ireland. The small band of dedicated enthusiasts at Howth has saved so much of Ireland's transport history for future generations. I trust that those generations will support the Museum at Howth.

I would like to make special mention of two people who, without their assistance, this work would not be as complete as I would have wished or desired; I acknowledge their willingness to give of their time and energy.

Cyril McIntyre kindly allowed me to consult the GNR archive held by Bus Éireann. If it were not for the foresight of Cyril a number of years ago when he saved many official documents from being burned, this book would not have been as comprehensive as I would have wanted, or transport history would have demanded. Geoff Lumb of Huddersfield, a lifelong enthusiast who has specialised in two particular subjects; that of the Karrier Company who produced buses, lorries and trolleybuses in his native Yorkshire town, and Irish bus and rail operations. He has amassed an unrivalled collection of artifacts and knowledge and was a prodigious photographer of Irish subjects, many of which are used in this book. The transport history of Ireland owes them both a great debt.

Grateful thanks also go to Liam Kelly, Des McGlynn, Gerry McAuley, Joe Robinson, Gary Manahan, Albert, Catherine and Leonard Switzer, Monica Lindsay, Val Owens, Geoffrey Hilditch, Christopher G Hilditch, Davy Byrne and his colleagues in Drogheda Fire Brigade, Peter Waller, Vic Nutton, Pauline Watkis, Robert Grieves, Gordon Barron, Steve Brady, Eugene Field, Marcus Bailie-Gage, Charles Meredith, Brendan Pender, Clifton Flewitt and sadly the late Paddy Mallon, Charlie Martin and Bryan Boyle, Alan Pritchard of the British Commerical Vehicle Museum and the Venture Team, Bob, John and Mark. Most importantly I want to thank my wife Joan for putting up with me whilst I wrote this.

I apologise if I have omitted to mention anyone by name.

Sam Simpson
October 2008

Explanatory Notes

Abbreviations

ACV	Associated Commercial Vehicles
AEC	Associated Equipment Company
ASLE&F	Associated Society of Locomotive Engineers & Firemen
BCT	Belfast Corporation Transport
B&I	British & Irish Steamship Company
B&CDR	Belfast & County Down Railway
BOC	Belfast Omnibus Company
CDRJC	County Donegal Railway Joint Committee
CIE	*Córas Iompair Éireann*
DUTC	Dublin United Tramway (later Transport) Company
DNGR	Dundalk Newry & Greenore Railway
GNR I	Great Northern Railway of Ireland (1877-1953)
GNRB	Great Northern Railway Board (1953-58)
GOC	General Omnibus Company
GSR	Great Southern Railways
IOC	Irish Omnibus Company
IFS	Irish Free State
IRA	Irish Republican Army
L&LSR	Londonderry and Lough Swilly Railway
LMS (NCC)	London Midland Scottish Northern Counties Committee
LNER	London & North Eastern Railway
NI	Northern Ireland
NIRTB	Northern Ireland Road Transport Board
NUR	National Union of Railwaymen
PRV	Park Royal Vehicles
RASC	Royal Army Service Corps
RUC	Royal Ulster Constabulary
SLNCR	Sligo Leitrim Northern Counties Railway
SMW	Service Motor Works
TD	*Teachta Dala*
TMSI	Transport Museum Society of Ireland
UTA	Ulster Transport Authority

Irish Language

Bord na Móna	Irish Peat Board
Ceilidhe	Traditional Irish social dance
Córas Iompair Éireann	Ireland's transport company
Cumann na nGaedheal	Irish political party (led by WT Cosgrove 1922-33) later became *Fine Gael*
Dail Éireann	Lower House of Irish Parliament
Fianna Fail	Irish political party (led by Éamonn de Valera 1932-37)
Garda (pl *Gardai*)	Civic Guard (police) – the official title is *Garda Siochana*
Oireachtas	Legislative bi-cameral Parliament
Saorstát Éireann	Irish Free State (1922-37)
Seanad Éireann	Senate Upper House of Irish Parliament
Sinn Féin	Irish political party, founded in 1905 by Arthur Griffith
Taoiseach	Irish Prime Minister. Prior to 1937 this office holder was known as the President of the Executive Council
Teachta Dala	Member of Parliament

Currency

Both the United Kingdom and Ireland adopted a decimal currency system on 15th February 1971. Traditional units are used throughout this book and it is felt no useful purpose would be served in showing present-day equivalents. Prior to this date each £1 was divided into 20 shillings (s) and each shilling into 12 pence (d). One shilling (1s) was the equivalent of 5p and one penny (1d) the equivalent of 0.416p

Today's £1.60p would therefore be shown as £1 12s 0d, a contemporary method of displaying prices which is utilised throughout this book.

The effect of inflation does however make comparison of prices very difficult. For example, a daily newspaper which cost 1d in 1930 had increased to around 3d in 1960 and is today around 45p, equating to roughly a 100-fold increase. Many other commodities showed comparable increases.

Time

All references to time in the book are in the 12 hour system, *ie* 8.00pm as opposed to the 24 hour system of 20:00

Photo Credits

AEC	AEC - British Commercial Vehicle Museum
AM	Alan Mortimer
AS	Albert Switzer Collection
CM	Charles Meredith Collection
CMc	Cyril McIntyre Collection
DN	Official GNR(I) Photo by Duffners Dundalk
GL	Geoff Lumb Collection
JAS	John A Senior
JG	John Gillham
LM	Leyland Motors - British Commercial Vehicle Mus.
MC	Michael Corcoran Collection
ML	Monica Lindsay Collection
RB	Roy Brook
RG	Robert Grieves Collection
RP	Bobby Pellissier Collection
SS	Sam Simpson Collection
VN	Vic Nutton
WM	William Montgomery Collection

Chapter One
Railway to Busway

Inevitably the history of the Great Northern Railway of Ireland (GNRI) Road Motor Services is inextricably linked to that of the Railway itself. Logically therefore many references in this work will of necessity mention events which would be considered railway matters, although a significant number of these had a bearing on the Road Motor Services. The Great Northern Railway was the largest, most prosperous and certainly the most innovative and enterprising of any Irish Railway Company. Its formation took place on 1st April 1876 following amalgamation of various railway companies. On 1st March 1875 the Dublin and Drogheda Company and the Dublin and Belfast Company joined forces to form the Northern Railway Company. The Irish North Western Company joined together with the Ulster Railway Company and others to form the Great Northern Railway Company. The formation of the GNR saw the introduction of the heraldic device (which adorned most rolling stock) quartered the arms of Dublin, three burning castles, top left; Londonderry (the badge of the City of London), on which is superimposed an Irish Harp, and below which the skeleton of Sir Cahir O'Doherty sits on the ruins of his castle, in which he was starved to death – top right. Enniskillen, a three-tower castle, bottom left, Belfast a sailing ship – bottom right. In the centre of the device is a shield carrying the Red Hand of Ulster. In 1897 the GNR promoted the Hill of Howth tramway

The Great Northern Railway Board Shield as applied to vehicles from 1953 until 1958. *(GL)*

Bill in Parliament which system eventually opened in 1901 and could really be said to mark a change in railway attitudes with its stated objective to encourage suburban and tourist traffic in the northern part of the Irish Capital. Unfortunately the Hill of Howth tram was never profitable and its history was punctuated by frequent attempts by the Board of the GNR to close it, despite the building of residential homes close to its line out on the Hill.

The GNR acquired a half share in the County Donegal Railway on 1st May 1906 in partnership with the English Midland Railway, which had a few years before bought the Belfast and Northern Counties Railway. The County Donegal Railway then became known as the 'Joint Committee', its management reporting to both companies. For 77 years the GNR enjoyed absolute independence until the Northern Ireland and Irish Republic Governments compulsorily acquired it jointly on 1st September 1953. Under this joint authority the Company became known as the Great Northern Railway Board (GNRB) until its dissolution on 1st October 1958, when the Company and its Railway assets were divided between the Ulster Transport Authority in Northern Ireland and *Córas Iompair Éireann* in the Irish Republic.

At the turn of the twentieth century road transport was being taken more seriously as improvements in the design and construction of lorries and buses became apparent. Competition from the omnibus posed a serious threat to the viability of the railway companies even in Ireland during the early part of the twentieth century. On 3rd June 1900 the first regular scheduled omnibus service in Ireland began when the Enniscrone and Ballina Motor Car Company began operating four trips each daily between Ballina and Enniscrone and this was quickly increased to seven trips. In the Ireland of the period railway companies were looking to the bus and lorry to perform a complementary role to that of the railway. In fact the Belfast and Northern Counties Railway commenced an omnibus service between Greenisland Station and Whiteabbey on 1st April 1902 and was the first railway company in the British Isles to do so. In later years the B&NCR's successor the LMS (NCC) developed a substantial bus operation, which at its peak numbered about 130 vehicles, until it was nationalised in 1935. Even the severely undercapitalised Belfast & County Down Railway started running a bus service, linking its railway at Newcastle with the busy fishing town of Kilkeel on 1st August 1916, using a contractor called Norton. By 1935 they were running 14 buses and 8 lorries and would have developed this further had the necessary finances been available. The Great Southern Railways, formed in 1924 through the amalgamation of the Dublin and South Eastern Railway, the Great Southern and Western Railway and the Midland Great Western Railway, inherited very limited road operating powers from its main constituents. The first two merely authorised road services between hotels and local tourist sites, whilst the last provided for the company to run coaches or lorries for the carriage of parcels, passengers and goods connecting with or in extension of the railway system. As early as June 1924 the GSR began operating its own road motor coaches in the County Kerry tourist region under its own name, providing an onward road link from important railheads where significant traffic existed during the summer months from: –

- Sligo-Bundoran-Ballyshannon
- Clifden-Mulrany
- Macroom-Glengarrif
- Kenmare-Parknasilla
- Killarney-Kenmare-Glengarrif-Bantry

Immediately after the First World War many independent motorbus operators took to the roads in Ireland, just as they did in Britain. In a wholly unregulated market it was a free for all with small motor buses racing each other from stop to stop to beat off the competition, which could just as easily have been another bus or a tram. In Ireland they became known as 'independents' or more commonly 'pirates', as many attained a bad reputation for running unsafe vehicles, scurrying around the streets and roads in a cavalier manner. The vehicles often carried trademarks or names and were usually 20-seaters or smaller. In the 1920s such exotic names as the Gladiator, Contemptible, Magnet, Pirate, Lone Star, Cosy, Chieftain, Tonic, Master McGrath and Viking Auto existed just to make life that little bit more interesting. On 17th April 1919 a company called the Clondalkin Motor Omnibus Company was formed, to initiate a bus service from the Inchicore Tram Terminus of the Dublin United Tramways Company out to Clondalkin Village, thus exploiting a passenger demand. On 10th November 1926 an Altrincham entrepreneur, Frederick Thomas Wood, armed with experience of running buses in Cheshire, bought the Clondalkin undertaking. Wood later turned out to be a highly controversial figure after he had formed a business called the Irish Omnibus Company (IOC), on 18th December 1926, to effect the takeover of the Clondalkin.

Under Wood the IOC expanded rapidly following an agreement of June 1927, approved by the IOC Board on 15th June, under which the IOC would operate on behalf of the GSR bus services for which the GSR obtained approval under the Railways (Road Motor) Act 1927. The agreement became effective from July 1927. The IOC gradually acquired its principal competitors from 1928 onwards. At the same time, difficulties arose between the IOC and the GSR over the agreement; mainly in relation to the operation by the IOC of services other than those covered by the GSR contract. Protracted and acrimonious wrangling ensued; of which the outcome was the acquisition of the IOC by GSR nominees through a 'vehicle' called the United Irish Investment Company. Thus the IOC effectively became a subsidiary of the GSR from 13th June 1929. FT Wood and the other original Directors resigned from the Board and were replaced by GSR people. On 22nd November 1933 it was agreed that the IOC would be wound up voluntarily and it became the Omnibus Department of the Great Southern Railway on and from 1st January 1934.

Whilst all of this road service activity was going on around them the shrewd traffic managers and railway mechanical engineers of the Great Northern were devising and planning their strategies. The Irish Civil War and the partition of Ireland posed significant problems for the GNR, which found itself cast in the role of an international railway forced to operate in two jurisdictions. During the Civil War Republican irregulars of the IRA kidnapped the GNR's General Manager, John Bagwell, who was also a *Cumann na nGaedheal* nominated member of the Irish Free State Senate. On the evening of Tuesday 30th January 1923 Bagwell was abducted by armed men from his Hill of Howth residence in front of his wife. The ordeal ended on the morning of Thursday 1st February when the vigilance of his captors was relaxed and Bagwell managed to climb through an open window over a wall, and into a field. Crawling along a hedgerow for some distance, he made it cross-country until he reached the Ashbourne Road close to the village of Swords. He hailed a passing motorist who took him the eight miles to Dublin where he presented himself to the authorities. The Government had earlier declared that it would execute IRA irregulars held in custody if Bagwell was not released within 48 hours. Bagwell, unhurt during his ordeal, immediately repaired to his Kildare Street club where he was visited by the President of the Executive Council and head of government WT Cosgrave, who immediately

An IOC Leyland PLSC pictured in Lancashire before delivery to Ireland, where it would have possibly been in competition with the GNR on the Navan Service. *(LM : LM 4099)*

Irish Free State Senator John Bagwell, the departing General Manager of the Great Northern Railway of Ireland *(SS)*

Jonathan Barton Stephens, the new General Manager of the Great Northern Railway of Ireland from July 1926. *(SS)*

arranged for Bagwell to have an armed guard at all times until the end of the civil war. The civil war ended in May 1923, after which the GNR set about concentrating on the development of the business. In July 1924 John Bagwell submitted a report to the Board, which recommended a strategy of meeting road competition by reducing long-distance railway passenger fares. Following a period of three months deliberation a decision was finally reached. At the Board meeting in Belfast on 2nd September 1924 it was decided not to reduce railway fares. Bagwell was instructed to return to the Board with a more comprehensive policy to deal with passenger and goods transport by road and establish how the Company should protect its interests. He had disappointed some on the Board with his unimaginative policies to deal with the threat of road competition and his single-track approach of offering passengers limited fare decreases and discounted season ticket rates. An impatient GNR Chairman, Sir George Clark Bt, favoured a more proactive approach, possibly occasioned by his good contacts with the Northern Ireland government who were at the time considering a legislative change. Contemporary speculation opined that the government would introduce some regulation into the market at the same time providing opportunities for railway companies to compete more effectively. The GNR quickly recognised that buses were for certain journeys (railway feeder services), the most convenient means of transport, especially as many GNR railway stations were located quite a distance from the town they purported to serve.

It was resolved at a Board meeting in Belfast on 28th April 1925 to adopt a strategy of contracting local operators to provide feeder bus services in certain areas. Contractors had to be used because the railway companies possessed limited powers to operate road services at that time. Bagwell's policy of selective reductions in passenger fares was also agreed upon in conjunction with an approach to the Northern Ireland Government, where road competition was at its most damaging to railway revenues. The first of the railway fares initiatives was agreed at the Board meeting in Belfast on 22nd December 1925, when Belfast suburban fares as far as Lurgan were slashed. The 'Belfast Bus War' began a short time afterwards as a direct result of the passing of the 1926 Motor Vehicles (Traffic & Regulation) NI Act. Ironically this measure was designed to assist the railway companies. It removed the licensing powers from local to central government, who promptly opened the floodgates to all comers, causing widespread chaos in the Northern Ireland Capital until an agreement which put an end to the free for all was reached between the parties concerned in November 1928. The GNR sent a delegation to meet Sir Dawson Bates, the Northern Ireland Home Affairs Minister, on 25th March 1926 to ask for road motor operating powers for the railways as part of the 1926 Act on equitable terms. The railway companies, some of whom were loss making, had to operate as licensed by the Railways Acts and were forced to charge according to railway tariffs, which penalised companies and were very difficult to vary in favour of the railway companies themselves. On 24th February 1926 the GNR Board meeting in Belfast were being asked by Bagwell to consider the substitution of buses in lieu of the Hill of Howth Trams because of mounting losses. The fact that the GNR didn't have any bus running powers, let alone any buses, at that stage ensured that the proposal was deferred.

Bagwell packs his bags

John Bagwell announced his intention to retire as General Manager effective from 30th June 1926. He had served the GNR in this capacity since 1911 when he in turn succeeded Henry Plews. His successor was Jonathan Barton Stephens of Holywood County Down, who was educated at the Corrig School, Kingstown (Dun Laoghaire). He had been a Civil Engineering Apprentice from 1885-1890 under the tutelage of the Belfast City Surveyor JC Bretland. Stephens joined the GNR as a junior assistant in the Civil Engineers department in 1890. At the turn of the 20th Century he was appointed assistant to John Bagwell and in April 1919 combined the role with that of Company Secretary. While attached to that department Stephens gained Parliamentary experience in connection with the GN Railway (I) Acts of 1892 and 1897 authorising the construction of the Ardee Branch line and the Hill Of Howth electric tramway respectively. He took up his appointment on 1st July 1926 at a salary of £2,000 per year and was at the time living at Rathruadh, Glenageary, County Dublin. As a result of the Stephens appointment a new Company Secretary, Mr Frank Campbell Wallace, formerly Stephens's Chief Clerk, was engaged on a salary of £800 per year thus permitting Stephens to concentrate on the General Manager's role. Jonathan Stephens immediately injected new energy into the running of the GNR, quickly moving a hand picked team of officials into key positions. WA Foster Graham was appointed to Stephens' former position as Chief Clerk to the General Manager on a salary of £375 per year. Stephens reorganised the Traffic Department at the end of 1926, retiring three elderly officials. Mr WJ Baillie was appointed to the Belfast based position of Traffic Manager from 1st October on a salary of £1,250 and Mr WJF Horne was appointed to the Dublin based position of District Superintendent (effectively the Traffic Manager's representative) at Amiens Street, Dublin on an annual salary of £650. Stephens' other priority was to establish another review of the Company's strategy to combat ever increasing road competition. On 24th September 1926 the GNR Board meeting at the Great Northern Hotel in Rostrevor Co Down decided to introduce a further reduction in passenger fares and season ticket rates in Northern Ireland. At a Board meeting in Belfast five months later on 16th February 1927 the GNR now faced the prospect of a potentially damaging direct bus service between Belfast and Dublin. The Board responded by slashing the Belfast/Dublin fares and those of intermediate stations where road competition was at its most intense.

The GNR Board, now feeling increasingly squeezed by road competition, decided to take a political course in conjunction with the Great Southern Railway. Sir George Clark, exploiting his exceptional Unionist Party credentials, led a GNR Board delegation on 13th May 1927 to meet with the Northern Ireland Prime Minister, James Craig (then recently ennobled as Viscount Craigavon on 20th January 1927), as a follow up to the earlier meeting with Dawson Bates. Sir George made a strong case for a change in legislation allowing the railway companies to compete on a level playing field against road transport operators. The Board of the GNR met their GSR counterparts who were similarly being pressured by road competition within the Irish Free State. As a result of that meeting the GSR officials agreed to invoke their political contacts with the government in Dublin to lobby for a similar change of legislation within its territory.

The combined efforts of the GNR and GSR resulted in a spectacular success. Jointly they had managed to persuade the two governments to act together. This resulted in the Irish Free State government enacting the Railways (Road Motor Services) Act of 27th May 1927. The Northern Ireland government passed the Railways (Road Vehicles) Act 17&18 on 31st May 1927. Both legislative Acts in their respective territories enabled railway companies to provide, own, maintain and run Road Motor Services. Both governments recognised the disadvantage the railway companies found themselves in, and by acting simultaneously proved the benefits of co-operation.

Having prevailed in the Civil War the *Cumann na nGaedheal* government was a deeply conservative one, characterised by following contemporary British policy rather than pursuing a revolutionary programme. It relied upon Protestant (and by implication Irish Unionist) money to keep it going. Two of its main financiers were Mr Henry Guinness, Governor of the Bank of Ireland, and Mr Andrew Jameson, a wealthy financier. Both men were nominated to serve in the Irish Free State Seanad. Its Northern counterpart, similarly conservative and outwardly pro-British, was not going to pursue a radical approach in anything it did for the simple reason that it relied on the British Treasury subvention for its continued existence. In a bizarre way both governments probably had more in common with each other than either would care to admit at the time.

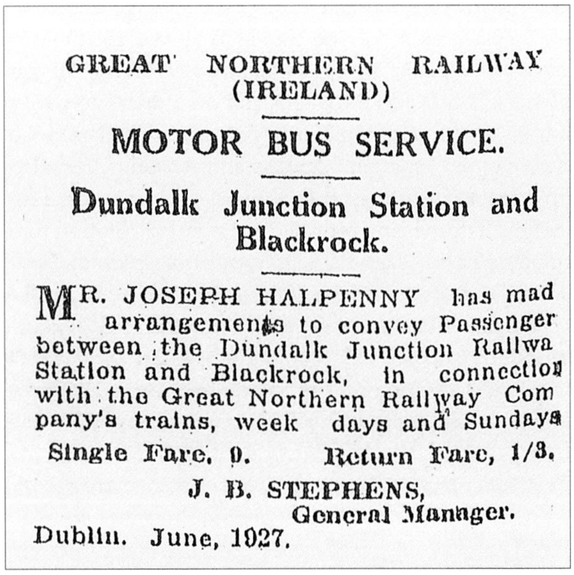

GREAT NORTHERN RAILWAY
(IRELAND)

MOTOR BUS SERVICE.

Dundalk Junction Station and Blackrock.

MR. JOSEPH HALPENNY has mad arrangements to convey Passenger between the Dundalk Junction Railwa Station and Blackrock, in connectio with the Great Northern Railway Com pany's trains, week days and Sundays

Single Fare, 0. Return Fare, 1/3.

J. B. STEPHENS,
General Manager.

Dublin. June, 1927.

An early example of the press announcements made by GNR following the securing of what would today be called a feeder service to the railway. *(GL)*

Contractors to the GNR

Earlier on, while the serious politics were taking place at Board level, the first bus contractor to be appointed in terms of Board policy, designed to circumvent the prohibition on railway companies running buses, was Hugh McAnulty of Church Street, Warrenpoint who was paid £50 per annum to run a connecting bus from Warrenpoint Railway Station to the Great Northern's Hotel at nearby Rostrevor. The bus was introduced on 19th May 1925, just in time for the summer season. McAnulty continued to operate this service on behalf of the GNR until 31st December 1935. On 15th April 1930 the GNR purchased a 14-seater bus for McAnulty, who agreed repayment terms in return for the operation of a Mourne Mountains Circular Tour. The Mourne Circular, as this popular tour was called, connected with the GNR Railway at Warrenpoint then to Newcastle by the scenic coastal road and back to Warrenpoint again for return rail connections. The GNR entered into another financial and contractual agreement with Ernest McDonnell of Virginia County Cavan on 27th November 1926. They purchased a new 14-seat bus for McDonnell to run a railway feeder service between Virginia Road Station and Kilnaleck. Repayment terms were agreed and such was the success of this venture that a further service was introduced between Virginia Road Station/ Virginia Town and Ballyjamesduff for an annual subsidy of £260 4s 9d and this arrangement persisted until May 1932. Skerries, County Dublin was next to benefit from the GNR's contractual relationships with local operators to provide railway feeder services. The Pratt Brothers of Skerries began working a bus between Skerries Railway Station and the town, a distance of about one mile, in February 1927. They charged a fare of 2d and were guaranteed a minimum of £10 of revenue a week by the GNR, irrespective of loadings. This arrangement continued until 1st July 1929 when the GNR bought out Pratts to run the service themselves. The Karrier CX type bus inherited from the Pratts, for which the GNR paid £100, was converted into a Garage Tender in October 1929 at a cost of an additional £80 and was used from Dublin Garage.

Portadown was a busy County Armagh town well served by the GN Railway. It was, however, unfortunate that the Railway Station was situated at Watson Street, in the Edenderry area, and just over half a mile distant from the town centre and entailed a brisk walk to get there. Back in July 1922 a local taxi operator called James Grew had agreed to pay the GNR an annual rental of £52 a year for the use of a car stand outside the railway station. In 1927 the GNR bought

A Commer bus loading passengers at Garristown for Dublin *(GL)*

Grew a 14-seat Morris T bus, contracting him to operate it between the railway station and the town, connecting to and from principal trains until May 1931, when they bought him out. John Murray had been running his bus from Lusk and Rush GNR Station to Rush Village for some time without subsidy. In September 1926 he approached the GNR, asking for £53 to effect repairs to his bus in order that the service might continue. Terms were agreed between Murray and the Company. Payment was made to him by the GNR on 22nd September. Murray later formalised his agreement with the GNR to provide his service under subsidy as from 9th February 1927. This agreement was short lived, passing to another man called Michael Jones in December. Jones charged a fare of 3d per passenger with a GNR guarantee of £10 per week under terms similar to that pertaining with the Pratt Brothers at Skerries. In early February 1928 the GNR bought a 14-seat Morris bus with bodywork by the Dublin firm of Potters to enable Jones to operate the service on their behalf.

Jones continued under contract until he too was bought out on Thursday 21st February 1935, following which he was employed as a Motorman performing the same service, this time in full-time employment with the GNR. The GNR roster for working this service called for the first six weekday workings to be performed by buses from Dublin Garage. Subsequent workings by Motorman Jones, now based at Rush, entailed him working from 10.40am until 11.00pm with a boy porter acting as conductor. An 11 hour 20 minute day was not uncommon in that era but would not be permitted in this day and age.

Charles McAllister from Beaverstown, Donabate was another GNR contractor providing a bus service between Portrane Asylum and Donabate Railway Station. The 2d fare charged attracted a subsidy of 1.75d per mile from the GNR who in turn received subvention from Dublin Corporation, owners of the asylum. McAllister's Morris bus was bought by the GNR for £460, the cost of which was repaid on the instalment system over a number of years. On 3rd January 1933 the McAllister bus failed, due to a damaged radiator, which leaked coolant, causing the engine to overheat resulting in a piston seizure. A substitute GNR bus was dispatched from Dublin Garage to work the service while McAllister's bus was undergoing repairs. The McAllister bus resumed its workings on Saturday 7th January but the writing was on the wall for it as the GNR bought out McAllister on Monday 1st January 1934.

As far back as June 1908 the GNR promoted the 'Boyne Valley Tour' from Dublin Amiens Street Station. Tourists could catch the 9.00am train to Drogheda, where they were met by a charabanc, taken to the Boyne River, where they boarded a steam launch for a trip to Slane and Navan. Alternatively a trip to Melifont Abbey and Monasterboice was offered by charabanc before being returned to Drogheda Station for the rail journey back to Dublin. A Drogheda bus operator, Charles M Markey, ran local bus services under the name 'BAM Bus Company' and came to the attention of the GNR, who contracted him to work the road portion of the combined road/rail 'Boyne Valley Tour' during Wednesdays and Saturdays in the summer of 1928. The BAM bus met tourists at Drogheda Station and followed the prescribed route taking in the Vale of the Boyne, Baltray, Monasterboice, Melifont Abbey, Slane, Navan, Newgrange and Dowth before returning them back to Drogheda Railway station for the train journey back home to their starting point. The contract was not renewed in 1929, as by this time the GNR had its own buses, which were used on this most popular of tours. In Dundalk the GNR entered into an arrangement with Joseph Halpenny of the Violet Bus Service for a bus connection with principal trains between Dundalk Junction Railway Station and Blackrock effective from Saturday 18th June 1927. Meanwhile Jonathan Stephens decided to apply in terms of the new Railways (Road Motor Services) Act for authority to operate a bus service between the GNR's Dublin Amiens Street terminus, across the Carlisle Bridge, fording the River Liffey on O'Connell Street to St Stephens Green. The objective was to provide an onward link with the burgeoning commercial district south of the river. Permission was denied, largely as a result of objections by Dublin Corporation, who did not want large numbers of buses crossing the Carlisle Bridge. The GNR did manage to obtain permission in January 1930 to operate a bus service from the main line arrival platform at Amiens Street Station (which had road access) to Eden Quay in connection with the 7.50 and 8.25am trains from Drogheda. Reverse workings in the evening from Eden Quay connected with the 5.15pm Malahide train and the 5.30pm train to Dundalk. This link was maintained until wartime emergency restrictions ended it on Monday 16th June 1941.

Yet another special GNR Board meeting was convened to discuss the question of Road Motor competition on 26th September 1928 in Dublin, at which the Stephens report commissioned two years previously was presented. This document, dated 12th September 1928, contained an analysis of where and what competition was adversely affecting railway revenues and recommended 'the establishment of a distinctive department of the Railway to operate its own buses and lorries to be known as the Road Motor Services which would operate the railway bus service network and the Road Merchandise Service which would provide railhead and cartage services to the Railway'. Additionally the report recommended the acquisition of the bus companies listed in the table below:

Company Name	Services Worked
HMS Catherwood	Belfast/Dublin
International Bus Service	Belfast/Dublin
Fairways Limited	Dublin/Clones/Monaghan
Duffy's Bus	Dublin/Drogheda/Dundalk
Irish Omnibus Company	Dublin/Kells/Navan
Magnet Bus Service	Dublin/Cavan/Enniskillen
McDowells	Dublin/Castlepollard
Louth & Meath Omnibus Service	Dublin/Bailieborough
Pirate Bus Service	Dublin/Portrane
Dublin United Tramway's Omnibus Service	Dublin/Malahide, Dublin/Killester, Dublin/Swords
Excellence Bus Company	Dublin/Howth
Alliance Bus Company	Dublin/Howth
Grafton, Emerald, Contempible, International Bus Companies	Dublin/Howth
Garryowen Bus Company	Dublin/Portrane
Pratts Motor Service	Dublin/Skerries
Alliance, Reliable, Contempible, Pirate, Garryowen, Cosy, Mac Bus Companies	Dublin/Dollymount/Killester & Killester/Clontarf services

Leyland PLSC3 Leyland Lion ZI 2725 with 32-seat bodywork built by City Wheel Works Dublin, to a Leyland design, seen outside Amiens Street Station, Dublin in 1929. *(RG)*

The Board decided to establish a sub-committee to deal with Road Motor matters, which consisted of the following GNR Officials:–

Sir George Clark Bt (GNR Chairman)

Mr William Burton Carson (GNR Deputy Chairman)

Captain Alexander Ronald Stanley Nutting (GNR Board Member and Governor of the Bank of Ireland 1924-28)

Mr Jonathan Stephens (GNR General Manager)

The first decision reached by the sub-committee was to agree that a professional manager with Road Motor experience be recruited by the Company to run the new Road Motor Department. Early in October 1928 adverts appeared in the press for the position of Road Motor Superintendent. Approval was also given for the immediate purchase of three new 31-seat Leyland PLSC omnibuses, for use at Drogheda and elsewhere, at a total cost of £4,781, including Irish Free State import duty, from the Dublin based dealer Messrs Ashenhurst and Williams. The first new machine was a Leyland Lion PLSC1 with a Leyland 31-seat body costing £1593 13s 4d. Two further pioneering machines of the Leyland PLSC3 type were given 32-seat bodies by City Wheel Works of Pearse Street Dublin to a Leyland design. Interviews were held during the first week in December, following which a candidate was selected. At a Board meeting held in Belfast on 19th December 1928 the appointment of Mr Joseph Mackle was approved, effective from 1st January 1929, on a salary of £500 per annum. Joseph Mackle actually started work in his Dublin Office on 4th January 1929 as the first Road Motor Superintendent and was universally known as Joe. He was born in Portadown in 1897. Following his schooling there he became an engineering trainee with the Glasgow firm of Halley Industrial Motors, between 1912-15, during which time he was finally employed as an outdoor mechanical inspector. George Halley built lorries from about 1905 and was eventually taken over by the Ministry of Munitions in 1915 for war production. When this occurred Joe Mackle joined the Royal Berkshire Regiment, serving between 1915-1919 on the French, Belgian and Italian fronts as a Motor Transport Officer.

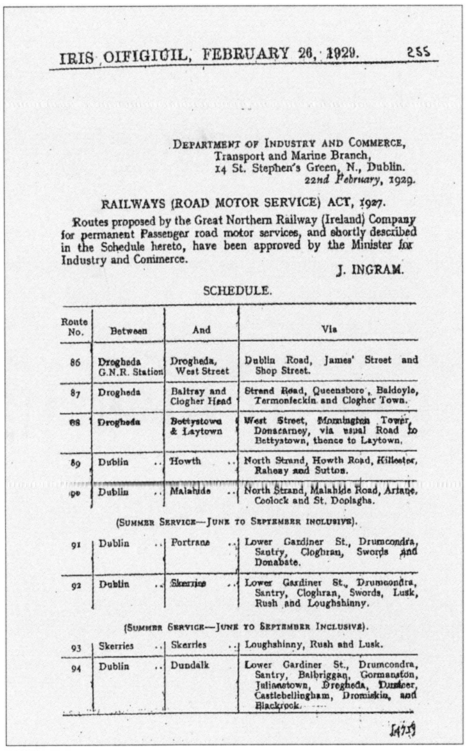
IRIS OIFIGIUIL, FEBRUARY 26, 1929. 255

DEPARTMENT OF INDUSTRY AND COMMERCE,
Transport and Marine Branch,
14 St. Stephen's Green, N., Dublin.
22nd February, 1929.

RAILWAYS (ROAD MOTOR SERVICE) ACT, 1927.

Routes proposed by the Great Northern Railway (Ireland) Company for permanent Passenger road motor services, and shortly described in the Schedule hereto, have been approved by the Minister for Industry and Commerce.

J. INGRAM.

SCHEDULE.

Route No.	Between	And	Via
86	Drogheda G.N.R. Station	Drogheda, West Street	Dublin Road, James' Street and Shop Street.
87	Drogheda	Baltray and Clogher Head	Strand Road, Queensboro', Baldoyle, Termonfeckin and Clogher Town.
88	Drogheda	Bettystown & Laytown	West Street, Mornington Tower, Donacarney, via usual Road to Bettystown, thence to Laytown.
89	Dublin ..	Howth ..	North Strand, Howth Road, Killester, Raheny and Sutton.
90	Dublin ..	Malahide ..	North Strand, Malahide Road, Artane, Coolock and St. Doolaghs.
(SUMMER SERVICE—JUNE TO SEPTEMBER INCLUSIVE).			
91	Dublin ..	Portrane ..	Lower Gardiner St., Drumcondra, Santry, Cloghran, Swords and Donabate.
92	Dublin ..	Skerries ..	Lower Gardiner St., Drumcondra, Santry, Cloghran, Swords, Lusk, Rush and Loughshinny.
(SUMMER SERVICE—JUNE TO SEPTEMBER INCLUSIVE).			
93	Skerries ..	Skerries ..	Loughshinny, Rush and Lusk.
94	Dublin ..	Dundalk	Lower Gardiner St., Drumcondra, Santry, Balbriggan, Gormanston, Julianstown, Drogheda, Dunleer, Castlebellingham, Dromiskin, and Blackrock.

[475]

As a result of the Railways (Road Motor Services) Act it was necessary for the Department of Industry and Commerce to publish appropriate schedules. *(GL)*

At the end of his wartime service Joe relocated to Belfast where he obtained employment with the local Leyland dealer Alister Kirk of Ballarat Street. Joe, exposed as he was to the Leyland product, developed a fondness for that marque which was to be evident in his later career. In 1926 he moved to join a new bus company called HMS Catherwood as its Chief Engineer, where he was instrumental in introducing many new Leyland buses. He was acknowledged as a highly successful Chief Engineer during his time with Catherwood, where he established most of the engineering and traffic management systems introduced by that firm.

Birth of the Road Motor Services

The plans were in place (well almost!) the staff recruited, the vehicles purchased and the route selected for the very first Road Motor Omnibus service operated by GNR staff with a GNR owned bus. Accordingly it pulled away from Drogheda Railway Station at 7.20am on Monday 28th January 1929. Appropriately the GNR's only bus, Leyland Lion fleet No. 1 performed the honours. A 31 year-old Motorman called O'Brien, who had been recruited only days previously, was at the wheel. O'Brien set off for the Post Office in West Street Drogheda, a distance of just over three quarters of a mile. The service was given the route number 86 by the Department of Industry and Commerce. Its introduction provided a welcome link between the town and the Railway Station, which is at the top of a hill on the Dublin Road. Such was the success of the service that it was quickly decided to extend it to Baltray Golf Links (often referred to in GNR documentation as the 19th Hole) and Clougherhead from 4th February, for which a single fare of 2d was charged this was given the route number 87 by the Ministry. This was introduced as a one person bus, with no Conductor on board and tickets were issued by the Motorman as appropriate, except at Drogheda Station where a boy porter issued tickets on the forecourt before the bus departed. The GNR's own bus replaced a bus operated on contract for some months previously by the BAM bus service that proved to be somewhat limited in accommodation and its reliability. Not everything went according to plan though, as Mackle discovered that the letter sent to the Department of Industry and Commerce requesting authority under the Railway (Road Motor Services) Act to operate the service had not been favoured with a reply. Technically therefore the GNR did not have in its possession at the time of commencement of the service the necessary authority to operate it. This was but a mere formality as the Minister could only refuse to give consent if the road motor service was being run by a 'railway company on a route substantially the same in whole or part as the route on which a road motor service for passengers is at the time of the submission run regularly by some person other than such railway company'. As this did not apply in

Joseph Mackle the first Road Motor Superintendent of the GNR(I). *(SS)*

this instance Mackle took the decision to proceed, given that all other aspects of the planned service were in place. The authority from the Department of Industry and Commerce was issued on 22nd February 1929, three weeks after the service started and over two weeks after the route had been extended, again without the necessary authority. In Joe Mackle's original submission to the Industry and Commerce Department he described the GNR bus livery in the following terms: dark blue body, white superstructure, gold lining, red lettering, illuminated roof sign 'GNR' showing white lettering on a blue background. Joe Mackle, ever quick to see an opportunity that would give the railway buses a unique advantage over the competition, correctly deduced it was ticketing.

In March 1929, return portions of bus tickets between Dublin and Dundalk and intermediate stops, now became available for return by train on the day of issue or the following day upon payment of a modest supplement. This was the first in a series of important ticketing, territorial agreements and purchases of independent bus operators that was to become central to the GNR's new strategy to develop the Road Motor Services, in line with the Stephens' proposals. The first of many takeovers of independents followed just days after the first GNR bus began running in Drogheda. Francis Duffy's Bus Service, with vehicles plying between Dublin and Dundalk was an obvious acquisition target. Duffy was paid £6,500 for four AEC buses. The acquisition of Duffy's Bus Service allowed the GNR to introduce an integrated Road/Rail timetable between Dublin and Dundalk and a pruning of the rail service. This model was adopted in respect of Rail/Road services between Dublin and Howth from 1st May 1929, followed by Dublin and Malahide (via the Coolock route and the Baldoyle route) and Belfast with Lurgan. For each coordinated service a timetable and fare card was issued showing the combined rail and bus times. Rail times were printed in black ink and bus times in red and a route diagram was also included. The Dublin based District Superintendent, Mr WJF Horne, who was nominally Joe Mackle's superior resigned on 20th March 1929, the result of continuing ill health. Much to Mackle's satisfaction his successor was John H Scott, on a salary of £550 per annum. Although Scott was a railwayman he was, however, an enthusiastic supporter of the Stephens' strategy of running buses and lorries. Future changes in the management hierarchy would not be so favourably received by Mackle. An event that was to have a profound effect on the personalities that would shape the future of the Company took place in March 1929. The Chief Civil Engineer, Freddie A Campion, announced his intention to retire aged 65 during May of that year after 20 years in the post and so the search for a replacement started.

George Bruce Howden – 20th Century Transport Colossus

George Bruce Howden took up the position of Chief Civil Engineer on 1st July 1929, some weeks after the retirement of Freddie Campion. Howden was to become one of the most authoritative figures on the Irish Transport scene of the 20th Century and would exert a profound influence on the future development of the railway company. Born in Naples in 1891, the son of a Scottish engineer, his early education was in Italy after which he attended a private boarding school in Scotland. He trained as a Civil Engineer under John Gray, District Engineer of the former North British Railway at Glasgow. Following extensive experience on constructional and maintenance work he was, towards the end of 1926, appointed District Engineer on the Border District of the Scottish Area of the London and North Eastern Railway, with headquarters in Carlisle. Two years later he became the Assistant Engineer, Scottish Area at Edinburgh, the post he left to take up his GNR duties. There is no doubt that Howden was attracted to the GNR by the very attractive salary of £1,400 per annum. Unlike many of the senior GNR officials he never lived in Dundalk, preferring the more refined surroundings of Proby Lodge, Dalkey where he lived for many years. Despite his early upbringing in Italy George Howden had a very distinctive Scots 'burr', always referring to himself as a Scotsman, with frequent trips there for holidays and for visiting relatives. Nonetheless he quickly became a highly committed, and as time wore, on an increasingly valued senior officer of the company.

On one famous occasion during the 1933 Railway Strike George Howden even had a live bomb thrown at him. It was Tuesday 7th March 1933, when a GNR petrol railcar, driven by Mr Charles H Slater, on which George Howden was travelling, together with Inspector Peter Allen of the GNR, was heading along the main line to examine storm damage between Dublin and Drogheda. As they approached Killester bridge a lorry was observed travelling over the bridge towards Malahide, the driver of which threw what they originally thought to be a stone out of the cab. They quickly discovered that the smoking object was in fact a bomb, which exploded on the line, derailing the rear wheels of the railcar. Fortunately no one in the party was injured. Two men were later apprehended and charged in the Dublin District Court.

As the year of 1929 came to an end the GNR had established its Road Motor Services, developing bus and lorry operations on an on-going programme, purchasing nine independent bus companies and entering territorial agreements with others. The railway bus and lorry was here to stay!

George Bruce Howden *(SS)*

Chapter Two
The Turbulent Thirties

It was not until 1935 that the GNR had developed an extensive network of services north of a line between Dublin and Sligo, which included the important high-density commuter services of Northeast Dublin and south of Belfast to Lurgan. In the rural Ireland (North and South) of the thirties the GNR Road Motor Services provided an indispensable mode of transport at cheaper fares than the railway. The GNR were not alone in developing high-density urban services in Ireland. The GSR operated these types of services principally in Cork City and to a lesser extent in Limerick and Galway.

The consolidation of the GNR's dominance in its operating territory was achieved firstly through challenging competition and secondly through important territorial and co-ordination agreements with the GSR/IOC and the DUTC which were actively encouraged by the Eire government.

Competition, Cartels and Carve Ups

Cavan Town was served by the Great Southern Railway from Dublin in the south and from Belfast via a northerly route run by the Great Northern Railway. The GSR owned the Railway station although the GNR leased part of it for their use. The railway was the sole provider of regular transport to Dublin until 1926, when bus competition arrived.

On 30th August 1926 Gordon's Motor Service commenced operating two daily services in each direction between Dublin and Cavan introducing special single and return fares of 7s 6d and 13s respectively, thereby providing a cheaper alternative to the GSR railway service. Contemporary accounts of the introduction of this service claimed that it was the first long-distance bus service to operate into Dublin from the rural areas. In June 1926 Francis Duffy of 67 North Lotts Dublin began a bus service from Shercock to Dublin via Bailieborough, Kells, Navan and Dunshaughlin, together with a Dundalk/Dublin service, to the annoyance of the GNR, as it was in direct opposition to its railway. Just to confuse matters to a greater degree another operator named Alexander McDowell, also based at 67 North Lotts trading as the Classic, began running to Dublin from Trim and Castlepollard in August 1926. It has been suggested that McDowell and Duffy were related in some way through marriage. The North Lotts area of Dublin is at the rear of the GPO and an ideal location for running buses from the City Centre. On 18th October 1926 Maurice Healy of Dublin Road Drogheda and Michael Sheridan of 'Ardcairn' Cabra Road, Dublin started a service from Carrickmacross to Dublin via Kingscourt, Nobber and Navan. Initially this ran via Dunshaughlin but was later altered to run via Kentstown and Ashbourne. Healy and Sheridan traded as the Louth and Meath Omnibus Company, although at the time no such Company was registered, and used the operating name 'Red Lion'. Francis Duffy had also at that time been operating a service from Dublin to Kells via Navan and Dunshaughlin under the name of Duffy's Bus Service (Tara) providing competition to the Louth & Meath. On 28th January 1927 Duffy, Healy and Sheridan agreed to amalgamate into the expanded Louth and Meath, which was formally incorporated on 4th February 1927, having offices at Watergate Street, Navan. On the same day a new service began from Kentstown to Ashbourne Road.

Both the GNR and GSR Railway companies lowered their fares in September 1926 as a direct result of omnibus competition. The GSR announced that the 3rd class fare from Dublin (Broadstone) to Navan was reduced to 4 shillings single whilst the GNR matched this fare. Then 1927 witnessed the arrival of Irish Omnibus Company bus services between Dublin/Navan/Kells; Dublin/Oldcastle; Dublin/Shercock and Dublin/Carrickmacross, increasing competition on all the major routes in the Cavan/Meath area. In an act designed to consolidate its position, the IOC bought part of the Louth and Meath operation for £6,274 *ie* the Shercock and Carrickmacross routes, together with three Leyland Lions and one AEC bus. The Dundalk route was not acquired but later passed to the GNR in 1929. Immediately after this purchase was complete the 'Contemptible' Omnibus Company under the ownership of Mrs Kathleen Gilbert started to run on the Dublin/Shercock and Carrickmacross services as a result of being squeezed out from some of her Dublin City and County routes. This was a short-lived enterprise resulting in her early withdrawal after which the IOC and the Magnet had the road to themselves.

The IOC, as the bus-operating arm of the Great Southern Railway, was determined to get the Magnet off the Cavan route. Concurrently the GNR threw a spanner in the works by applying for permission to operate a bus service between Sligo and Lough Derg, which elicited an immediate objection from the IOC and GSR to the Minister of Industry and Commerce, Patrick McGilligan. One could be forgiven for thinking 'what has an application by the GNR to operate a service in Sligo/Donegal got to do with bus services in the Cavan area?' The answer lies in Minister McGilligan's reply to the letter of objection from the IOC and GSR. Paddy McGilligan was a native of County Derry and was renowned for his plain speaking. In his response to the Great Southern Railways on 7th May 1929 he berated the GSR and IOC for engaging in wasteful competition with the GNR in the Cavan and Donegal areas. Minister McGilligan went on to suggest a pooling arrangement between the IOC and the GNR, who had just lodged their application to start a Dublin/Cavan omnibus service. The Directors of the IOC, reeling from Minister McGilligan's strident criticism of their opposition to the development of road motor services by the GNR, initiated discussions to obtain an agreement on the suggested pooling arrangements. The IOC made clear their rationale for entering such an arrangement was to drive the Magnet off the road. There was no sign of an early agreement between the two parties. An interesting feature of the GNR's dealings with the Ministry of Industry and Commerce at this time is that the Secretary to the Ministry was none other than the Hon. Gordon Campbell, who would himself join the Board of the GNR as Chairman between 1938 and 1952 as Lord Glenavy, following the death of his father. Many readers will recall with particular fondness the television personality Patrick Campbell, who for many years in the 1960s and 70s featured as a team leader on BBC TV's 'Call my Bluff' quiz show – he was the son of the Hon. Gordon Campbell.

The GNR entered the fray on Monday 2nd September 1929 using two AEC Reliance buses, numbers 24 and 30, one working from Cavan Garage and the other from Dublin, operating three trips in each direction daily. Authority to operate this service was granted by the Department of Industry and Commerce on 6th August 1929 and given route number 109. GNR and IOC officials again met on 1st October to discuss co-operation on the Dublin/Kells section. This meeting ended without agreement. The IOC was dismayed that the GNR should have started to operate buses from Dublin to Cavan; they regarded this corridor as the preserve of the GSR train and the IOC bus. By early 1930 the IOC had determined that they were going to go onto the Cavan route and that GNR's buses were taking rail passengers from the GSR. Discussions continued between the two companies in search of an accommodation. At the end of June 1930 Mackle and the GNR team reached agreement with the IOC for a pooling arrangement on the Dublin/Cavan/Shercock and Carrickmacross services for an initial period of one year. Soon after the IOC felt that the GNR was distinctly uncooperative on the ground, alleging that instead of competing against the 'Magnet' they were in fact chasing the IOC along the route. Joe Mackle responded by organising an anti-competition 'squad bus', introduced on Tuesday 1st July 1930, using an additional Leyland TS2 from Dublin Garage to sandwich the Magnet company's first up service and return back to Cavan, in conjunction with revised timings of the normal daily departures. A further GNR/IOC meeting to discuss co-ordination took place in Dublin during August, at which the IOC proposed to give up their Garristown services and reduce the Carrickmacross to Kingscourt route, if the GNR gave up their Cavan operations. It was suggested at that meeting that the level of unpleasantness between GNR/IOC staff had reached serious proportions with the allegation that IOC conductors were engaged in fare cutting on the Cavan road. The GNR went on to assert that IOC staff in Sligo were handing over Donegal passengers to Catherwood instead of the GNR. The IOC countered claiming they had evidence that GNR staff in Sligo were handing Dublin passengers to the Magnet. It was hardly surprising, given the tone of the discussions, that no agreement was reached. After six months operation of the IOC/GNR pooling arrangement it was discovered that the IOC lost £976 and the GNR losses amounted to £4,138. The IOC Directors realised their losses were entirely due to a very costly strike of platform staff from 1st May 1930 to the 20th July 1930, the effects of which continued until the end of that year. The IOC were not prepared to continue with the pooling arrangements, serving immediate notice of their intention to withdraw from it, at the same time proposing to the GNR that they should withdraw from the Cavan/Meath area, leaving the IOC a free hand to deal with the Magnet which the IOC would fight at its own expense. Trust had broken down between the GNR who now decided that they could not rely on the IOC to assist them to remove the Magnet. At the same time Minister McGilligan intervened again by suggesting that the GNR/GSR and the Dublin United Tramway Company should meet and agree to remove all competition from among them. The GNR and GSR could not agree as to the division of road operations in the Meath and Louth areas. The sticking point was that the GNR held the Cavan district within its territory or sphere of influence, while the GSR contended that the Cavan district was the most westerly section of the area that lay between their parallel lines Dublin to Kingscourt, and Dublin to Cavan, and that it was out of the question that they should concede this territory to the GNR. Deadlock ensued resulting in an appeal to the Minister for intervention.

By the middle of 1930 the GNR's railway services northwards from Cavan town were facing intense bus competition from the following operators: –

Operator Name	Route
Phair Brothers, Belturbet	Cavan/Enniskillen
McGirr Bus Service, Cavan	Cavan/Monaghan
Boyd's Omnibus Service Clones	Clones/Monaghan
Erne Bus Company, Enniskillen	Cootehill/Enniskillen/Bundoran
Nugent's Pioneer Bus Service, Keady, Co Armagh	Ballybay/Cavan; Cavan/Dundalk; Ballybay/Bailieborough

The GNR's chief troublemaker – the private bus, now served almost all major towns and villages in the Cavan/Monaghan area! The GNR responded to this attack on its revenue by introducing many new bus services of its own on 1st July 1930 in direct competition with the private operators. The GNR's Joe Mackle turned his attention towards adopting an alternative strategy to get the Magnet off the Dublin/Cavan road. He took the Great Northern into a ticket interavailability and co-ordinated timetable agreement with the Magnet, effective from 1st November 1931. Higher fares were introduced and return tickets were also made available on GNR 3rd class rail services. Additionally Mackle agreed a joint co-operative timetable between Dublin and Cavan passing through Navan and Kells. The joint GNR/Magnet timetable had been altered to conduct an intense war on the IOC in their opinion. The IOC was furious with Mackle and the GNR but did agree to continue the interavailable ticketing, which had first been agreed during the brief pooling arrangement. The IOC saw this as a way of keeping a dialogue open with the GNR, which might lead to a future friendly settlement. The IOC reacted immediately with a Dublin/Cavan service of its own which started on Wednesday 11th November 1931 that was timed to run in front of the joint GNR/Magnet service charging fares to meet the combined attack. The IOC hastily arranged for their buses to be garaged in Cavan at the premises of James

An AEC 426 35/50hp bus for Gordon's Motor Services, trading as the Magnet, which later became a GNR(I) Railbus. *(GL)*

Cullen & Sons in Mill Street for the sum of 10s 0d per week. Mackle's plan to rid the Cavan road of the Magnet came to fruition on the 15th December when its Dublin/Cavan and Cavan/Virginia Road services were bought by the GNR for £6,000 following agreement with the owners Matthew and Norman Morrow. The residual Magnet operations to Ballina, Westport and Sligo etc. were acquired by the IOC from 13th June 1932. Five poorly maintained buses were taken into GNR ownership, one of which, a 26-seat AEC was dispatched to Dundalk Works to have a broken chassis repaired; such was the diabolical condition of the Magnet buses.

Now that Mackle had driven the Magnet off the Cavan road his hand was strengthened in discussions with the IOC. He rapidly turned his attentions towards concluding an agreement for interavailability of bus tickets between Dublin and Cavan on GSR/GNR trains and IOC omnibuses. Mackle's big prize was to obtain GSR/IOC agreement on a territorial carve-up. The discussions started in early January 1932 between Robert D Griffith, General Manager of the IOC, James Lockhart, John H Scott and Joe Mackle of the GNR, to agree territorial delineation between the Irish Omnibus Company through its owners the Great Southern Railway. An agreement was reached, the terms of which were implemented on 1st February 1932 and provided *inter alia* for the following: –

- The establishment of a Louth/Meath and Meath/Cavan pool area for a period of 25 years
- within the pool areas the Dublin/Cavan and Dublin/Carrickmacross services became jointly operated, being described in the timetables as 'co-ordinated services'
- rationalisation of all fares within the pool areas
- on the Dublin/Cavan services a four-way interavailability would apply *ie* GSR, IOC, GNR rail and road
- on the Dublin/Carrickmacross services a three-way interavailability applied *ie* IOC and GNR rail and road
- all net revenues to be shared on a fifty-fifty division within the pool areas
- joint supervision of the co-ordinated services
- the IOC service between Dublin, Garristown and Naul although within GNR territory would continue to operate outside the pool arrangements
- the IOC would continue as they had since August 1931 to provide the GNR with facilities to garage a bus (7s 6d per week) and wash vehicles at 2s a time. Fuel would also be provided at the prevailing IOC prices.
- the IOC would continue to offer the GNR bus passengers facilities at their Aston's Quay Bus Office for the sum of £1 10s 0d per week
- the GNR would facilitate IOC omnibuses at their garages at the above rates
- the IOC would garage buses at Shercock (2), Carrickmacross (1), Garristown (1), Kells (1), and Cavan (1) to facilitate the operation of the co-ordinated services.

This agreement between the GNR/GSR and the IOC outlived the existence of the latter two companies and was continued by CIE up until the demise of the GNR. Some facts that have not been previously reported in relation to the Louth/Meath services came to light recently. By 1932 the new Road Transport Act was in place and this provided the first system of Road Service Licensing. As the GNR was now the longest serving operator on the Cavan Road it, not the IOC, was granted the licence under the new Act and from Monday 25th July 1932 the Great Northern were the sole providers of bus services on the Dublin/Cavan route for several weeks as the IOC had to withdraw temporarily. The increased commitments handed to the GNR caused some headaches for John Scott, the GNR's Dublin District Superintendent, who had to resort to hiring three buses from the GSR on 2nd August. The buses concerned were ZI 8752,

ZI 8755 and ZI 8757, two of which were used on the Skerries, Howth and Baldoyle services whilst the third was used on the Carrickmacross route.

Dublin United Tramways Company (1896) Limited

In line with the Eire government's policy, the GNR entered into discussions with the DUTC to protect its Dublin bus services and proposals for three pooled areas were tabled on 11th December 1928 as follows: –

1. All Howth branch rail traffic including the Hill of Howth Tram and the Dollymount/Howth DUTC tram and the joint (GNR/DUTC) Dublin/Howth bus service
2. Clontarf/Killester rail traffic and the DUTC Killester bus traffic
3. Malahide rail and bus traffic from Dublin.

GNR rail passengers were thus permitted to travel by tram or bus between Amiens Street Station and Sackville Street in a seamless ticketing arrangement providing a link with Central Dublin, which was a long held ambition. Protracted negotiations between the two companies took place during which period the GNR moved to consolidate their omnibus services in Northeast Dublin. The GNR were by now successfully marketing the Dublin/Howth corridor as a joint rail and road service on a single timetable card with rail departures in bold type. This initiative, which included integrated timetabling, won considerable business from the DUTC Tram as travellers took advantage of the GNR's attractive rail/road interavailability features.

A further act of consolidation designed to guard its territory occurred on 25th January 1929 as the GNR proposed the introduction of a bus service between Dublin and Howth routed through Fairview, Killester, Raheny and Sutton; the service commenced on 18th February 1929 despite DUTC objections. In anticipation of the GNR service starting up the DUTC introduced a highly competitive 6d return fare on the 6th January 1929 between Nelson's Pillar and Sutton, where the bulk of the traffic existed. The DUTC fought back dramatically by reducing all fares on the Howth services, season tickets were discounted to pre World War One rates on the Nelson's Pillar/Howth tram service to both Sutton and Howth from the 23rd February 1929. Undaunted GNR buses started running between Eden Quay and Malahide on 3rd June 1929 in competition with the DUTC bus. The GNR introduced a return fare of one shilling, which forced the DUTC to reduce their return from 1s 2d to 1s. Once again the GNR successfully employed the integrated rail/road service marketing technique on the Malahide services replicating the earlier improvements on the Howth road. The ruthless Joe Mackle sought to undercut the DUTC by selling books of fifty 6d single tickets at £1, which represented a 20% discount. The DUTC alleged that Mackle was pirating DUTC services by putting more buses on the road than permitted.

The war continued between the GNR and the Tramway Company and it was not until a draft agreement was prepared by officials from both companies on the 16th January 1931, that there appeared to be the basis of an agreement. Continuing negotiations resulted in a further revised draft presented to both parties on the 10th February 1931, which was based on the co-ordination of timetables and interavailability of return tickets as opposed to the pooling arrangement, which had featured in the earlier discussions. Final agreement to end the bus war was achieved on the 24th March 1931. GNR officials John H Scott and Joe Mackle met with Dublin United Chairman Dr William Lombard Murphy and Director James McCann to sign a three year deal from 1st March 1931 which provided for the following: –

An unidentified AEC Reliance passing Clontarf Station, *en route* to Dublin from Howth, in early 1930. *(MC)*

Co-ordinated timetables came into effect from 1st May 1931.

Return tickets issued as follows were available for the return either by DUTC or GNR:

- Malahide Rail and Bus
- Howth, Sutton Cross Rail Tram and Bus
- Black Banks on the Howth Road Tram and Bus

The implementation of the agreement was deferred until 1st June 1931, after which books of GNR contract tickets would no longer be sold. Additionally, from that date Baldoyle and Corr Bridge tram and bus tickets were added to the list. In all instances any difference between return fares had to be paid by passengers. The DUTC for its part agreed to discontinue selling season tickets on the Howth and Dollymount trams. During 1935/6 the GNR agreed by the exchange of correspondence with the DUTC, to permit Hill of Howth through ticket holders to return to Nelson's Pillar on the DUTC No. 31 tram service. Despite the DUTC/GNR agreement there were still moments of discord. The DUTC in a letter of 6th February 1934 to Jonathan Stephens of the GNR, complained that his company was 'pirating' on the Swords Road following the recent take over of the operations of the HMS Catherwood Company. The DUTC contended that the GNR was failing to provide the guaranteed three buses on the Malahide Sunday services, running only one while flooding the more lucrative Howth road with every bus they could get their hands on. However, DUTC/GNR relations did improve to the extent that by 30th April 1938 the DUTC agreed to discontinue monthly season tickets from 2nd May between Dublin, Swords and Lissenhall. Interavailability arrangements were extended as follows:

1. Howth – DUTC was credited with 6d in respect of the return portions of Rail and Omnibus tickets between Dublin and Howth, and 5d in respect of return portions of rail tickets between Dublin and Sutton Cross and Bus tickets between Dublin and Corr Bridge.
2. Malahide interavailability arrangements between rail and bus to be continued on the basis of crediting the bus with 6d out of the return rail fare of 1s and collecting an excess payment of 2d from each passenger.

Further discussions took place in May 1940 between Foster Graham, Chief Clerk to the GNR General Manager and JB Martin, the Passenger Services Manager of the DUTC, in a bid to establish the closest possible working relations between the two companies. Both undertakings held that there existed considerable scope for economies in expenditure by the elimination of wasteful mileage, coupled with the prospects of increased receipts, without impairing the efficiency of the services provided by the two companies, at the same time continuing to meet the requirements of the travelling public through a pooling arrangement. The discussions continued right up to March 1941 with additional impetus being provided by the acute fuel shortage. The DUTC, which was by now bizarrely abandoning trams as fast as Percy Reynolds could manage, changed its title to the Dublin United Transport Company. The two heavyweight figures from both administrations, George Howden, General Manager of the GNR and Percy Reynolds, his DUTC counterpart quickly concluded the following agreement:–

1. DUTC to have no further interest in the Howth route (a) beyond Killester and (b) beyond Dollymount, subject to the subsequent development of immediate suburban areas. The DUTC would discontinue its tram service (No. 31) to Howth from March 29th 1941.
2. GNR(I) to have no further interest in the main road bus service between Dublin and Malahide via Coolock, which ceased operation on the night of Saturday 5th April 1941. The following day the DUTC commenced operating an amended service on this route. The GNR also abandoned the bus service between Dublin, Portmarnock and Malahide (via The Bawn) from Saturday 5th. The following day the GNR commenced operating to Malahide via the new Coastal Road.
3. DUTC abandoned all rights they might have had to the operation of a bus service between Dublin and Malahide via the new Coast Road.
4. GNR(I) to be the sole provider of road passenger transport in the Sutton, Howth, Baldoyle, Hole-in-the-Wall, Portmarnock and Malahide (via Coast Road) area.
5. The DUTC would be the sole provider of road passenger transport between Dublin and Malahide via Coolock. (The existing Church service between Hole-in-the-Wall and Kinsealy would continue as a GNR operation).
6. The DUTC discontinued its Dublin to Portrane service in favour of the GNR service.
7. GNR to provide transport for 25 to 30 scholars who had previously travelled by DUTC tram between Sutton and Clontarf (Vernon Avenue) in the mornings with a reverse working in the afternoons.

The DUTC renewed the agreement annually, by written reaffirmation right up to the take over by CIE. The latter company continued to respect the agreement although it did not enter into any official correspondence on the matter.

Irish Free State Regulation

The GNR Chairman, Sir George Clark, deputy Chairman Mr William B Carson and Captain AR Stanley Nutting met with the Industry and Commerce Minister Paddy McGilligan on 7th August 1931, together with representatives of the IOC, GSR and DUTC to lobby the Minister to throw a lifeline to the railway companies and the Dublin Tramways in their fight with rampant road competition. In his forthcoming bill, which was about to be introduced to the *Dail*, Paddy McGilligan just managed to get it through the *Oireachtas* before the defeat in the election of 1932, of the Cumann na hGaedheal Government Act No. 2 of 1932, known as the Road Transport Act 1932 (still current today), which provided for a system of Road Service Licensing and repealed the earlier Railway (Road Motor Services) Act of 1927. The new law introduced three categories of licence on 25th July 1932:

1. Continuous – services operate on every week of the year but not necessarily on every day of every such week.
2. Occasional – service is provided on only one or more specified occasions.
3. Seasonal – services carried on during every week of a specified part of the year but not necessarily on every day of every such week.

The Act gave the Minister wide-ranging powers of veto over the granting of licences if a 'substantially identical' or 'identical' service already existed. It was said that this provision was designed to 'eliminate wasteful competition'. When licences were granted under the Act a series of conditions including the under noted were applied:–

- Rigid adherence to published timetables as a condition of licensing.
- Permission given for the operation of duplicate services where the number of passengers patronising any one service is in excess of the seating capacity of the bus operating that service.
- Services may not be operated beyond or short of a terminal to which it is scheduled to run.
- Roads traversed by services may not be altered except in emergency where the roads are impassable owing to weather or other conditions without prior consent of the Minister.
- A copy of the current timetable and fares list must be displayed on the front bulkhead of all vehicles in service, with a copy of each held by the Conductor.
- Destination blinds and boards must be displayed and adjusted to show the point to which the vehicle is travelling.

Licences had to be renewed annually from 31st October each year and operators were required as a condition of the granting of the licences to furnish the Minister with detailed statistics, including a statement of accounts, records of traffic and in fact any information which the Minister deemed necessary, all of which he could elect to publish if he felt it prudent to do so. The government included conditions in the 1932 Act to give effect to the protectionism policy of local industries, which would irrevocably shape the GNR's Road Motor Service policy for years to come. The relevant clauses included the following:–

- When considering whether or not to issue a licence, 'the Minister shall have regard to the extent to which the vehicles used or intended to be used on the passenger road service to which such application relates are or will be manufactured (in whole or in part) in *Saorstát Éireann* and also the extent to which such vehicles are or will be kept in repair by *Saorstát Éireann* labour'.
- The Minister could 'attach to a passenger licence a condition requiring the use (either exclusively or to a specific extent) on the passenger road service to which such licence relates of vehicles manufactured in whole or in part in *Saorstát Éireann*.

The Acts of the Apostles

On 9th March 1932 Eamon de Valera's *Fianna Fail* party formed a government for the first time, following the foundation of the Irish Free State, with the seven votes of the Labour party. Elected on a mandate to withhold the payment of land annuities to Britain they embarked upon a prolonged and highly damaging economic war in June, which lasted until 1938. Britain retaliated by imposing a 20% levy on agricultural imports from the Free State. De Valera countered with a series of punitive duties on imports. Free trade between the United Kingdom and Ireland was not properly achieved until December 1965 with the ratification of the Anglo-Irish Free Trade Agreement. *Fianna Fail* policy in this area led to the virtual elimination of the cattle industry in favour of tillage. Economic protectionism, industrial self-sufficiency and isolationism led to de Valera's Minister of Industry and Commerce, Sean Lemass, setting about the introduction of yet more legislation, which would have a dramatic affect for years to come on the Great Northern Railway. The repercussions of the economic war initiated by de Valera prompted Sean Lemass to issue this warning to the Irish people on 1st November 1932, a mere eight months into their administration; "we have reached the point where a collapse of our economic system is in sight. By a collapse I mean famine conditions for a large number of our people". Sean Lemass had a mind-boggling belief in state intervention in all aspects of Irish life, with the intention of protecting Irish industries. Lemass began his protectionist policies by introducing a tariff regime, which led to the promulgation of an increasing number of government orders limiting imports as the noose steadily tightened. One of his first legislative acts was to introduce the Control of Manufacturers Act of 29th October 1932, which was designed to develop indigenous Irish industries using local capital and severely limiting foreign control of enterprises operating in Ireland. The policy devised by Lemass and enacted over a period of thirty years was a spectacular failure, almost leading to bankruptcy. The protectionist measures Lemass applied to industry generally were replicated in the transport sector with the introduction of a series of Acts, some of which are briefly dealt with.

Road Transport Act 1933

This legislation entitled 'The Road Transport Act 1933 (No. 8, 12th June 1933)' provided for compulsory acquisition by the 'authorised companies' (effectively the railways and the DUTC) of road passenger and freight operators. It also placed restrictions on the carriage of goods by road through the introduction of a licensing regime, limited to existing operators in a tightly defined geographical area. A system of binding arbitration in the event of a dispute arising between the acquiring organisation and the company being bought was arranged. The GNR resorted to this Tribunal on several occasions and did not always get its way! On 31st August 1933 Jonathan Stephens wrote to The Secretary of the Department of Industry and Commerce advising the government that the company intended to apply for orders under the 1933 Road Transport Act to compulsorily acquire a number of bus companies. It had just obtained an order to acquire HMS Catherwood. The list below illustrates the companies that the GNR intended to buy out:–

Carlingford Motor Service
General Motor Service
Tourist (McGowan's Bus Service)
Boyd's Omnibus Service
Erne Omnibus Service

The General Motor Service was bought by the DUTC; the story of the outcome of the Erne is dealt with later. The remaining operators were eventually acquired by the GNR.

The Carlingford Motor Service, which ran buses to Dundalk, was one of two operators in direct competition with the Dundalk Newry & Greenore Railway (DN&GR) and this undertaking made a financial contribution to the purchase of the Carlingford. The GNR had assumed responsibility for the running of the DN&GR in 1933 and were determined to eliminate private road competition where it affected this railway company's revenues. The Omeath Motor Service, who ran between Newry and Carlingford, was bought out in December 1932 with financial support from the DNGR's parent, the London Midland & Scottish Railway Company.

Road Traffic Act 1933

The Road Traffic Act 1933 (No. 11, 29th June 1933) provided for a weekly rest period for drivers and conductors of Public Service Vehicles and specified the maximum daily driving periods and minimum rest periods as outlined:

- Every omnibus driver and conductor must have a period of not less than 24 consecutive hours rest in every seven days.
- No driver to be rostered to work in excess of five and a half hours without a break, such break to be of not less than 30 minutes duration.
- No driver to be employed for more than 11 hours in one day (24 hours beginning at 2:00 am)
- A rest period of at least ten consecutive hours between the last turn of duty on one day and the first turn of duty on the next day to be granted to drivers.

Control of Imports Act 1934

This Act made provision for the control of imports and authorised the imposition of quotas across a wide range of materials, some examples of which were tyres, body parts, engines, machinery and building materials all of which had a detrimental effect upon the working of the GNR.

International Bus Service Gilford LL166 ZI 710 working the Belfast/Dublin service at Dundalk in July 1929. *(SS)*

Road Transport Act 1935

It was the introduction of this Act of the *Oireachtas* which gave the GNR the final inducement to start producing its own buses at Dundalk. It also spelt the death knell for those independent bus and lorry operators who wanted to purchase new vehicles. The Act introduced severe controls on the importation of any mechanically propelled vehicle, which was to be used for the carriage of passengers or merchandise. The Act expressly stated in section 6 'It shall not be lawful for any person (other than an authorised (passenger carrying/merchandise) company) to import into *Saorstát Éireann* on or after 1st July 1935 any mechanically propelled vehicle'. The 'authorised companies' referred to in the 1933 Road Transport Act could and did apply for licences to import buses and lorries, although in most cases very high levels of import duty had to be paid. The implications of these Acts of the *Oireachtas* were quickly realised by the GNR management who immediately set in train a series of actions designed to ensure compliance with the legislation to minimise the effects of it and the imposition of import duties on profits. Some of the measures introduced by the GNR over the succeeding years included:–

- The transfer of 15 buses from Northern Ireland to the Irish Free State on Sunday 24th July 1935.
- The splitting of the Road Motor Service fleet (buses and lorries) into vehicles operating in Northern Ireland and those working in the Irish Free State; the latter fleet also included the cross border vehicles, which could operate in either territory.
- The construction of two omnibus rail trucks to convey buses by rail duty free from the Irish Free State into Northern Ireland and back into the Irish Free State again.
- The rapid expansion of bus and lorry body building facilities at Dundalk works thus ensuring conformity to the strictures on *Saorstát Éireann* vehicle manufacture using local labour.
- The eventual establishment in 1937 of the GNR Gardner bus-building programme.

Harold Catherwood, second left together with Viscount Craigavon, Prime Minister of Northern Ireland (middle) and the Governor of Northern Ireland, the Duke of Abercorn, whilst visiting the Catherwood stand at the Balmoral show in 1930 *(SS)*

Harold Matthew Stuart Catherwood

Harold Matthew Stuart Catherwood began running buses in Northern Ireland from 7th July 1925 with a service from Toomebridge to Belfast. Development of further services continued apace with the establishment of a Belfast/Dublin service on Tuesday 19th July 1927, which provided for two Monday to Saturday departures at 8.00am and 6.00pm from either end. Catherwood was not the first operator on the Belfast/Dublin service; that accolade belongs to two Belfast businessmen SH Weir and AS Baird, who established a company known as the International Bus Service with its fleet of predominately Gilford vehicles. Baird and Weir quietly started their service on 1st July 1927 just in time to beat the new requirement in Northern Ireland to first seek authority to operate bus services. Both companies undercut the GNR rail fares by 4s 0d on a single and 11s 6d on a return ticket, thus taking the lion's share of their traffic from the railway. In October 1929 Catherwood bought the International from Baird and Weir for £8,000. Harold Catherwood founded his bus company on money which his wife inherited from her father. Catherwood, a devout member of the Plymouth Brethren believed in the Calvinist tradition that the Lord had put us here to fulfil our earthly calling and that hard work together with whatever talent we possess would bring about positive results. His strongly held Christian conviction ensured that he never ran any bus services on Sundays. Many Catherwood staff were members of the Plymouth Brethren sect.

Mackle immediately seized the opportunity for the GNR. On Sunday 4th September 1929 he inaugurated Sunday only services with two double workings between Belfast and Dublin. Mackle cleverly offered comparable fares to Catherwood and introduced a heavily discounted 3-day excursion fare at 1s 0d less than Catherwood, with the opportunity to take the return trip taken by train at no extra cost. This had a great effect in clawing back revenue to the GNR. Motorman Harold Pentony and Conductor William Collier, who pulled away from College Square at 8.30am in their AEC Reliance bus No. 32 for the 4 hour 50 minute journey to Dublin, inaugurated the service from Belfast. This GNR service continued to operate until 28th April 1935. Catherwood's peripatetic operations included services between Londonderry and Sligo with feeder connections to Glenties and Portnoo. He introduced a short-lived service on 16th December 1927 between Belfast and Londonderry via Portadown, Omagh and Strabane on the one hand, and Belfast to Warrenpoint via Markethill and Newry with one journey each day serving Armagh. They ended as a result of a territorial agreement signed between HMS Catherwood, Bell & Paisley and the BOC on 17th February 1928. On Friday 15th November 1929 Catherwood began another feeder bus from Clones, Newbliss,

A Leyland PLSC1 (fleet No. 21) with bodywork by Hall Lewis (later Park Royal), specially constructed with underfloor luggage lockers and toilet at the offside rear, for the Belfast/Dublin service. *(GL)*

The Leyland-bodied PLSC Lions were unusual in having bucket seats, in addition to the luggage compartment. *(LM: LM 4362/4361)*

Ballybay, Castleblaney, Carrickmacross and Dundalk where a connection with the Belfast/Dublin service was made. At the same time they audaciously began running a bus service from Eden Quay in Dublin and The Bailey on the Hill of Howth but both services were short lived. Catherwood's Howth service managed to upset not only the GNR but also the DUTC as well. In 1930 Catherwood extended the limited stop Belfast/Dublin service to Cork and in a direct tilt at the GNR introduced a Drogheda/Clogher local service – these became the last ventures of this enterprising company in the Irish Free State transport scene.

Harold Catherwood epitomised the Protestant work ethic with his innovative, reliable and progressive company. His Cambridge blue liveried buses with the HMS Catherwood

Catherwood PLSC Lion Fleet No. 7, typical of the type, operated on the Catherwood Donegal services in competition with the GNR. *(GL)*

Half-a-dozen HMS Catherwood Leyland PLSCs are seen here prior to delivery to Belfast to participate in the Belfast Bus War of 1926-8. *(LM: LM 5258)*

legend, always well presented and maintained with friendly staff, were serious competitors in an increasingly crowded bus market. He even established a coach building department at premises on Belfast's Donegal Road, adjacent to the Maguire and Patterson match factory where bus bodies and overhaul activities took place. On the 22nd April 1932 those marked characteristics attracted the attention of the giant mainland based Thomas Tilling transport organisation, who agreed to guarantee the Northern Bank in Belfast the sum of £25,000 to service an overdraft. Tilling took a £70,000 stake in HMS Catherwood giving them the 58.36% control, leaving Harold and nominees with a 41.64% minority share. Harold's nominees were his wife Mrs JEM Catherwood and her sister Mrs M Agnew. Tilling appointed Harold Managing Director of HMSC on a ten year contract and allowed him to nominate one other director to the board of HMSC. He was further rewarded with a directorship with the National Omnibus Company. Tilling appointed Henry Charles Merrett of Finsbury Square, London as their nominated HMSC Chairman. From that point forward all dividends were paid to Tilling. The company was dormant after the NIRTB take over in 1935 when all accounts were transferred to the Midland Bank in Northampton until it finally went into voluntary liquidation on the 11th February 1936.

Catherwood were the first company in Ireland to introduce toilets on their long distance buses, decades before any other operator, such was the concern for passenger comfort, which led unsurprisingly to high levels of popularity. The GNR, using its newly acquired powers of compulsory purchase, applied to the Minister for Industry and Commerce for permission to buy HMS Catherwood's cross-border services between Dublin and Belfast and in the areas of Derry, Donegal and Sligo. The Ministerial order issued on 29th November 1933 also assigned the Dublin/Cork service to the Great Southern Railway. Discussions between Catherwood and the GNR on the mechanism for the transfer actually started in September of that year, with meetings between James Lockhart and Tom Hutcheson together with Messrs Culbert, Ellis and Kelly from Catherwoods. Harold Catherwood bitterly opposed the transfer and immediately instructed Messrs Thomas Crozier and Sons, Dublin Solicitors, to fight it. Arthur Culbert, Catherwood's Dublin Traffic Manager, set about organising a public campaign to oppose the transfer. On 27th September 1933 Culbert arranged to have thousands of leaflets handed out on buses and outside GNR stations. These leaflets denounced Lemass and the transfer, which Catherwood said would result in the GNR enjoying a monopoly of the passenger traffic on the Dublin/Belfast and Londonderry/Sligo roads. In the Sligo/Donegal area Catherwood's had two doughty defenders in the shape of a Sligo Auctioneer Alderman John Jinks, a National League Party Councillor on Sligo Corporation who had occupied the position of First Citizen on no less than five occasions. Jinks was also a TD and good friend of Robert Smyllie, then a journalist on the local Conservative Sligo Times newspaper. Smyllie went on to become the legendary editor of the Irish Times. The second champion was a Bundoran businessman and Sligo Councillor Patrick Conlon, who organised a petition opposing the transfer of Catherwood's licences to the GNR. By 14th November he had obtained 42,000 signatures. The petition was sent to Sean Lemass, supplemented by a campaign of letter writing to members *Dail Éireann*. The issue was regularly discussed in Sligo Corporation meetings. Resolutions in opposition to the transfer were sent to the Minister. One Sligo Councillor, Mr Kelly said on 16th November 1933 that "Catherwood's were the most Christian employers on the road. They never asked their employees to work on Sunday" and they should be supported. The campaign of opposition, despite being well organised and broadly based, failed to make an impression and get the decision reversed.

There now followed a period of interminable wrangling between the GNR and Catherwood, relating to the financial settlement and the numbers of vehicles to be handed over. The GNR was insistent that its Works Manager Richard Meredith should carry out a mechanical inspection of every vehicle. It was agreed that Captain Stagg, the Chief Engineer of Catherwood, would accompany him. Both men eventually completed this exercise after visiting all the Catherwood depots by early December. Catherwood's garages at Dublin, Drogheda, Dundalk, Ballyshannon and Sligo, some of which had long leases to run, were of no interest to the GNR. The company did however take over Catherwood's Quay Street Bus Office in Sligo. Harold Catherwood did not enter direct negotiation himself with the GNR at any stage, although he was present at the Gresham Hotel in Dublin whilst a meeting was underway between his Managers and the GNR at Amiens Street Station. This was surprising, as he had taken such a direct interest in the development of his business. Some of Catherwood's drivers and conductors of whom there were 16 of each grade working services in the Irish Free State were offered employment with the GNR at a lower rate of pay. On Monday 11th December 1933 the services of HMS Catherwood passed to the GNR together with 24 Leyland buses, some of which were delivered at midnight to GNR garages in Dublin, Dundalk, Belfast, Londonderry, Portnoo and the IOC garage in Sligo. There was a certain reluctance on the part of Catherwood's to hand over to the GNR documents relating to the buses acquired and this resulted in Albert Switzer having to make visits to Catherwood premises in Belfast and Londonderry between Friday 5th January 1934 and Tuesday 16th January 1934 to obtain vehicle log books, which were urgently required in order that customs formalities could be completed by their new owners.

The Catherwood purchase resulted in the GNR appointing several officials to manage its new routes, especially in the Donegal area. Revenue Inspector Magee was transferred to Donegal Town as the first Bus Foreman reporting directly to Belfast Traffic Manager James Lockhart. Magee was responsible for all omnibus services in Donegal, liaising with Henry Forbes, the CDRJC General Manager. Inspector Bertie Irwin, based at Londonderry Foyle Road, was responsible for local services between Londonderry and Ballybofey via Lifford and the main road as well as the main trunk service to Sligo as these were considered pure GNR routes. Bertie Irwin, one of two brothers who ran their own bus company in Lurgan, had been bought out by the GNR in 1929 and was previously a GNR Inspector in Ballyshannon from September 1930, when he took over from Inspector Mick McGeough who returned to his native Dundalk. The management appointed its first female Bus Controller, Mrs Gillespie, at a period in history when the transport industry was seen as a wholly male preserve. She worked at Ballyshannon, which was a strategic location for controlling the all-important Sligo service, and reported directly to Magee in Donegal Town. Control of the Sligo/Londonderry service later passed to the Dublin based District Superintendent on 30th June 1934 as part of a re-organisation of the Road Motor Services following the end of the Mackle era. The GNR agreed to honour Catherwood return tickets up to the 8th January 1934. Fares were revised on the Dublin/Newry, Donegal/Portnoo and Londonderry/Ballybofey services. No increases were implemented on the other former Catherwood services that were less well patronised. The agreement provided for Catherwood to provide a bus connection at Newry to the GNR buses arriving and departing southwards although in practice it never happened. The GNR buses to and from Dublin made connections with the GNR train at Edward Street Newry thus maintaining a bus/rail link with the two Capital cities. Harold Catherwood submitted a claim of £181,958 to the Tribunal established to arbitrate on matters concerning compulsory acquisition of licences in April 1934. The GNR resolutely opposed such a settlement and argued their case at the Tribunal. The Catherwood saga finally ended through the binding arbitration clause being applied on the 20th March 1935 which saw the GNR pay £50,000 for the Catherwood licences and 24 buses that were compulsorily purchased. Seven days later the offer was accepted. The County Donegal Railway contributed £2,500 to the settlement figure in recognition of the elimination of the Catherwood competition in the county.

GREAT NORTHERN RAILWAY (IRELAND).

ROAD PASSENGER SERVICES.

Commencing on MONDAY, 11th DECEMBER, 1933, the Services on the under-mentioned Routes, hitherto operated by Messrs. H. M. S. Catherwood, Ltd., will be conducted by the Great Northern Railway Company, as from which date the existing Time Tables will be cancelled, and the times of the Services will be as shown on the Company's Handbills:—

DUBLIN—DROGHEDA—DUNDALK.
DUNDALK—NEWRY.
DROGHEDA—CLOGHER.
DROGHEDA—ARDEE.
SLIGO—LONDONDERRY.
DONEGAL—PORTNOO.
LONDONDERRY—BALLYBOFEY (Via Lifford).

Return Portions of ORDINARY TICKETS issued for Sections on the abovementioned Routes by Messrs H. M. S. Catherwood, Ltd., will be valid for travel on the G.N.R. (I.) Omnibuses up to and including 8th January, 1934.

MONTHLY AND WEEKLY SEASON TICKETS will also be valid on the G.N.R. (I.) Omnibuses during the period of their currency.

J. B. STEPHENS, General Manager.
Dublin, December, 1933.

This modest press announcement by GNR following the takeover of the Catherwood services rather belies the extent of the negotiations which led up to this event. *(GL)*

Bad Boy Boyd

The operation of Isaac and Thomas Boyd who ran a service between Clones and Monaghan was compulsorily purchased on 30th December 1937. Boyd's omnibuses made their mark on the GNR ten years earlier in Clones on 31st December 1927 when Isaac Boyd crashed his bus through the level crossing gates, causing £37 of damage. Boyd, who at that time ran a bus between Cavan and Monaghan known as the 'Tirconnail Queen' wrecked the crossing gates at the foot of Churchill Street and derailed two wagons which were being shunted at the time. Four passengers escaped shaken but unhurt. The Boyd brothers actually lived at Carryduff Co Down and had links with the owners of the Tonic Bus Company in Bangor Co Down and were colourful characters. In August 1934 Isaac Boyd was jailed in Northern Ireland for 12 months in connection with an armed hold-up. After serving nine months in jail he was keen to sell the bus operation to raise some cash. He first approached Maurice Cassidy, owner of the Erne Bus Company who told Boyd he was not interested. In October 1937 Chief Inspector Albert Switzer went to Clones to investigate the operations of the Boyd Brothers. Extracts of his report make interesting reading; 'Boyd rents a garage at Gas Lane Clones, from a Mr Rodgerson. I went there and observed an old Reo 20-seater bus practically dismantled following the crossing gate accident. There is also an old Austin Car, which was involved in an accident some time ago. Both these machines are the property of Mr Boyd; they are both definitely un-serviceable and are only value as scrap. A Mr Mohan (Police Pensioner) of Cara Street, Clones, presently controls the service. The vehicle presently in use is a Reo 20-seater of 1929 vintage with an expired tax disc. It was bought from the Northern Ireland Road Transport Board for about £40'. Boyd's Reo bus was loaded onto an omnibus rail truck at Clones Station and sent to Dundalk in a deplorable condition. A GNR 20-seat Dennis Ace omnibus, fleet No. 33 was allocated to Clones to operate the former Boyd service from Saturday 1st January 1938, being garaged overnight under the Veranda of the Goods Store at Clones Station.

All Ireland Tours

On 15th October 1931 an agreement was reached with the LMS (NCC) to introduce 'All Ireland Motor Coach Tours' during the summer of 1932. This agreement provided for the joint purchase of four Leyland TS3 24-seat tour coaches, three active with one spare. Both railway companies allocated a total of £7,000 to finance set-up costs including the purchase of the vehicles, joint publicity etc. The tours departed from Belfast on Saturdays (between April and mid-September) were Trans-Atlantic steamers arrived in time to permit passengers to join a tour right around the country including Dublin, Cork, Kenmare, Killarney, Galway, Sligo, Donegal and the Glens of Antrim on their 'All Ireland Tour'. Tourists were met at the boats by representatives dressed in attractive blue uniforms complete with caps in a shade similar to the colour of the coaches. The all-Ireland coach tours represented excellent value for money including meals and accommodation, in addition to the services of an experienced courier on the coach. In the summer of 1932 an eight day tour cost £13 10s 0d or a shorter 2 day break could be had for £3 10s 0d. The early tours were marketed using the slogan 'Let us show you the beauties of our Island Home'.

Steps were taken by the GNR and LMS (NCC) to persuade the Irish Omnibus Company to participate in the All Ireland Tours programme at a meeting held in Belfast on 27th November 1931. Robert Griffith of the IOC was personally prepared to come to an amicable settlement of the matter, and join in running the tours, but the Directors of the Great Southern Railways, who were not prepared to agree, tied him down. Negotiations continued between April and December 1932 with Major Sandy Spier of the LMS (NCC), James Lockhart of the GNR and Robert Griffith of the IOC with the objective of achieving an agreement in time for the 1933 season. The IOC was offered the facility to buy a third share in the four tour coaches, their payment to the LMS (NCC) and the GNR to be on the basis of the original capital cost less one year's depreciation calculated on a five year life. The IOC declined this offer from the other two administrations. The IOC's Robert Griffith rightly contended that the company had important interests in Cork, Galway and Dublin in terms of its customer base. He wanted the tours to start from these centres in addition to Belfast but the two Northern Companies resisted. The GNR and LMS (NCC) had suffered a loss of £1,000 each in the operation of the tours during the 1932 season. The chief cause of the loss in working, apart from the general question of the trade depression, was undoubtedly the fact that after the buses had been obtained there was an unfortunate turn of political events in the Irish Free State, as

Number 261 arrives at the GNR Hotel at Bundoran; note the GNR Shield above the hotel entrance door. *(WM)*

a result of the General Election in the Spring of that year. This caused unsettled conditions in the country, and there were numerous alarmist rumours, which deterred many people from visiting the Free State and even from visiting Northern Ireland. It was most unfortunate that this state of affairs coincided with the inauguration of the 'All Ireland Tours'. The experience gained enabled reductions in costs to be effected by the elimination of poorly patronised tours and by the combination of others. From the information available to the Railway companies it appeared that their 'All Ireland Tours' did a good deal better that those of their opponents, namely the Belfast Omnibus Company and Messrs Catherwood, even though they had both been in the field before the GNR/LMS (NCC).

There was no doubt that the railways were in a better position to cater for the tours because of the large number of agencies they had in Great Britain through the LMS Company's Stationmasters, District Manager's and various offices. When the tours were being planned it was anticipated that the depreciation of the pound sterling would result in a large transference of holiday makers from Continental resorts to home resorts. In the case of Ireland this unfortunately did not prove to be the case, chiefly owing to the fact of the troubles, which had been taking place and which had frequently been greatly exaggerated in the British press. The Great Southern Railway, through the Irish Omnibus Company, also ran 'All Ireland Tours' and an attempt was made by the GNR and LMS (NCC) to get them to combine the tour programme. The Great Northern and the Northern Counties Committee thought they had obtained an agreement with the Irish Omnibus Company. The Great Southern Railway Directors decided in January 1934 that in view of the transport position in the Irish Free State that it did not wish to carry out the arrangement reached. They advised the GNR and the LMS (NCC) that all passenger bus transport south of a line drawn from Dublin to Sligo should be run by them, and that all north of that should be in the hands of the Great Northern Railway and the LMS (NCC). They stated that they would have been quite willing to run their services from Dublin to Sligo in connection with the services working north thereof, but this would be a somewhat difficult proposition. The matter was discussed between Jonathan Stephens of the GNR and Mr Morton of the Great Southern Railway and it had been decided to draw up a scheme of joint tours comprising tours in the area of the Irish Free State north of Sligo – Dublin line, and also to run joint tours in Northern Ireland. Arrangements were also made to connect with the Irish Omnibus Company's services at Sligo and Dublin.

Tourist Treasures

Away from the 'All Ireland Tour' programme the GNR paid considerable attention to regular day tourist traffic from an early stage of the Road Motor Services development. An extensive network of tours was operated from the main centres within the company's operating area. Many were self-contained excursions by road, but the majority consisted of combined rail and road services. Devised as circular tours, it was possible for passengers to join at intermediate points or to start from points outside the area of the tour. On 15th June 1930 the company introduced 'Land Cruises' to the Mourne Mountains from Warrenpoint Railway Station during the summer season, using a local contractor Hugh McAnulty. Carlingford and the Cooley Peninsula Land Cruises operated

Leyland TS3 No. 236 at Rochester before delivery by Short Brothers – note the joint fleet owner names of GNR(I) and LMS (NCC). *(SS)*

from Dundalk Station well into the late 1950s. The GNR was particularly fortunate in that many of the country's tourist treasures were to be found within its territory, such as Tara, seat of the High Kings of Ireland, Old Mellifont Abbey, founded by St Malachy in 1142 which was the first Cistercian monastery in Ireland. The company exploited the tourist potential all over its omnibus network as an important source of additional revenue. A popular contemporary concept was the Mystery Tour, which the GNR operated from all its major centres. During these three and half-hour tours some 50 miles of sightseeing was covered at speeds not in excess of 25mph. Percy Bogle and Bobby Navan of the GNR Commercial department produced detailed routes for Motormen and commentaries for Conductors, ensuring that passengers were fully acquainted with every interesting fact and statistic concerning features *en route*. In 1935 the GNR entered into a joint tour venture with the London Midland & Scottish Railway and the Great Southern Railway to develop excursion traffic from North Wales to Ireland. Excursionists travelled by LMS train and ship to Dublin via Holyhead and Dun Laoghaire where they boarded the GSR train to Westland Row Station, being met there by GNR omnibus for a tour of Dublin and North Coastal Tour. This took in Malahide, Howth, Portmarnock, Baldoyle, Killester and Clontarf, followed by a brief stop for afternoon tea and shopping in O'Connell Street, before being returned to Westland Row Station for the return journey to Wales. The LMS North Wales Tours, as they became known, were an important source of revenue to the GNR in the years between 1935 and 1939 when they were suspended because of the wartime emergency. In 1935 1,601 passengers bought tickets and the traffic reached its zenith in 1936 as 2,668 customers sampled the delights of Dublin City. The Omnibus Department of the GSR also operated an alternative Dublin City and South Tour.

Eire's economic war continued and in 1938 the government appointed a Tribunal of Inquiry on Public Transport, which would examine tariffs, service levels, future traffic predictions etc. Its deliberations and recommendations would not affect the GNR, which was by now undergoing a financial crisis. The Belfast News Letter of 8th February 1939 stated that 'The Directors of the GNR reported a substantial deficit in the net revenue account for 1938 and cannot recommend a payment of the dividend on the guaranteed stock or of a dividend on the preference and ordinary stocks. In 1937 the dividend on the guaranteed stock was only paid after transferring £9,000 from the reserve'.

Room at the top

On 25th January 1939 Lord Glenavy was elected Company Chairman to succeed the late Mr William Carson who died on 6th January. On the same day Jonathan Barton Stephens retired as General Manager after a long and distinguished period of nearly 13 years and was now able to spend more time at his Rathruadh, Glenageary home. He represented the Great Northern at the Rome Congress of the International Railway Association in 1922 and also in Madrid in 1930 and Paris in 1937. Among the outstanding events of his tenure he inaugurated road passenger and freight services and kept the GNR going during the 1933 strike. He was also keenly involved with the Eire government in the development of the various Road Transport Acts and with the Northern Ireland government in the formulation of the legislation, which established the Northern Ireland Road Transport Board. During his long service of nearly 50 years with the GNR Jonathan Stephens had the unique experience of serving under each of the nine Chairmen of the Company since its incorporation in 1876 and three of these (Sir George Clark, Sir Lingard Goulding, and Mr WB Carson), died in office whilst he was General Manager. Such was the esteem in which he was held by the GNR that he was immediately elected to the position of Deputy Chairman, a post he held until the formation of the GNRB.

George Bruce Howden succeeded Jonathan Stephens and upon assuming the role of General Manager was immediately faced with the prospect of running the Company, which was by now almost bankrupt. Howden, desperate to improve the revenue stream, immediately introduced fare increases of between 5 and 33%. On 20th November 1939 he unwisely abolished all omnibus return fares excluding the Dublin suburban routes. The effect of this for the thousands of rural folk who relied on GNR buses was to reduce return travel by about 27%. GNR bus passengers voted with their feet, deserting the Road Motor Services as alternative were found. They resorted to using cycles, horse drawn vehicles, lorries, car sharing. Recreational trips to cinemas, football matches and even hospital visits were drastically reduced. By March 1940 senior officers of the company implored Howden to restore return tickets, which had been favourably discounted prior to their abolition. In April Howden instructed James Lockhart (the Belfast Traffic Manager) to carry out a thorough review of levels of fares and services. Lockhart resisted pressure from Howden for further potentially fatal service cuts, instead recommending the introduction of a new fares policy and a pruning of operating costs. The Lockhart proposals included the widespread introduction of Motorman/Conductors (one-person operated) working buses. It was suggested that a start be made on the Donabate/Portrane and Skerries services. There was also a proposal to introduce 'composite' vehicles, which had been tried out in the Ardee area in 1937 with the introduction of a local bus network. This involved the removal of a number of seats in the rear of the bus to create a goods compartment for the conveyance of mails, parcels and small consignments. It was suggested that a trial be initiated on the Donegal/Portnoo service although this never happened. The Board of the Company endorsed the Lockhart proposals on fares. On 1st May 1940 return tickets were reintroduced to and from principal towns except these arrangements did not apply to the pool area services. This action stimulated bus travel once again and saved the Road Motor Services from collapse. However on 5th April 1943 return tickets were once again abolished outside the Dublin suburban services. Finally on 1st June 1943 the company decided to abolish the return tickets on the Dublin suburban services as well. Revenues held up remarkably well only as a result of the wartime emergency restrictions. George Howden now had to adapt to running a Company in wartime Northern Ireland and neutral Eire.

Chapter Three
The Strike, which nearly ended it all

Tuesday 30th January 1933 witnessed the start of a strike by members of the National Union of Railwaymen and ASLEF trade unions. In response to the withdrawal of labour the Board of the Great Northern Railway Company issued the following statement:–

'The company regrets that, owing to the majority of its employees having withdrawn their labour as from midnight last night, a great number of train services, both goods and passenger, have had to be suspended.

This is particularly the case at the southern end of the system, notwithstanding that during the continuance of the Irish Free State Government subsidy the remuneration of the employees in the Free State would remain unchanged.

This regrettable situation has arisen out of the decision of the Irish Railways Wages Board, dated 25th November 1932 given after close scrutiny of the evidence submitted concerning the financial position of Irish Railways. The finding was arrived at under the procedure laid down in the machinery of negotiation as agreed by the Irish Railways Companies and three railwaymen's trade unions; it provided for a reduction in wages and salaries equivalent to about 6 % on earnings. The wages board finding was due to come into effect from 26th December last, but the Free State Government decided to give a grant for a limited period, equal in amount to the reduction due to the finding. Accordingly, within the Free State, the Railway Company is providing so much for wages and salaries as results from the application of the finding, while the Government makes up the payments to their previous amount.

The Great Northern Railway Company had no alternative but to adopt the same course. The grant of a subsidy in the Free State, while there is none in Northern Ireland, necessarily creates a difference in the amounts which employees would receive. It is from the attitude of the Governments that the difference results, not from any action by the Company, whose position is that it must treat all its employees alike. Since on the Great Northern system expenses have for some months exceeded receipts, the company is unable to forego the reduction in expenditure resulting from the finding, and regrets the circumstances should have rendered that course inevitable'.

The Great Northern Railway Road Motor Service staff were not subject to the Railway Wages Board ruling although there were some doubts, which led to sporadic stoppages. Thus the strike was portrayed in its early days as the Northern Ireland Railway strike affecting all railways in Northern Ireland as the Government were not prepared to subsidise railwaymen's wages. The Londonderry and Lough Swilly and County Donegal Railway also became enmeshed in the strike. In an act of solidarity with the Northern Ireland railwaymen GNR employees in the Irish Free State went out on strike. The reality of the strike was that it quickly developed into a highly bitter, acrimonious industrial conflict characterised by rampant intimidation, vandalism, sabotage, terrorism and worse still, murder.

On the first day of the strike the disruption to rail services was widespread with pickets on most railway stations from the early hours. For those not so directly affected by the strike – the bus and lorry men and members of the Railway Clerks Association – no clear instructions were issued by their respective unions. Some Motormen and Conductors at Dublin Garage were unsure what action they should take, if any, and as a result some early morning buses from Dublin left up to an hour late. By contrast in Belfast most Motormen were working normally. The normal lorry service was even supplemented by additional vehicles formed into convoys to convey goods, which would have normally been transported by rail to various parts of the province. The RUC provided armed guards for these convoys, which provided a lifeline for many towns and villages. A limited train service also ran throughout the system albeit erratic and subject to termination *en route* if a particular signal cabin was unmanned.

The Trade Unions involved in the strike were the National Union of Railwaymen, whose President was Mr W Dobbie, and the Associated Society of Locomotive Engineers and Firemen, represented by the Assistant General Secretary Mr WJR Squance. James Lockhart, Traffic Manager and Foster Graham, Chief Clerk in the General Manager's Office represented the Great Northern Railway in negotiations with the Trade Unions. During the course of the strike Mr JM Andrews, the Northern Ireland Minister for Labour (and a future Prime Minister) and Mr Sean Lemass, the Minister for Industry and Commerce in the Irish Free State Government (and a future *Taoiseach*) represented their respective governments in discussions with parties to the dispute.

Day two of the strike was marked by an outrage, which resulted in the death of two men, employees of the Great Northern Railway Company and in injury to six others including a young boy. Two rails had been removed from the permanent way at a point near Dromiskin, about two miles north of Castlebellingham, County Louth. At 10.30am the Belfast bound train from Dublin approached, and was derailed being thrown down a steep embankment. At the inquest into the death of the two men killed at Dromiskin, which was held in Dundalk on Wednesday 29th March 1933 George Howden then Chief Engineer of the GNR, gave evidence of examining the track on the afternoon of the derailment. "He had no doubt that the rails had been removed before the accident by persons experienced in that class of work. The position of the removed rails on the down line was the most suitable that could be found if the object was to produce a thoroughly satisfactory disaster". On the day of the Dromiskin outrage the National Union of Railwaymen called upon GNR busmen, who were members of the union, to cease work as from midnight. The call was widely ignored with the notable exception of the Dublin area. At local meetings in other areas the overwhelming majority of Road Motor Services staff voted to continue normal working.

GNR Chairman Lord Glenavy held an urgent meeting with Sean Lemass in Government Buildings to discuss the Dromiskin tragedy. The Minister said afterwards that the outrage was the work of criminals and as such the *Gardai* would carry out an investigation into it. The strike leaders suggested that the derailment was not due to interference with the permanent way and earned a sharp rebuke from James Lockhart who stated in reply that the company had evidence that the work of removing the rails was done deliberately and regardless of the consequences. Sean Lemass announced the discontinuance of the wages subsidy to the Great Northern Company as a direct result of the strike. The next day another act of sabotage was carried out in County Donegal when thirty yards of rail was removed from the line near St Johnston, about six miles from Londonderry. No trains ran to or from Dublin and GNR busmen from the Sheriff Street Garage joined the strike, which resulted in Free State Army lorries providing a service to Skerries and Balbriggan. In Dundalk the Army in armoured cars carrying machine guns was patrolling the streets and the Civic Guards were reinforced from country districts to protect buses and lorries. Four armed men stopped a bus belonging to HMS Catherwood at 'The Thatch' between Santry and Whitehall, which had departed from Eden Quay *en route* to Dundalk. The driver, William Cairns of Dundalk and Conductor William Drysdale of Belfast were ordered to get into a waiting taxi and were eventually dumped at Glasnevin before being transferred to another car. They were then taken to a trade union meeting in Parnell Square where after about 10 minutes they were harangued and denounced as drivers of the Catherwood Bus Company and warned not to drive any more buses before being released. A Civic Guard who was escorting the bus and who was sitting at the back of it, was ordered by one of the armed men to put up his hands and told not to move from his seat. As soon as the armed men left the crewless bus the stranded passengers walked to Santry *Garda* Station whereupon the Guards pursued the armed men in cars. A relief bus crew was sent out from Catherwood's headquarters in Dublin to take the bus to Dundalk.

In Northern Ireland the railway companies ran limited services and GNR busmen continued to work normally. On Friday 4th February all GNR bus and rail services were cancelled in the Dublin area resulting in the use for the second day of military lorries morning and evening conveying passengers to towns and villages north of Dublin as far as Balbriggan. The Free State Government announced Police Guards in touring cars would escort all Catherwood buses to protect that Company's staff. In Northern Ireland there was some improvement in the level of railway services and Road Motor Service staff continued to refuse to join the strike. One early effect of the strike was the marked increase in the volume of road traffic between various centres; most of these people would never again return to the railways, a factor which would in later years sound the death knell for many railway lines within the GNR system. After five days of the strike it was evident that it was more effective in the Free State than in Northern Ireland. The unions recognised this and sought to coerce the Transport and General Workers Union representing men employed at the deep-water docks in Belfast to support the strike, this they agreed to do. The dockers issued a warning to the maize millers that if they used either the Great Northern Railway or the London, Midland and Scottish Railway lorry services, their supplies of grain would be stopped.

Leyland Tiger TS2 No. 98 with Potter bodywork on Eden Quay on 20th February 1933 following the sabotage attempt during the railway strike. *(SS)*

On Monday 6th February GNR General Manager Jonathan Stephens announced that the Company intended issuing notices terminating the employment of members of its salaried and clerical staff and members of those grades who have not been affected by the strike or have not obeyed their unions order to cease work. Stephens in his notice to staff thanked them for their loyal services since the beginning of the strike and explained that should the strike end in most cases the notices would be withdrawn and

Strike scenes in Dundalk on 4th February 1933 as strikers picket the GNR Bus Office and Irish Army soldiers guard the Bus Garage on Ardee Road. *(SS)*

was being taken as a purely protective measure. Senator JT O'Farrell, the Irish Secretary of the Railway Clerks Association, responded by saying that if the notices were enacted they would arrange to pay unemployment benefit to its members if necessary.

The following day Jonathan Stephens was asked by the press to respond to reports that the unions had made approaches to the Company. He responded by saying "there has been no approach to the company, on behalf of the men on strike, with a view to settlement". The Company resolved to maintain its position and conversely the strikers would not accept reductions based upon the findings of the Railway Wages Board. GNR bus services throughout the Irish Free State did not operate except in the Dundalk, Monaghan, and Cavan districts where they continued under police and military protection. As a result of the situation Sean Lemass announced that from February 8th the Dublin United Tramways Company buses as a result of an agreement with the striking unions would provide all GNR bus services in the Dublin area. In Northern Ireland railway lines were now being patrolled on foot by armed RUC officers as the railway companies reported continued improvements in the level of services being operated. The GNR omnibus and lorry services continued to operate normally and were said to be doing huge business.

No sooner had the DUTC substitute bus service begun in the Dublin district than the objections came from the striking unions. Subsequently a union deputation waited on Mr JD Stuart of the DUTC objecting to the level of replacement services. Mr Stuart assured the unions that the DUTC had no wish to take unfair advantage of the situation and were quite prepared to limit the service between Dublin and Balbriggan and Skerries to runs made the previous week by military lorries. This proposal appeared to satisfy the unions.

By Tuesday 7th February the GNR in Northern Ireland had taken on extra road motor staff and moved buses from Dublin and Drogheda garages to provide additional bus services running from station to station in place of or in addition to the ordinary train services. For example, the service between Londonderry, Omagh and Enniskillen was increased by three bus journeys in each direction. Similar auxiliary bus services in addition to the normal timetable operations were provided between Belfast and Portadown, Belfast and Banbridge, Belfast and Armagh, Belfast and Antrim and Belfast, Dungannon and Cookstown. James Lockhart and Joe Mackle drew up the plans with the active assistance of his deputy Tom Hutchinson.

At 3.30pm on the afternoon of the 7th the GNR's Belfast Garage Tender a converted AEC 413 bus arrived under RUC armed guard at the Glasgow shed in Belfast Docks to collect a case of stores for the Belfast Garage. The dockworkers immediately refused to load the case onto the vehicle following which it was eventually loaded by Great Northern employees and RUC men. As a result of this the Dockers walked out on strike until 4.30pm when they were instructed to resume work by their union leaders. On the same day James Lockhart was reporting to the media a continuing drift back to work by striking railwaymen, which enabled them to initiate further improvements in the railway services. The unions immediately denied any such return to work saying that had received a large number of telegrams from their branches all over Northern Ireland denying the return to work. The propaganda war was clearly in full swing as both sides made claims and counter claims supporting their respective positions.

The improvement in the level of services being operated by the railway companies clearly exasperated supporters of the strike. Subversives now saw an opportunity to resort to terrorism and cold-blooded murder in a bid to further their cause. On a frosty moonlit Saturday February 11th Dunmurry residents were alarmed and houses shaken when an explosion occurred on the GNR main line underneath the bridge carrying Black's Road over a railway cutting. The explosion, which was heard all over south Belfast occurred at about 9.30pm. Constable T Bunting, who was one of a large police patrol, which had kept constant watch on the Great Northern permanent way, had his attention attracted by the

A Rolls Royce armoured car patrols Dundalk streets during the Railway Strike. *(SS)*

headlights of a car, which appeared to be stationary near the bridge. He started to walk towards the bridge at which point the car drove off in the direction of Hannastown. He took a few steps more when he recoiled before a loud explosion occurred. Fortunately little damage was done, and the line was re-opened the following day.

In the lonely Barnesmore Gap in the Donegal Highlands, at Cashelnavane, more than a mile from the nearest house, a ganger making a dawn patrol of the County Donegal Railway's track between Donegal and Stranorlar on the same Saturday morning discovered a bridge over a ravine partially wrecked by explosives. The ganger flagged a railbus to a standstill before it reached the damaged bridge, and all traffic was suspended pending an examination of the bridge. Many of the stones and supports were split and dislodged but after temporary repairs the service was restored using railbuses until permanent repairs were made thus permitting locomotive hauled trains. Henry Forbes, General Manager of the Donegal Railway said in an interview with the Northern Whig "that the chief trouble in County Donegal was that pickets from Northern Ireland came into the Free State and endeavoured to intimidate those who remained loyal to the Company. This matter of terrorism is one of the greatest difficulties the Company has to face". On Monday 13th February the first train to operate on the Londonderry and Lough Swilly Railway since the strike began left Londonderry for the Free State heavily laden with consignments of coal, maize and other merchandise, further evidence that the drift back to work among railway workers continued. The deadlock between the railway companies and the trade unions concerned in the strike remained with no sign of a move towards a settlement.

A Road Motor Inspector from the GNR was kidnapped on Saturday 18th February whilst *en route* from Dundalk Garage to Dublin Garage with another official for the purpose of bringing one of the Company's buses back to Dundalk. A short distance outside Dublin a group of men accosted and surrounded the two GNR officials. The Inspector was seized and taken to a hall in Dublin. There he was forced to sign an undertaking not to drive a Great Northern bus, and was then released. The following Monday the first GNR bus to make the journey between Dundalk and Dublin since the railway strike began three weeks earlier was partly destroyed when set on fire in Dublin by a crowd which gathered on Eden Quay. The vehicle had arrived shortly before 11.00am and was due to return in the afternoon to Dundalk. The Motorman, Hugh Lewis of Dundalk Garage, reported an uneventful trip from Dundalk that morning. The bus, a Leyland TS2 fleet No. 98, was parked on the Liffey side of Eden Quay being prepared for its northward journey at about one o'clock when a crowd had gathered on the quay as if anticipating some disturbance. Some of the younger members of the crowd, youths aged between 18 and 25, began to shout 'blacklegs' at the GNR crew when suddenly the crowd rushed towards the bus sweeping away the Civic Guards who had formed a cordon around the vehicle.

One of the youths succeeded in disconnecting the autovac, through which the petrol flows, and ignited the fuel. The engine compartment and bonnet was quickly engulfed in flames. Motorman Lewis made an attempt to seize a fire extinguisher from the driver's cab but received a very rough handling by some members of the crowd, who hustled him towards the wall of the River Liffey with the obvious intention of throwing him in. A Civic Guard went to his rescue and following a hard struggle succeeded in breaking up the crowd using his baton. A number of additional Guards arrived on the scene, together with three sections of the Fire Brigade and the flames were quickly extinguished with hand pumps. The damaged vehicle was removed to Dundalk works where it was repaired and returned to service some weeks later. Two young men aged 20 years appeared in the Dublin District Court charged with malicious damage.

At the end of February secondary action by dockers in Belfast who were refusing to handle 'diverted' goods resulted in 100,000 tons of goods and general merchandise including the all important linen exports lying in sheds on the docks. Such was the seriousness of the matter that the Northern Ireland Minister of Labour John Miller Andrews interceded with Mr Bevan, the President of the Amalgamated Transport and General Workers Union in an unsuccessful attempt to get the dockers to handle the merchandise. The Northern Ireland government was coming under increasing pressure especially from the Linen Companies, most of whom were significant financial donors to the Unionist Party, to intervene in the dispute with a view to reaching a settlement.

An attempt to burn down the GNR bus office at the Market Square Dundalk on Monday 27th February was foiled by Sergeant Flood who had been on Guard duty in the vicinity and noticed flames blazing at the rear of the small office. He extinguished the fire by throwing snow on it (there had been a severe blizzard two days previously) before any serious damage could be done. A GNR convoy of lorries was about to leave Grosvenor Street Goods sheds loaded with goods and mails on the night of Tuesday 28th February under RUC guard when a serious incident happened. At 11.00pm Constable John Ryan, a native of Tipperary, was shot dead at the junction of Durham Street and Albert Street after a fusillade of shots rang out from six armed men making their escape from the railway goods sheds after firing on the RUC convoy guards. An RUC Sergeant on convoy duty immediately opened fire at a number of figures lurking in the shadows on the opposite side of the road. The men decamped towards the Falls Road district. Constable Ryan managed to return the fire with his .45 revolver before falling in the street with four bullet wounds. Two known IRA men were subsequently arrested and charged with Constable Ryan's murder. Earlier in the day a bomb was found in the GNR locomotive sheds at Adelaide and was safely defused.

Another major horror occurred on Thursday 2nd March when a Great Northern passenger train from Belfast to Enniskillen was derailed and completely wrecked near Omagh and although no one was killed, all twenty-four passengers were injured. The train narrowly missed crashing through a bridge into the river below. The engine and tender remained on the rails, but telescoped and battered carriages and goods vans were hurled in all directions, the scene being one of indescribable confusion. GNR Traffic Manager James Lockhart and Deputy Joseph Walker together with a breakdown gang of 40 men complete with crane and civil engineers staff arrived on the scene that afternoon and immediately set about removing the wrecked train. It consisted of four passenger carriages, guards van, two cattle wagons, two fish vans, and five other vans and had left Belfast at 08.30 am. The train had been travelling at about 40mph as it approached the points where the lines branch off to the goods station at Omagh. A subsequent investigation revealed that the points had been set to divert the train to the goods branch in a diabolical attempt to throw the train into the river. Omagh railwaymen passed a subsequent resolution denouncing the outrage and dissociating the railwaymen from it.

The Northern Ireland Minister of Home Affairs Sir Dawson Bates speaking at a dinner of the County Grand Orange Lodge of Belfast on the day of the crash said:–

"We may have difficulties in the future, but the Government are prepared to take such measures as are necessary to ensure the safety of Northern Ireland. I refuse to believe that the outrages that have recently taken place have been brought about by the railwaymen". Clearly the government had deduced that sinister elements were exploiting the difficulties then being experienced. There was a widespread belief at the time that the IRA was behind much of the violence.

There have been many railway strikes in the British Isles since the invention of the railways; no other dispute witnessed such persistent outrages or reckless disregard for human life. The Omagh outrage was the sixteenth since the strike began, other outrages are summarised in the following table:–

Date	Incident
1 February	Train derailed at Dromiskin 2 killed
2 February	Track torn up St Johnston, Co Donegal
6 February	Crossing gates and points tampered with at Coleraine LMS (NCC). Bolts placed on the line at Whiteabbey
11 February	Attempt to blow up the line at Dunmurry. Bridge damaged in explosion at Barnesmore Gap, Co Donegal
14 February	Rail car collision with ganger's trolley left on the line at Glenties, Co Donegal
20 February	Bus set on fire in Dublin and attempt to throw the driver into Liffey
21 February	About 60 feet of line lifted at Dromore, Co Tyrone
25 February	Bombs thrown at the LMS and GNR Belfast termini
28 February	Belfast police constable shot dead by gunmen escaping after firing at goods and mail lorry convoy. Bomb found at GNR locomotive sheds at Adelaide
1 March	Attempt to blow up the line outside Larne. Fishplates, bolts, and a chair removed near Coleraine and attempt to blow up the line

The pressure to settle the strike continued to mount as more and more railwaymen drifted back to work allowing the railway to plan a normal Easter schedule of services for early April. Drogheda was the scene of great excitement on Tuesday 14th March when a group of five Dundalk Motormen were sent to the GNR Garage, which at that time was located beside the Railway Station. The Motormen were dispatched to Drogheda to retrieve five buses, which had been garaged there since the beginning of the strike and were required elsewhere to supplement the normal bus timetable. A group of about 20 strike pickets was on duty at the station premises, but the Motormen gained access to the garage by a ruse. They crept into the yard adjacent to the garage from the Navan branch line, unobserved by the pickets, who were greatly surprised when they heard the buses being started up and driven at speed towards them and the main Drogheda to Dundalk road.

The pickets rushed to close the railway yard gates, and when they were almost closed the first bus reached them. The Motorman driving the first bus instead of pulling up increased his speed and dashed through the gates, which were flung back scattering the crowd of pickets. This first bus escaped but when the second one came along the pickets formed a human chain in an endeavour to get the Motorman to pull up. This Motorman fearing being beaten up increased his speed and dashed through, the pickets having to jump aside quickly to avoid being knocked down and injured. The pickets then stoned the remaining three buses as they approached the gates, smashing several windows, fortunately there were no injuries. All the buses were driven to Dundalk Works by a circuitous route, via Duleek, Slane, Collon and Ardee without further incident. Dundalk now witnessed scenes of terrorism on Thursday 16th March as a bomb was thrown into a GNR bus within one hundred yards of the *Garda* Station in Anne Street. Civic Guard J McElroy, who was travelling in the bus, was seriously injured and a mechanic Patrick Comiskey sustained slight injuries. Motorman Michael McCabe and Conductor Joseph Mulcahy both escaped injury. The bus was travelling from Carrickmacross reaching Dundalk at about 9.30pm, when passing Wynne's Terrace the bomb was thrown through the window and exploded inside the bus with great violence. The bus windows were smashed, seats were torn and a 3ft hole was blown in the floor of the vehicle. Guard McElroy, who was sitting at the back of the bus and sustained most of the force of the explosion, was badly wounded in the arms and on his right leg. Bomb fragments were later recovered inside the bus, which revealed that the device was made from home made explosives.

Saint Patrick's Day 1933 arrived after seven weeks of railway strike and the situation in Northern Ireland was becoming desperate. Farmers were unable to obtain fertilisers for the sowing season, industry was dislocated and unemployment was rising. The government was under further pressure in Parliament from Northern Ireland Labour Party MPs who were asking embarrassing questions enquiring how much the strike was costing industry and the Ministry of Home Affairs (who were responsible for the RUC) to provide additional policing. The Northern Ireland Prime Minister Lord Craigavon had by now decided that John Miller Andrews, the Minister of Labour, had to intervene as a negotiator and shortly after summoned representatives of all parties to talks. The talking continued between the unions, railway companies and the Northern Ireland Government acting as facilitator. At first the talks seemed to be getting nowhere and then the breakthrough came.

On Thursday 6th April 1933 in Belfast's Grand Central Hotel representatives from the Association of Irish Railway Companies, which included some of the most important officials from many famous railways, attended. The delegation consisted of:–

Major Malcolm Spier Manager and Secretary of the LMS (NCC) accompanied by his Operating Superintendent Mr W Getty and Accountant Mr FL Smith. The GNR team consisted of James Lockhart the Traffic Manager and Foster Graham the Chief Clerk of the General Manager's Office. The Great Southern Railways, although not on strike, was represented by Mr PJ Floyd and Mr J Harty. Mr SC Lyttle, General Manager of the Sligo Leitrim and Northern Counties Railway, represented that administration. The Londonderry and Lough Swilly Railway delegate was its General Manager Mr J Whyte. Belfast and County Down Railway General Manager Mr WF Minnis was the final delegate. The LMS (NCC) and GNR jointly represented the interests of the County Donegal Railway as joint owners of that railway.

The Union delegations consisted of:–

National Union of Railwaymen

Mr W Dobbie, MP President
Mr CT Cramp, General Secretary
Mr CD Watters, Irish Secretary
Mr J Campbell, Irish Organiser
Messrs J Convery, AJ Byrne, P Harity, JB Figgins
Members of the Negotiating Committee.

ASLEF

Mr W Steele, Vice-President
Mr WJR Squance, Assistant General Secretary
Mr JG Stobie and Mr G Tyler, Executive Members.

Railway Clerks Association

Mr FB Simpson, President
Senator GT O'Farrell, Irish Secretary
Mr HH Oatts, Executive Committee Member

At 4.55pm Major Malcolm Spier issued the following statement in his capacity as Chairman of the Irish Railway Manager's Association:

'The meeting has arrived at a basis of agreement which in the case of the NUR and ASLEF has to be submitted to their Executive Committees on Friday. In the case of the RCA the delegation approved of the agreement on behalf of the Executive Committee to whom a report will be given at the weekend'.

The terms of the agreement were deliberately shrouded in secrecy at the request of the Unions who wanted the opportunity to present it to their Executives for ratification. The sticking point in the negotiations had always been the terms of reinstatement of striking rail workers. The agreement provided for the suspension, for four weeks from the resumption of work, of the guaranteed week, after which it will be restored, the companies agree to retain such staff as is adequate to meet the needs of the traffic, the choice being determined on a seniority basis. As a result of the settlement, the ban on diverted traffic at the docks was removed and normal conditions were resumed. The dockers and carters who had ceased working earlier in the week in support of the railwaymen resumed work. The Northern Ireland Prime Minister Lord Craigavon and his Labour Minister John Miller Andrews both expressed their pleasure that agreement had been reached. The secrecy surrounding the terms of the settlement did not last for long as word leaked out in advance of the various Union meetings that were taking place the next day Friday 7th April. The terms of settlement provided for the following:–

The general principle agreed upon is that all men who ceased work shall be reinstated in order of seniority; the men will be taken on as required to work the services in operation; the companies will reopen and extend their services as rapidly as the traffic warrants; the guaranteed weeks shall be suspended for a period of four weeks as from the date of resumption of work; during this period the work shall be shared equally between the men. At the end of this period the guaranteed week shall be restored. On the restoration of the guaranteed week the companies will retain sufficient staff to deal adequately with the traffic on their railways and will give consideration to any representations made by the unions regarding redundant men; the companies will when engaging a staff for railway or road transport services give preference to suitable men who have been discharged as redundant; where men have been convicted in the courts for a criminal offence their re-entry is precluded by the companies usual procedure. The companies will give consideration to any representations the unions may wish to make on any particular case; the agreement concerning deductions from earnings and variations in conditions of service, separately concluded between the Associated Irish Railway Companies and the National Union of Railwaymen, the Associated Society of Locomotive Engineers and Firemen and the Railway Clerks Association shall apply immediately on the resumption of work to the companies whose men withdrew their labour. It is agreed that on and from 1st May 1933 the following deductions from earnings and variations in conditions of service shall take place: – all conciliation grades including drivers, firemen and cleaners but exclusive

A Weymann-bodied, Albion PT65 No. 253, at Grosvenor Street Garage Belfast – note the garage allocation code W above the fleet number. *(SS)*

of road motor passenger staff; a 7% deduction from earnings based on the rates in force prior to May 1931.

Holidays without pay – all holidays for the year 1933 provided for in accordance with the February 1922 agreements shall be taken without pay.

Stationmasters and goods agents, male and female clerks and supervisors – 10% deduction from earnings based on the rates of pay in operation prior to May 1931.

The deductions from earnings provided for above shall operate until 1st May 1934 and shall be 7¼ % for the year ending 1st May 1935, provided that in March 1934 the companies respond to the unions that their financial position is such that additional relief is necessary. A meeting shall take place for the purpose of considering such representations and agreeing on the method of providing such relief.

The trade unions took the settlement proposals to their respective executives who endorsed the agreement that had been reached with the railway companies. By Saturday 8th April 1933 the message was going out to the strikers to return to work and that the dispute was over. But all was not well, especially in the Irish Free State and more particularly in Dublin. At a meeting of about 500 National Union of Railwaymen members in the Ardee Hall Dublin on the evening of Friday 7th, addressed by the Irish Organiser Mr Campbell, there was considerable opposition to the terms of the settlement. Following a stormy and acrimonious debate at which several motions were proposed to continue the dispute the meeting broke up in chaos without a vote being taken. This confusion and rancour resulted in some railwaymen returning to work and many more in the Dublin area staying out. A further complication arose out of the way in which the NUR meeting broke up in that an *ad hoc* 'Central Strike Committee' was formed determined to continue the dispute. They issued a call to all railwaymen to embark upon a lightning strike commencing at midnight on Sunday 9th April and this would include the Great Southern Railway. This was a new and worrying development, as the GSR by virtue of the fact that its employees enjoyed a wages subsidy did not join the strike that had just been settled on the Great Northern. The prospect of a GSR strike would inevitably lead to a withdrawal of the subsidy by the Free State Government as it had been on the Great Northern as soon as they went on strike.

The unofficial strike of Irish Free State railwaymen went ahead as from midnight Sunday in spite of a meeting with Sean Lemass the Minister of Industry and Commerce who told the strike committee that no better terms could be obtained. The lightning strike resulted in widespread loss of railway services on Monday and Tuesday 10/11th April. It was immediately condemned by the NUR, as an unofficial action, with the warning that strike pay would not be made. Locomotive staff reported for work as normal and attempts were made by the strikers to coerce them and the combined workforce of the Irish Omnibus Company and the cartage men of John Wallis and Sons (both owned by the GSR) to support the strike.

The response to the strike call resulted in a complete suspension of all Great Northern trains from Amiens Street station. The Great Southern Railway disruption extended to services on the Midlands lines to Athlone, Galway, Mayo and Sligo. No trains ran from Kingsbridge southwards or from Broadstone westwards. Services from Harcourt Street and Westland Row stations operated on the Monday morning but were suspended by lunchtime following a march of strikers from Kingsbridge to Harcourt Street and after a meeting with signalmen they decided to strike. The position in the south and west of the country was completely different as railwaymen in Cork, Limerick and Waterford remained on duty and most services other than those to or from Dublin operated.

GNR Road Motor Service staff in Dublin returned to work on Tuesday 11th April prefacing a return to work that occurred over the succeeding couple of days by the die hard striking railwaymen. Railway services began to return to normal from Thursday 13th April following the realisation by many rail workers that they were not going to improve upon the settlement terms agreed.

The Effects of the Strike

The most obvious effect of the strike was the highly regrettable deaths, injuries and mayhem that ensued during the sixty-six days of the dispute. Railway customers were severely inconvenienced both passenger and freight, appreciable damage was done to the economy in both Northern Ireland and the Irish Free State as exports lay on the docks and vital supplies were late arriving in the shops. For the striking railwaymen of the NUR and ASLEF they endured financial hardship, passing this on to their family and loved ones. This when combined with the terms of the settlement that was finally achieved meant that they were all far worse off than they would have been had they accepted the recommendation of the Irish Railway Wages Board prior to the commencement of the strike. The lasting effects of the bitterness and hatred engendered between the strikers and the railway companies were to sour industrial relations for generations to come.

The railway companies, and in particular the Great Northern, suffered a haemorrhage of passenger and freight traffic much of which failed to return to the railway. Road transport, which customers had resorted to using during the strike, proved that they were capable to providing a cheap, safe and efficient alternative. Although the road competitors did not take undue advantage of the railway's predicament, they were 'handed a gift' once normality returned. Already in a parlous financial position prior to the strike the loss in revenue caused by the stoppage almost led to the demise of the Great Northern. The company's finances were so weakened by the strike that arguably it could be said that the company was trading whilst technically insolvent. The company's fortunes improved temporarily during the war years when traffic was buoyant. Industrial relations between the company and its employees were never the same again as trust and confidence had broken down. Traffic Manager James Lockhart did, however, win plaudits for his handling of a difficult period in the Company's history

The strike encouraged those in the Northern Ireland Government who were intent on ensuring that the railway companies would not remain the principal transport providers in the land. There is evidence that the case for nationalisation of road transport from the Linen merchants, Ulster Farmers Union and various industrialists, many of whom were members of the Unionist Party, was being won among Ministers. During the strike there were many calls for the railway's road services to be bought out by the government and run under state control. Two years after the strike nationalisation of all road services became a reality with the creation of the Northern Ireland Road Transport Board. The seeds of that nationalisation were sown in the strike. Many of today's commentators blamed the Northern Ireland Government's perceived 'anti-rail' bias as being the rationale behind their lack of support for rail transportation. I contend that displeasure with the railway companies originated from the strike when the Province so nearly collapsed during those 66 memorable days in 1933 only eleven years after the introduction of self-government.

A 1934 line up of buses in Sheriff Street with Leyland LT5A No. 301 heading the queue waiting to depart. *(MC)*

Chapter Four
Donegal – Partition and Early Development

Following the partition of Ireland on 6th December 1922, County Donegal found itself in the unenviable position of being virtually isolated from the remainder of the Irish Free State for almost the entire length of the county. As in so many parts of Ireland, the development of bus services was interrupted by the Irish Civil War, which raged between the pro and anti treaty forces from June 1922 until 24th May 1923. Although partition established a territorial frontier between the Irish Free State and Northern Ireland (in the beginning it was not difficult to cross), this did not initially lead to a reduction in cross border traffic. It was in fact the Irish Free State government that established the 'Customs Barrier' between North and South on 1st April 1923 by introducing trade regulations, and with that measure authorised crossing points were established all along the frontier. These soon became institutionalised.

Lough Derg is known the world over as a place of pilgrimage – to the Irish people this romantic lake has been known and cherished for over 1500 years, and its history has been a succession of romantic and frequently tragic events. The lake is dotted with islands, the principal of which is Station Island or St Patrick's Purgatory, half a mile from the mainland shore. It is on this island that the pilgrimage was made. The Lough lies four and a half miles from the town of Pettigo, which was served by the Great Northern Railway from Bundoran Junction. The pilgrimage season, from 1st June to 15th August each year, became highly lucrative for transport operators. Upwards of 8,000 would travel by train from Dublin alone with totals from all over the country of about 16,000.

Pettigo Problems

Pettigo had the distinction of witnessing the last British troops to leave the territory of the Irish Free State. The Great Northern Railway played a part in these events. Pettigo is a *cul de sac* in County Fermanagh. There is only one road out to the Irish Free State, a mountainous road to Laghy. All other roads run through Northern Ireland. In December 1922 the local majority Protestant and Loyalist population of Pettigo feared the imminent arrival of Irish Free State troops who were to establish a garrison in their part of the village. A repetition of widespread murder and intimidation visited upon them by Republican forces the previous May and June struck fear into their hearts. The Loyalists on the British side of Pettigo were under the protection of 'D' Company 2nd South Staffordshire Regiment, commanded by Captain Horden and the Royal Ulster Constabulary led by County Inspector Gerrity, together with elements of the Ulster Special Constabulary led by Captain Sir Basil Brooke, Fermanagh County Commandant. Between 40 and 60 Protestant families left the village of Pettigo in fear of their lives at the hands of the Free State forces. The spokesperson for the remaining Loyalists, the local Church of Ireland rector Rev EW McKegney, eventually agreed for the 150 Free State soldiers from 'B' Company 3rd Southern Battalion, under the command of Captain McNaughten, himself a Protestant, who had been appointed the Civil Commissioner, to enter Pettigo and establish a garrison. Thus on Tuesday 9th January 1923 the Union Flag was hauled down for the last time as the 20 men of the Staffordshire Regiment boarded the GNR train for Omagh, leaving behind a small Headquarters party. Although the morning was cold, dark and a blustering wind blew, quite a number of the residents of Pettigo gave the Tommies a hearty farewell. The Free State troops arrived by a special GNR train under Royal Ulster Constabulary special escort as it had passed through Northern Ireland to reach Pettigo. The RUC men marched straight to the Constabulary station, which was located in the Northern Ireland part of the village. The Free State soldiers entered Pettigo from the Railway Station. There was no waving of flags; there were no cheers or shouts of joy. Most people stayed indoors, sullen and dour. General Yapman, Captain Horden (Stafford's OC) and other officers were at their Headquarters and as the Free State troops came along, the British took their departure. The Free State troops gave a general salute, which General Yapman acknowledged. The incoming forces relieved the small residual British party of 20 men at the Mill Street post. The Free State forces established quarters in Flood's Hotel, the Courthouse and the Market House. Rival barracks were quickly established within a stones throw of each other. Each sent out patrols that it was suggested came within speaking distance of the other, although a word was never exchanged. The Termon River formed the Border between north and south. Pettigo is a village of three streets; Main Street climbs the hill past the Protestant Church and then the Roman Catholic Church. Mill Street, narrower and more worn, flanks the river Termon and High Street crossed the river straddling both north and south territory.

The advent of the border between North and South created particular problems in Pettigo. In January 1923 two Post Offices were established in the town, one a 'Loyalist' in the Northern territory where letters could be posted at 1½ d, and the other a Free State Post Office with Mr Andrew Brennan as Postmaster, where the charge was 2d. Loyalists had declared that there was a bigger turnover at their establishment. Andrew Brennan, the Free State Postmaster decided to turn to running buses as a means of supplementing his income. In February 1924 he began running his charabancs between Ballyshannon and Sligo through the Irish Free State. Brennan, who operated with the benefit of aid in the form of a subsidy for providing an Irish Free State postal service from Pettigo to Sligo via Laghy and Ballintra adopted this route along the road now numbered the R232, which was not the direct method of gaining access to Ballyshannon. Had he chosen the direct route along the road leading to Ballyshannon through Belleek this would have necessitated crossing into Northern Ireland territory, which he could not do as a result of his mail contract.

In May 1928 Brennan was successfully sued for £1,500 plus costs by Bridget Meehan who was knocked off her cycle in August 1927 by one of Brennan's buses. This case plunged the Brennan Bus Service into financial ruin. Brennan also ran a service between Sligo and Ballina, which for a brief period put him in competition with the IOC on that road. In April 1929 Andrew Brennan sold his bus service to RH Curran of 19, O'Connell Street, Sligo who withdrew the Sligo – Ballyshannon service at the end of that year. Curran continued to use the Brennan Bus Service name and was himself bought out on the 28th February 1933 by the IOC. Another obscure local operator who ran a bus from Sligo to Ballyshannon County Donegal Railway Station established in 1924 was Mr Peter McKenna of 8, Charles Street, Sligo. The Great Southern Railway decided to contract the Sligo Motor Engineering Company during the seasons 1925/6 to run a charabanc service connecting the GSR Sligo railhead with that of the GNR stations at Bundoran and Ballyshannon where Lough Derg bound pilgrims could travel to Pettigo by GNR train. By March 1927 the GSR wanted to extend its road motor services into County Donegal by proposing two return workings daily from Sligo to Ballyshannon outside the pilgrimage season. On 29th May 1928 an application for a service from Sligo to Donegal Town was made.

Such was the magnetism of Lough Derg traffic for bus operators that during the pilgrimage season of 1929 the Erne Bus Company commenced operating a daily bus to the Mainland Shore from Enniskillen. The following season the Erne provided the same service from Enniskillen in conjunction with the Phair Brothers (whose bus operated from Cavan to Enniskillen) and the Magnet Motor Services with its Dublin/Cavan service. The 1931 season provided further interest with the through service from Cavan to Lough Derg being run by the Phair Brothers as far as Enniskillen with a connecting bus operated by W Clarke of Belmore Street Enniskillen. The Erne continued to offer an Enniskillen/Lough Derg/Bundoran service extolling the virtues of through ticketing from places served by the Magnet. The GNR bought the Magnet on 15th December 1931 and the Phair Brothers operation on the 23rd April 1932 thus ending this alliance. John McGowan of Wardhouse, Tullaghan, Co Leitrim who traded as the Tourist Bus Service, launched a Sligo – Bundoran service in 1927 with two International buses and a very down-at-heel Ford charabanc. McGowan engendered loyal patronage by undercutting other operator's fares between Grange and Cliffoney to Sligo.

The GSR decided in July 1927 to contract the Irish Omnibus Company to run bus services on its behalf, and for which it had obtained authority under the Railway's Road Motor Act 1927 – these were designated as 'approved' services. IOC unapproved services were those operated commercially and largely independently from the GSR. The Sligo/Donegal area featured in this arrangement. In June 1928 the IOC suggested to the GSR that it extend its proposed unapproved service from Sligo to Donegal northwards to Derry. The IOC eager to establish a local base for its Sligo/Donegal area services rented garage premises in Lord Edward Street Sligo from the 10th July 1928. The rivalry between the GNR and the GSR and its surrogates in the IOC led to discussions concerning Donegal competition on 19th July 1928. The GNR expressed the view that they would not object to IOC buses south of Ballyshannon from Sligo working through the County Leitrim salient (that part of Leitrim which extends westwards to the coast at Donegal Bay just south of Bundoran), which the GSR considered its territory. Jonathan Stephens, GNR General Manager, warned the GSR that it would retaliate in respect of any services which pushed north of Ballyshannon. The IOC then informed GNR that it was proposing to run an unapproved omnibus service from Sligo to Londonderry and some preparatory work was completed in July 1928 including the publication of a fares handbill, although it never ran. The GSR obtained approval on 29th September 1928 from the Dublin Ministry of Industry and Commerce for the operation of a Sligo-Donegal service (Route No. 83) and a summer seasonal service between Ballyshannon (where a connection was made with IOC buses) and Lough Derg (Route No. 84). The Great Northern Railway now became active in the provision of a service for Lough Derg pilgrims. On 5th May 1928 it contracted Michael John Mullally of Bessboro Avenue, North Strand, Dublin who traded as Lally Motor Transport to inaugurate a seasonal Pettigo to Lough Derg bus service conveying pilgrims to the mainland shore. The GNR came in for some criticism on the 16th March 1929 at a meeting of Donegal County Council for charging five shillings in respect of the bus journey from Pettigo the previous season, which was considered predatory. The Council instructed the County Surveyor Mr Steadman to suspend operations on road widening up to the mainland shore until the GNR reduced their fares for the 1929 season. The Council's tactics worked resulting in lower fares together with a new development from the GNR. The Irish Omnibus Company quickly reacted to the GNR service by providing a rival unapproved one from Sligo (GSR) Railway Station to Lough Derg, which began on 7th June 1928.

Again in June 1928, responding to increased competition, McGowan (Tourist Bus Service), appealed to his customers to remain loyal to his services by taking out adverts in the Sligo Champion newspaper entreating customers to 'Support Local Enterprise'. Additionally he extended his services to Donegal Town with three journeys on weekdays and two on Sundays introducing competitive fares. He supplemented his main service from Sligo to Ballyshannon by projecting the operation to Donegal Town via Rossnowlagh and

Ballintra to cater for the summer seaside traffic effective from Monday 18th July 1932. The McGowan move was in response to the GNR Ballyshannon – Rossnowlagh summer service that began on 5th June 1932. During September 1928 in an attempt to raise additional revenues, he entered the excursion business running day trips to Galway. In October 1929 McGowan commenced day excursions to the recently constructed power station at Ard-na-Crusha on the Shannon a few miles north of Limerick.

Another operator with considerable entrepreneurial skills, HMS Catherwood, who also had strong personal connections with County Donegal, now commenced bus operations in the County. A Monday to Saturday service between Sligo-Londonderry began with two workings in each direction on 20th December 1928. On Tuesday 25th June 1929 a connection at Donegal to Glenties via Killybegs was added. Catherwoods appointed a Donegal Town Chemist, Britton and Sons, in the Main Street as its agent, garaging its bus behind the Commercial Hotel in the Diamond. On 1st June 1929 the GNR inaugurated a retaliatory bus service, which was being regulated by Chief Inspector Albert Switzer (in opposition to the IOC) between Sligo, Ballyshannon and Lough Derg (Route No. 104). A Dublin contractor, J Holmes of Granby Place, was employed using a red and white 14-seat Crossley bus complete with GNR stickers on the side. A Bundoran Station Porter acted as Conductor to collect the 3/6d return fare. Mr Holmes was paid 9d per mile for the duration of the contract. The service ran on Irish Omnibus Company timings. Albert Switzer correctly viewed it important for the contractor to get his bus positioned advantageously just outside Sligo Railway Station to maximise the number of passengers. On the first day of operation the bus arrived at the Railway Station to meet the mail train from Dublin and the driver cheekily parked beside the IOC bus. An angry GSR stationmaster was summoned who quickly evicted the offending vehicle from railway property. On that first day of operation Albert Switzer managed to obtain a record of the IOC takings on the route. Relations between the GNR and the IOC/GSR now became very strained. The GNR quickly introduced cut-price fares undercutting the competition, which by now was intense. The IOC responded by running a 'chaser' bus clearing the road from the GNR and handing over to the normal service car at Ballyshannon, then returning back to Sligo in front of the 1.00pm GNR service. Concurrently the GSR took effective control of the Irish Omnibus Company as its new board consisting of GSR nominees met for the first time between 1st and 2nd July 1929.

An agreement between the rival GNR and GSR (including the IOC) was ever closer as further discussions on September 1st 1929 resulted in a compromise. The IOC agreed in principle to discontinue its Sligo/Donegal service. The GNR applied to the Dublin Ministry for authority to operate a Sligo-Carrigans (for Derry) service (Route No. 111), which was granted on 3rd October 1929, and with this its intentions became clear. A formal agreement between the GNR/GSR and the IOC was reached on Monday 14th October 1929, which provided that:–

The GSR/IOC agreed that the GNR would assume responsibility for operating all bus services between Sligo and Donegal as soon as they were in a position to do so. The road between Sligo and Ballyshannon would for the purposes of the agreement become joint GNR/GSR territory, all revenue to be split on a 50/50 basis between the two railway administrations. This was referred to as the 'pooled area'. The agreement date is significant, as it became the anniversary for subsequent agreements between the two railway concerns in respect of road freight territory and the operation of a joint GNR/GSR lorry service between Sligo and Ballyshannon.

HMS Catherwood Bus Station in Foyle Street, Londonderry, such was the extent of Catherwood operations in this area. *(GL)*

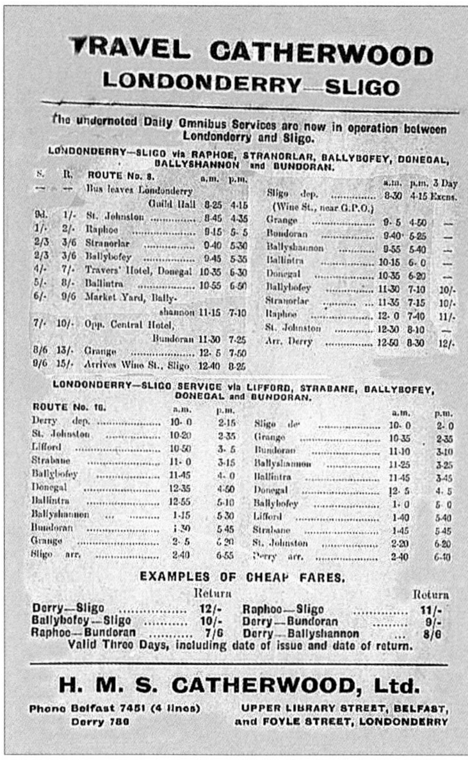

TRAVEL CATHERWOOD
LONDONDERRY—SLIGO

The undernoted Daily Omnibus Services are now in operation between Londonderry and Sligo.

LONDONDERRY—SLIGO via RAPHOE, STRANORLAR, BALLYBOFEY, DONEGAL, BALLYSHANNON and BUNDORAN.

S.	R.	ROUTE No. 8.	a.m.	p.m.
—	—	Bus leaves Londonderry Guild Hall	8-25	4-15
9d.	1/-	St. Johnston	8-45	4-35
1/-	2/-	Raphoe	9-15	5- 5
2/3	3/6	Stranorlar	9-40	5-30
2/3	3/6	Ballybofey	9-45	5-35
4/-	7/-	Travers' Hotel, Donegal	10-35	6-30
5/-	8/-	Ballintra	10-55	6-50
6/-	9/6	Market Yard, Ballyshannon	11-15	7-10
7/-	10/-	Opp. Central Hotel, Bundoran	11-30	7-25
8/6	13/-	Grange	12- 5	7-50
9/6	15/-	Arrives Wine St., Sligo	12-40	8-25

	a.m.	p.m.	3 Day Excns.
Sligo dep. (Wine St., near G.P.O.)	8-30	4-15	
Grange	9- 5	4-50	—
Bundoran	9-40	5-25	—
Ballyshannon	9-55	5-40	—
Ballintra	10-15	6- 0	—
Donegal	10-35	6-20	—
Ballybofey	11-30	7-10	10/-
Stranorlar	11-35	7-15	10/-
Raphoe	12- 0	7-40	11/-
St. Johnston	12-30	8-10	—
Arr. Derry	12-50	8-30	12/-

LONDONDERRY—SLIGO SERVICE via LIFFORD, STRABANE, BALLYBOFEY, DONEGAL and BUNDORAN.

ROUTE No. 16.	a.m.	p.m.
Derry dep.	10- 0	2-15
St. Johnston	10-20	2-35
Lifford	10-50	3- 5
Strabane	11- 0	3-15
Ballybofey	11-45	4- 0
Donegal	12-35	4-50
Ballintra	12-55	5-10
Ballyshannon	1-15	5-30
Bundoran	1-30	5-45
Grange	2- 5	6-20
Sligo arr.	2-40	6-55

	a.m.	p.m.
Sligo de[p.]	10- 0	2- 0
Grange	10-35	2-35
Bundoran	11-10	3-10
Ballyshannon	11-25	3-25
Ballintra	11-45	3-45
Donegal	12- 5	4- 5
Ballybofey	1- 0	5- 0
Lifford	1-40	5-40
Strabane	1-45	5-45
St. Johnston	2-20	6-20
Derry arr.	2-40	6-40

EXAMPLES OF CHEAP FARES.

	Return		Return
Derry—Sligo	12/-	Raphoe—Sligo	11/-
Ballybofey—Sligo	10/-	Derry—Bundoran	9/-
Raphoe—Bundoran	7/6	Derry—Ballyshannon	8/6

Valid Three Days, including date of issue and date of return.

H. M. S. CATHERWOOD, Ltd.

Phone Belfast 7451 (4 lines) Derry 780

UPPER LIBRARY STREET, BELFAST, and FOYLE STREET, LONDONDERRY

GREAT NORTHERN ROAD MOTOR SERVICES.

SLIGO—LONDONDERRY
— AND —
SLIGO—DONEGAL
via Bundoran and Ballyshannon.

WEEK-DAYS.

		a.m.	p.m.	p.m.	p.m.
SLIGO	dep.	11-35	1-15	3-30	7-30
GRANGE	,,	12-15	1-55	4-10	8-10
BUNDORAN	,,	12-50	2-25	4-40	8-40
BALLYSHANNON	,,	1- 0	2-45	5- 0	9- 0
BALLINTRA	,,	—	3-10	—	9-25
DONEGAL	arr.	—	3-30	—	9-45

		a.m.	p.m.	p.m.	p.m.
DONEGAL	dep.	9- 0	—	4- 0	—
BALLINTRA	,,	9-18	—	4-18	—
BALLYSHANNON	,,	9-45	1- 0	4-45	9-30
BUNDORAN	,,	10- 5	1-20	5-10	9-50
GRANGE	,,	10-35	1-55	5-45	10-20
SLIGO	arr.	11-15	2-25	6-15	11- 0

SUNDAYS.

		* a.m.	p.m.	p.m.	* p.m.	p.m.
SLIGO	dep.	10. 0	1-30	2-45	5-30	—
GRANGE	,,	10-35	2-10	3-20	6-10	—
BUNDORAN	,,	11-10	2-40	3-50	6-40	8-40
BALLYSHANNON	,,	11-25	2-50	4- 0	6-55	8-50
BALLINTRA	,,	11-45	—	—	7-15	9-10
DONEGAL	,,	12- 5	—	—	7-35	9-45
BALLYBOFEY	,,	1- 0	—	—	8-30	—
STRANORLAR	,,	1- 5	—	—	8-35	—
CONVOY	,,	1-20	—	—	8-50	—
RAPHOE	,,	1-35	—	—	9- 5	—
ST. JOHNSTON	,,	2- 5	—	—	9-35	—
CARRIGANS	,,	2-20	—	—	9-50	—
LONDONDERRY	arr.	2-40	—	—	10-10	—

		a.m.	* a.m.	p.m.	* p.m.
LONDONDERRY	dep.	—	10- 0	—	5-30
CARRIGANS	,,	—	10-20	—	5-50
ST. JOHNSTON	,,	—	10-35	—	6- 5
RAPHOE	,,	—	11- 5	—	6-35
CONVOY	,,	—	11-20	—	6-50
STRANORLAR	,,	—	11-35	—	7- 5
BALLYBOFEY	,,	—	11-40	—	7-10
DONEGAL	,,	10-30	12-35	—	8- 5
BALLINTRA	,,	10-50	12-55	—	8-30
BALLYSHANNON	,,	11-10	1-15	4- 0	9- 0
BUNDORAN	,,	11-30	1-30	4-10	9-15
GRANGE	,,	12- 5	2- 5	4-45	9-50
SLIGO	arr.	12-45	2-40	5-15	10-25

* These Services will operate between Sligo and Londonderry on each Sunday as from Sunday, 31st August, 1930.

J. B. STEPHENS, General Manager.

DUBLIN, AUGUST, 1930.

Competition on the Sligo/Londonderry service as exemplified by the handbills of the GNR(I) and HMS Catherwood. *(GL)*

The 1930s Consolidation & Concerns

Some members of the Donegal County Council adopted a position of opposing the involvement of bus companies in the county. Companies with a Northern Ireland base were the target of the particular criticism such as Catherwood and Roberts. The County Council meeting in Lifford on Tuesday 28th October 1930 debated the matter of cross-border bus services and the contribution or otherwise they made to the life of the county. This debate was taking place at a time when the cash strapped County Council was struggling to maintain the existing road network let alone paying for the desired improvements particularly to the trunk road network. Councillor Manus O'Boyle speaking in the debate, enquired from the County Secretary what contribution the GNR made to the upkeep of the County's road network. The Secretary pointed out that the GNR made a significant contribution through the payment of rates in the county on property, which it owned. The Secretary continued by stating that inquiries made on its behalf showed that of eight Catherwood buses used on the Sligo-Londonderry and Portnoo service, only two-paid road tax in the Irish Free State, the remainder being taxed in Belfast. This revelation drew wide criticism and engendered a strong anti-Northern Ireland sentiment. Councillor Neil Blaney TD said a railway company was trying to get a monopoly of roads, and he did not think this was fair. It is clear that this remark was directed at the GNR who had recently bought the Roberts service. Some Councillors wanted to restrict cross border bus services, the main champion of this cause being Councillor Nyhan. He contended that buses running from Donegal into Derry resulted in a loss to Donegal business and were almost exclusively run by 'Northerners' for the sole benefit of 'Northerners'. Fortunately the anti-Northern Ireland sentiments subsided and the County Council settled down to work in constructive partnerships with bus operators who through the passage of time turned out to be the railway companies.

The 1930s began with the GNR committed to taking over the Sligo-Donegal services of the IOC as soon as buses and staff were available. Together with the County Donegal Railways, the GNR viewed the Catherwood buses as the most damaging to the future viability of both railway administrations. The County Donegal Railways Joint Committee (CDRJC), to give its full title, was jointly owned by the GNR and the London Midland and Scottish Railway. Its General Manager, Henry Forbes a former GNR railway man originally from County Armagh, was one of the great railway characters of Ireland. He gained encyclopaedic knowledge of both the Donegal Railway and the inhabitants of the County. This provided him with an excellent insight into where the revenue and traffic could be maximised. Forbes was a railwayman through and through and his dislike of buses was well documented; however he recognised the part they could play in complementing his railway operations. HMS Catherwood forced the CDR and the GNR to develop a common strategy in an effort to protect the railway traffic and provide feeder services from outlying districts. The CDR Board meeting in Stranorlar on Thursday 26th September 1929 instructed Henry Forbes to apply to the Irish Free State Minister of Industry and Commerce for approval to run six bus routes. The Catherwood Sligo/Londonderry bus introduced in December 1928 and the Londonderry/Glenties service running from June 1929 with shorter journey times and lower fares severely dented CDR revenues.

On 27th November 1929 Ministerial approval for five routes was obtained:

Donegal/Glencolumbkille (Route No. 112)
Letterkenny/Milford (Route No. 113)
Glenties/Ardara (Route No. 114)
Glenties/Portnoo (Seasonal Service 1st April to 10th September) (Route No. 115)
Ballybofey/Carrigans for Londonderry (Route No. 117)

There is no evidence that the CDR were intent on running a bus between Ballybofey and Londonderry although the GNR were most certainly interested in doing so, indicated by the fact that they too had applied to the Minister in Dublin to operate a bus service between Sligo and Carrigans for Londonderry (Route No. 111). Although Dublin approval was obtained, the Northern Ireland government refused

Number 305 is a Leyland LT5A, despite the GNR Gardner radiator, side by side with a true GNR Gardner No. 250 outside Foyle Road Station in Londonderry in 1951. *(MC)*

Former Roberts Dennis G bus now in GNR ownership, at Foyle Road Goods yard in July 1931 which was then used to garage GNR buses. *(SS)*

permission for the GNR bus service to enter Londonderry from the Carrigans frontier. This refusal resulted in the GNR changing tactics. They then sought and obtained approval from the Irish Free State for a single daily Sligo-Lifford service on the 7th February 1930 (Route No. 135). Albert Switzer was called to Dublin to meet Joe Mackle on Thursday 13th March 1930 to discuss the introduction of a Sligo/Strabane service, although approval was again refused by the Northern Ireland government to operate the section between Lifford and Strabane, a tantalisingly short distance of about one mile resulting in the proposal being still born. The CDR Board meeting in the GNR's Board Room in Belfast on Wednesday 19th February 1930 authorised Forbes to establish a bus service between Ardara and Portnoo via Glenties and for him initially to hire in buses for this purpose. He was unable to obtain the hire of suitable buses and was subsequently authorised by the CDR Board meeting, this time at the LMS's York Road Station on Thursday 29th May 1930, to purchase from the GNR four Reo buses for £270. These machines had just been acquired by the GNR from the United Motor Services of Tanderagee fleet. They were dispatched to Stranorlar following an overhaul and repaint in Dundalk Works and were used to inaugurate the CDR's first railway feeder bus service, which ran as a summer seasonal service at that time between Glenties and Rosbeg from the 20th July 1930. This service was unprofitable from its inception despite the fact that preference on the bus was given to passengers connecting with the railway at Glenties. Its efficacy was soon questioned by Forbes who pointed out to his Board that it was only profitable on Sunday when the Catherwood buses with which they competed were not on the road. Forbes now lost interest in buses and was content to let the GNR develop services in County Donegal on behalf of the CDR from then on.

A startling turn of events within the IOC now worked ultimately in the GNR's favour. Mayday 1930 unleashed a widespread and particularly violent strike resulting from the GSR's refusal to recognise the National Union of Railwaymen as the representative group for bus drivers. Many IOC services failed to operate during the 12 weeks of industrial turmoil. Some buses did manage to run using compliant labour and this resulted in some scenes of serious civil disorder. In July 1930 armed men attacked two IOC buses returning to Sligo from Ballinamore. The IOC Depot Manager at Sligo, Mr Brannigan, was wounded when the bus he was driving was fired on near Gurranmount. On Monday 7th July 1930, the GNR, now under immense pressure resulting from the inability of the IOC to operate their Sligo-Donegal service since May, took over the service in accordance with the agreement of the previous October. The new Leyland TS2 buses delivered to the GNR's Dublin Garage permitted the cascading of two Leyland PLSC buses to the Donegal Area to work the service. Several IOC drivers joined the GNR, as did the IOC representative in Ballyshannon, Mr Gillespie and whose wife became the GNR agent in the town. The IOC strike was finally settled on Friday 20th July 1930.

With the GSR/IOC agreement now in place regarding services in South Donegal similar dialogue was taking place in Londonderry between the GNR and local bus operator Roberts and Sons. The initial impetus for the discussions arose from the refusal by the Northern Ireland government in October 1929 to grant the GNR authority to run a bus service from its border into Londonderry as part of a proposed Sligo-Londonderry service and thus compete with Catherwood, so another strategy was devised. GNR Chairman Sir George Clark, whilst on a routine visit to Londonderry in May 1930, took the opportunity to open up discussions with the Roberts brothers concerning the purchase of their services, which ran in GNR and CDR territory. The three Roberts brothers, Hugh Eccles, Reginald and Charles were pioneers in bus operations in the Counties of Londonderry and Donegal. In early 1912 Roberts began running a bus between Londonderry and Greencastle via Moville. Further services were added to Claudy, Feeny and Park in the County Londonderry hinterland. On 1st January 1913 a Roberts's night mail van began running to Strabane, Letterkenny, Milford and Portsalon from Londonderry under contract to the Royal Mail. During the First World War a Roberts's bus powered by town gas ran to Limavady from Londonderry. They were also sub-contractors to the Admiralty for the repair and maintenance of all the motorboats in connection with the warships and mine sweeping fleet in the North West as well as munitions manufacture. Further bus service development came in the twenties with routes from Londonderry to Strabane, Victoria Bridge, Castlederg (either via Fyfin or Ardstraw) to Killeter and Aghyaran. In late 1928 the Roberts Company gained a highly profitable two and a half year contract to convey 200 men daily from Londonderry City to the Banagher where a new reservoir was under construction, together with the pipe main linking it to the City. The major prize for the GNR was the Roberts service, which they had initiated on the 1st June 1927 with two journeys daily between Londonderry and Ballybofey using the St Johnston and Convoy route. A month later the frequency was doubled with a bus being stationed overnight at Ballybofey. The acquisition by the GNR of the Robert's operation unlocked the gates of the Maiden City breaking the siege permitting the GNR to run buses the four miles from County Donegal into the City.

On the 10th July 1930 the GNR paid the Roberts brothers the sum of £2,850 for their Ballybofey and Aghyaran routes and a collection of six buses. The County Donegal Railways contributed £500 towards the purchase. The GNR and CDR quickly agreed that the existing GNR Sligo-Donegal service should be linked up with the Ballybofey-Londonderry service thus providing a through bus service from Sligo to compete with Catherwood and so the GNR first through bus service from Sligo to Londonderry, as a Sunday only operation (when HMS Catherwood did not run) began on 31st August 1930 using a mixture of former Roberts and GNR machines. A GNR weekday Sligo/Londonderry service started on Monday 22nd September 1930 as an additional cascaded Leyland PLSC Lion bus became available. Albert Switzer was again in charge of translating plans into reality having been in the area since Wednesday 10th September. It was also agreed that the new service would be operated wholly by the GNR and that net receipts (or net loss) would be divided between the two railway administrations in respect of all costs north of Ballyshannon. The Roberts bus services were eventually

GNR Gardner No. 246 at Sligo GNR Bus Office on 2nd August 1950. Note the large departure board just to the right of the vehicle. *(JG)*

split three ways with the LMS NCC who had acquired their third on 7th October 1929 to be joined by the GNR and later still the Londonderry and Lough Swilly Railway acquired the Inishowen services. The expansion of bus services by the GNR in County Donegal facilitated the singling of the double track railway between Londonderry and St Johnston in 1932.

The introduction of the 1933 Road Transport Act by the Dublin government resulted in the compulsory purchase of the HMS Catherwood services within the Irish Free State on 11th December 1933 as already mentioned. Using the same powers the Dublin government sanctioned the compulsory acquisition by the GNR on the 29th July 1934 of the McGowan's Tourist Bus Service between Sligo (Wine Street) and Ballyshannon (Market Yard). McGowan, livid by this turn of events, went personally to the Ministry of Industry and Commerce in Dublin with the intention of protesting to the Minister Sean Lemass. He failed to obtain an audience with the Minister, settling instead for a fruitless encounter with his officials. McGowan said he was not willing to hand over the licence and would continue to operate the service and if need be apply for a new licence, until his staff and the machines were taken over by the GNR on terms that were acceptable to him. A farcical situation ensued with McGowan continuing to operate his services in full alongside the GNR who were now the legal licence holders until he was forced to desist by the *Gardai* on Monday 6th August 1934, following personal representations to them by Chief Inspector Albert Switzer who remained in the area until Thursday 9th August 1934. McGowan, who enjoyed a certain local notoriety, had a number of entanglements with the law. On Friday 7th September 1934 he appeared in the Sligo District Court to answer charges of 'running a bus on an unauthorised route without an occasional licence' after being stopped by the *Gardai* at Dromahair whilst *en route* to Hazelwood Races and was fined ten shillings. This incident happened a mere six weeks after losing his licence to the GNR. The GNR acquisition of the Tourist Bus Service and the Catherwood service gave the company complete dominance of all bus services on the Sligo/Londonderry corridor. McGowan eventually received £2,000 compensation in return for his licences from the GNR who did not purchase any of his vehicles.

Lough Derg

Leaving aside the intense competition on the Sligo-Londonderry corridor, by 1931 the increasing demand for summer season omnibuses to convey rail passengers from Pettigo Station to Lough Derg Shore led the GNR(I) Board to authorise purchase of six second hand former London General Omnibus Company double-deck buses at a cost of £360 each with a further sum of £660 set aside for overhaul at Dundalk Works. Although Board approval was granted at the meeting in Dublin on the 21st January 1931 the purchase did not proceed, principally as a result of the poor road conditions in Donegal. Instead six former Ribble Leyland SG7/SG9 vehicles were purchased on 25th March 1931 from Blakes, a Manchester bus dealer, at a total cost of £1,480 including freight, import duty and reconditioning. The Ministry of Industry and Commerce very nearly vetoed the purchase as the vehicles were fitted with solid tyres until an assurance was received that pneumatics would be fitted at Dundalk Works before the buses entered service. The purchase of these vehicles was preferred as the Board noted that the chassis could be utilised if necessary as 4½ ton lorries. Lough Derg traffic reached a peak on the 17th May 1931 as thousands of pilgrims from all over Ireland converged for the consecration of a new Church. This was the first occasion on which the GNR used the former Ribble buses. The vehicles saw service for 6 weeks during July and August being garaged at night in the yard of Pettigo Railway Station. Their primitive construction ensured they were quickly cascaded onto other duties. Four of these buses were converted into goods lorries in 1932 at a cost of £432.16.0. The remaining two vehicles were converted into railway engineer's railcars. The annual Lough Derg summer services continued largely unchanged until 1955 when the Great Northern severed the direct omnibus connection between Sligo, Ballyshannon and Lough Derg. The connecting bus service from trains arriving at Pettigo Station to the Mainland Shore continued to operate. The Sligo connection was reinstated in the Summer of 1958 as a joint service operated by the Great Northern and the Ulster Transport Authority as part of the agreement reached following the closure of the Bundoran Railway in September 1957. The Great Northern omnibus operated between Sligo and Ballyshannon where it connected with an Ulster Transport vehicle, which conveyed passengers to Lough Derg. From 1958 the UTA ran buses during the summer pilgrimage period from the nearest railhead of Omagh to Bundoran via Lough Derg right up to the closure of the Londonderry Foyle Road line in 1965.

GNR Dominance in Donegal

In 1933 in the aftermath of the railway strike the County Donegal Railway was saved from extinction by the parent company's general policy of which the Great Northern's acquisition of its road services was an integral part. The GNR, by acquiring the Donegal road services, which initially ran at a loss, actually provided the best form of insurance for its railway operations. There is no doubt that had the GNR not obtained control of road services in South Donegal rampant road competition would have ensured the railway's demise much sooner than actually transpired. The formal agreement entered into on 1st January 1933, which replaced an earlier verbal accord of July 1930, entered into in the aftermath of the Roberts purchase called for the Great Northern to provide

GNR Gardner No. 399 at the GNR Agency Abbey Hotel, Diamond Donegal. Note the white outlining of mud guards. This was a distinctive feature of buses operated by this garage. *(JG)*

and develop omnibus services. The progressive development of the under mentioned routes in the CDR area eventually became known as the Donegal Area Joint Services, the net revenue/loss was apportioned 80% to the CDR 20% to the GNR as shown in the table below:–

Route	Date of Commencement
Londonderry – Ballyshannon	31 August 1930
Donegal-Glenties-Portnoo	11 December 1931
Ballyshannon – Rossnowlagh	5 June 1932
Killybegs – Malinmore	1 September 1944 after Bogagh Bus purchase.
Glenties – Dungloe	1 May 1946
Ballybofey – Letterkenny	1 July 1946
Stranorlar-Glenties-Portnoo	15 December 1947

Lough Derg services were not considered jointly operated. The first joint service ran from Killybegs to Portnoo via Glenties, which began on the 11th December 1931. However after the HMS Catherwood take-over on December 11th 1933 that year a connecting service to Donegal Town was added.

The GNR(I) and LMS (NCC) jointly entered into a territorial co-ordination agreement with the Londonderry and Lough Swilly Railway Co effective from 12th June 1934. The agreement recognised 'the necessity of co-ordinating their respective omnibus services with the object of avoiding wasteful duplication.' The L&LS Railway territory was defined as the area north of a line drawn from Londonderry through Kildrum, Newtowncunningham, Manorcunningham, Letterkenny, Swilly Bridge, Cumick Bridge, Fintown and Doochery to Dungloe. Territory to the south and east of this line was recognised as belonging to the GNR and LMS (NCC). Traffic between Londonderry and Letterkenny was regarded as common to both the CDR and L&LSR but recognised the L&LSR's existing rights to operate an omnibus service on the direct road.

In December 1938 the GNR, in a drive to reduce a substantial loss on its Donegal bus operations (£2,372), proposed a reduction in services involving the cancellation of one of the two Londonderry–Lifford-Ballybofey services saving £260 per annum. The Minister of Industry and Commerce objected, stating that the provision of a Rail Service could not be regarded as an adequate substitute for existing omnibus services. The company made further representations to the Minister agreeing to a restoration of the service if subsequently the public demanded it! The Minister on reflection agreed to the cancellation and lo and behold there was no public outcry. By June 1939 Forbes was writing to the new GNR General Manager, George Howden, in increasingly desperate tones calling on him to take drastic action to reduce the loss on omnibus services, the County Donegal share of which was running, at £2,000 per year. Forbes entreated Howden to exploit a strike then taking place of Road Motor Service staff by 'wiping out a lot of the services altogether'. Forbes claimed in this letter 'the railway strike of 1933 was our [CDR] salvation'. Howden in reply proposed a joint working party to examine the future of all road services in Donegal composed of the Dublin based District Superintendent John H Scott (a keen proponent of bus operations) and Forbes. This working party produced a plan for the elimination of road services, which ran parallel to the railway between Donegal and Ballybofey and Donegal and Killybegs. Howden was opposed to any further reductions, as this would have allowed private competition into the county. Forbes still wanted to abandon all bus services in the county claiming that the railway could adequately cater for all the transport business. Howden, although very respectful of Forbes' position and local knowledge, decided to go over his head and consulted the LMS Railway who agreed with his analysis and in the end no alterations were made. Sadly Forbes died prematurely in post on 7th November 1943. Bernard L Curran, who had come to the CDR from the LMS (NCC) some years earlier where he had been an accountant, immediately succeeded him. He was regarded by some as a 'lightweight' particularly by those who knew him during his NCC days. Curran was more amenable towards bus operations, largely because he could grasp the fact that some sections of his railway empire would never pay their way even allowing for the introduction of more diesel railcars. He might have been a lightweight but he was a realist!

Bogagh Bus Company

The County Donegal Railway purchased the operations of the long established Bogagh Bus Service of Carrick County Donegal for £2,500 on 2nd October 1944, which had been established by Johnny O'Donnell. The service, which included Posts and Telegraphs mails and newspaper delivery contracts, ran between Killybegs, Carrick and Glencolumbkille. Johnny O'Donnell suffered a fatal heart attack on 27th August 1942. His widow took over the running of the company in addition to the running of a shop in Carrick. There was considerable wrangling with Mrs O'Donnell concerning the purchase price resulting from the fact that the only company records were a crudely kept account book written in pencil. Passengers were not issued with tickets, all fares were collected when passengers alighted from the bus. The acquired Bogagh service was operated by the GNR on behalf of the CDR using a GNR Gardner bus (fleet No. 322) dispatched from Donegal Garage to Killybegs. This was their most westerly bus service. The GNR extended the service to the Glen Bay Hotel at Malinmore on 10th December 1944. Shortly after, on 22nd January 1945, a coordinated timetable was introduced providing improved connections to the CDR train at Killybegs, the success of which was illustrated by an additional journey from Killybegs to Malinmore, which began on the 15th April 1946. The one man operated and badly worn out 20-seat Bedford bus which was the mainstay of the Bogagh fleet, together with a near derelict Ford machine, were both sent to Stranorlar for conversion by the CDR into road freight lorries. Curran wanted to use the Bogagh buses to introduce a new service between Stranorlar and Letterkenny via Convoy, Raphoe, Pluck and Manorcunningham. The GNR agreed that such a service was desirable and socially necessary. Operations commenced on 1st July 1946 and resulted in a GNR Gardner bus (No. 208) being garaged at Letterkenny for the first time. Curran at the same time proposed to eliminate

Leyland Tiger TS2 No. 277 with Catherwood body, having originated with that operator, being dug out of the snow near Sligo in March 1947. *(RG)*

Donegal Garage on 9th June 1953 with Leyland LT5A No. 305 and unique Northern Ireland registered GNR Gardner No. 220. The lorry (No. 151) began life as a Leyland Lion LT2 bus, fitted with Service Motor Works bodywork and was then converted to a lorry in 1946 and was scrapped in 1955. Note the extended turf creels fitted to the sides. *(JG)*

AEC Regal IV No. 270 being refuelled before heading for Londonderry at the CIE Garage in Lord Edward Street Sligo, which began life as the IOC base in the town. *(RG)*

the railcar service on the Glenties Branch line from Stranorlar replacing it with omnibuses. A bus service linking Stranorlar with Portnoo via Letterkenny Cross, Shallogans, Glenties and Maas was introduced on the 15th December 1947, the day on which the CDR closed the Glenties branch to passenger traffic. Additional bus services linking Glenties with Donegal were instituted. This flourishing led to the extension of the service northwards to Dungloe. This road between Glenties and Dungloe, followed an exceptionally winding course alongside the estuary of the Gweebara River for about four miles, crossing the river by an iron bridge about seven miles from Glenties. The bridge was in a much neglected state; the iron latticework, which formed the sides, had been eaten through in many places by the effects of salt water. Donegal County Council placed a 3-ton weight restriction on the bridge thus preventing the GNR from operating a large bus over it. This presented the Company with a logistical problem. Howden arranged for a Dennis Ace bus, which had been used at Dundalk Works as an ARP Ambulance and was originally number 34 in the GNR fleet to be converted back to a 20-seat bus. Following this it was numbered 225 in the fleet and dispatched to Donegal garage on 20th April 1946. The service commenced on 1st May 1946 and the Dennis Ace bus was authorised to operate as a driver only service. Unique arrangements were put in place for the operation of the service across the Gweebara Bridge, where it had to cross empty the passengers following on foot. The Dennis Bus was a failure as it was mechanically unreliable, and more often than not it languished in Donegal garage under repair. In desperation the GNR finally stationed a bus in Dungloe, working to and from the Gweebara Bridge replicating the arrangement on the Glenties side until 1st February 1954 when a new bridge was opened.

Twilight Years in Donegal

George Howden initiated discussions with RHW Bruce, General Manager of the LMS (NCC) in Belfast on the 8/9th November 1945 with a view to terminating the 1933 agreement and handing over all road services in Donegal north of Ballyshannon to the CDR. It was proposed that the vehicles would be maintained at Stranorlar and painted into the railways standard colour scheme, overhauls etc. being carried out at Dundalk. The senior officers of the GNR, Harold S Knott (Traffic Manager), Harold McIntosh (Mechanical Engineer) and John Shanahan (Accountant) were opposed to Howden's proposals on the basis that it could result in all services north of Ballyshannon being taken over by the newly created CIE at the Government's behest. Howden's plan was never actioned although the story didn't end there. A joint GNR/CDR report was sent to the Minister for Industry and Commerce on the 25th February 1953, regarding transport in Donegal recommending (a) the substitution of road for narrow gauge rail transport and (b) that the GNR should operate all services in the County.

On 4th August 1954 Harry Patterson, the GNR Accountant for the recently established GNR Board, produced yet another joint report, this time involving Dick Meredith who had now assumed the Mechanical Engineer's position, Harold Knott, Mr B Smith, British Railways London Midland Region Accountant and BL Curran, the CDR General Manager. Bernard Curran of the CDR wanted to assume control of all omnibus services in the CDR territory, which would result in the Derry/Sligo service terminating at Ballyshannon, thus breaking the direct omnibus link. In the end nothing was carried forward and the GNR continued to operate Donegal services until the end of its existence, when CIE took on these operations themselves and when the CDR ceased railway operations they hired a number of CIE buses which were painted in CDR livery operating rail substitution services. The CDR bus operation finally came to an end as a result of the British Minister of Transport Barbara Castle introducing legislation effective from 31st May 1968 to break up the British Transport Commission, who was the half-share owners of the CDR, together with CIE. CIE then had to obtain legislation in *Dail Éireann* to enable the CDR bus operations to be wholly operated by CIE.

Dennis Ace No. 225 parked on the Gweebara Bridge in the summer of 1946 where it had to cross empty such, was the unsteady condition of the bridge. *(RG)*

Chapter Five

Northern Ireland Notions

It was during the period 1922/3 that the many new independent bus and charabanc operators took to the roads in Ulster. The ever-increasing numbers of operators, many of whom were ex-servicemen, invested their wartime earnings in vehicles and equipment. By 1925 there were 400 buses operating across the Province. In September of that year Harry Brook's Pilot Bus Company later referred to as the Six County Motor Services began running buses between Dungannon and Stewartstown. A later Six County service between Dungannon and Belfast via Portadown and Dungannon to Omagh services operated by the Blytheswood Bus Company sharply dented railway revenues. The rapid increase in bus operators spurred the railway companies into action.

In March 1926 the management of the GNR, LMS (NCC) and B&CDR issued a joint statement to the Northern Ireland government expressing concern at these developments. The railway companies demanded legislation to control the operation of road motor services in view of the serious financial position they found themselves in due to the growth of road motor transport in areas served by the railways. Large numbers of buses and lorries were charging low rates and fares resulting in considerable damage to railway revenues. The joint statement made clear the disadvantage the railways found themselves in having to provide their own permanent way and carry all manner of traffic whether remunerative or not. Conversely, the road motor operators were free to run when and where they liked for minimal contribution towards the construction and upkeep of the roads system. Bus operators were permitted to operate from the kerbside in towns and villages without making any payments to local councils. The railway companies were on the other hand normally the largest ratepayers in districts in which they operated. Road motor operators were thus able to charge low fares and rates, which the railways were being forced to attempt to match in order to retain the business. The railway companies levelled the accusations that some road operators were using mere boys of 18-20 years as motormen and children aged 12-14 as conductors. Similar claims that uninsured vehicles were overloaded and regularly exceeded the speed limits were undoubtedly true in certain cases.

The railway companies urged the Northern Ireland government to introduce legislation compelling road motor operators to:–

- Make road operators responsible for damage caused to roads, which according to one county surveyor averaged at £300/500 per annum.
- Regulate services and only permit their operation by experienced employees.
- Introduce compulsory third party insurance for buses and lorries
- Place controls on working hours, loading and speed limits.

The Northern Ireland Cabinet discussed this but immediately ruled out any form of subsidy arising out of the entreaties of the railway companies' financial plight. An illustration of the intensity of bus competition in the GNR operating area by mid 1927 can be seen from the following detail. On the Belfast-Lisburn service no fewer than 100 daily bus journeys in each direction were being run by operators such as William Jellie, Courtney's, Cosy and Violet. Other services passing through Lisburn to Lurgan (Belfast Motor Service and Irwins) and Armagh (McGlades Criterion and The Classic) provided greater headaches for the railway. The government did however act in favour of the railways by introducing two important pieces of transport legislation the first of which came in 1926 and was known as the Motor Vehicles (Traffic & Regulation) Act which established a new system of vehicle inspection, licensing, mandatory third party insurance, standards of construction, design and condition of vehicles together with the licensing of both drivers and conductors. The Northern Ireland government by introducing this legislation preceded similar laws introduced in Great Britain by some years and it was to become a model for such. The second element of the Stormont government's transport policy was the introduction of The Railway (Road Vehicles) Act 1927 which conferred upon the railways powers to operate road services. They responded by becoming large operators of road vehicles. The effects of the new laws were felt almost immediately as some of the more adventurous pirates were forced off the roads although by 1927 there were some 700 buses operating on Ulster's roads.

GNR bus services in Northern Ireland almost predated the commencement of Irish Free State operations. The Company applied to the Home Affairs Ministry on 6th December 1928 to operate a bus from Warrenpoint to Kilkeel and on 25th January from Banbridge to Scarva. The Home Affairs Minister Dawson Bates replied to the GNR on 11th April 1929 refusing consent for both planned services. Company strategy now turned to the acquisition of bus companies; accordingly Sir George Clark and the Rt Hon J Milne Barbour were authorised on 20th March 1929 to approach James and Robert Irwin, owners of a shoe shop in Market Street and a pawnbrokers in Edward Street, Lurgan. The Irwin brothers operated seven buses from Belfast to Lurgan. A mere ten days later the GNR had bought its first bus company in Northern Ireland from the Irwins. The Northern Ireland Bus Owners Association approached the GNR on 24th July 1929 offering membership as a result of the Irwin purchase. The Company declined to take up the offer being content by its association with other Irish railway companies.

An unidentified Irwins Dennis E 28-seat bus which competed with the GNR on services between Belfast and Lurgan. *(WM)*

An unidentified Belfast to Lurgan competitor, believed to be the Balmoral Buses, who operated an hourly service between the two centres. *(SS)*

Northern Ireland Agreements

The company introduced many inter-availability schemes supporting its desire to provide an integrated rail-road transport network. Northern Ireland gained such a scheme on 3rd July 1929 when the company permitted holders of omnibus return tickets on the Belfast/Lurgan service to return by 3rd class rail at no additional cost. This permitted the GNR

to thin out its suburban train service between Belfast and Lurgan. On 1st November 1929 Joe Mackle introduced limited inter-availability arrangements on the Belfast/Dungannon bus service. This scheme allowed for holders of omnibus return tickets to return by selected off peak trains, four days a week between Belfast and Portadown, passengers then continuing their journey by bus between Portadown and Dungannon. In early 1931 agreement was reached with the London Midland & Scottish Railway Northern Counties Committee (LMSNCC) allowing holders of GNR return portions of ordinary rail tickets, Belfast with Antrim, and Belfast with Cookstown, to return using LMS (NCC) omnibuses without extra charge. LMS (NCC) omnibus ticket holders were permitted to return via GNR rail service (3rd class) between Antrim, Cookstown and Belfast.

Northern Ireland fares were fixed by the Road Transport Fares Tribunal, which was set up by the Motor Vehicles and Road Traffic Act (NI) 1929. The GNR and LMS (NCC) jointly opposed the application of HMS Catherwood made in November 1931 to this Tribunal for reduced minimum rates for excursion bus fares. Had the Tribunal permitted the reduction it would have resulted in the loss of considerable rail revenues by both companies. The joint campaign of opposition to the Catherwood proposal was a success and both the GNR and the LMS (NCC) regarded this as tangible evidence of the benefits of increased co-operation. On 7th March 1934 the GNR entered into an agreement with Fawcett Hotels Limited for the provision by the GNR of suitable omnibuses in connection with their Motor Coach and Rail Tours from Antrim and Portrush during the summer of 1934. The agreement was enacted again the following season for the final time as a consequence of the establishment of the NIRTB. A second contract was agreed with the proprietors of the Laharna and McNeill's Hotel of Larne Co Antrim to provide group travel facilities by rail from Belfast to Dublin. Hotel parties were met at Amiens Street Station by omnibus to be taken on a nine mile Dublin City Tour before being returned to the railway station for the journey home. The GNR actually ran a bus service in Belfast, which never at any time appeared in its timetables. This was an inter-station service providing a road connection from Great Victoria Street Station to the LMS (NCC) York Road Station for through boat passengers going to Scotland. This service began in June 1932 finishing in December 1934.

Belfast Omnibus Company

The Belfast Omnibus Company (BOC), formed in April 1927 through the fusion of several operators, represented the greatest competitive threat to the rail and road services of the GNR. The BOC ran bus services radiating from Belfast to Lurgan, Crumlin, Armagh, Newry, Dromore and Enniskillen all centres served by the GNR railway. In November 1927 the BOC placed orders with the Associated Daimler Company for 30 model 416 and 25 model 422 buses, a move which heralded rapid expansion of its operations. On 24th April 1929 Jonathan Stephens met BOC officials in Belfast with the intention of entering an agreement which would have resulted in the BOC operating railway feeder services to the GNR in the Down and Armagh areas. There was an outright refusal on the part of the BOC management who felt quite correctly that they had the GNR on the ropes and were winning passengers from the railway. An unwritten 'gentleman's agreement' (effective from 31st January 1931), with the BOC relating to fare levels, was an endeavour to minimise the effects of revenue loss resulting from BOC buses. The BOC unilaterally terminated it with two years later on 31st January 1933. On 27th May 1931 the GNR Chairman Sir George Clark, together with fellow Board member The Rt Hon J Milne Barbour, met with representatives of the Belfast Omnibus Company to propose the joint acquisition of the Duchess Bus Service of Thomas Morgan and Martha Chambers, who ran two 20-seat buses between Donacloney and Belfast. The Duchess was damaging railway revenues from Hillsborough and Dromore areas and was a source of cheap competition against the BOC in the area. The BOC did not react favourably to the GNR's idea of a joint purchase as their negotiations with the Duchess were already well advanced and indeed were satisfactorily completed a short time later.

The Managing Director of the BOC, James McCrea, viewed with alarm the impending take over of HMS Catherwood in the Irish Free State. The BOC mistakenly thought that the GNR would take over the operation of the through Belfast/Dublin bus service including the portion within Northern Ireland between Belfast and the border, which would be in direct competition with the BOC's Newry service. In response to the ending of the BOC's 'unwritten agreement' deal on fares, the GNR reduced some of its rail fares and increased the frequency of competing trains. The BOC responded by making an application to the Railway Fares Tribunal for the revocation of a prohibition on more than two double journeys being made daily by bus season ticket holders, a move which would further harm the railway. The Tribunal agreed with the BOC and the GNR had to quickly slash railway fares in the greater Belfast area to meet the BOC competition especially from workers going to and from their places of employment. On Sundays when important GAA football matches were being played in Dundalk, the BOC would convey busloads of supporters from Warrenpoint, Newry and Hilltown at very cheap fares. GNR Inspectors monitored the activities of the BOC and on more than one occasion BOC buses were observed picking up passengers in the Irish Free State in clear breach of their licence. Despite complaints to the *Gardai* in Dundalk by Chief Inspector Albert Switzer the BOC seemed to enjoy complete immunity. The reality was that the *Gardai* did not want hundreds of northern GAA supporters left on their doorstep with no transport home and the headache that would cause them. Various Northern Ireland independent operators 'creamed off' valuable railway revenues such as Omagh based William Simpson who ran his 'Fleetwing' buses between Omagh Enniskillen and Castlederg from 1927 until the formation of the NIRTB in 1935. In 1927 Clarkes Blue Buses running from Enniskillen to Pettigo provided faster journey times than the comparable rail service, which resulted in a drift towards the road service.

GNR bus services in Northern Ireland were developed by the company almost exclusively as a result of the acquisition of the small independent operators and were largely used to

A line up of BOC buses at their Belfast North Street Bus Station on 20th May 1930, many of which would compete against the GNR. *(WM)*

A BOC AEC Regent I stands by the distinguished McKee clock tower in Bangor, Co Down. *(AEC:AEL 1991)*

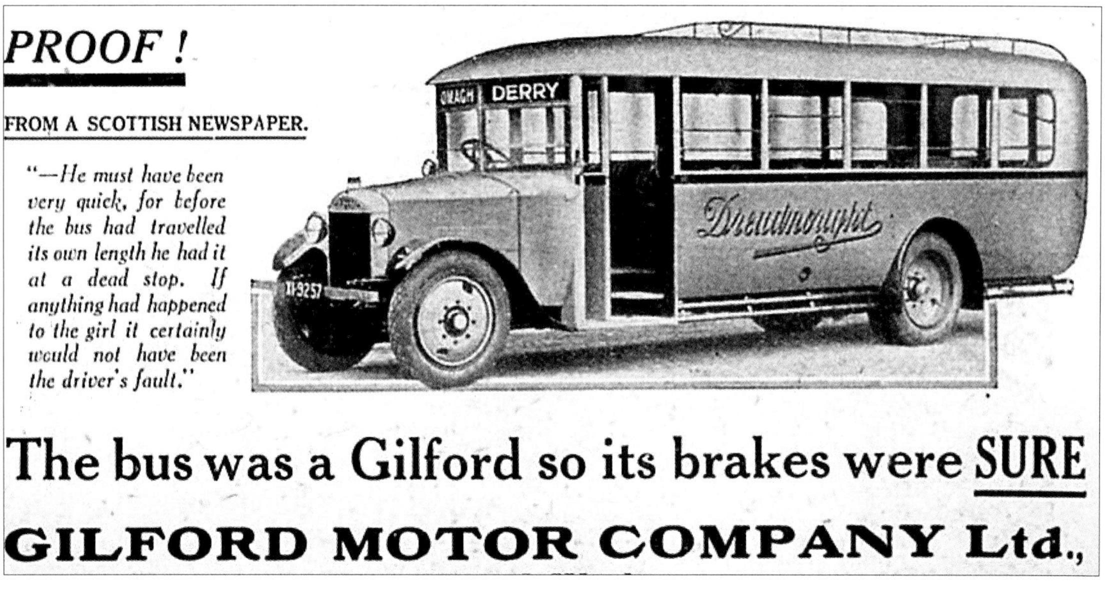

Gilford bus with a 30-seat Metcalfe body belonging to the Dreadnought Bus Company, who competed with the GNR railway between Londonderry and Omagh. *(GL)*

act as feeder services to the railway operations and provide a cheaper alternative to train travel particularly over shorter distances. The company introduced services linking railway stations with town centres where distances were considered a disadvantage to rail travellers such as Armagh, Omagh and Portadown, the latter through the acquisition of a private operator who had previously provided this service. The Home Affairs Minister Dawson Bates exhibited a truculent streak by refusing the GNR permission to operate a new bus service linking Cookstown and Omagh on 26th June 1929 on a road where there was no direct railway connection. The GNR sought to introduce this service in order to reduce the number of passenger trains running on the Cookstown Branch from Dungannon where an onward rail connection was made with Omagh. The acquisition by the GNR of the Pioneer Bus Service of Keady, owned by Thomas Nugent on 20th November 1931 permitted the GNR to close the Armagh/Keady railway line to passenger traffic, saving £1,290 per year according to a report presented to the GNR Board on 16th December 1931. Railway passenger services between Armagh and Keady ended on New Year's Day 1932.

The Castlederg and Victoria Bridge Tramway was a 3ft gauge line that ran from the curving bay platform at Victoria Bridge GNR station to Castlederg via Fyfin and Spamount, a distance of some seven miles and opened for traffic on 11th July 1884. The last tram journeys operated on Monday 30th January 1933 as a strike commenced the next day, which continued until Friday 7th April 1933. The owners of the Tramway decided not to resume its operation eventually winding up the company on 30th September 1933. The GNR Road Motor Services stepped in to provide a substitute bus service to replace the tramway. The GNR had inherited the former Roberts bus service from Strabane to Aghyaran via Victoria Bridge on 10th July 1930 with three return workings on weekdays. The Tramway replacement service, which commenced exactly four weeks after the strike ended on 17th May 1933, resulted in the following service amendments. The weekday Newtownstewart – Ardstraw – Castlederg bus service which provided an onward connection with principal GNR trains on the Belfast – Londonderry line was downscaled to operate on a Monday, Friday and Saturday only. The tramway replacement bus service between Victoria Bridge – Castlederg, which followed the same route as that of the tram began with eight return workings on weekdays of which three were projected to Aghyaran so as not to disenfranchise the people of that area.

First Aid for the Railway

The Great Northern Railway, the Belfast and County Down Railway and the LMS Northern Counties Committee submitted a comprehensive memorandum to the Prime Minister of Northern Ireland, Viscount Craigavon, in October 1932 setting out the seriousness of their financial position. The Railway companies urged the government to introduce legislation to establish equitable conditions of competition between rail and road transport and to enable the companies more effectively to co-ordinate rail and road services. The Railway companies met with Viscount Craigavon on 10th October 1932 at which they were afforded an opportunity to present their proposals before the Prime Minister. In formulating these proposals they kept in mind that any legislative measures must provide the public with a transport service, functioning without waste and with the maximum of efficiency in methods and speed, and providing the greatest possible reliability and convenience at the lowest rates consistent with its cost and with a reasonable return on the capital necessarily invested in its provision. The effects of discussion between the railway companies and the Prime Minister, taken together with the effects of the 1933 Railway Strike, undoubtedly prompted the appointment of Sir Felix Pole's investigation of transport in April 1934.

Some new services were provided by the GNR to cater for Church services in the Armagh/Keady area in June 1933. In the previous year a service was introduced linking Omagh with Londonderry, two centres already served by the GNR railway. However it was felt that the remoteness of some railway stations from the population centres, which they purported to serve, together with cheaper bus fares offered would be attractive enough to win new passengers. This strategy was proved correct as revenues steadily improved. Unusually the company also ran special buses in competition with its own train services illustrated by an evening run from Belfast to Dungannon in connection with Greyhound racing, promoting it with a special return fare of five shillings in April 1933.

As a consequence of the 1933 Railway Strike passenger train services did not return immediately on certain routes. One affected line was the Scarva to Banbridge section. The Road Motor Services started running buses on 11th September 1933 between Banbridge Railway Station and Goraghwood Railway Station in lieu of the passenger trains. The service, which called at the intermediate railway stations of Scarva and Poyntzpass on its 40-minute journey, was provided to give trains to and from Dublin at Goraghwood a connection with stations in the West Down area. It represented an excellent example of how the GNR could use the bus to complement its rail services. The service was discontinued on 15th October 1934 as a result of the introduction of Railcar 'A' which went on to give many years of excellent service between Scarva and Banbridge. The last new GNR bus service introduced in Northern Ireland was the Sunday only Church service between Laurelvale and Banbridge on 1st April 1935. Just a few months later GNR bus operations wholly within the Province would disappear.

As referred to previously, in April 1934 the Northern Ireland government decided to appoint Sir Felix Pole, formerly General Manager of the Great Western Railway and Chairman of Associated Electrical Industries Ltd, to report on the conduct of road transport (bus & lorry) in Northern Ireland. The government was concerned with the problem of road and rail transport where co-ordination was considered a matter of extreme emergency, given the small population of the Province, in an area about the size of Yorkshire, and the dire financial position of the railway companies. At the enquiry, which opened in Belfast on 30th April, Jonathan Stephens represented the GNR. It was joined by an organisation, called 'Great Northern Railway

A quintet of GNR Albions with Weymann bodies outside the imposing Great Victoria Street Station, Belfast on 25th July 1934. *(WM)*

Dennis F bus with Strachan & Brown bodywork when new and just prior to delivery to James Winter's Eclipse Motor Transport, for service between Belfast and Omagh, in competition with the GNR train. *(GL)*

Shareholders' Protection Association', both naturally opposed to nationalisation of its assets. On 23rd July Pole recommended the formation of the Northern Ireland Road Transport Board (NIRTB), which would take control of road passenger, and freight services through an amalgamation of the larger road transport companies and the road services operated by the railways. Following the enquiry, the Northern Ireland government hosted a conference with representatives of all the Railway and Omnibus Companies at Stormont on 5th October 1934 at which it announced in broad measure its intention to nationalise all road transport in the Province as recommended by Pole (this excluded Belfast Corporation).

Northern Ireland Road Transport Board

The Northern Ireland Government's decision to accept the Pole Report resulted in an enabling act on 16th July 1935. The GNR operations in Northern Ireland, buses and lorries, were accordingly taken over by the newly created Northern Ireland Road Transport Board on Tuesday 1st October 1935. All GNR road motor services staff, including Superintendents HF Hutcheson (who had been heavily involved in the GNR take-over of Catherwood's two years previously) and Bertie Irwin (one of the two Irwin brothers from Lurgan) now became employees the NIRTB. The new Board quickly found itself embroiled in difficulties of an industrial relations nature with its driving staff. Inherited former Belfast Omnibus Company drivers continued to be paid £3 5s a week. Former Catherwood drivers were paid £3 per week while the ex-Railway Company drivers were the poor relation, on £2 18s per week. All drivers were required to work a 48-hour week and do the same kind of work. The pay differentials were the recipe for industrial conflict, which lasted for a number of years and contributed to losses in the early years of the NIRTB's existence.

The GNR, although opposed to nationalisation, quickly accepted it and pragmatically played a significant role in the early development of the NIRTB with weekly and monthly omnibus tickets being sold at GNR railway stations in Dungannon, Omagh, and Strabane. Indeed the level of co-operation between the Great Northern and NIRTB was very extensive. This co-operation resulted in the establishment of several NIRTB depots on GNR land. On 25th February 1937 the NIRTB approved the erection of a garage adjacent to Armagh Railway Station at a cost of £2,582 after the purchase of the land from the GNR for £60. A further portion of GNR land, which had been a siding at Armagh, was sold to the NIRTB on 10th February the following year for £26. Banbridge and Crumlin saw the establishment of NIRTB depots on GNR property, leased to the Board for 999 years at an annual rent of £5. The Banbridge garage building was approved on 6th May 1937 at a cost of £1,934 16s 6d. On Thursday 10th March 1938 the NIRTB agreed the purchase of a parcel of GNR land at Victoria Bridge for £60 on which was built a garage and washing plant at a cost of £1,056. Alterations to the GNR goods shed to facilitate the NIRTB were also carried out. The GNR Road Motor Garage at William Street in Lurgan was acquired from the railway in 1937 following eighteen months of dereliction and suitable repairs and renovations were completed costing £393 10s 0d. In Londonderry one half of the Foyle Road Goods Store was rented at an annual cost of £65 for the NIRTB lorry operation.

Hands Across the Border

The international nature of GNR operations continued even after the formation of the NIRTB, which at no time in its brief history ever operated cross-border scheduled services in its own right. These services tended to be enmeshed in political controversy between the governments north and south. As far back as December 1929 the GNR proposed the operation of a bus service from Crossmaglen to Dundalk. The Northern Ireland authorities vetoed this proposal, as it would have taken valuable commercial trade away from Newry. Agreement was however given for the GNR to operate a bus from Dundalk to Newtownhamilton effective from Monday 7th July 1930, competing with the private bus operated by Thomas Nugent of Keady, which was bought out by the GNR in November 1931. Another private operator, John and Robert Steen of Newtownhamilton, who had established a bus service in July 1920 linking the town with Armagh, augmented its services to Dundalk on 28th July 1930 as a result of increased bus activity.

Very soon after the formation of the NIRTB, an inter-territorial agreement was reached which continued right through into the days of its successor Ulster Transport Authority. This agreement provided for a series of consents and working agreements between the two administrations. The GNR was authorised to use omnibuses from any point on the land boundary to any destination in Northern Ireland and back again to the land boundary for the conveyance of:–

- private parties which originate in the Irish Free State
- merchandise which originates in the Irish Free State
- use motor vehicles from any point in Northern Ireland served by the GN Railway to the land boundary for the conveyance of merchandise which is for a destination in the Irish Free State
- regular timetable cross-border omnibus services operated by the GNR as under:–
  Dundalk-Newry
  Newry-Omeath-Carlingford
  Londonderry-Sligo
  Castleblaney-Keady
  Cavan-Enniskillen
  Aughnacloy-Monaghan
  Monaghan-Middletown

The operation on the Monaghan-Tyholland-Middletown service was eventually ceded to the UTA in October 1957 as a result of railway closures.

In January 1936 the NIRTB reached agreement with the GNR(I), Great Southern Railways and Londonderry & Lough Swilly Railway for reciprocal arrangements in respect of the operation of one-day tours, private hires and special parties between Northern Ireland and the Irish Free State. There were three interesting and significant elements to this agreement namely:–

- The NIRTB agreed not to operate any day tours, private hires or special parties from Londonderry, Strabane, Enniskillen and Newry into the Irish Free State where these activities could adversely affect railway revenues.
- The railway companies for their part agreed not to lodge any objection to the Minister for Industry and Commerce (Irish Free State) to his authorising the issue of Licences to enable the NIRTB to operate one day tours, private hires and special parties from Northern Ireland into the Irish Free State.
- The NIRTB recognised pre-existing railway territorial agreements and thus agreed to pay railway companies in respect of any NIRTB buses passing through the delineated areas.

Upon the formation of the NIRTB three cross border services became jointly operated with the GNR as overleaf:–

Armagh-Keady-Castleblaney-Ballybay

Although the NIRTB had planned to take over this service from 1st October logistical difficulties prevented them from doing so until 25th October when the service ran as follows. The NIRTB buses worked the section between Armagh and Keady connecting with GNR buses, which worked the service to Ballybay on weekdays only. On Sunday no through service was provided although NIRTB buses worked through to the Carnagh Northern Ireland Border Post. How passengers were expected to get any further is anybody's guess. With effect from 14th September 1936 the GNR took over the Sunday operation handing this back to the NIRTB again on 30th May 1937.

Monaghan-Middletown-Lislea-Milford-Armagh

The NIRTB were not in a position to take over their element of this service from day one. The result was that up until 5th November 1935, the GNR bus worked through from Monaghan to Armagh before the agreed arrangements could be introduced, which were as follows:–

The GNR bus worked between Monaghan and Tyholland Border Post, which connected with an NIRTB bus to convey passengers to Armagh.

This arrangement continued until fuel restrictions forced the GNR to suspend their leg from Monaghan from 1st June 1940 on the same day the NIRTB cut their service back to Middletown providing a link to Armagh Railway Station and the Belfast trains. The GNR service between Monaghan and Tyholland Border was not resumed until 26th September 1948 and then limited to a Monday and Saturday operation. This was further restricted to a Saturday only operation effective from 10th October 1949 and remained so until the service was extended on 23rd June 1957 to serve Middletown in anticipation of the closure of the railway between Monaghan and Armagh. The service was withdrawn by the GNR on 1st October 1957, the day the Ulster Transport Authority commenced a through bus service between Armagh and Monaghan, which is still operated today by Ulsterbus.

Monaghan-Aughnacloy-Dungannon

The GNR bus operated the section between Monaghan and Aughnacloy connecting with an NIRTB vehicle which ran between there and Dungannon. The NIRTB quietly dropped the Aughnacloy/Dungannon connection during the war. At the same time the GNR reduced the frequency of its leg and it continued running at this level right up to 1958. A total of 50 omnibuses and 58 motor lorries, together with all the active bus routes wholly within Northern Ireland were transferred to NIRTB ownership. It was said at the time that the GNR transferred all of its Leyland buses to the Irish Free State to prevent them from being acquired by the NIRTB. I have examined all the vehicle allocation tables available to me from 1930 but I cannot find any evidence to support this view. There had been a transfer of omnibuses in July as a result of the new Albion and Dennis machines that arrived in March and April 1932 at the request of James Lockhart the Belfast Traffic Manager. This was a devious way of getting buses into the Irish Free State without paying import duty at the time. Ten Leylands and five AEC machines were moved to the Irish Free State but this was over three years in advance of the NIRTB formation. In Belfast all former GNR bus services under NIRTB control operated from the Central Bus Station at Upper North Street. Prior to the NIRTB take-over, all GNR omnibuses and lorries based in Northern Ireland carried the legal address 'Great Northern Railway (I), Great Victoria Street, Belfast, JB Stephens General Manager'. Irish Free State vehicles had Amiens Street Station, Dublin as their address. Following the NIRTB take-over of GNR operations in Northern Ireland GNR vehicles carried dual Belfast and Dublin addresses for legal purposes. The GNR valued the assets consisting of vehicles; garages and services handed over to the NIRTB at £80,500. Compensation was given to the GNR in the form of 39,763 shares in the NIRTB in lieu.

Mckeown and McClaughan-bodied Leyland Lion LT2 No. 112 loads a group of female excursionists for the return journey to Belfast from the Phoenix Park in Dublin during 1932, possibly in connection with the Eucharistic Congress. *(MC)*

A Night of Keady Chaos

On the evening of Sunday 21st April 1940 GNR Motorman Charlie Scott and Conductor PJ Woods, both from Monaghan Garage, were in charge of Leyland Lion LT2 bus fleet No. 109 with 18 passengers on board *en route* from Keady to Dundalk. A Keady Band who were engaged to play at a *Fianna Fail Ceilidhe* in Dundalk had hired the bus. Their journey was to become far more eventful than anyone on board the bus ever imagined. Charlie Scott takes up the story; "At about 6.10pm I was driving up the steep hill at Aughnaguran, two and a half miles from Keady, when I suddenly noticed five men spread across the road. Four of them wore masks, which consisted of handkerchiefs. As I approached they shouted to stop the bus. As the bus pulled up one of the men came up beside me, while another entered the bus and ordered the passengers out with their hands in the air. As the man came beside me in the cab he shouted, 'stand back'. With that I pulled the mask off his face. The leader shouted 'plug him' and a shot was fired that went right through my trouser leg, but did not wound me. I came out of the cab onto the roadway and the fellow who had fired walked around the bus sprinkling it with petrol. Two armed men then fired five or six shots into the fuel tank, which immediately burst with a fierce explosion. Then a motorcar came on the scene; the gunmen got into it and drove off pointing their revolvers at us until they had gone out of sight. The RUC at Darkley were summoned, who arranged for another bus to come out from Dundalk Garage which conveyed the Band to the border under Police escort where we were met by the Civic Guards who accompanied us to Dundalk". The bus was completely gutted and was subsequently removed by GNR engineers to Dundalk Works on Tuesday 23rd April following which it was scrapped. This incident, which was undoubtedly the work of the IRA, did little to enhance GNR bus operations in the area at the time.

On 9th September 1940 the NIRTB curtailed the service on Sundays at Keady. Wartime fuel restrictions forced the GNR to cut back the Castleblaney/Keady leg to a Wednesday and Friday only operation with two workings in each direction effective from 16th June 1941.

The service never really recovered from the wartime constraints although the GNR continued to operate a downscaled timetable right up to 1958.

GNR Gardner No. 212 waiting to depart for Cavan outside Monaghan Railway Station in North Road. *(SS)*

Ulster Transport Authority

The Ulster Transport Authority was constituted under the Transport Act (NI) 1948 and operations commenced on 1st October as the direct successor to the Northern Ireland Road Transport Board. Its initial composition included that of the Northern Ireland Road Transport Board, Belfast & County Down Railway and from 1st April 1949 the London Midland & Scottish Railway (Northern Counties Committee). The duty of the Authority was to provide an efficient, economical, convenient and properly integrated system of public inland transport in Northern Ireland for passengers and goods by rail and road. The Authority was required to so conduct its undertaking that, taking one year with another, it shall pay its way. This last statement was a particularly important one in the determination of the GNR's future existence, as we shall discover later.

On 13th October 1947 in the lead up to the establishment of the UTA, George Howden and the Directors of the GNR held a meeting at Stormont with the Minister of Commerce, Sir Roland Nugent, together with two senior officials from his department, Major Percival Maxwell and Mr GHE Parr, to lobby against incorporation of the GNR into the UTA. The Northern Ireland operations of the Great Northern Railway were originally earmarked for incorporation into the UTA. However, along with the County Donegal and Londonderry & Lough Swilly Railway Companies, they were specifically excluded due to the cross border services undertaken by all three concerns. Many commentators have claimed an anti-rail bias within the upper echelons of the UTA pointing to the wide scale railway closures, which took place during its formative years. What is often overlooked is that the UTA authorities were required by statute to run the undertaking on a commercial basis. Accordingly they were forced to close uneconomic railway lines in a bid to achieve a quick fix. The UTA saw no prospect of making loss making lines profitable with a staff streamlining and dieselisation programme and failed to encourage or attempt to generate new traffic for the railway.

With the formation of the Great Northern Railway Board in 1953 the Northern Ireland government ensured that its nominees to the GNRB reported to UTA officials. All GNRB property located in Northern Ireland became vested in the UTA. The GNRB concluded a freight coordination agreement with the UTA in fulfilment of the latter's statutory obligation to ensure an integrated transport network. The UTA was very much in the driving seat as far as Northern Ireland operations of the GNRB were concerned, particularly as they were expected to meet the Belfast government's share of the losses of the GNRB. On 1st November 1954, almost four years prior to the end of the GNRB, a UTA official, Mr RL Streight was appointed by the GNR (on the instructions of the UTA) as the officer appointed to oversee the integration of the GNRB into the UTA on an annual salary of £1,150. Evidence if it were necessary of the UTA's ultimate intentions towards the GNRB. When the GNRB was dissolved on 1st October 1958 the Ulster Transport Authority became responsible for half the accumulated debt and purchase price (£2¼ million) as a result of the Northern Ireland government's insistence that its publicly created corporation be responsible for all aspects of land transportation costs. The government's decision to saddle the UTA with this liability almost resulted in its early demise.

GNR AEC Regent No. 65 at the Irish Free State Carrickarnan Border Post on 15th February 1948 as passengers endure thorough roadside baggage searches. *(DN)*

Road Motor Services in Bondage

One effect of the inter-territorial nature of GNR Road Motor Service operations from the Irish Free State into and out of Northern Ireland was the requirement for GNR buses and lorries to comply with two sets of legislation in order to cross the land frontier legally. The following cross border services were operated by the GNR from the dates shown below:-

Cross Border Route	Date Service Commenced
Dundalk and Newry	1 July 1929
Dundalk and Newtownhamilton	7 July 1930
Belfast and Dublin	4 September 1929
Sligo and Londonderry	22 September 1930
Keady, Castleblaney and Ballybay	2 November 1931
Armagh, Monaghan and Ballybay	2 November 1931
Cavan and Enniskillen	1 May 1932
Dungannon, Aughnacloy and Monaghan	11 July 1932
Newry, Omeath and Carlingford	17 December 1932

The Irish Free State government were the principal legislators with regard to the movement of vehicles across the border. They introduced The Customs (Land Frontier) Regulations 1924, which on 17th June introduced for the first time a 'pass book' which was required in respect of every vehicle moving between the Free State and Northern Ireland and vice versa. A motor vehicle owner resident in Dundalk wishing to take his/her vehicle to Newry had to present the vehicle to a Customs Official who upon being satisfied that the vehicle was free of any duties that might be owing would issue a passbook. The driver would then have to enter details of the route to be taken to the Frontier Post by way of an approved route. Upon arrival at the Frontier Post the Customs Officer would stamp and sign the book before leaving the State. The Northern Ireland authorities would stamp and sign the passbook on the inward and outward journey.

The Irish Free State authorities introduced a further piece of legislation in the form of The Motor Cars (Temporary Importation) Regulations, 1926, which placed additional restrictions on vehicles. A 48 hour time limit was imposed on non Irish Free State vehicles entering the jurisdiction; additionally a 'Carnet de Passages en Douanes' issued by a recognised Automobile Club was now required to be presented to the Frontier Customs Official upon entering the Free State. For the unlucky motorist who was not a member of either the AA or RAC they were required to pay an importation deposit at the Frontier which was calculated to be the import duty applicable. The deposit was refunded once the vehicle was presented to an approved Frontier Post on the way out. Whether importation took place through a motoring organisation or upon the payment of a deposit to Customs a single pass-sheet was issued at the Frontier Post and these became known as Triptyques. The triangular Triptyque applied to a vehicle's windscreen was to become a feature of cross-border vehicle travel right up until Britain and Ireland joined the EEC. Omnibuses crossing the frontier were required to comply with the provision of the Act.

A year later the Dublin government introduced the Motor Cars (Temporary Importation) Regulations, 1927, which provided some relief for bus operators. Providing a bus was registered in Northern Ireland it could be imported into the Irish Free State free of duty between 1st June and 30th September in any year subject to the 48-hour rule. This concession was designed to facilitate foreign holidaymakers entering the Free State by bus or tour coach. In 1931 the United Kingdom HM Customs required the GNR to pay duty on all buses crossing into Northern Ireland at considerable cost to the company. This measure limited the opportunities for the development of cross-border services. In 1934 the Irish Free State government introduced its Finance Act 1934 which instituted a new regime of duty in respect of the temporary importation of vehicles registered in Northern Ireland, which required the Company to lodge a bond with the Revenue authorities in Dublin of £450 per machine. A strange consequence resulting from the formation of the NIRTB in 1935 permitted buses owned by the Great Southern Railway (who had no scheduled cross border services) into Northern Ireland under bond and NIRTB vehicles were similarly allowed into the Irish Free State under the same conditions. The Bond, which was refundable as soon as the Company took it off the list of bonded vehicles supplied to the Revenue, was less pernicious than duty paid on every cross-border trip which was not refundable.

As the GNR now only operated short sections of its cross border routes in Northern Ireland as permitted by the NIRTB and given the fact that the GNR was precluded from operating services wholly within Northern Ireland, this put the GNR at a decided disadvantage. Representations were made to the NIRTB and the Northern Ireland Government, which resulted in the GNR being able to operate buses on scheduled and private hire operations under new arrangements. The result was that thirty-six buses were bonded for cross-border operations when the first agreement was signed on 8th July 1937 at a cost of £13,000 – a large sum of money at the time. The figure was increased the following year to £25,000, as more buses were needed for cross-border services. The number of vehicles operated on cross border services determined the size of the bond. A few new GNR buses were registered in Northern Ireland from 1937 onwards thus avoiding the need for bonding. The GNR was in bond to HM Customs until the formation of the Ulster Transport Authority when this requirement was eliminated. GNR buses operating into Northern Ireland also had to pass the Public Service Vehicle Test, the standard of maintenance required to achieve this was much higher than in Eire, resulting in further additional expenditure.

Chapter Six
The Frugal Frosty Forties

Second World War Emergency

The advent of the Second World War brought with it peculiar difficulties for the GNR, operating on both sides of the Irish border, where in neutral Eire it was referred to as 'The Emergency', whilst in Northern Ireland it was truly a 'time of war'. Northern Ireland enjoyed considerable supplementary wartime passenger and goods traffic as a result of the population being greatly increased through an influx of servicemen. The cross border bus services of the Road Motor Services filled with passengers who travelled from Northern Ireland to Eire in search of commodities such as razor blades, tea, watches, clocks, clothing and jewellery all of which were in plentiful supply in Eire. Similarly passengers from Eire came North in search of arcane items such as spark plugs and electrical wiring, freely available in Northern Ireland. Smuggling became a national obsession in both directions but northern folk also travelled south to enjoy hotel holidays in Dublin where food was in plentiful un-rationed supply. This improved the company's financial position and railway revenues in Northern Ireland, where two-thirds of railway operations were located, yielded a three-fold increase in turnover. Timetabling cross border bus services became nightmarish during the war thanks to the application in Northern Ireland of double summer time. Complications arose for travellers crossing the frontier by bus. For example passengers leaving Londonderry on the 9.05am bus to Sligo found themselves arriving at Raphoe County Donegal at 8.30am, thirty-five minutes before starting their journey from Londonderry!

Fuel rationing was introduced in Northern Ireland on 16th September 1939 and was followed by similar restrictions in the Irish Free State on the 2nd October. It was particularly severe south of the border, which relied entirely on Britain for all of its refined liquid fuel. Harold McIntosh, the Mechanical Engineer, in a circular dated 14th February 1942, also highlighted another acute problem facing the GNR. He reported, "there is a serious shortage of vehicle tyres as a result of damage. The present position is such that as unfit tyres are removed from taxed machines the former have to be replaced with tyres from untaxed machines and when this source of supply is exhausted the vehicles may have to be withdrawn". The decline in omnibus journeys wholly within Eire during the early years of the 'emergency' is illustrated by an examination of the peak vehicle requirements of the period. During the summer of 1939 the figure was 122; during the same period in 1942 the requirement had fallen to 57, almost entirely brought about as a result of strategic material shortages. The company introduced service cuts in five separate phases so as to spread the grief for the travelling public and in the benign hope that fuel restrictions would ease. The five phases were as shown overleaf:–

Table 34. DERRY—RAPHOE—SLIGO.

WEEK-DAYS.

	A				B	C									
	a.m.	a.m.	a.m.	a.m.	a.m.	a.m.	p.m.	p.m.	p.m.	p.m.	...	...	...	...	...
DERRY (Foyle Rd. Stn.) dep.	...	...	...	9† 5	10*†0	10*†0	...	4† 0	5†45	6†45	...	...	...	...	...
Carrigans .... "	...	...	...	8 30	9*25	9*25	...	3 25	5 10	6 10	...	...	...	...	...
St. Johnston............... "	...	...	...	8 35	9*30	9*30	...	3 30	5 15	6 15	...	...	...	...	...
Raphoe .... "	...	...	...	9 0	——	9*55	...	3 55	——	6 40	...	...	...	...	...
Convoy .... "	...	...	...	9 10	...	——	...	4 5	...	6 50	...	...	...	...	...
Stranorlar.................arr.	...	...	...	9 30	...	...	...	4 25	...	7 10	...	...	...	...	...
" ....dep.	...	...	...	9 30	...	...	...	4 25	...	7 10	...	...	...	...	...
Ballybofey.................. "	...	...	...	9 35	...	...	...	4 30	...	7 15	...	...	...	...	...
Donegal (Diamond)......arr.	...	...	...	10 25	...	...	...	5 20	...	——	...	...	...	...	...
" (Rly. Stn.)...... "	...	...	...	...	...	...	...	...	...	...	...	...	...	...	...
" " " ......dep.	...	...	9 0	...	...	...	...	...	...	...	...	...	...	...	...
" (Diamond)...... "	6*30	...	9 5	10 35	...	...	...	5 30	...	...	...	...	...	...	...
Ballintra .... "	6*50	...	9 25	10 55	...	...	...	5 50	...	...	...	...	...	...	...
B'shannon (Mkt. Yard) dep.	7*15	7 30	9 50	11 20	...	...	4 15	6 15	...	...	...	...	...	...	...
" (Rly. Stn.)...dep.	...	...	...	...	...	...	...	...	...	...	...	...	...	...	...
Bundoran (Rly. Stn.)... "	7*30	7 45	1010	11 40	...	...	4 35	6 35	...	...	...	...	...	...	...
Grange .... "	——	8 20	1045	12 15	...	...	5 10	7 10	...	...	...	...	...	...	...
Drumcliffe .... "	...	8 35	11 0	12 30	...	...	5 25	7 25	...	...	...	...	...	...	...
Sligo (Quay Street)......arr.	...	8 55	1120	12 50	...	...	5 45	7 45	...	...	...	...	...	...	...
SLIGO (G. S. Rlys.)...... "	...	...	...	...	...	...	...	...	...	...	...	...	...	...	...

A—Runs only on Manorhamilton Fair Days

B—Wednesdays and Saturdays only. C—Raphoe Fair Days only. **NO SUNDAY SERVICE.**
Services noc run daily are indicated thus *.

†— Double Summer Time.

The impact of double summer time in Northern Ireland is clearly shown on this time-table for the Derry – Sligo cross-border service; the last journey from Derry arrives in Raphoe, some 12 miles distant, five minutes before its journey has commenced! *(SS)*

GNR Gardner No. 248 seen during 1944 at Londonderry Foyle Road Station – note the offside headlamp cover and wartime white lining of mudguards and liferails. *(WM)*

Monday 10th February 1941

- all Sunday services other than those operated in the Dublin suburban area were discontinued
- Dublin/Hole in the Wall; Dublin/Strand Road/Skerries Station/Holmpatrick services withdrawn completely
- Dublin/Skerries; Dublin/Cavan; Dublin/Carrickmacross; Sligo/Londonderry; Cavan/Kilnaleck/Virginia Road Station. Thinned out dramatically
- Dublin City Suburban last bus departures were cut back to 10pm.

Sunday 6th April 1941

- Dublin/Malahide via Coolock service was discontinued in favour of the Dublin United Transport Company bus service to Malahide
- The GNR service between Dublin and Malahide via Portmarnock and the Bawn was diverted to operate via the then new Coast Road between Portmarnock and Malahide.

Monday 16th June 1941

- The following services were discontinued
  Amiens Street Station/Eden Quay
  Monaghan/Clones
  Monaghan/Newbliss
  Monaghan/Tyholland Border Post
  Cootehill/Bailieborough
  Castleblaney/Ballybay

Monday 19th April 1942

- Temporary suspension of selected services in the Dublin, Drogheda, Omeath and Sligo areas.

Monday 27th April 1942

- Specific services in Dublin, Drogheda, Cavan and Sligo areas were truncated.

The aggregate savings in mileage amounted to 11,857 per week, which represented a reduction of 26%. The GNR estimated the savings in fuel oil to be 4,250 gallons per month. GNR buses could be fuelled in Northern Ireland at Newry, Londonderry and Enniskillen where petrol and diesel was in more plentiful (although still rationed) supply than in the Irish Free State. In late 1939 Billy Smyth, Garage Superintendent at Donegal, devised a plan to rotate his whole fleet of buses onto duties that went into Londonderry where diesel and petrol could be obtained. This initiative ameliorated an otherwise difficult situation in the Irish Free State. Cavan and Dundalk Garages followed Billy Smyth's example and sent most of their buses to Enniskillen and Newry respectively on a rotational basis to obtain fuel in Northern Ireland.

Before the advent of war over 90% of vehicles operating in Eire were running on petrol or diesel. The numbers involved were roughly 50,000 private, 10,000 goods, 5,000 public service, 3,000 motor cycles, 100 steam, 70 electric battery and 2,000 miscellaneous vehicles, including farm tractors etc. the remainder being horse powered. Eire consumed some 40,000,000 gallons of petrol, 18,000,000 gallons of kerosene, 10,000,000 gallons of diesel and 4,500,000 gallons of crude oil annually. The Eire Government, now only able to obtain 25% of its normal consumption during the war, illustrates the seriousness of the fuel situation. Eire introduced emergency wartime controls on bus operations under an Emergency Powers Order of 30th May 1941 in an effort to conserve precious fuel and eliminate duplication of services. The ever worsening fuel crisis in Eire forced hundreds of Dundalk residents to go digging turf at Annaverna just north of the town at Ravensdale. Their major difficulty was getting it back to Dundalk. In July 1941 the County Council looked to Harold McIntosh and Richard Meredith of the GNR for help. They very quickly arranged for Dundalk works to convert an AEC Reliance bus, fleet number 25, to a turf lorry with specially modified low ratio differential to handle the stiff gradients on the mountain path. Following the success of the conversion a Dennis G 20-seat bus, obtained in 1932 from DJ Davidson of Aughnacloy was also turned into a turf lorry. The objective was to move up to 100 tons of turf a day to Dundalk for winter heating. The GNR's contribution was greatly valued by the local Dundalk community. The GNR road motor services turned to buses using producer gas generated on a trailer accompanying the vehicle in a bid to improve a critical fuel shortage. On 14th April 1944 Major General McNeill of the Irish Army asked the GNR to provide two gas producer buses to convey parties from Dublin to entertain troops digging turf on the bogs for electricity generation. Harold McIntosh arranged for two buses based in Dublin Garage, Nos. 91 and 92, to be fitted with gas producer trailers. A description appears later in this book.

In Northern Ireland the evacuation of civilians from Belfast added to the difficulties, as daily rail services had to be augmented to cater for workers and others engaged on essential work. On Easter Tuesday 1941 Hitler's Luftwaffe embarked on a concentrated blitz of Belfast in an attempt to destroy factories producing war material. The ferocity of this bombing can be appreciated by the fact that over 700 people were killed and 1,500 injured. The blitz managed to destroy part of the NIRTB's workshops at Duncrue Street with the resultant loss of a number of vehicles. The GNR readily agreed to lend 21 buses to the NIRTB to supplement those destroyed by enemy action and to assist with the increased wartime traffic. The Great Southern Railway loaned the NIRTB 30 buses for the same purpose. The £35 per vehicle per calendar month rental charged for buses, which would have been in storage anyway, was extremely valuable to the GNR. The buses were handed over to the NIRTB at their Marcus Square depot in Newry.

The following GNR vehicles were seconded to the NIRTB from April 1941 until December 1942:–

GNR Bus Fleet No.	Registration No.	Type	Notes
40	ZI 3553	AEC Reliance	
41	ZI 3554	AEC Reliance	
79	ZI 4262	Leyland Tiger TS2	
82	ZI 4265	Leyland Tiger TS2	
84	ZI 4267	Leyland Tiger TS2	
86	ZI 4269	Leyland Tiger TS2	
93	ZI 4276	Leyland Tiger TS2	
94	ZI 4277	Leyland Tiger TS2	
96	ZI 4279	Leyland Tiger TS2	
97	ZI 4280	Leyland Tiger TS2	
98	ZI 4281	Leyland Tiger TS2	
110	AZ 5078	Leyland Lion LT2	
149	AZ 7642	Leyland Lion LT2	
151	AZ 7644	Leyland Lion LT2	
233	AZ 9134	Leyland Tiger TS3	Tour Coach
235	AZ 9136	Leyland Tiger TS3	Tour Coach
263	ZI 8544	Leyland Tiger TS4	
264	ZI 8545	Leyland Tiger TS4	
276	AZ 4059	Leyland Tiger TS2	Ex Catherwood
278	ZI 9198	Leyland Tiger TS2	Ex Catherwood
296	AZ 1514	Leyland Tiger TS2	Ex Catherwood

GNR Gardner No. 200 running on anthracite producer gas, complete with trailer in tow and seen speeding along the Ardee Road in Dundalk during 1941. *(DN)*

GNR Leyland LT2 (fleet No. 110) with Service Motor Works body on loan to the NIRTB, seen at Rathfriland depot complete with Sangar during 1941. This vehicle was later converted into a lorry a picture of which appears on page 46 in this book outside Donegal Garage. *(MC)*

During the period of hire to the NIRTB they remained in the GNR Oxford Blue and Cream livery devoid of all Great Northern lettering, coat of arms and fleet numbers. The NIRTB did apply their own fleet numbers and many had the lettering 'NIRTB' applied to the front scuttle.

Howden's Reshuffle

George Howden reshuffled his pack of Senior Managers and Officials, promoting those who identified with his management approach. On 30th June 1940 the Dublin based District Superintendent John H Scott retired, to be succeeded by Paddy A Foley the next day on a Salary of £600 per year. Paddy was an inspired choice as the new District Superintendent, being a Major in the Irish Army's reserve Local Security Force and at the time the GNR Official who was responsible for all wartime emergency preparations. In the summer of 1940 the strength of the part time component of the Irish Army, known as the Local Security Force numbered 140,000. Many GNR men served in the LSF. The Army held LSF exercises on 27th July 1940 in the Howth area, the scene of regular manoeuvres during the emergency, which involved the commandeering of many GNR buses from Dublin Garage. The Howth Company of the LSF, which was headquartered at Howth Demesne under the command of Captain Sir Lauriston Arnott (a World War One veteran, and Managing Director of the Irish Times), was one of the most active elements in the country. Miss Gaisford St Lawrence, daughter of the owner of Howth Demesne was in charge of the Howth and Sutton Nursing Division of the St John's Ambulance who acted as a First Aid Detachment to the LSF. It is ironic that today the Gaisford St Lawrence family are the benevolent hosts to the Transport Museum Society of Ireland located at Howth Demesne, a facility which houses many GNR vehicles. Paddy Foley controlled the Road Motor Services until his retirement on 31st December 1945. His successor was Tommy Carton, appointed on 26th September 1945 on a salary of £650 per annum. Carton, a native of Dun Laoghaire, had previously been the Acting Operating Assistant to the Traffic Manager and a Stationmaster at Amiens Street Station in Dublin.

On 25th September 1940 a series of management changes took effect, the most significant of which saw John Frederick McCormick who had been George Howden's Chief Clerk in the Civil Engineers Office, promoted to the position of General Manager's Chief Clerk. The position of John McCormick was further enhanced when on 18th November 1942 he was appointed to the new position of assistant to the General Manager. Joseph Walker, who had been the Assistant Traffic Manager, retired on 30th September 1940 after 55 years service. WA Foster Graham succeeded him on a salary of £900 but his tenure in the post was very brief as he passed away in February 1942. McCormick in turn brought J Campbell Baillie and Cecil Rue, two friends of long standing into the General Manager's Office as Clerks. PKM Carey was appointed to the Solicitor's Office on 18th December 1940 in preparation for the impending retirement of the highly respected Company Solicitor Cecil Bailie-Gage, who eventually left the GNR on 28th February 1943. The retirement of Cecil Bailie-Gage presented the GNR with a future conundrum as he was an officer of the Court on both sides of the border and could thus practice in Belfast or Dublin. Carey on the other hand was limited to practice in the Irish Free State, resulting in the GNR having to instruct Solicitors in Belfast for future legal work there.

GREAT NORTHERN RAILWAY (I.)

OMNIBUS

TIME TABLES

4th APRIL, 1943

AND

UNTIL FURTHER NOTICE.

During the continuance of the present emergency the Omnibus and Train Times shewn herein are subject to alteration or cancellation, without notice. Intending passengers are, therefore, advised to enquire beforehand for the latest information available concerning services.

The Company cannot undertake to provide more than one Bus for each Service.

NOTE.—Double Summer Time is shown so far as Placès in Northern Ireland are concerned (thus 8†20) and Normal Summer Time so far as Places in Eire are concerned.

The notes on this page of a 1943 time-table neatly sum up the problems of war-time operation. *(SS)*

Córas Iompair Éireann

The Transport Act 1944 amalgamated the GSR and DUTC to form CIE, which became a statutory undertaking with shareholders of the same status as the GSR and DUTC had been. On 2nd January 1945 AP Reynolds was installed as the first Chairman of CIE. The Irish Government again commissioned another report into Transport Strategy, this time chaired by Sir James Milne who had been the General Manager of the Great Western Railway up to nationalisation. They presented their report on 6th December 1948 after five months of deliberation. The commission declared that 'the time does not appear to be opportune for embarking on any drastic change in the constitution of the Great Northern Railway'. They did however suggest some form of joint authority by the two Governments, north and south, although this was not acted upon immediately. Milne was highly critical of the then Chairman of CIE, Augustus Percy Reynolds, who had been personally appointed by his good friend and Skerries Golf Club co-member Sean Lemass, the *Fianna Fail* Minister. Reynolds was portrayed as a moderniser but his tendencies were directed more towards modernising buildings rather than rolling stock and services. He was a racehorse owner and through this pursuit became friendly with the well-known Dublin Architect Michael Scott. Scott was responsible for alterations to Reynolds' house 'Abbeyville' at Malahide, now the home of the late disgraced former *Taoiseach* Charles J Haughey. Scott, through his close friendship with Reynolds, gained the commissions to design and build Busaras and CIE's Donnybrook Bus Garage. Reynolds was singled out for criticism in respect of the almost total power he enjoyed without scrutiny together with a number of very contentious management decisions made at the time. A new inter-party government had been elected in February 1948. The new Minister, Daniel Morrissey, after reading the Milne report, immediately dismissed AP Reynolds as CIE Chairman. In retrospect Morrissey probably used the report to settle some latent political scores. The *Transport Act 1950* amalgamated CIE and the Grand Canal Company and brought the combined undertaking into State ownership. The name CIE was retained for the new State-owned organisation, which commenced operations on 1st June 1950. The two distinct legal entities CIE (1945) and CIE (1950) are often confused but were in reality different organisations without any distinguishing qualification as to date or status.

The new CIE Chairman designate TC Courtney made a startling decision in March 1949 as he appointed George Howden, who was still the GNR's General Manager (then still a private company) as a consultant to CIE. Barely 12 months later Courtney consolidated Howden's position in CIE by appointing him to the post of General Manager. Howden's dual General Managerial position in both companies, whilst unusual, ensured greater co-operation between the two undertakings. This was symbolised by the introduction in October 1950 of a jointly operated Enterprise Express train between Belfast and Cork via Dublin and the purchase of 60 AEC Railcars by CIE, which were almost identical to the earlier GNR fleet. The appointment of George Howden to the position of General Manager of CIE led directly to a further series of management changes at the GNR. On 29th June 1949 John F McCormick was appointed to the oddly titled position of Managerial Executive Officer (effectively the General Manager in all but name). J Campbell Baillie was appointed Operating Superintendent. The District Superintendent's position in Omagh was dispensed with, which resulted in the incumbent, H Evans, being moved to the post of Staff Superintendent in Belfast. A Max Beaton, who had been the assistant to the Traffic Manager (for Commercial Outdoor Activities) became the Advert and Publicity Superintendent and was the man responsible for the new design of GNR bus timetables which featured a photograph of a GNR double-deck bus on the front cover. Max Beaton was born in 1907 and joined the GNR(I) in 1924 serving at various stations throughout the system. He was transferred to the Road Motor Superintendent's Office in 1930 and in 1932 was transferred to the same office in Belfast to look after the Northern Ireland fleet.

Nationalisation of CIE by the Government in 1945 specifically excluded the Londonderry and Lough Swilly Railway. Although 98% of its operations were in the Free State it was in fact registered in Northern Ireland. The County Donegal Railway, which was jointly owned by the GNR and the LMS companies, was also excluded from incorporation into CIE. This left the Great Northern Railway as an independent company with railway operations on both sides of the border and road transport operations concentrated south of the border. Dublin was very wary of the GNR and its management – this was partly borne out of the perception in the minds of government Ministers that the GNR was a Unionist controlled Trojan horse. It would be fair to say that the vast majority of the shareholders probably considered themselves Unionists. GNR chiefs, in common with those of most other Irish Railways, were invariably Protestants and it is reasonable to assume that they identified far more with Britain than with the emerging Irish nation. The Eire government were concerned to learn that during the Second World War the GNR in Dublin were collecting funds to buy Spitfire aircraft for the Royal Air Force. Meanwhile the irrepressible Howden continued to serve two masters until March 1953. He then resigned from CIE after having been courted by the Northern Ireland Government to become the Chairman of the Ulster Transport Authority, such was the esteem in which he was universally held.

A Final Acquisition

Keenan Brothers were the last independent bus company bought by the GNR under section 51 of the Road Transport Act 1933. The GNR paid John Keenan £2,750 on 29th October 1945 in respect of the bus service he and his brother ran from Carlingford Co Louth. They operated the following services:–

Carlingford/Dundalk via Ravensdale
Carlingford/Dundalk via Bellurgan
Dundalk/Ballybinaby
Grange/Boherboy via Greenore
Carlingford/Ferryhill
Dundalk/Ferryhill

Nine years previously, on 19th March 1936, Keenan's Northern Ireland PSV plate was removed by the Royal Ulster Constabulary at Newry due to the poor mechanical condition of his bus. His Newry, Carlingford and Dundalk services were immediately truncated at the Ferryhill border post as a result of the RUC action. Keenan's never regained a Northern Ireland PSV plate. On acquisition the GNR immediately scrapped three former DUTC ADC buses. A 14 seat Reo Speedwagon did enjoy a brief sojourn as a bus before becoming a store at Dundalk works. Keenan claimed that the business was worth £35,000 and took the GNR to the Transport Tribunal after reducing his claim to £20,200. He agreed to abide by the ruling of an arbitrator appointed by the Tribunal who eventually ruled, on 23rd May 1947, that the GNR should pay £4,169 plus 3% interest from the take over date.

Acquisitions too far

Hezekiah Appleby ran the Central Bus Service from Enniskillen to Sligo. On 4th February 1936 he wrote to John McCrea, General Manager of the NIRTB, seeking to operate a summer service from Enniskillen to Bundoran daily. At the time he ran this service on Sunday, Tuesday, Thursday and Saturday only. The GNR lodged a strong objection to McCrea at the NIRTB, claiming that the existing Appleby buses had already adversely affected rail revenues. McCrea wrote to Appleby on the 21st March 1936 refusing his application. The NIRTB took over the Northern Ireland portion of his Enniskillen/Sligo service on 30th June 1938, however he continued to operate between Blacklion (Irish Free State Frontier) and Sligo. During November 1940 Hez Appleby approached Howden of the GNR to enquire whether they were interested in buying him out. Howden consulted James Lockhart who in turn suggested that the Sligo Leitrim and Northern Counties should be approached since he operated in their territory. The SLNCR did not have powers of compulsory purchase under the 1932/3 Road Transport Act as they were registered in Enniskillen Northern Ireland. Howden didn't want the Appleby service although he did want to keep the Erne Bus Service out of Sligo, which was the probable outcome of Appleby surrendering his licence. The Omnibus Department of the GSR had also expressed little interest in taking over the service. Appleby had not approached SC Little, the General Manager of the SLNCR directly and in turn he was not disposed to take any action even if he could. Howden acted by applying to the Department of Industry and Commerce to compulsorily acquire the Appleby business on 17th December 1940 (Licence No. 315 Blacklion Frontier Post to Sligo Stephen Street) although it did not proceed as a result of the emergency conditions pertaining at the time. An eventual approach by Appleby to Little was made in October 1944. On 28th October Little wrote to Howden seeking advice on taking over the Appleby licence. An interesting by product of the 1944 Transport Act, of 8th December 1944, which established *Córas Iompair Éireann*, was that any Railway Company in the state could apply for road passenger and merchandise licences of independent operators within their territory. Howden advised Little to take advantage of the new legislation and to buy Appleby out which he did in 1945.

Little again wrote to Howden on 24th November 1944 asking him if the GNR could sell the SLNCR two second hand buses. Two Leyland Tiger buses 86 and 96 were offered for sale at £350 each. On 10th March 1945 Little wrote to Howden informing him that the SLNCR were taking two of Appleby's buses and that they would now buy only one GNR bus. After inspection at Dundalk by the SLNCR engineer GF Egan, bus No. 96 was repainted into the SLNCR colours and dispatched by rail omnibus wagon on 25th June 1945 to Manorhamilton. Three months later, because of the unreliability of the former Appleby buses, Little looked to Howden for another bus. On 20th September 1945 the GNR again offered No. 86 for sale at the same price. Then, days later, the GNR changed their mind and offered Little one of the ex Catherwood Leyland Tigers No. 296 for the same price, which they accepted and it was delivered to Manorhamilton on 5th February 1946. By the middle of 1947 the SLNCR were in trouble again with vehicles. At this time Howden refused to sell the SLNCR any vehicles, but he did allow Little to approach Billy Smith, the GNR Foreman in Donegal Garage when failures occurred, in order to hire GNR vehicles and crew, which became an all too often occurrence.

On 28th November 1955 Tommy Carton, the Dublin based Deputy Traffic Manager of the GNR, was instructed by Howden to prepare for the substitution of all SLNCR rail services between Manorhamilton/Sligo, Dromahair/Manorhamilton, Blacklion/Sligo and Dowra/Ballinaglera. As soon as the SLNCR ceased all operations the GNR decided, largely through a combination of poor revenue and diabolical roads, especially between Manorhamilton and Dromahair through the townland of Bohy, to limit the bus substitution to a single service, which was introduced on 1st October 1957 between Carrick on Shannon and Bundoran, running on Monday, Wednesday and Saturday. By 14th October 1957 a Carrick on Shannon to Sligo service was operating on a Tuesday, Thursday and Friday. CIE provided substitute buses between Sligo and Manorhamilton (two routes) and Manorhamilton to Enniskillen. The Sligo Enniskillen service meant that CIE for the first time in its history began operating a cross border service into Northern Ireland territory.

Joseph Halpenny of Blackrock Co Louth, proprietor of the Violet Bus Service, was advised on 11th April 1945 that the GNR intended to acquire his business under section 51 of the Road Transport Act of 1933. Halpenny, a well liked and respected local businessman, objected strongly to any suggestion of a take over. Paddy Foley dispatched Chief Inspector Albert Switzer to make discreet enquiries prior to the proposed acquisition. Switzer reported back that the Violet was essentially a summer season operation with low levels of patronage during the winter on the 4½ mile route from Roden Place, Dundalk to Blackrock Pavilion. The Violet buses (2 Dennis and 2 Leyland) all dated from 1931 to 1935 and were considered by Switzer to be in poor condition. John Shanaghan, the GNR accountant also examined two years worth of Violet books, following which he reported back to the Board that he could not recommend the purchase. In May 1955 the GNRB again considered acquisition of the Violet; this time a plan had been devised by the Traffic Manager in Belfast to integrate the Blackrock service with the existing GNR local bus network in the Dundalk area. This scheme did not progress beyond the planning stage. It is worth mentioning that the Violet Bus Company was formed in 1920 and is still a thriving concern today, having recently added a Dundalk/Newry service using brand new vehicles.

The Last Days of Independence

Following the Second World War the GNR, faced with bankruptcy caused by the need to maintain an obsolete fleet of rolling stock and renew worn out permanent way, was in

The GNR(I) Board and Senior Officers.
Front row left to right: The Hon Lord Glenavy (Chairman), John M Cairnes (Director), Raymond A Burke (Director), Senator Kennedy Stewart (Director), John B Stephens (Deputy Chairman), T Frederick Stokes (Director), JP Herdman (Director), R Stanley Stokes (Director), Major CAM Alexander (Director).
Back Row left to right: FC Wallace (Company Secretary), GB Howden (General Manager), CH Sleator (Civil Engineer), PKM Carey (Solicitor), JF McCormick (Management Executive Officer), HS Knott (Traffic Manager), JS McCormick (Stores Superintendent), RW Meredith (Mechanical Engineer), C Johnson (Hotels and Catering Manager). *(SS)*

dire straights. The winter of 1947 will long be remembered in Ireland for its severe blizzards and massive disruption to the transport industry. It was also the last full financial year that the company had traded profitably, although the Road Motor Services operated in profit consistently from 1935 onwards. Industrial relations degenerated on 15th August 1947 when 100 road motor staff employed in the Drogheda, Dundalk and Newry garages staged an unofficial one day strike demanding pay parity with CIE staff, which amounted to a five-shilling weekly increase. The company did not yield to the demands of the strikers; although the issue subsided it remained a source of discontent for some years to come. Then 1949 saw crisis meetings between the Company's Accountant John Shanaghan and the banks. The Bank of Ireland and Royal Bank of Ireland struggled with the GNR to ensure short-term liquidity and keep the business going. The banks eventually agreed to facilitate additional loans against assets, which only succeeded in buying a little time for the company. John Shanaghan retired on April Fool's Day 1949 in the middle of the crisis, handing over the financial reins to Harry Patterson, who assumed his responsibilities as Accountant and who promptly demanded that Howden introduce immediate cost cutting. An internal examination of costs was instituted within the Road Motor Services focusing on the staffing of omnibus garages. In August 1949 the following economies were introduced:–

Dublin	Reduction of one Ticket Examiner and one Ticket Picker
Drogheda	Reduction of a Parcels Attendant
Dundalk	Reduction of a Ticket Picker
Cavan	Reduction of a Ticket Examiner
Donegal	Reduction of One Clerk

The reductions in staff were made possible as a direct result of the introduction of new Setright ticket machines. By the end of the 1940's severe weather had given way to the most forbidding financial crisis facing the GNR.

G N R (I)

Furniture Removed by Road or Rail

GOOD VANS
NO WORRIES
RELIABLE SERVICE
INQUIRIES INVITED

Skilled Packers and Attractive Rates

Phone, write or call to the District Supt., Amiens St. Station, Dublin, or apply at any of the Company's Stations. Phone : Dublin 72941.

GEO. B. HOWDEN, General Manager.

An extract from a GNR bus timetable promoting the Road Merchandise Service. *(SS)*

Chapter Seven
The Fighting Fifties

The 1950s began with the Great Northern Railway fighting for survival, and by the close of the decade it had vanished into the annals of the transport history of Ireland. At a stormy shareholders' meeting of the GNR in Dublin during November 1950 they demanded that the company act to curtail deficits by wholesale railway closures. The Chairman of the Board, Lord Glenavy, addressing a shareholders' meeting in Belfast on 8th December 1950, announced that the company had a surplus of liquid assets of £1,000 at 30th November with losses running at £8,000 per week which would result in widespread job losses. On 20th December 1950 a dramatic announcement was made from the GNR to the effect that it was to terminate all rail services from 1st February 1951. Repeated warnings from the directors of the GNR to both governments from 1948 were largely ignored. Reserves had been so drawn down that the maintenance of solvency was critically in doubt. No one who took heed to the many public warnings that GNR solvency was in question should have been surprised at the closure announcement. The respective governments required the GNR in Northern Ireland to follow the standards of British Railways and in the Irish Republic that of CIE. The costs in both territories were shown to be beyond the GNR's capacity to meet them. The directors consistently told both governments that the company's finances had been prudent, the management competent and indeed heroic in the way it had faced such handicaps as the stricture of a customs border across the middle of the GNR. This final action rang immediate alarm bells in the corridors of power in Belfast and Dublin who began taking the threat of closure seriously.

The crisis provoked initial dialogue between the two Governments, which began in August 1950. Mr Liam Cosgrave (Parliamentary Secretary to the Irish Minister of Industry and Commerce Daniel Morrissey and a future *Taoiseach* in the 1970s), met the Northern Ireland Minister of Commerce WV McCleery. Cosgrove was assisted by senior civil servants such as the long serving Secretary to the Department, John Leydon and a very formidable Principal Officer in charge of Transport Miss Thekla J Beere, whose knowledge of her brief was acclaimed by all. Miss Beere was a rare species amongst senior Irish Civil Servants being both a female and a Protestant long before equal opportunities came into vogue. Discussions were elevated to Ministerial level on both sides as Daniel Morrissey and Minister WV McCleery met in Dublin for discussions. This was the first official visit by a Northern Ireland government Minister for over 35 years. The previous one had been when Lord Craigavon went to talk to Michael Collins at the time of the treaty negotiations. The GNR's announcement regarding its future focused the minds of the two ministers and their officials into taking joint action to save the company. Within a matter of days the two governments advised the GNR that they had jointly agreed to acquire the company for the sum of £3.9 million and that until such arrangements could be approved by the two parliaments both governments would assume responsibility for operating losses. The GNR Board meeting to consider the intentions of the two governments agreed to postpone closure of the railway network. However, they emphatically rejected the offer of £3.9m for purchase of the company, as the Board knew that the strength of feeling among the shareholders was such that it would not be approved.

Dublin and Belfast were thrown into further crisis by the GNR's unexpected rejection of the offer. Mr McCleery held further meetings with his Dublin counterpart to consider what action to take. This was interrupted by a general election in the Irish Republic during June 1951 which saw a new *Fianna Fail* government and Minister Sean Lemass given the task of sorting out the GNR mess. The two Ministers met with the Board of the company advising them that both governments would if necessary compulsorily purchase the GNR for the sum of £3.9m. They went on to say that if a proposal came from the company shareholders on slightly more advantageous terms both governments would look sympathetically at this. A shareholders' vote was taken in September 1951 at which a Board recommended purchase figure of £4.5m was approved.

Great Northern Railway Board Formed

On 30th October 1951 both governments announced jointly that they had agreed to purchase the Great Northern Railway for the sum of £4.5m. The ministers went on to say that they had no agreed mechanism for running the railway but that discussions would continue. The two governments and the Board of the GNR continued to talk during 1952 in order to establish arrangements for the administration of the company. It was clear from discussions that both governments had separate and specific agenda objectives from which they were not going to yield concessions. The Dublin government wanted to protect the jobs at Dundalk Works in the constituency of Frank Aitken TD, the leading member of a die-hard Republican faction in *Fianna Fail* and Minister for Foreign Affairs. Belfast, with its fiercely Unionist government, was equally determined that Dublin would not gain any foothold or have any authority joint or otherwise over any GNR asset in Northern Ireland. Dublin offered to amalgamate the GNR into CIE but as one can imagine this met with a swift rejection by Mr McCleery on behalf of the Northern Ireland government. Once the two sides got out of their respective trenches the agreement that did emerge was for a new corporation to be established in October 1953 called the Great Northern Railway Board (GNRB). Both governments agreed that all GNR land within Northern Ireland would be vested in the Ulster Transport Authority. The GNRB would then be permitted to use the land and assets for the purposes of operating the railway. The ownership of Dundalk works was to be vested in the Dublin government and both administrations would fund its operation on behalf of the GNRB.

The purchase price was shared equally by both administrations; however various funding formulae were devised. For example the GNRB was to be funded 60/40 between Northern Ireland and the Irish Republic, which took account of the fact that 2/3 of the rail network was in the North. All of the Road Motor Service buses, lorries, garages, depots and staff costs were borne by the South as its operation was based there. The provision of all new railway rolling stock was to be shared equally. Conversely any capital project to upgrade GNRB infrastructure was to be funded by the relevant government after agreement from the respective minister. The composition of the new Board was ten directors, five being nominated from Northern Ireland and five from the Republic. A 'senior member' from each administration, George Howden for the North and Percy Reynolds from the South, alternated annually between the positions of Chairman and Vice-Chairman. George Howden's old friend John F McCormick was appointed to the position of General Manager (Designate) of the GNRB on 1st September 1953 at a salary of £3,000 a year.

On Monday 10th August 1953 in the conference room of the Royal Courts of Justice in Belfast the agreement between the two Governments to acquire the GNR was signed by both Ministers. The GNRB came into existence formally on Thursday 1st October 1953. Born of necessity. it was immediately plunged into a crisis. The independent GNR had lost £675,284 in 1951. This increased to £945,000 during 1952, which both governments had to provide for, despite the fact that both were cash strapped. The earlier assurances were however honoured North and South. It was very clear given the legacy inherited by the GNRB of antiquated rolling stock and a permanent way requiring major renewal that the new corporation was not going to enjoy an easy ride. Board members were frustrated by the necessity to obtain prior approval from both governments for a programme of capital expenditure. This cumbersome procedure often took months and even years to get an agreement from each administration.

The Northern Ireland government agreed to pay the salary (£1,150 per annum) of Mr RL Streight who was appointed on 1st November 1954 as the officer for the integration of the GNRB and UTA in the Province, in a move which clearly signalled their intentions for the recently established Board. Mr Streight joined the LMS (NCC) in 1916 and later worked at integration of road freight and passenger services with the Northern Ireland Road Transport Board. It was during the GNRB years that the largest single Private Hire operation was undertaken with organisation and preparation, which would have done justice to the military planners of the D Day landings. On Sunday 19th September 1954 the Pioneer Total Abstinence Association held its National Pilgrimage at Knock at which 50,000 adherents attended. The GNR provided 52 buses from throughout the company's operating area, all converging on Knock. Arrangements were made to have Garage Tenders and mechanics available along the Longford and Sligo routes leading to Knock to ensure that the 1,900 pilgrims in the care of the GNR enjoyed a smooth journey.

Earnestly Seeking The Erne

Maurice Cassidy's Erne Omnibus Service established in 1929 running between Enniskillen and Cootehill via Lisnaskea and Clones was always well turned out in its brown and cream livery. In 1930 he began running to Bundoran from Enniskillen and then from Clones to Cavan. Cassidy had his head office at 27 Belmore Street Enniskillen where he garaged seven of his eventual nine buses. The remaining two were based in the Republic at Carrigallen and Clones. He had become very active in the private hire sector during 1932 causing considerable infuriation to the GSR in the areas to the Southeast and Southwest of Sligo. At the request of the GSR the *Gardai* stopped a number of Cassidy's specials. Frightened, he then resorted to operating his buses as special hires to John McGauran's omnibus service of Ballinamore who also ran the Commercial hotel in the town. In July 1935 the GSR acquired McGauran's licences to run Ballinamore/Sligo and Ballinamore/Bundoran services. On 6th August 1935 the GSR sold the Ballinamore/Bundoran licence to the GNR. Cassidy, now unable to use the McGauran cover, applied for a licence to operate between Enniskillen and Monaghan via Clones and another service between Ballinamore and Ballyshannon in November 1936. The GSR and GNR jointly opposed the granting of the licences, a stance endorsed by the Minister. Undaunted, Cassidy proposed operating a service between Cavan and Mullingar in April 1937, which immediately initiated a strong challenge from the GSR because it would have run mainly within its area. The Minister again spurned Cassidy, at the same time warning the GSR that he would not continue to turn down applications from Cassidy indefinitely. Cassidy then turned his attentions towards the Breffni Bus Company established in 1934 by James McInerny of Carrigallen County Leitrim. From 1st November 1938 Cassidy bought out McInerny, the upshot of which was that he gained new services, which caused serious concern in the GSR and GNR. Additionally he applied for licences to operate the following services:-

- Carrigallen and Bundoran (Competing with the GNR between Drumshanbo/Bundoran)
- Carrigallen and Manorhamilton (Competing with GNR between Drumshanbo/Bundoran)
- Longford and Abbeyshrule (Competing with GSR services)
- Cavan and Oldcastle (Competing with GNR Cavan/Kilnaleck/Virginia services)

In spite of the combined opposition of the GSR and GNR he was permitted to operate services between Carrigallen and Cavan/Longford/Carrick on Shannon the result of the Breffni purchase. The activities of Cassidy caused the General Managers of the GSR and GNR to agree to ensure the removal

of Cassidy from the district. As a direct result of Cassidy's activities, the GSR proposed to the GNR a formal extension of the Meath pooling area in 1939 which would have provided for the following:–

- A line of demarcation between the Great Southern Railway and the Great Northern Railway would place the section Drumkeeran/Carrick on Shannon, the area North of Sligo as far as Grange and East of Sligo as far as Manorhamilton as GSR territory. The GSR would continue to offer garage and maintenance facilities to the GNR at their Lord Edward Street garage. Receipts were to be split 80% to the working company on a route, which crossed into the other company's territory 20% to the non-working company of receipts within their area. Lockhart of the GNR opposed the agreement and it became still born as a result of the advent of hostilities in September.

Following the end of the war the acquisition of the Erne Bus Company by the GNR was proposed with contributions (based on gross receipts of the Erne in the respective areas during the agreed period) from CIE and the NIRTB towards the costs of licences in their respective territories. The GNR would operate the bus services and retain the gross receipts paying 3% on their contribution to CIE and NIRTB as well as a share of the receipts earned in their respective territories (to be calculated by apportioning gross receipts pro rata to the share of compensation for the licences). In Northern Ireland Cassidy ran timetable services under consents granted by the NIRTB on the same day as a vesting order was issued on Friday 31st December 1937, which was never enacted. In the Republic Cassidy held licences granted by the Ministry of Industry & Commerce. Cassidys' six routes were:–

- Enniskillen/Bundoran
- Enniskillen/Clones, with extensions each to Cavan and Cootehill three days weekly.

Erne Bus Company Leyland Comet CP01 with Murphy 32-seat bodywork seen in Sligo during 1958 working the recently acquired service to Carrigallen which the GNR and GSR had fought for years to prevent. *(GL)*

- Enniskillen/Rosslea a service wholly within Northern Ireland.
- Carrigallen/Cavan
- Carrigallen/Longford
- Carrigallen/Carrick-on-Shannon

In March 1954 the Passenger Manager of the Ulster Transport Authority, Robert Hughes and the Commercial Superintendent of the GNRB, John F Atkinson, recommended to their respective undertakings the joint acquisition of the Erne Bus Company for £80,000. The proposal obtained provisional agreement on 28th July 1954. Jointly both administrations examined the Erne accounts but due to its impossibility of eliminating private hire operations together with the uncertain future of the GNR branch lines it did not proceed. The UTA was facing increasing pressure by the politically powerful Ulster Farmers Union which was pressing for new routes to be opened in Fermanagh, which were on Cassidy's roads, and there was trouble deciding whether he, or the Authority was to provide them. In August 1956 the UTA decided to go it alone setting up a holding company called the Devenish Carriage and Wagon Company Limited which purchased the Erne Bus Company from Cassidy on behalf of the Authority thus gaining cross border services to Clones and Bundoran from Enniskillen.

Rising to the challenge

During the night of 8th December 1954 one of the piers of the GNR mainline railway bridge number 3 over the Tolka River at East Wall Road was washed away following a hurricane force gale accompanied by torrential rain, snow and sleet. Amiens Street station was cut off from the rest of the network; it was to the road motor services that the company looked to get passengers moving again. Four summer buses stored at Abercorn Road garage (Nos. 286/8, 381/2) were pressed into immediate service to meet the emergency demand. GNR bus services themselves were disrupted as a result of the gales. The Dublin-Portmarnock service had to be abandoned when the sea at high tide flooded the road at Moyne Bridge, Baldoyle. On the Dublin-Dundalk route services were delayed due to flooding at Swords whilst other disruptions occurred on the Cavan and Carrickmacross services as a result of flooding and fallen trees. Between 9th December 1954 and 4th January 1955 Clontarf and Killester Stations effectively became the main passenger terminus for Dublin. The Road Motor Services were operating a bus substitution between Amiens Street and Clontarf/Killester Stations. The Amiens Street train departure times were observed from Clontarf, the feeder buses leaving the top of Carriage Drive in front of Amiens Street fifteen minutes earlier. All Dublin – Howth rail services were operated by bus during this period and where necessary services were augmented to cater for additional passengers. By 4th January contractors had erected a temporary Bailey bridge; a new concrete structure was opened a year later constructed by the Dublin firm of Collins Brothers who were Ireland's foremost authority on pre-stressed concrete structures.

In fact the Company was often called upon to provide rail substitution services. Some years earlier in November 1938 part of the Dundalk Newry and Greenore Railway was washed away by floods, which saw GNR buses providing replacement services for a British Railway. The Road Motor Services came to the railway's rescue again. This time it was called upon to provide a bus substitution from 26th September 1956. The Bundoran branch railway line was closed between Pettigo and Castlecaldwell stations when heavy rains at Ross Harbour washed part of the embankment along the Lower Lough Erne shore away. Omnibuses worked from Pettigo to Bundoran a distance of about ten miles calling at Castlecaldwell, Belleek, and Ballyshannon observing train times. Additional vehicles were drafted in from Dundalk and assistant motormen from Donegal were used as crew for the extra workings until the line was re-opened to traffic on 18th October 1956. Sadly just less than a year later the railway line closed forever.

Adapt or Die

Despite an increase in road motor service receipts the GNRB losses over the next four years ran at about £1m per annum; it was evident from this that the Board would not enjoy a long life. The Northern Ireland Government was now insisting that the Ulster Transport Authority bear the losses on behalf of the government. This placed in jeopardy the continued existence of the UTA, which risked the possibility of bankruptcy. The Stormont government was not going to allow the GNRB to bring down the UTA, insisting that all modes of public transport pay their way in Northern Ireland. In October 1955 William McCleery announced the proposed closure of secondary railway lines in the south and west of the province all of which ran through to the Republic of Ireland thus promoting a crisis for both governments. The Irish Minister, who was by now William Norton, objected to the proposals. A Joint North/South Transport Tribunal was established under the Section 22 of the Great Northern Railway Act 1953. The Rt Hon Sir Anthony B Babington QC, the Northern Ireland Transport Tribunal Chairman commenced sitting at the County Court House in Belfast on 8th and 9th May 1956. His southern counterpart, Dr James P Beddy began taking evidence at the City Hall, Dublin on 23rd April 1956. Mr JF McCormick, General Manager who was the Board's principal witness at the public hearings, represented the GNRB. Mr J Campbell Bailie, Traffic Manager, Mr PH Patterson, Accountant, Mr AM Beaton Staff Officer, Mr WHC Stone, Civil Engineer and Mr RW Meredith, Mechanical Engineer accompanied him. Eventually the scheme went ahead after exhausting all the appeal mechanisms. The closures took place on 30th September 1957 as directed by the new Minister of Commerce in the Northern Ireland government Lord Glentoran who dropped a further bombshell by announcing that the Belfast government would not extend the first five year term of the GNRB. This, taken with the decision to close the secondary railway lines, was not greeted with unanimous approval within the ruling Unionist Party. The late Mr Harry West, the Fermanagh MP and a regular GNR customer, along with other Unionists from west of the Bann were opposed to the closures and dissolution of the GNRB, however they could not move the government into a reversal of its policy.

The closures resulted in the GNR having to provide additional omnibus services in the Clones-Monaghan-Cootehill and Cavan areas from Tuesday 1st October 1957. In addition the closure of the Sligo, Leitrim and Northern Counties Railway resulted in substitute buses being provided mainly by CIE with assistance from the GNRB. Additional buses were transferred from Dublin, Drogheda and Dundalk to Cavan, Clones and Monaghan to meet the new requirement. Following the withdrawal of the residual rail services in the Irish Republic between Dundalk Junction and Clones, Glaslough to Cavan and Ballyhaise to Belturbet with effect from 14th October 1957 further buses had to be found to provide substitute services. In December 1957 a review of substitute services was carried out which resulted in fine-tuning of all the timetables in the Monaghan/Clones/Ballybay/Cootehill/Cavan area effective from 6th January 1958. The Friday only service between Cootehill and Clones via Newbliss, which had been operated by the Erne Bus Company prior to its demise, was operated by Great Northern bus from Friday 3rd January 1958. Meanwhile the GNRB General Manager John F McCormick, who had been unwell since early 1958 retired following 52 years service. It is said that the 1957 railway closures caused him considerable stress from which he found it difficult to recover. McCormick and Campbell Baillie put up a magnificent campaign at the Transport Tribunals in an attempt to stop the closures by arguing for a stay of execution whilst dieselisation of the lines could be introduced. They argued and produced figures to support their contention that this action would quickly see them in profit. Heartbroken, McCormick fell ill and never

GNR Gardner working the rail substitution service in 1957 from Cootehill to Clones at a roadside stop with the helpful conductor unloading merchandise. Note the 3173 Northern Ireland licence plate. *(JG)*

returned to his position with the company. His assistant Percy Bogle who was Chief Clerk to the General Manager oversaw the arrangements for the transfer of undertakings to *Córas Iompair Éireann* becoming the acting General Manager.

The Road Motor Services were called upon for the last time to provide rail substitution services on Monday 14th April 1958 as a result of the withdrawal of passenger train services between Drogheda and Oldcastle. The pre-existing bus service connecting with trains at Virginia Road Station was cancelled and a revised timetable was introduced on the Virginia Town-Kilnaleck-Cavan service and on the Drogheda/Oldcastle service. In the early GNRB years new services continued to be introduced that were not the direct result of the withdrawal of railway services. On 28th February 1955 Dublin gained one such route from Eden Quay to Raheny, serving a newly constructed high-density housing development called St Anne's. This was the last new service initiated in Dublin.

Tommy Carton, the Dublin based District Manager, revived a service between Drogheda and Mullingar, which had originally been inherited from CM Markey in 1930 who began operating his service on 22nd October 1928. One of Markeys' former employees called McCabe bought a 14 seater Chevrolet bus and started working a Drogheda/Mullingar service under the name of the Boyne Bus Service from 1st March 1930. McCabe played cat and mouse with the GNR resulting in heavy losses for the Company, which terminated its Mullingar service in February 1931. The GNR reached an agreement with McCabe, which resulted in him running the service at times fixed by the GNR with an option for the company to buy him out. In May 1931 a man called McDonnell appeared on the road called Macs Bus Service, which ran for six months before ending. Macs now faced further competition from an operator called Culligan who ventured onto the route for about three weeks. Culligan had his bus seized for non-payment of a debt. McDonnell started running to Mullingar again on 8th February 1932 this time running via Navan and Athboy. He came off the road at the end of 1932 after which there was no service to Mullingar. The GNRB reincarnated service began experimentally on Monday 14th February 1955. It was a limited stop route

John Frederick McCormick, General Manager of the GNR from 1953 to 1957 following which he retired due to ill health. *(SS)*

between Drogheda and Mullingar and was worked by the AEC Regal III vehicles, which were celebrated for speed. Mullingar was outside the traditional GNR operating area and was introduced as a result of requests from customers and enjoyed the active support of CIE. It was never a paying proposition; however the service was continued being regarded as socially necessary.

In 1956 the IRA embarked upon a terrorist campaign concentrated on the border between the Republic and Northern Ireland. The Northern Ireland Ministry of Home Affairs took action to seal a number of cross-border roads, mainly 'unapproved roads' that is those without customs posts. However a series of attacks on Northern Ireland Customs posts at Upper Fathom led to the road, which was the main Newry to Carlingford route, being spiked on 28th January 1957. The effect of this action was to severely disrupt the Dundalk to Newry via Carlingford and Omeath bus service. The GNR responded by allocating an additional car and crew to Newry depot to work a shuttle service from Newry at the one end and Dundalk at the other to the point where the road was spiked. Buses from either end of the route met at the road spikes of Upper Fathom. Through passengers from either end had to get out of one bus walk a short distance and board the bus waiting on the other side to continue their journey. The GNRB decided to sue the Northern Ireland Ministry of Home Affairs who were technically and in law owners of 50% of the Company. Following a brief Court hearing in Belfast the Company was awarded £474 compensation on 26th September 1957 for the loss of revenue on the disrupted service. An examination of the GNR passenger statistics for the first three months of 1956-1958 illustrates the drop in passenger numbers:–

Dundalk/Newry via Omeath Omnibus Service			
Jan/Feb/Mar	1956	1957	1958
Passenger Numbers	33,553	29,212	21,547

The outlook for the GNR was not promising despite an increase in road passenger journeys between 1938 and 1956 of 79%. Improvements in road freight tonnage in the corresponding period of 152% and the fact that unlike the railway operations, gross receipts have increased at a rate greater than expenditure were not enough to ensure a secure future. In fact the Road Merchandise Service of the GNR though much smaller, was far more profitable than its CIE counterpart. In its final year of operation the GNRB declared a loss of £1,103,174. The omnibus department of the Road Motor Services declared a profit of £31,090 and would have continued trading independently had the recommendations of the Urwick Orr and Partners consultants' report been enacted. On 1st October 1958 after just five short years of existence both governments ending an era in the transport history of Ireland dissolved the Great Northern Railway Board. The GNRB handed over to *Córas Iompair Éireann* 36 double-deck buses, 122 single-deck buses, 130 lorries, 12 service vehicles and 12 staff cars together with hundreds of employees with thousands of years experience running a Road Motor Service within a Railway.

AEC Regent No. 67 at Dundalk Bus Station on 20th August 1948 when double-deckers were first allocated to the busy cross border service to Newry. *(JG)*

Chapter Eight
Dundalk Works – innovation & support

In 1880, four years after the formation of the Great Northern Railway, work commenced on the construction of a central works on lands owned by the earls of Roden. Twenty acres of land to the west of the Dublin to Belfast main line comprised the works area. The GNR required a well-equipped works to support additional rolling stock and railway infrastructure such as track, buildings etc. The town was also readily accessible from all parts of the GNR railway network and was strategically positioned between the country's two capitals being about 50 miles equidistant from Belfast and Dublin. At the time the works was being built the company had in its inventory 114-railway engines, almost 200 carriages and some 2,900 wagons. It was in 1881 that the works formally opened with the completion of the erecting shop, machine shop and smithy's shop which meant that locomotives and other rolling stock could be repaired and overhauled. Over the next 40 years or so the works developed into a facility where locomotives and rolling stock were built from scratch. By 1900 21 locomotives and 60 carriages and wagons had been built at Dundalk.

Unfortunately in September 1891 fitters at the works decided to strike in support of their claim for a 2s increase in weekly wages together with a reduction in working hours. The strike dragged on with the GNR bringing in skilled labour from England and then after some time returning them again. The works continued production, albeit at about 50% of its capacity as the attitudes hardened on both sides. This dispute was finally resolved on 6th February 1892 when the by now sacked strikers were re-employed with an increase in weekly wage. Industrial unrest in Dundalk works did not end there. For decades to come there were strikes, threats, intimidation and acts of violence and sabotage, which demonstrably weakened the Great Northern Railway down through the years. In 1907 the level of industrial unrest in Dundalk was such that the GNR thought seriously about moving the works to a location in Belfast, in all probability adjacent to Adelaide where there was a highly skilled labour force eager to fill the 700 or so jobs currently in Dundalk.

The establishment of the Irish Free State and the formation of a Government in Northern Ireland which gave effect to partition of the island of Ireland created the bizarre result that Dundalk works was in a foreign territory to that of two-thirds of the GNR rail network. Rumours began to circulate in Dundalk that the GNR, who were by now despondent at the continuing industrial unrest at the works, would move it to Northern Ireland. The economic prospects for Northern Ireland looked much brighter than those of the Irish Free State. On 20th February 1923 at a meeting in Belfast, the GNR Board considered a proposal by the Northern Ireland government to grant financial assistance to the GNR in terms of the Loans Guarantee Act (NI) 1922 to relocate the works. The GNR examined the purchase of land at Knockmore near Lisburn County Antrim as a potential new location for the works. At the end of February the GNR informed the Northern Ireland Minister of Labour John Miller Andrews that they would not be transferring the works as the costs would have been prohibitive despite the offer of government funding.

In the Irish Free State a bitter civil war raged from June 1922 until May 1923, engulfing Dundalk in this conflict, which caused the GNR further disruption to production at the works. Opposing forces gained and lost control of the town as armed gangs, sometimes mere boys, roamed the streets with revolvers and rifles. Eventually matters settled down when the pro-treaty forces drove the anti-treaty factions northwards from the town after which law and order was re-established. The early 1920s were characterised by buoyant revenues. However by the mid-1920s serious inroads into the companies' finances were being made by the emerging road transport competition. Such was the concern in the GNR that over 200 redundancies had occurred in the works by 1926. Towards the end of the decade financial uncertainty in the international markets, coupled with another damaging GNR strike, almost resulted in the Company going bankrupt.

A New Works Manager – A New Era

Mr AW Denniss, the Locomotive Running Superintendent, was granted extended sick leave in April 1925, which resulted in Harold McIntosh, the Works Manager being appointed to that position in an acting capacity, the upshot of which was that Mr Michael Cremin was appointed Acting Works Manager. There was no sign of Mr Denniss returning to work, a consequence of which was that Harold McIntosh was appointed to the substantive position of Locomotive Running Superintendent. The Company advertised the Works Manager's position in the press, which garnered twenty-four applications. The Board decided on 24th November 1925 to interview three candidates named Cremin, Meredith and Robinson, following which it was decided to offer the position to Richard Walsingham Meredith, then a 34 year-old native of Dublin, educated at Aravon School and the Royal College of Science in Ireland. Richard Meredith entered the service of

Richard Walsingham Meredith in his Dundalk Office 1949.
The locomotive depicted behind him on the wall is one of the five famous 3-cylinder 4-4-0s of the GNR(I). They were built in 1932 by Beyer, Peacock to the design of Gerge T Glover, GNR(I)'s CME. Numbered 83-87, they were named after birds of prey, and carryed a striking sky-blue livery lined out in black and white. *(CM)*

the Great Southern & Western Railway in 1912 as a pupil of the late REL Maunsell, who at the time was the Chief Mechanical Engineer of that Company. In March 1916 Meredith obtained a commission in the Royal Army Service Corps, serving for three years on the French and Italian fronts as a workshops officer in a mechanical transport section attached to siege artillery. Following war service he returned to the GS&WR in 1919 as Materials Inspector. Three years later he became the Locomotive Running Assistant. Following the creation of the Great Southern Railways he was promoted to the position of Assistant Works Manager at Inchicore.

He took up his new position on New Year's Day 1926 at a salary of £600 per annum. The Works Manager's position also came with a five bedroomed house on the Carrickmacross Road (near the Railway Station), which still stands and bears the name 'Capard' that Dick Meredith gave it, and for which he paid £50 rent per year. Dick Meredith and his wife were to remain there for thirty years. Meredith was a quiet, charming and kind man, with an outstanding intellect coupled with a very clear vision of the future for transport motive power. He was a keen fisherman and enjoyed this pursuit in the nearby River Dee after which the County Louth town of Ardee takes its name. An enthusiastic traveller he visited many European countries with his wife long before it became accessible to the masses. During the summer months when he was not travelling abroad Meredith could be found at the family home in the Slieve Bloom Mountains near the Ridge of Capard, hence the name given to his Dundalk home. He was a frequent visitor to the Reichwald factory in Germany from September 1926 onwards to inspect steam engine boiler tubes and copper plates on behalf of the GNR. It was here that he first learnt of early diesel experiments as a form of motive power for railways. His German experiences fashioned his determination to introduce diesel power on the GNR.

Dick Meredith worked for the mysterious English born Chief Mechanical Engineer of the GNR, Lieutenant Colonel George T Glover who had been appointed in 1912 with a break for Military Service in the Royal Engineers between 1914-18, wherein he gained a commission in the British Army. George Glover liked to be addressed using his military title and was deeply distrustful of the GNR workforce in Dundalk. He regarded them as a rebellious lot, not to be trusted, and with something of the night in them. He refused to live in the GNR house set aside for the CME on the Carrickmacross Road, Dundalk. He preferred to travel to and from his home in Belfast to Dundalk every day by train. He retired from the GNR on the 30th July 1933, an event which was widely celebrated by many of the Dundalk workforce.

Shortly after taking up his appointment Richard Meredith encountered two major difficulties at Dundalk Works, the first of which was the lack of space, the second was the antediluvian working practices and methods, which he considered adversely affected production. The establishment of the Road Motor Services added further pressure on Dundalk's resources. It was vital that suitable infrastructure capable of supporting its development could be found from within a finite resource. During Richard Meredith's first four years he achieved a remarkable degree of success. The most notable achievements attributed to him were:

- Elimination of piecework in the erecting and fitting shops resulting in increased output. This meant that heavy repair of engines in Belfast was discontinued.
- The scheduling of all processes connected with locomotive repairs which reduced average unit downtime from 16 weeks in 1927 to 11 weeks in 1929.
- The reorganisation of the carriage lifting shop with interchange bogies and bogie traversers introduced, resulting in the lifting process taking one day as opposed to two weeks previously. Carriage repairs were now concentrated during the winter months, ensuring improved availability during the peak period. During the 12th July holiday in 1925 18 carriages were in the works whilst during the period 12th July to 5th August 1929 not a single carriage was in the works.

- The repair of carriage underframes was put on a mass production basis, 24 having been dealt with in 1929 as opposed to only two in 1926. In the sawmill and carriage building shop greatly improved working practices resulted in a 30% increase in output between 1926 and 1929.
- Spray painting of railway rolling stock was introduced resulting in piecework prices being cut by 75%.
- The Brass shop was entirely reorganised enabling the Belfast foundry to be closed down and the work absorbed at Dundalk without any increase in staff.

Meredith's reorganisation of Dundalk Works is all the more astounding when considered in conjunction with the decrease in works staff together with a shorter working week. Had it not been for this revamp Dundalk would certainly not have been able to cope with the introduction of the Road Motor Service activity. Most railway aficionados have tended to ignore Meredith's achievements simply on the basis that he was not favourably disposed to steam traction as a form of motive power and thus was guilty in the eyes of many of heresy.

In the latter part of 1930 a section of the existing carriage and wagon building shop was converted to a road motor garage, Board agreement having been earlier given on the 23rd October the previous year. It consisted of a paint shop, engine repair shop and five workstations. It was used to carry out routine maintenance of buses and lorries as well as mechanical overhauls. In addition some of the north side of the other carriage and wagon shop, which was on the Dublin end of the works, created a dedicated motor body repair shop. The first bus to emerge from the GNR works on 20th May 1930, with a body built in Dundalk (fleet No. 87) on a Leyland LT2 chassis, was built in the carriage and wagon building shop under the stewardship of foreman Josie McKee. The bus body shop took quite some time to start serious production of bus bodies, largely due to the dilapidated state of some vehicles acquired by the GNR on which repairs were urgently required. In addition production was concentrated on the development of the railbus, a particular favourite of Richard Meredith.

In August 1932 yet another strike broke out, the complete workforce of the locomotive shops having downed tools. Many other GNR workers came out in sympathy, but the company refused to talk to the strikers until they resumed normal working. There was intimidation of sections of the GNR workforce who continued to work normally. Slogans were daubed on GNR property and pickets demanded to inspect GNR omnibuses returning to the works to ensure that no mechanics were hiding inside the vehicles preparing to work a night shift. Ten days later after intervention from Government officials the mechanics returned to work after the company agreed to allow the staff grievances to be put to the Board of Directors. No sooner had the mechanics returned to work but another crisis developed in the form of widespread salaries and establishment cutbacks all across the GNR caused by the severe state of the company's finances. After notice had been served on the relevant Trade unions they promptly announced their intention to strike.

Despite moves to avert a strike on 31st January 1933 the entire GNR railway network came to a halt with angry pickets being established in most of the major centres including the works. This 1933 strike disrupted production of railbuses, which were considered a highly important element in the GNR management's strategy to keep open less well-patronised lines to passenger traffic in the face of increasing costs. A further setback suffered that year was the company's inability to purchase any new bus chassis and build bodies. New vehicles were desperately required to fight competition and improve reliability of services. Old vehicles had to be rebodied, such was their deterioration, the direct result of poor roads. Once again Richard Meredith's continued achievements astonished many. Even in the turmoil of strikes a dedicated bus body building shop was established in 1933. This was a wooden building, which was located close to the main offices and vehicle entrance off Brook Street. It consisted of an office, trimmers shop, body parts store and work area which could accommodate 3 or 4 buses in the course of construction. It had previously been a timber store from about the turn of the century.

To facilitate the establishment of the Road Motor Shop extension, which was opened on 27th September 1933, Richard Meredith commissioned the construction of a new timber building at the old Dundalk Junction station. It was some 300 yards north of the works, at Traffic Place and was used to spray paint railway rolling stock. In 1934 six Leyland LT5A bus chassis were bodied at Dundalk marking the resumption of this activity at the works. Later that year further work was undertaken to support the road motor services with the construction of a bus repair shop opposite the general stores building which was on the western side of the Dublin/Belfast main line. Access to this facility was gained from a separate entrance off the Ardee Road; it included an open bus parking area, staff mess room and a single vehicle wash bay. All bus and lorry washing carried out by hand.

The search for a standard diesel engine

On 13th January 1932 the Board gave Meredith the authority for the purchase of a Gardner 4LW engine at a cost of £524 and a Leyland 6-cylinder diesel engine for £651 10s to be experimentally fitted into two omnibuses for evaluation purposes. In June of that year the petrol engine was removed from a Dennis E 32 seat bus of 1928 vintage. The vehicle (fleet No. 57) had previously belonged to the Eclipse Bus Company of James Winter. The vehicle was fitted with the Gardner 4LW 68bhp oil engine, which was returning an average of 14 miles per gallon in service. This was the first GNR bus to receive a Gardner diesel engine, the result of intensive development work by Richard Meredith. The Leyland Diesel engine was fitted to a Leyland Tiger TS2 bus No. 88 at the same time.

Serious testing and evaluation of various engines fitted to Leyland and AEC vehicles began in February 1934. A Leyland Tiger TS2 vehicle, fleet No. 91 was fitted with a governor, limiting the maximum speed to 40mph in May 1934 for the purposes of ascertaining the petrol consumption. This vehicle was used as the benchmark petrol vehicle against which all the diesel engines were measured. The vehicle itself was fitted with a Beardmore engine in 1937 after trials had been completed. Beardmore designed their

AEC Reliance No. 24 with City Wheel Works front entrance bodywork seen at Dublin Sheriff Street Garage in original teak livery. This bus was converted to rear entrance in 1936. *(MC)*

Leyland LT5A No. 314 at Dundalk works after being re-powered with a Gardner 4LW engine, necessitating the lengthening of the bonnet as evident in this view. Note the absence of mirror, wiper blade and destination blind, signifying additional work to complete the overhaul. *(MC)*

six-cylinder diesel engine to fit both Leyland Tiger and AEC Reliance vehicles with the flywheel housing being drilled to take both makes of gearbox and with a choice of flywheels available. Richard Meredith was attracted to the Beardmore diesel with its 100 hp and lightweight integral cylinder block and crankcase. With the exception of the starter motor, exhaust manifold and decompressor mechanism, all the ancillaries were mounted on the nearside and very accessibly arranged. Of particular interest to Meredith was the Beardmore fuel pump and injection equipment, since it provided automatic timing that ensured the correct degree of advance or retard of the injection period according to the speed of the engine and quite independent of the driver's control. A valve coupled to the accelerator pedal operated the hydraulic governor. A sliding member with straight and helical splines accomplished variable timing, and rotation of hardened plungers in the pump affected by a rack coupled to the governor. The first two Beardmore diesel engines were purchased on 15th August 1934 at a cost of £378 each and were fitted into two AEC Reliance buses (Nos. 24/5) where they supplanted AEC petrol units. Two further AEC Reliance vehicles were fitted with Beardmore diesel engines in 1934, one of which was subsequently removed and replaced by an AEC diesel unit. During 1935 eight further petrol-engined AEC Reliance vehicles had AEC A165 diesel engines fitted followed by a single conversion a year later. In the same year a hydraulic dynamometer and tachometer was purchased for the Road Motor Shop for £187.19.6 from the English specialist manufacturers Hennan and Froude Ltd to assist with the testing and performance monitoring of diesel engines.

In 1935 three AEC Reliance vehicles were fitted with Gardner 4LW engines. The following year saw the installation of Gardner 4LW engines to three Leyland TS2 and one Leyland LT2 vehicle. In the same year one Leyland LT2 vehicle had a Leyland diesel engine fitted to replace a petrol unit. In 1937 Beardmore diesel engines replaced petrol engines in nine Leyland TS2 buses and Gardner 4LW engines replaced petrol units in four older Leyland LT2 vehicles. By this time, armed with some operating experience of AEC, Beardmore, Leyland and Gardner diesel engines, the company selected the Gardner as the most reliable, fuel efficient and lightweight engine. The price of the four-cylinder Gardner engines had been reduced as a consequence of Richard Meredith's negotiations with Gardner Engines Ireland Limited to £391 19s 6d per unit. The comparative prices of the AEC six-cylinder diesel was £834 14s 2d from the Dublin agent, Doyle's Motors. Beardmore's six-cylinder diesel was £433 10s 0d from William Beardmore in Glasgow and the Leyland six-cylinder reduced to £587 10s 0d. Five-cylinder Gardners were now available to the GNR at £419 5s 0d each. The Beardmore failed to live up to its earlier expectations of significant improvements in fuel economy, longevity and performance.

Between 1937 and 1939 ten Leyland Lion LT5A vehicles were fitted with Gardner 4LW engines. The LT5A, with its short 3ft 11¼ins bonnet, had to be lengthened to accommodate the longer Gardner four-cylinder engine. This resulted in the bonnet and radiator projecting some six inches forward of the front windscreen and scuttle, which created a somewhat ungainly appearance. In all other respects they were very satisfactory. The larger Gardner 5LW units were fitted to six AEC Regent double-deck vehicles during the years 1941/2. The last bus to be re-engined was an AEC Regal II that received a Gardner 5LW engine in 1952. All the development, research, re-engineering and production of components necessary to carry out the replacement of bus engines was performed at Dundalk works. In total Dundalk works re-engined 49 vehicles between 1934 and 1952. In August 1937 the Dublin Company of Joyce and Brady supplied a high-speed connecting rod boring machine to assist with the local overhaul of engines at the works. At the same time Leyland gearboxes were purchased through Ashenhurst, Williams in Dublin for assembly in Dundalk as spare units for Leyland Lion LT5A buses, thus avoiding Irish Free State duty as the GNR claimed that they were built in the works using local labour.

In 1941 the open bus parking area at the Ardee Road garage was enclosed to provide additional covered parking and maintenance facilities on that site. This building existed largely unchanged until it burnt down in 1997. Consequent with the improvement and expansion of facilities at the Ardee Road Garage the area of the wagon building shop, on the Dublin end of the works, which had been converted earlier for road motor use, was returned to its original use. In addition the road motor shop in the works was extended to provide a further five workstations and a paint shop at the expense of part of the sawmill. This was the last planned infrastructure development at Dundalk to provide the necessary support for the road motor services. It permitted all planned preventative maintenance and running repairs to be carried out at the Ardee Road Bus Garage as distinct from Dundalk works, which now concentrated upon the locomotive overhaul programme for buses and lorries. Another important element of the works programme was the on-going Gardner bus building programme and the completion of bus bodies on imported chassis. The AEC Regal IV buses on Park Royal frames completed in 1956 were the last vehicles turned out from the works.

Productivity Problems

By 1947 the senior management of the GNR, particularly Richard Meredith and George Howden, were seriously concerned at the poor climate of industrial relations at the works, combined with very low levels of productivity and highly entrenched lines of demarcation. Meredith felt that the workforce, although highly skilled and capable, were refusing to co-operate with the company in its desire to introduce new working practices for fear of the inevitable redundancies that would logically follow. The reality was that the cost of maintaining a large unproductive works was pulling the company down into the arms of the receiver. No significant improvements were made by the time the Company was jointly nationalised and became the Great Northern Railway Board. The retirement of Chief Mechanical Engineer Harold McIntosh prompted a series of new appointments on the 1st January 1951. Richard Meredith was appointed to the short-lived position of Assistant Mechanical Engineer on an annual salary of £1,400. Harry Wilson was chosen to replace

Meredith as Works Manager. Mr CE Turner in turn replaced him as Chief Draughtsman. Marcus Bailie-Gage became the Assistant Works Manager. Richard Meredith was formally appointed to the position of Chief Mechanical Engineer seven months later on the 1st July 1951, the interim position of Assistant falling away. Unfortunately once the GNRB ceded control of the works to the Dublin government in 1953 they were interested in one thing and that was preserving every single job at the works whatever the cost. The GNRB management did eventually get the two governments to agree the appointment of three management consultants from Urwick, Orr and Partners who arrived at Dundalk on Monday 1st November 1954 to examine and report on the future organisation, methods and control of all aspects of the Great Northern Railway Board. George Howden and Richard Meredith held secret meetings with Colonel Urwick's representative in Ireland, a Mr Atkinson. The meetings took place in Atkinson's Mespil Road home in Dublin during 1954 to establish the terms of reference in examining the running of the works and consider future structures of the company in general. The consultants were not universally welcomed at the works and quickly earned the nickname 'The Dooleys' after a family sitcom then being broadcast on Radio Éireann. By the time the consultants' report was in the hands of the two Governments and had been considered by the Company's management it was irrelevant, as the GNRB was about to be dissolved. This fact together with the massive bills in having the consultants at Dundalk ensured that their services were quickly terminated. The initial contract called for three consultants to work for three years at a total cost of £19,000.

The Great Fire of Dundalk

On Wednesday 7th September 1955 in the early hours Dundalk suffered its biggest fire since the concert hall at the Town Hall was gutted in 1947. The bus building shop at the GNR works was engulfed by fire. Part of the timber store with its valuable contents extending in line with and under the same roof as the bus shop was destroyed. Two AEC Regent III double-decker buses, 300 and 305, were totally destroyed, as was GNR Gardner 380. A further three vehicles were fire damaged but were returned to service after repairs they were 215, 366 and 299. Some of the content of the timber store was saved although the greater part of the material was destroyed. Uppermost in the minds of those who were employed in the Dundalk works who looked at the remains of the fire was the thought of how serious it might have been. That was not to minimise the loss, which was suffered by the company. Had the fire spread to other shops the loss to the company and the town would have been disastrous. It was fortunate that the burned shop was at the extreme western end of the works and that a wide enough passage ran between it and the adjacent shop forming a firebreak. Across a ten yard passageway stands the sawmills and the road motor shop, which thankfully survived almost unscathed. The fire was

GNR Gardner No. 380 photographed on the south side of Eden Quay in this 1954 view. A little over a year later this bus was totally destroyed in the Dundalk works fire. This was one of the batch of vehicles that had their bodies framed in Belfast by local bodybuilder Harkness with very angular construction. *(MC)*

discovered at 4am by the night watchman Paddy Copas who immediately called out the fire brigade. Railway workers living in nearby Brook Street and Ardee Terrace used the company's fire fighting appliance to assist. In the meantime the flames were seen by the signalman on duty in the South Cabin and by a Civic Guard, G Comerford, who was on duty in the nearby Crescent *Garda* Station. Dundalk Fire Brigade, which was a part time unit, reached the scene twenty minutes after the alarm was raised. On arrival they found that the highly combustible materials stored in the bus shop had ensured that the fire had already got a complete grip. The two Dundalk appliances were unable to cope. It was therefore decided to summon the Northern Ireland Fire Authority's Newry brigade with its superior equipment. Thirty minutes later the Newry brigade arrived but by this time the fire had actually spread across the 10 yard passageway to reach the sawmills and, more dangerous, a wagonful of sawdust and a wooden paint store which stood against the wall of the sawmill caught fire and was burned out. The Newry fire fighters concentrated on preventing the fire spreading by keeping other buildings doused with a stream of water and ultimately saved the sawmill. Many GNR employees ran to the works to assist with the task of fighting the fire. By 8.30am as the main body of employees at the works had reported for duty the fire was under control and largely subdued and was confined to a heap of smouldering debris which kept the fire brigade busy until mid afternoon.

Also lost in the blaze were the tool kits of 84 men who worked in the destroyed shops. Many of the men who ran to fight the fire worked under the direction of Peter Byrne, the bus shop foreman and his deputy Barney Mulholland. The explosions caused from pneumatic tyres bursting under the heat awakened the men in the first instance. There was considerable praise for the way GNR employees responded to the fire and for the way the Dundalk and Newry Fire brigades reacted. Many employees and fire fighters took risks to tackle the blaze and remove valuable material and equipment. Work in the sawmills and other shops was delayed for a good while on Wednesday morning as the power had been turned off as a safety measure during the battle to put out the fire.

The clear up operations took some weeks to complete, the entire bus body shop was demolished and repairs were carried out to the remaining half of the timber store left largely intact. Seventy thousand pounds of damage was caused and the Bus Body Shop was never re-built by the company. Marcus Bailie-Gage, then Production Manager at Dundalk commented at the time that the fire represented the beginning of the end for the Works. Many others shared this view and with the benefit of hindsight were proved correct. The damage and destruction of the buses in the fire resulted in some vehicles, which would have been de-licensed for the winter, being retained for service. As double-deckers were a highly valuable asset the company approached CIE to obtain second hand replacements. The story of these replacements is to be found in Chapter Ten. A very senior former GNR official who worked at Dundalk during this period told me recently that just prior to the fire he was proceeding on annual leave to the GN Hotel at Bundoran. He was approached by some works employees who said to him "when you come back there won't be a works here". The suggestion being made by this official was that the fire was a deliberate act of sabotage, a view shared by others who have spoken to me on this matter.

On 31st March 1957 Richard Meredith retired from the company aged 65 years. His contract contained an option to continue until his seventieth birthday but Meredith elected to go; he hated the political interference by both governments in the affairs of the GNRB particularly that of Percy Reynolds, the senior member of the Board nominated by Dublin. He retired to a bungalow on the main Bray Road at Cabinteely Co Dublin, which he named 'Capard' after those family house parties in the mountains during the twenties and thirties. The GNR gave him a retirement lump sum of £5,000, which he invested in stocks and shares, this providing him with a retirement income.

Regrettably Richard Meredith died in December 1971 having cut himself off from all his transport contacts following his retirement. He has not been given adequate recognition for his outstanding contribution to modern rail and road mechanical engineering in Ireland. He was after all the man who developed diesel powered rail and road buses and railcars for the GNR long before others had dared experiment with them. It is a measure of the man that following his death he left a considerable amount of money. This six-figure sum was the proceeds of that initial £5,000 investment in 1957. It is known that he hated the patent railbus wheel being registered as the 'Howden/Meredith' wheel. Not without justification as Howden was not directly involved in the development. Howden's name was included for no other reason than the fact that he was Meredith's boss at the time and felt that he should garner some of the kudos.

Harry Wilson succeeded Meredith as Chief Mechanical Engineer effective from 1st June 1957 on a salary of £2,050 and for the first time a Deputy Mechanical Engineer, Mr NC Carter was appointed on a salary of £1,550. Harry had been the very capable Works Manager in succession to Meredith when he got the Chief Engineers job, although he was not Howden's first choice. He wanted to bring in another Scot, REB Price, a native of Fort William who was employed by British Railways. Howden was unable to offer sufficient assurances to Price regarding the GNRB's long-term future, which resulted in him declining the appointment. Marcus Bailie-Gage in turn succeeded Harry Wilson as the Works Manager in 1957. Marcus had been a pupil apprentice to the LMS (NCC) at their York Road Works until he was recruited by Howden as Dundalk Works Inspector in 1942 and then became Production Manager in 1955. He could not envisage a stable future with CIE at Dundalk following dissolution of the Board in October 1958. His father had been the highly successful Company Solicitor until his untimely death in 1952 and he in turn had been a loyal GNR officer for sixteen years. It was therefore with a feeling of considerable sadness that he left the company. On 10th January 1958 the Dundalk Works was hived off from the GNRB by the government in Dublin and formed into a separate company, Dundalk Engineering Works Limited. It continued to fully service the needs of the GNRB right up to the dissolution of the Board on 30th September 1958. The 1,000 employees were

Leyland Titan PD3A/6 double-deck buses built at the former GNR Works in Dundalk using Park Royal body frames in 1964/5 for *Córas Iompair Éireann*. *(MC)*

left facing unemployment and all the uncertainties and instabilities associated with it. Most employees were issued with protective notice letters. Harry Wilson, now in the employ of CIE, was retained for a short time to look after its interests as far as the Works was concerned. He and Barney Lennon, the former Under Manager of the Timber Section of the works moved into offices up at the Railway Station from where they conducted their activities. DEW did in fact complete the building of the last few BUT railcars for the GNRB and continued to overhaul buses as per the laid down programme. Following the dissolution of the Board CIE gave DEW a limited contract to maintain railcars and locomotives, but this could not continue on economic grounds. This work ended about 1960 as CIE found that all of its maintenance and overhaul could be undertaken elsewhere without having to send rolling stock to the northern extremity of its rail network. The former GNR BUT railcars were transferred for use on the Wexford line where CIE drivers quickly trashed them. *Bord na Móna* contracted DEW to produce turf cutting and conveyor machines although there was insufficient work to guarantee a long-term future.

Two days before Christmas 1957 Percy Reynolds, now Chairman of the Dundalk Engineering Works, wrote to Sir Henry Spurrier of Leyland Motors with a proposal to grant them exclusive rights to assemble and sell Leyland buses and lorries in the Irish Republic. Leyland rejected the entreaties by Reynolds on behalf of DEW mainly because CIE enjoyed favourable terms in respect of vehicles to meet their requirements and Ashenhurst, Williams employed 43 people erecting chassis for other users. The Nottingham based firm of Frank Bonsor and Co used part of the works to produce agricultural machinery including a small farm truck, a potato harvester and agrotiller range of rotary cultivators. The German Company Heinkel, of Luftwaffe bomber notoriety had after the war diversified into the production of 'cabin scooters', which in this country were known as 'bubble cars'. They used part of the works to assemble these little vehicles and slowly started modest production of some parts at Dundalk. Their plans for future expansion failed to materialise and after three years they closed down.

The former GNR works foundry was sold to a company called Dealgan Steel Foundries Ltd, who initially produced pressings and other components for the Heinkel operation in another part of the works. Some castings, springs and brackets for the dwindling number of GNR Gardner buses now in CIE ownership were also produced. Another part of the former works was utilised by a company called CRV, (Commercial Road Vehicles) which was formed by Ivor McCullough (nephew of Harold McIntosh the former Chief Mechanical Engineer of the GNR) the former road motor superintendent in charge of the GNR's road merchandise service. CRV became the AEC agent for Ireland carrying out truck assembly and distribution at Dundalk. In order to sustain the business they diversified into production of Sylvan caravans for export. In 1961 the company was in trouble in spite of a large grant from the government through the Industrial Credit Company.

The company had to be downsized to ensure its continued survival. CRV concentrated their activities on the former road motor shops to carry on their business. Remarkably in 1964/5 CRV produced some buses for CIE who at the time encountered a severe shortage of double-deck vehicles the last new deliveries of such having been in 1961. CIE engineers struck upon the plan to salvage driveline units from surplus Leyland OPS2 Tigers, suitably overhauled, and then married to new Leyland Titan double-deck chassis imported and assembled complete with the fibreglass St Helens front by CIE at their Spa Road works. The idea for this scheme came from a plan which the Ulster Transport Authority put into action a decade earlier, when they were experiencing a shortage of double-deck vehicles. They had taken Leyland PS2 vehicles, removed the bodies and built MCW framed double-deck bodies on them. Once CIE had produced 26 new Titan chassis frames with reclaimed and overhauled units they were dispatched to CRV at Dundalk who had obtained from Park Royal a similar number of double-deck body frames. They were completed in contemporary CIE style at Dundalk, entering service from Dublin City Garages in two batches as R901-910 in 1964 and R911- R926 in 1965 – the last of this class was withdrawn in 1981. A number of these vehicles have been preserved privately and are represented in the national transport collection of the Transport Museum of Ireland at Howth just north of Dublin.

In 1966 CRV went bankrupt and this led Ivor McCullough to re-launch the company together with some former GNR managers and local businessmen. They obtained one part of the works, which was used for the AEC business and the caravans. They recommenced production of the caravans and by 1971 had produced over 1,000 such units. The AEC business restarted and continued until the Leyland take-over of AEC when truck cabs were bought in from outside suppliers. For CRV this meant a decline in skilled work such as bodymakers, sheet metal workers etc. all of whom had learnt their trade at the GNR. In 1977 Ivor McCullough, who was by now Chairman and Managing Director of CRV died suddenly. His wisdom, innovation and leadership was sadly missed.

CRV was taken over by the Smith Group in that year with just over 150 employees who were by then engaged in the production of municipal vehicles for councils all over Ireland. The post office provided work in the form of building van bodies as did the local Macardle Moore Brewery who took trailers built by CRV. By February 1986 with just 38 employees CRV closed its doors as all work simply dried up. A Company called S&S (Stein & St Ives) took over the CRV premises in May of 1986 to design and produce machinery for the manufacture of corrugated paperboard and boxes. S&S very quickly got into difficulties and a receiver was called in. These were the phoenix like industries that arose from the ashes of the Great Northern Railway of Ireland Dundalk Works.

Craftsmen Built Buses from Dundalk

The coachbuilder's craft was being practised in Dundalk works for decades before GNR buses and lorries appeared. Craftsmen in wood produced a wide range of carriages and wagons for the extensive GNR railway network. Although wood was used at Dundalk for early bus and lorry building, many of these bodies suffered badly from vibration on the hideous Irish roads. The early buses were of course all timber framed reinforced at vital points by forged steel plates. The skin of the vehicles was mainly composed of aluminium although some steel sheets were pinned or screwed to the timber framework.

Ash was used almost exclusively for the framing of bus bodies it was seasoned naturally in the timber store where air may circulate freely – the stacked timber being separated by sticks placed transversely. The stack was kept up by careful forward buying against the time the timber would be used in production and to allow time for the natural seasoning to take place. Oak or teak was used for the under-frame, as these were moisture-resisting timbers. Plywood was used for saloon flooring with the resin-bonded variety a particular favourite. Pine and other softwoods were used for seat and lining boards. Mild steel angle, channel and tee sections were used as body-stiffening plates. Brackets were sometimes used for windscreen and body pillars, where it was required to reduce the bulk of the framing to provide the minimum obstruction to vision or where a sounder structural job can be made by the use of a metal pillar. On completion of the timber framework, the whole vehicle was given two or three coats of lead primer. Generally steel parts were treated with a protective primer before assembly.

Aluminium components, and the reverse side of any aluminium panelling, were treated with aluminium primer. Where aluminium and steel components are in contact, di-electric paint was applied to the components before assembly. The undersides of wheel arches were treated with a bitumastic compound to ensure the exclusion of water and to prevent corrosion through damp conditions. The Works draughtsmen produced general arrangement drawings to one-eighth or quarter size to aid with shop floor assembly of the body. The sawmill would have required full sized drawings to make patterns in ¼in thick deal-board for side pillars, which gives their sectional contour 'tumble-home' that is the slope inwards towards the roof and the 'turn-under' that is the contraction towards the bottom. Further patterns would have been made for the cant rails hoopsticks and bottom sides. A timber schedule was prepared in the works offices, which would detail the kind of timber to be used, the length, width and thickness of each component.

When the body was being 'framed-up' it was stood on low trestles, carefully checked to ensure an absolutely flat foundation. Some later bus bodies were built directly upon the chassis such as on the 1934/5 Lions and later still on the Gardners. The trestle was often built up in the form of the chassis so that the body could be subsequently mounted more conveniently.

The lap or half-lap joint is the one most commonly used where the two pieces to be joined are more or less at right angles. The scarf or splice is used for joining two pieces in the same direction and for joining curved members. The bottom sides or runners being the foundation of the body were produced first. On completion of the bottom frame, the side pillars were erected. A tenon was cut at the top of each standing pillar to receive the cant rail. The elbow rails were lapped or tenoned into the rear standing pillars and a spliced joint made with the backrail. Wheel arches were generally built up by scarfing pieces cut with the grain running as much in the direction of the arch as possible. Some wheel arches were steamed and bent into shape. The fitting of a forged steel plate screwed on the inside braced the whole arch.

The pillars, lapped into the bottom sides, were temporarily held at the right distance apart by strainers screwed to them. As the top front rail and scuttle rail hold the front pillars together, these were now assembled and fitted. The roof, which was constructed entirely in aluminium, had to have insulation between the hoopsticks and roof panel to prevent 'drumming'. The cant rails, which form the junction of body side and roof, are mortised to receive the tenon at the top of the pillar and notched for the fitting of the hoopsticks, which form the framing of the roof and give it its shape, were cut parallel to the roof camber and lapped into the notches, provided in the cant rails. To support the roof mounted luggage racks the intermediate hoopsticks represent a gradual development from minimum at front to maximum camber at rear dome. Panel battens faced with felt were fitted to the inner panels to prevent 'drumming'. The skin or exterior panels were usually of 16 or 18 SWG aluminium sheet and were secured by screws through mouldings or cover strips.

The imported seat frames were trimmed in the different designs of moquette used by the company following the manufacture of its own seat cushions and squabs. All interior fittings and internal wiring was completed before seats, handrail, windows and doors were fitted. The bus was now ready for painting all of which was done by hand in several stages as outlined in the following standard process:–

Clean, scratch and prime
Fill-up
Stop-up as necessary
Rub-down
First coat undercoating
Face down
First coat finishing glaze colour
First coat hard drying varnish
Flat-down
Apply coach lines, coat of arms, legal lettering, transfers, etc
Varnish
One coat finishing varnish

The process described above undertaken at Dundalk works applied to the construction of timber framed bodies during the period 1930 – 1942 when the last timber framed Gardners were built. After the war the GNR, in common with most other coachbuilders, were unable to obtain seasoned timber, which accelerated the change to metal framing.

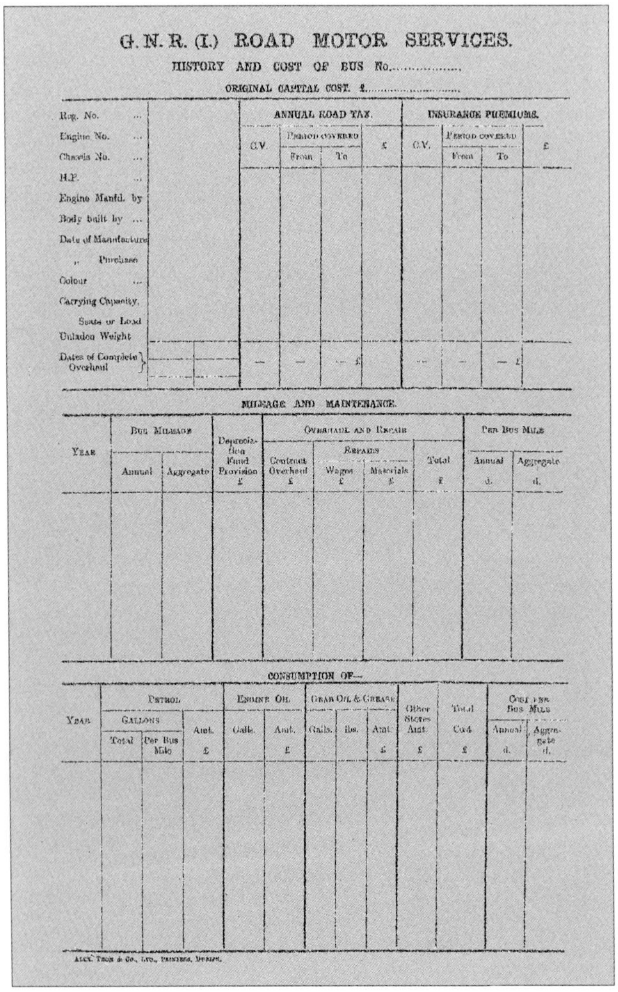
G. N. R. (I.) ROAD MOTOR SERVICES.

HISTORY AND COST OF BUS No.....................

ORIGINAL CAPITAL COST. £..............................

			Annual Road Tax				Insurance Premiums			
			C.V.	Period covered		£	C.V.	Period covered		£
				From	To			From	To	
Reg. No. ...										
Engine No. ...										
Chassis No. ...										
H.P. ...										
Engine Manfd. by										
Body built by ...										
Date of Manufacture										
" Purchase										
Colour ...										
Carrying Capacity, Seats or Load										
Unladen Weight										
Dates of Complete Overhaul			—	—	— £		—	—	— £	

MILEAGE AND MAINTENANCE.

Year	Bus Mileage		Depreciation Fund Provision	Overhaul and Repair				Per Bus Mile	
				Contract Overhaul	Repairs		Total		
	Annual	Aggregate	£	£	Wages £	Materials £	£	Annual d.	Aggregate d.

CONSUMPTION OF—

Year	Petrol			Engine Oil		Gear Oil & Grease			Other Stores Amt.	Total Cost	Cost per Bus Mile	
	Gallons		Amt.	Galls.	Amt.	Galls.	lbs.	Amt.			Annual	Aggregate
	Total	Per Bus Mile	£		£			£	£	£	d.	d.

ALEX. THOM & CO., LTD., PRINTERS, DUBLIN.

The GNR maintained meticulous vehicle history and costing records. An example of a vehicle record is shown here. *(SS)*

Chapter Nine
The Buses the Railway Built – The GNR Gardners

No history of the Great Northern would be complete without reference to the celebrated GNR Gardner buses built at Dundalk Works. In 1935 Dundalk Works Manager Richard Meredith proposed to Chief Engineer George Howden the construction of a fleet of buses engineered and designed to meet the prevailing operating conditions that the company endured at the time. Meredith gave three reasons for establishing a bus building programme and Howden readily agreed to support the proposal at Board level.

The rationale for this ambitious programme was based firstly on the company's dissatisfaction with the mechanical performance of two batches of Leyland Lion LT5A vehicles purchased in 1934 (Nos. 301-306) and 1935 (Nos. 307-316). The LT5A's had a new 5.7 litre 4-cylinder oil engine fitted. They were underpowered; thirsty and noisy for duty in Ireland. Motormen quickly resented having to drive them. The company experienced fuel injection and cylinder head problems with the engines. The average life of these diesels was about eighteen months at best and the company was determined to improve upon this performance. This sub-standard performance led to a serious disagreement between Richard Meredith and senior engineers at Leyland In June 1936 Leyland sent a Service Mechanical Inspector named Pendleton to Dundalk for two weeks to assist with the rectification of problems with the Leyland Lions, but Meredith remained un-impressed with this Leyland product. A January 1936 option with Leyland for the supply of seven Lion LT7 chassis was cancelled as a direct result.

Secondly, a compelling case for the production of buses at Dundalk had been mounting up for some time as new legislation began to take effect. In the Irish Free State of the 1930s punitive import duties had been applied for some time. There was the requirement under the 1932 Road Transport Act, which implied that preference would be given in the granting of licences to operators who used vehicles, built and maintained in the Free State. The Road Traffic Act of 1933 gave birth to pieces of legislation entitled Mechanically Propelled Vehicles (Construction Equipment & Use) Order 1934 – Statutory Rules & Orders No 150 of 1934; combined with the Large Public Service Vehicles Regulations 1935 Statutory Rules & Orders No. 259 of 1935, which jointly imposed new regulations in respect of vehicle construction on operators. A system of Public Service Vehicle Licences and Plates was also provided for under the main 1933 Act, which came in on 3rd May 1937. A significant number of older vehicles, which did not meet the requirements of the 1935 regulations, continued in operation until 1937, but on failing the Carriage Office inspection could not be licensed and so had to be withdrawn. Howden and Meredith soon realised that by declaring their intention to build buses at Dundalk they could circumvent the import duty requirement and save the GNR considerable sums of money and win the plaudits of the Government.

The final reason for the building of buses at Dundalk was Dick Meredith's objective to introduce a high degree of standardisation of major units and parts. He contended that once satisfactory standardisation of equipment was achieved, overhauls and reconditioning of parts would be performed cost effectively in Dundalk, thus reducing the GNR's dependence on external suppliers. Howden proposed to, and obtained authority for, the building of an initial batch of 21 buses, at the Board meeting in Dublin on 23rd September 1936. The Board had discussed the matter at great length for there were those members who were opposed to the project on the grounds of its seeming financial inviability. In the end it was agreed to allow Howden to assemble a team of engineers to work under the direct supervision of Dick Meredith.

John Henry Owens

The canny Scot Howden recruited a young engineer born in Falkirk in 1909, who received his engineering training at Glasgow University. His early experiences with the Central Scottish Motor Traction Bus Company made him the ideal man for the GNR and thus Johnny Owens became the first member of the Gardner team. This was for George Howden an inspired choice as Central SMT had encountered problems of their own with the Leyland LT5A. Owens was to bring to the GNR all of the valuable knowledge and experience gained as a result of his Scottish experiences. Johnny H Owens started work at Dundalk on 13th January 1936 as a Road Motor Technical Assistant on a salary of £250 per annum. He arrived at Dundalk with his new wife, Belfast born Madeline Flynn, whom he had met in Scotland whilst at Glasgow University. Johnny lived for a short period at his wife's Grandmothers house at Whitecross, Dromiskin near Castlebellingham before moving to Dublin, which necessitated daily travel to Dundalk Works. There he worked under the direction of Richard Meredith, ensuring that completed vehicles emerged from the works in accordance with his pre-determined programme and that the necessary parts etc were all available on time. In early 1941 as the Gardner programme was being run down, Howden moved Johnny Owens to the Civil Engineers Department to become Clerk of Works, managing the project to build the new road motor garage in Dublin's Abercorn Road. Concurrently Johnny now moved into the GNR Stationhouse on the Howth Road at Clontarf, which had previously been occupied by John F McCormick who went on to become the GNR General Manager. One of his four daughters still lives in that house to this day. As soon as the building of Abercorn Road Garage was completed Johnny continued to work in the Civil Engineers Department right up to the demise of the GNR. He joined CIE and was appointed to the position of Stores Examiner in the office of the Railway Chief Mechanical Engineer at Inchicore. In common with so many former GNR officials he quickly gained the impression that CIE held the GNR people in utter contempt, offering them worthless dead end positions. Johnny Owens, an intensely quiet and thoroughly professional man, could not find any synergy with his new colleagues in CIE. The frosty atmosphere of working in Inchicore soon led to Owens terminal decline when in 1965 he fell ill and died in 1968, a mere 59 years young.

Robert (Bobby) William Pelissier

Road Motor Technical Assistant Robert (Bobby) William Pelissier joined Johnny Owens on the Gardner project team. Bobby was born in Palace Street Drogheda in 1913. His father, Albert Alexander Pelissier was a pharmacist and worked for FW Brittain Chemists of 84 West Street, Drogheda. It was always expected that Bobby would follow in his father's footsteps, although he had other ideas. As his surname suggests, Bobby was of Huguenot extraction and was educated in Drogheda Grammar School, which was founded in 1669, during the reign of Charles II. In 1939 the school was under threat of closure after the Erasmus Smith trust to which it owed its existence withdrew funding. A committee was formed under the then Headmaster Mr W Fleming Thompson to save it. Bobby Pelissier became an active member of that committee which saved the school from extinction. Many famous men were educated at the school including the Duke of Wellington, Henry Grattan, the famous Irish Parliamentary leader, and the Rt Hon John Foster, the last Speaker of the Irish Parliament. An indication of its importance in past Irish life can be realised by the fact that in March 1782 the Irish Parliament went into recess so that many of its members could attend the prize day at the school. Bobby Pelissier continued to work on behalf of the school right into his retirement.

He became apprenticed to the GNR in 1928 and was thereafter employed in the works until he joined the Road Motor Services in 1933. Bobby had his own unique role to play in the development of the Gardner buses. He was the person tasked with trouble shooting, ironing out the in-service problems with the Gardner. A crucial element of this was to monitor the progress of the vehicles at the sharp end. Following the end of the Gardner project Bobby took on the role of an Operational Engineer, spending most of his time in the field supporting the garages. He was a highly respected and competent engineer who provided innovative solutions to a variety of technical difficulties over the years. After joining CIE he became the Engineering Training Officer and was the author of many CIE driver's instruction manuals. Latterly he was the officer charged with advising CIE on European Economic Community legislation, as it would affect its operations. I had the honour to meet Bobby in his office at Broadstone on several occasions in 1972. He was a perfect gentleman and the inspiration for this work. He retired from CIE in 1978. His retirement was tragically short, a fall from a ladder whilst painting his new bungalow at Bryanstown just north of his beloved Drogheda resulted in Bobby's death on the 5th October 1983.

Preparations Commence

In 1935 the GNR purchased a new Leyland LT7 chassis from the Erne Bus Company (fleet no. 317) and the following year a single new AEC Regal II (fleet No. 61) was purchased. Dick Meredith took the opportunity to have both vehicles stripped and examined by the Gardner project team at Dundalk in order that the first GNR Gardner buses would incorporate the best of contemporary engineering practice. This task was entrusted to Joe Webster the Road Motor Shop Foreman at Dundalk. This event led many commentators writing in the trade journals of the time to mistakenly contend that the Gardner chassis was a copy of the Leyland LT7. This was not the case. The chassis was a fusion of a 1926 Leyland design combined with a further section, which was to a Dennis Brother's design. When these elements were married with stock sections the finished product was very much a Dick Meredith GNR design.

The chassis frames were never produced in Dundalk; they were imported from John Thompson Motor Pressings Ltd of Ettingshall, Wolverhampton. On 8th October 1936 a set of drawings number 6536 was sent to Richard Meredith in Dundalk for approval. The drawings illustrated the detail of the chassis frame, an engine bar and the proposed cross-member brackets. John Thompson Motor Pressings were the pre-eminent specialist suppliers of most chassis frames to Leyland and other manufacturers of the period. The chassis side members were pressed hot in the large hydraulic presses, which contained the various dies. This ensured the correct profile was produced every time. Dundalk imported a specialist chassis frame-drilling machine from the English company Alfred Herbert Ltd at a cost of £97 11s 6d to facilitate the machining of the frames and this arrived in January 1937.

The first 21 chassis frames were transported from Thompson's to Dundalk on the merchant ship Liverpool. The frames were fully assembled including the bolted tubular cross members. The banjos (the drum shaped central part of the rear axle casing into which the differential was fitted) were supplied loose. All subsequent frames were marshalled into parts kits by Thompson's and then dispatched to Dundalk for assembly. The GNR Works cast the dumb-irons (the front extensions of the side members of the chassis frame to which were fitted the front ends of the leaf springs bearing the front axle) in bronze as the foundry could not cast in steel. The road springs were manufactured at Dundalk works in the hot and noisy smithy where the radiator frames were produced. The wire wound radiator tubes supplied from Clayton Dewandre were then fitted to complete the distinctive Gardner radiator. Fuel tanks made from rolled steel with riveted end plates were fashioned in the Dundalk smithy.

The relationship with Gardner Diesel and the GNR was through Gardner's Belfast Distributors. Gardner Engines Ireland Ltd, owned by the Edwards family, enjoyed a strong relationship with Dick Meredith going back to 1927. Meredith entreated the Edwards family to assist him achieve his ambition to introduce a family of diesel-engined railcars and buses to the GNR. In 1929 the Edward's family formed a subsidiary company called Gardner Railcar Ireland Ltd to promote such developments. Tony Edwards enjoyed an open-ended agreement negotiated personally with Joe Gardner in the 1930s, for the sole concession to sell Gardner engines throughout Ireland an arrangement that was very profitable for both parties.

In the highly competitive bus market of the period with many private passenger transport undertakings competing against each other, savings in fuel would give operators an advantage. During the early 1930s many bus operators in the UK who ran petrol-engined Leyland TD1 and TD2 vehicles replaced them with Gardner 5LW and to a lesser extent the 6LW unit. In the light of this favourable experience the 7.4 litre 5-cylinder Gardner 5LW engine developing 85-brake horsepower with its excellent fuel economy became the standard GNR bus engine and provided the power for the bus building project. The drive from the Gardner engine was taken through a normal friction type clutch and the 4 speed Meadows Gearbox having the following ratios:– top, 1/1; 3rd, 2.04/1; 2nd, 3.63/1; 1st 5.55/1; reverse 6.95/1. The propeller shaft was fitted with needle roller bearings, and the rear Kirkstall axle had a 4.8 to 1 ratio, giving a theoretical top road speed of 47mph, with 9.00 x 20in tyres. The actual top speed of the Gardners was about 42mph, adequate in the days when schedules were compiled using the IFS legal maximum permitted speed of 35mph. On test the designed speed was fully realised, the fuel consumption working out to approximately 14mpg, the average in service being 12.6mpg.

The first 21 Gardners turned out from Dundalk were fitted with 4 speed constant mesh gearboxes and clutches supplied by the Wolverhampton firm of Henry Meadows Ltd. They enjoyed a close association with Guy Motors and were major suppliers of gearboxes to the Bradford based Jowett company who were famous for their Javelin car. Leyland GB9 four-speed constant mesh gearboxes and Leyland C6 clutches were fitted to the remaining 75 machines supplied by Ashenhurst, Williams & Co whilst Kirkstall Forge of Leeds provided front and rear axles, which proved to be highly reliable throughout the whole production run of 96 vehicles. A CAV Bosch axial type starter motor and generator powered the 12-volt bus electrics, which were supplied through Major AJD Thomson of Portland Street North, just off the North Circular Road in Dublin. Lockheed hydraulic brakes with a Clayton Dewandre vacuum servo and engine mounted Gardner exhauster provided the stopping power. Gardner bus parts were sourced by the Dundalk based Stores Superintendent George Young who tragically died prematurely on the 6th June 1939. His successor, JS McCormick, the brother of the future General Manager, took over on the 30th of the month with clear instructions from Dick Meredith to stockpile materials for continued production of the Gardner buses in the face of the looming certainty of war and all the shortages that would bring.

On 25th March 1937 the first of 96 GNR Gardner buses emerged from Dundalk Works. The vehicle, given the fleet No. 200, was paraded on the Ardee Road adjacent to the works for Duffner's the official GNR photographers to record the momentous event for posterity. It was officially described by the company as a 'Streamlined service type omnibus' and was allocated to Dublin Garage for six weeks initial evaluation. The construction of the Gardners at Dundalk engendered a feeling of great pride and provided a much-needed boost in staff morale together with a confident outlook for the future. This feeling engendered by management hype belied the reality that the GNR Gardner buses were for the most part assembled at Dundalk using proprietary parts imported from the United Kingdom. This sleight of hand suited the company at a time when they were keen to demonstrate a willingness to be seen to be contributing to the creation of home industries.

The official launch of the GNR Gardners took place at Dundalk Works weeks later on Thursday 29th May 1937, when Government Ministers joined railway dignitaries from several companies to witness the building of the buses. The next day's Irish Times carried the following report of the launch:

Travelling almost daily on the railways of Ireland, few members of the public appreciate the work that is necessary to ensure the smooth and safe running of those railways. Yesterday the Free State Minister of Industry and Commerce (Mr Sean Lemass) and the Minister of Defence (Mr Frank Aitken) visited Dundalk to see something of what goes on 'behind the scenes' at the five-acre works of the Great Northern Railway and to observe the building of new buses.

The Ministers, who were accompanied by the Chairman of the Company (Mr William Carson) and some of the other Directors and officials, travelled northwards on a special train drawn by one of the first engines to be completely built at Dundalk. The journey ended in the yard of the works, where more officials, Mr James Coburn TD and representatives of local bodies greeted them. Outside of the works stood two recently completed omnibuses – a sunshine saloon coach and a standard bus – that later took the party to lunch at the nearby Great Northern Hotel at Greenore.

Their tour, which lasted an hour, took them through the road motor shop, where they saw omnibuses under construction. The only parts of these vehicles, which are assembled outside the Free State, are the engines. Mr Lemass showed a keen interest in the high-speed machinery in the sawmill, and in the finish of the various castings and other parts for the omnibuses.

After the lunch, the Chairman, Mr William Carson thanked the Ministers for their visit. Mr Lemass replied that he was very pleased to have seen what the company was doing at Dundalk. They deserved every credit for their efforts to overcome the difficulties, which they had encountered, and he trusted that in their future

Ministerial visit to witness the production of the GNR Buses at Dundalk Works of the GNR on 29th May 1937; from left WB Carson (Chairman GNR), Sean Lemass (Industry & Commerce Minister), GB Howden (Engineer GNR), Frank Aitken Louth (TD), L O'Brien (Parliamentary Secretary), RW Meredith. *(SS)*

enterprise they would meet with the same success.

The attendance at the lunch included:–

The Minister for Industry and Commerce, the Minister of Defence, Mr WB Carson (Chairman GNR), Lord Glenavy, Mr JJ O'Carroll, Mr RA Burke, DL; Mr AP Reynolds (General Manager Dublin United Tramways Co), Mr EC Breadon (Chief Mechanical Engineer, Great Southern Railways), Mr JB Stephens (General Manager GNR), Mr FC Wallace (Secretary GNR), Mr GB Howden (Chief Engineer GNR), Mr RW Meredith (Works Manager GNR), Mr JH Scott (District Superintendent GNR), Mr P O'Hagan (Chairman Dundalk Urban District Council), Mr JT Magee (Chairman Louth County Council), Mr TF McGahon (Chairman Dundalk Harbour Commissioners), Mr JB Hamill (State Solicitor), Mr B McGuinness (Chairman Dundalk Chamber of Commerce), Mr John Byrne (Chairman Dundalk Trades Council), Mr I Cleary (Revenue Commissioners), Mr Leo O'Brien (Private Secretary to the Minister of Industry & Commerce), Mr John O'Brien (Department of Industry and Commerce), Mr TJ Flynn (Assistant Secretary, Department of Industry & Commerce), Mr H McIntosh (Assistant Mechanical Engineer, GNR) and Mr JH Owens (GNR).

The first four batches of GNR Gardners built were Nos. 200-215/7/8/9 in 1937; 216 was completed in January 1938, 220-259 were out shopped in 1938. The next batches, 318-27 were not produced until 1941 followed by 328-30 in 1942. All were bodied using timber framing. This followed the well-tried principles of production detailed at the end of chapter four. The body frames and detail work of the bodies were fashioned from ash, oak, teak, plywood and pine. Because Masonite 'Presdwood' composite hardwood panels were extensively used in the production of railway carriages, it was decided that the same panels would be used on certain sections of the Gardners. The Masonite panels were instantly noticeable on vehicles as evidenced by the dull paint finish and ripple effect as the panels contorted after a period in service. Of the first tranche of Gardners, Nos. 201/4/5/9/10-2 were built as 'Streamlined Sun-Saloon' vehicles specifically to cater for the ambitious tours programme then being undertaken by the company. The vehicles received replacement bodies some years later at which point they reverted to standard saloons.

Dick Meredith's original concept for the Gardner project involved several different body designs to meet a variety of uses. Four design drawings were produced two of which entered production whilst the remainder failed to leave the drawing board. The design drawings, which I have in front of me, were as follows:–

1. Standard Luxury Coach – this design became known as the 'Streamlined look' many of its features were incorporated into the first 21 Gardner buses.
2. Service Type – the 1938-42 Gardner buses were produced to this design, which was less, streamlined although still attractive and functional. Interestingly a change of livery was proposed for these vehicles moving away from

the Oxford Blue to a Crimson Red rather similar to the contemporary GSR colours.

3. Tour Coach – a return to the streamlining effect was proposed with the application of plated mouldings with a white body combining Oxford Blue window surrounds and wheel arches finished by a splash of yellow along the bodyside just under the window line. A single outward opening tour bus door ensured the maintenance of a clean side appearance. No vehicles were ever produced to this design.
4. Full Front Long Distance Service Bus – this design was strongly redolent of concurrent American styling with steeply swept back rear roof profile with three bumper bars front and rear. It featured the distinctive 'submarine' type windows, which were to become commonplace in Gardners produced after the war. Unfortunately no complete vehicles ever saw the light of day.

The recent discovery of the drawings together with documentation from the archive of Bobby Pelissier illustrates the intensity of the work undertaken by Dundalk engineers to consider many bus body designs before entering production.

Early Gardners had cut away canopies on the nearside front, with destination blinds above the drivers cab window. Later versions had destinations fitted on the nearside above the front bulkhead window. Another experimental feature of the early vehicles was the fitting of a mesh section incorporated into the vertical leaf of the engine cover thus exposing the Gardner 5LW engine, for cooling purposes but not deemed necessary on later models. The first Gardner bodies were distinctive because of their angularity, the result of fitting Young's P-type half-drop single control constant balance windows as opposed to later examples, which featured sliding windows. Pre-war Gardners all had standard railway carriage door locks and handle fitted to the drivers cab doors. A practice which was discontinued as more attractive recessed handles became available. On the last three batches of GNR Gardners built (385-87 of 1950; 388-91 of 1951 and 392-402 of 1952), they had full width front canopies permitting destination displays to be fitted centrally on the front dome. Red patterned moquette supplied by the famous Halifax firm of John Holdsworth was used on all Gardner seats, which looked very attractive in an otherwise utility saloon.

One aspect of the Gardner that was common to the whole production run was the radiator. Indeed identical radiators were also fitted to GNR Leyland's that had been re-engined with the Gardner 4LW unit, for a time causing some confusion as to their origins. The radiator resembled a combination of contemporary Leyland and AEC designs. The top of the radiator was narrower than the bottom, which gave it the Leyland look. The radiator frame was finished at the top with a centrally positioned 'V' and at the bottom with an inverted 'V', which was akin to the AEC design. The radiator frame incorporated two mounting lugs one at either side in the lower third for bolting to the chassis frame; most had external Rexene rollup radiator blinds for winter running. Early Gardners were fitted with enamel GNR coat of arms which was fitted on the centre 'V' section of the radiator. These did not last long on vehicles, as they very quickly became a prize trophy for collectors. A starting handle was fitted to every Gardner right up to the very end, some had the front number plates fitted on the radiator others had the number painted onto the scuttle just below the driver's windscreen.

The first production run of Gardners was sufficient to start replacing some of the more exotic and less reliable vehicles inherited from former independent bus companies bought out by the GNR. A further batch of 20 vehicles was built in 1938 including 220, which was uniquely registered in Belfast and

The legendary GNR Gardner chassis, clearly showing the 5LW diesel engine and substantial side members, at Dundalk works before bodying takes place. ***(DN)***

The upper photo records the handover of the first GNR Gardner to Dublin Garage. The officials from left are: J Johnson (Foreman Railcar Shop), RW Pelissier (Road Motor Assistant), JH Owens (Road Motor Assistant), RW Meredith (Works Manager), P McGuinness (Foreman Engine Shops), J Webster (Foreman Road Motor Shop) and P Byrne (Foreman Bus Body Shop). *(ML)*

(Below) Interior of GNR Gardner No. 200 at Dublin Garage on the day of the handover. *(ML)*

GNR Publicity photograph of Gardner No. 200 taken on the Ardee Road Dundalk by the official photographers Messrs Duffner. *(DN)*

was allocated to Londonderry Garage for the Sligo service. It was not until 1941 that the next batch of ten Gardners was built, followed in 1942 by three more all of which were built using materials purchased before war started. Production then dried up then until 1947. Eight of the 1941/42 group had to have their bodies rebuilt using Metal Sections framing in 1948 as their wartime wooden bodies were literally falling apart. As a result they gained the peculiar looking side window arrangement of having a small sliding vent under which was mounted an oval glass. GNR staff referred to them as 'submarine' buses because of their 'porthole' style of appearance. In the run up to the Second World War (called 'The Emergency' in the Irish Free State) materials in Britain were being diverted to defence production or war production once hostilities commenced in September 1939. During the 'emergency' supplies of coal and other fuel including diesel were in short supply.

The GNR, determined to overcome the adversity, established a research laboratory in 1941 under Dr Brett who was appointed the Chief Chemical Engineer. The laboratory located adjacent to the Dundalk Works was very well equipped for its time, its immediate task was to try and develop a coal substitute and producer gas for road vehicles. Producer gas, essentially a mixture of hydrogen and carbon monoxide, is generated on the vehicle trailer from anthracite coal, coke, wood charcoal or pressed peat. In 1941 anthracite coal was the only material available in such quantities as the GNR required. Suitable modifications were made to twelve buses in Dundalk works, including the production of the trailers which they towed. The modifications were short lived as experience demonstrated that compression ignition engines lacked power when operating on producer gas. A further disadvantage of producer gas was the premature wear of friction components such as pistons, rings etc caused by the insufficient lubrication properties of the gas. Poor filtration of the gas on the trailers also led to debris entering engines. Gardner number 200 was the prototype producer vehicle. On September 1st 1941 the vehicle started operating on the Dublin/Dundalk service. The experiment was discontinued after only six weeks as No. 200's engine suffered detrimental power loss.

Some months previously on Saturday 5th April 1941 number 200 was almost written off. It was working a service from Londonderry to Sligo with Motorman A McCready at the helm when just outside Carrigans some 20 minutes after leaving Londonderry he swerved to avoid a cyclist. As a result the vehicle struck a bridge, lost control, and smashed into a mill wall. Motorman McCready was badly injured and never returned to work again following this incident. The vehicle was extensively damaged, requiring three fitters and the garage tender to go out from Donegal Garage on Monday 7th April to recover it. Three weeks of repairs at Donegal costing £227 saw 200 back on the road again and it survived until 1957.

With the 'emergency' over in 1945 the GNR settled down to resume normal operations, but it was not until 1947 that production of the Gardners resumed in Dundalk when 11 vehicles were constructed.

Metallic Machinations

The GNR and the LMS (NCC) jointly bought four Leyland TS3 buses with Short Brothers metal-framed bodies in 1932, all of which ended up with the GNR. These vehicles proved to be very sturdy and did not suffer from the same degree of degradation as contemporary timber framed bodies. Dick Meredith was impressed with the metal-framed vehicles as they did not require 'interchange bodies' (GNR terminology for re-bodying every five years as with timber framed

GNR Gardner No. 320 photographed following rebuilding with a new body on the Ardee Road, Dundalk on 4th October 1949. *(DN)*

machines) even after 12 years in service. The reputation enjoyed by all-metal bodies ensured the next batch of Gardners was provided by Metal Sections Ltd of Oldbury near Birmingham.

The GNR had an ambitious programme of railway rolling stock replacement and repair after World War Two to correct the deficiencies caused by wartime material restrictions. It was therefore decided that the Belfast coachbuilder Harkness and Son would erect the Metal Sections framing on 12 Gardner chassis in 1947/9. The chassis were conveyed to Belfast by the two omnibus rail wagons, delivered to the McTier Street works of Harkness. The frames for these vehicles were delivered by the GNR to Harkness in boxes.

The first four Harkness buses were very angular in appearance with flat-fronted full width canopies and conventional side windows. Subsequent Harkness buses were less angular with half width front canopies. Undoubtedly their most distinctive feature was the 'submarine' type side windows glazed with 'Claytonrite' rubber, which gave a highly unusual impression. The frames were assembled before being returned to Dundalk for completion on the same omnibus rail wagons. The rear windows were rectangular as opposed to earlier 'D' shaped design of pre-war vehicles. Eleven vehicles were completed between June and November 1947 with the twelfth (No. 380) being turned out on January 10th 1948. A second group of twelve chassis were sent to Harkness for framing in June/July 1949.

Just prior to the Harkness contract Bobby Pelissier highlighted weaknesses in the Dundalk built bodies in a letter to Richard Meredith in September 1947. The document stated

'A number of the 200 type buses are due for replacement bodies, which should of course have been constructed and fitted long ago. The nominal life of the body was reckoned at 5 years, but most of these have gone on to 10 and 11 years. They are now quite bad, but at 7 or 8 years were quite presentable and new bodies fitted now may be reasonably expected to serve for at least this period. Now the chassis to which they are to be fitted on an 'extended' 5 years further 'life' which will bring most of them to a total of 15 years. The company has built about 130 bodies on a variety of chassis. Despite all this experience, nothing seems to have been learnt, or at least we have not profited by any lessons. Since the first body was built there has been little or no improvement or important change in the method of construction, and framework still is prone to more or less rapid deterioration, by rot, loosening of joints and development of innumerable squeaks and rattles. Front bulkhead structure has always been a very weak point, and there are few machines in the fleet in which this part of the body is not loose and floating in relation to the rest.'

Eventually nine vehicles received metal-framed bodies before the programme was immediately halted. The GNR soon discovered that the Metal Sections framed Gardners were not robust enough to cope with potholes and adverse cambers which typified Irish roads. Most of the Metal Sections vehicles suffered premature fracturing of pillars, outriggers, window and roof framing. Bobby Pelissier started to receive reports from garages concerning premature fractures of these bodies and immediately stopped any further rework. Richard Meredith tried to cancel a further batch of Metal Sections frames for the 12 chassis, which were due to be produced in 1949 but was unsuccessful so the GNR modified these before sending them to Harkness for framing. A grand total of 24 new Gardners were framed by Metal Sections and over the next few years would require additional work to eliminate the weak points. Significant sums of money from company reserves had to be earmarked for repairs to the Gardner fleet. On 26th November 1946 the sum of £3,000 was transferred into the maintenance account for urgent repairs to 14 buses. It was not to end there; again on the 17th December 1947 £20,544 was transferred from the bus renewal fund to the omnibus body repair suspense account. On 22nd March 1950 a further 13 buses required heavy repairs at a cost of £15,693. But for the fact that the AEC Regal II vehicles had arrived in 1947 the Company would have faced a serious vehicle shortage. No further bus body frames from the Metal Sections Company were ever purchased by the GNR. One pre-war vehicle (No. 327) was rebuilt at Dundalk in 1949 following a serious road traffic accident when it skidded during icy conditions overturning and killing a pedestrian. It was re-registered ZJ2123 and given a new chassis number 12/49/327.

Production ends

In 1950 with the unfortunate experience of the Metal Sections frames under their belt the GNR turned to Park Royal Vehicles of London to provide frames. Three buses were completed at Dundalk between March and December 1950. The PRV frames were of a more substantial construction and deemed to be suitable for the prevailing road conditions. The finished product that emerged from Dundalk was a very gracious elegant well-proportioned vehicle. Built as 33-seat dual-purpose vehicles with Clayton Dewandre front bulkhead saloon heating units, full front canopies and interior luggage racks fitted, they were eagerly used on tour and private hire work. Four more Park Royal framed examples entered service in May and June 1951 just in time for the annual summer excursion and tours programme. Escalating production costs resulting in continued production of buses in Dundalk in 1952 saw the Gardner build programme coming to an end. Eleven machines entered service the final bus fleet number 402 entered service on 1st August. This was the very same day as an underfloor-engined Leyland Royal Tiger No. 226, representing the next generation of buses began it's career with the GNR.

A distinct feature of the 'Gardners', as they were commonly known to all that worked in the GNR, was the tendency of the company to perform regular changes of body and alter seating configurations. There is much to be said for a chassis that can withstand the rigours of the Irish country roads and outlive its first body. In 1948 though, all was not well within the GNR Road Motor Technical Department. The design of the engine mountings on early Gardners was very rigid and unable to absorb the vibration from the driveline. This vibration invariably travelled right through the body itself adding to the cause of early deterioration. This was corrected when in 1942 metalastik metal/rubber mountings were introduced. In August 1944 there was a proposal to fit shock absorbers to the front axles of Gardners although this was never adopted, despite the fact that they were a standard fit on Leyland Tiger buses the GNR bought new in 1929.

It was also remarked upon in 1944 that the Oxford Blue and Cream livery looked shabby after a relatively short period of time. The company was not going to change the livery but did carry out an experiment with Gardner No. 210 which had been repainted in the standard livery in June 1944 using a different make of finishing blue paint, together with a higher concentration of varnish, and it was deemed an improvement. There was little predictability of style, shape or presentation with the Gardner fleet, some had cream wheel flashes, some had advertisements on the sides of the

GNR Gardner No. 385 photographed following construction using Park Royal frames in March 1950. Again the location is the Ardee Road. *(DN)*

GNR Gardner No. 382, with an angular Harkness framed body, photographed loading a private hire party at the Liverpool Bar on Dublin's North Wall. *(MC)*

roof mounted luggage racks other not, some had flat single glazed windscreens others had split screens. The Gardners were used on all types of operations and their reliability was legendary so much so that celebrities travelled all over Ireland in these remarkable creations. One such bus (fleet No. 389) was used to convey Ted Heath and his band (then a popular orchestra) on their seven day all Ireland Tour from Tuesday 19th June to Monday 25th June 1951. The tour departed from Dublin's Mansion House; the first overnight stop was spent in Derry. The following night was spent at Bangor (Co Down) thereafter overnight stops were made at Portrush; Balbriggan; Cork and Ennis before returning to Dublin. Many other famous people travelled in GNR Gardners such as Joe Loss and his Orchestra during their all Ireland Tour of October and November 1950.

Joe Mackle, who was the first Road Motor Superintendent of the GNR and by now the Rolling Stock Engineer and the General Manager designate of the Belfast Corporation Transport Department, hired a GNR Gardner. Fleet No. 320 transported Mackle and his guests on a grand seven-day tour of Ireland from 12th-19th July 1951. His party was picked up from his brother's house at 403 Crumlin Road; Belfast at 8.15am on the very day thousands of Orangemen would parade down that road on their way to Finaghy. The first night of the Mackle Tour was spent at the Great Northern Hotel in Bundoran. Thereafter the tour continued with overnight stops at Claremorris; Limerick; Lakes of Killarney; Cork; Kilkenny returning to Belfast after completing a total of 1153 miles. Mackle had been running extended seven-day private tours using GNR buses since July 1938, with an interruption between 1940-48 due to the war, but the tours ended in 1953.

Shortly after the last batch of Gardners entered service withdrawals of the pre-war vehicles commenced in 1953. Increased production costs mainly as a result of massive hikes in materials and labour together with a view that the Gardner chassis was now dated conspired to ensure that no more vehicles would be produced. Further retirements took place following the arrival of the AEC Regal IV fleets in 1954-56 and this pattern of disposal continued unabated.

Three Gardners were sold to the Sligo Leitrim and Northern Counties Railway 214, 218 in 1953 and 208 in 1956; all three operated from Manorhamilton. Number 208 had been allocated to Donegal for many years prior to sale. In August 1958 the very last bus overhauled by Dundalk works was a GNR Gardner number 327 dating from 1941, which was rebuilt in 1948 with the metal-framed body - it was scrapped in 1962 by CIE. An illustration of the longevity of the Gardner is illustrated by the fact that the average age at withdrawal was 16 years. Fleet No. 212 was in service for 24 years while No. 243 served for 22 years. Fifty-five GNR Gardners passed to *Córas Iompair Éireann* and many were transformed from the beautiful Oxford Blue and Cream livery with its magnificent GNR Crest proudly displayed on each side, into the drab olive and eau-de-nil livery complete with the 'flying snail' emblem. This replacement livery did not do justice to the Gardners. CIE, in accordance with their 'Alexander' numbering system, classified the GNR Gardners as 'G' Class, simply prefixing this letter with the GNR fleet number.

Unfortunately the Gardner's days were numbered when CIE took over, especially in the Sligo/Donegal area as the new E Class Leyland Leopards entered service in 1961 and then a steady stream of new vehicles starting work right through to 1964. Serious withdrawals began in 1960 with all the Gardners out of commission by the end of 1964, although at least four remained available at Broadstone for service if necessary until mid-1965. In addition GNR Gardner No. 397 was stored under cover at the former GNR garage in Ballyshannon up to August 1965. It was reported to be in very good condition at that time. In the early 1960s many lay in yards exposed to the elements in bus graveyards at garages throughout the former GNR operating territory. Quite a number were eventually burnt at Donegal Garage then removed by scrap men.

There were two reprieves for the GNR Gardner as they approached the end of their proud careers. Firstly in 1960

CIE suffered a serious shortage of suitable coaches to service the successful and growing tours business. Some of the later dual purpose Gardners enjoyed a couple of seasons on coaching work, a real testament to their reliability. They were repainted into the primrose and grey coaching livery of CIE. Some Gardners retained their GNR livery up to about 1960, mainly because it was known that they would be early withdrawal candidates and it was not considered worthwhile repainting them into CIE colours. Secondly, four of these vehicles (386-389) were converted for CIE by a Dublin coachbuilding company called Ryan's in 1964 into special ambulances for the Knock shrine in County Mayo. They were capable of carrying eight stretcher-borne persons. Number 389 was painted into the ambulance livery of brown and cream at Donegal Garage and from there went straight into its new role. They were based at CIE's garage in Ballina Co Mayo finally being withdrawn in 1975 when cascaded E class Leyland Leopards, suitably modified, replaced them. These Gardners lay decaying in the open until 1978, 28 years after being built at Dundalk, before being disposed of.

Thankfully, due to the Knock Ambulance conversions a number of the later Gardners survive in tribute to the professionalism of the GNR and in particular the craftsmen in Dundalk. Joined by one earlier example which is resident in Northern Ireland they are:–

- 324 – Preserved by Ulster Folk and Transport Museum
- 389 & 396 Preserved by private individuals and housed at the Cavan and Leitrim Railway at Dromod.
- 387 & 390 are in the National Transport Museum collection.

Gardner No. 324 was donated to the Transport Museum which was then in Witham Street (since moved to Cultra). Before it was handed over to the Museum it was fully overhauled in 1961 at the former GNR garage in Donegal Town. The dock overhaul was carried out under the stewardship of Billy Smyth, the Garage Superintendent, who was related by marriage to Mr REM Hughes, who was the Ulster Transport Authority Passenger Manager at the time. He in turn was instrumental in preserving this marvellous specimen of Irish bus engineering. The vehicle was driven from Donegal freshly adorned in GNR livery including side flashing applied by painter Danny O'Donnell and was magnificence exemplified. Pioneering bus preservationists Bryan Boyle and William Montgomery contributed significantly to ensuring that this vehicle was saved in Northern Ireland by collecting it from Billy Smith on Saturday 5th August 1961 at Lifford County Donegal. The vehicle is currently undergoing further restoration work by William Montgomery.

Gardner Omnibus Parts Suppliers

Component or Unit Description	Supplier	Cost per Unit	Comments
Gardner 5LW Engines	Gardner Engines (Ireland) Ltd	£419 5s 0d	
Front Axle	Kirkstall Forge Leeds	£44	
Rear Axle	Kirkstall Forge Leeds	£88	
Spring Clamp Plates includes			
bolts and nuts	Kirkstall Forge Leeds	£5 17s 6d	
Chassis Frames complete with Crossmembers and banjos	John Thompson (Motor Pressings) Ltd Millfields Rd Ettingshall, Wolverhampton	£23 10s 0d	First 21 chassis frames arrived at Dundalk assembled Remainder arrived in CKD form
Prop Shafts 2 per bus	Hardy Spicer	£5 each	Used on early buses with Meadows Gearboxes
Prop Shafts 2 per bus (each)	Laycock Engineering	£12 6s 0d	Used on later buses with Leyland Gearboxes
Gearbox 4 speed	Henry Meadows Ltd Wolverhampton	£58 10s 0d	Used on first 21 buses built
Forward Control Clutches	Henry Meadows Ltd Wolverhampton	£18 5s 0d	Used on first 21 buses built
Leyland GB9 Gearbox	Ashenhurst, Williams	£74 18s 0d	Used for buses built from 1938 onwards
Leyland C6 Clutch assembly	Ashenhurst, Williams	£11 13s 3d	Used for buses built from 1938 onwards
Wheel Bearings (each)	Hoffman Bearing Manufacturers	10s	
Wheel Centres minus tyres	Joseph Sankey & Sons	£1 5s 6d	6 road and 1 spare per bus
Tyres (each)	Irish Dunlop Ltd	£1 17s 7d	
Saloon Heating Equipment (sets)	Clayton Dewandre	£13 10s 0d	
Vacuum Servos (each)	Clayton Dewandre	£7 15s 0d	
Radiator Tubes (finned) (each)	Clayton Dewandre	2s 7½d	Wire wound tubes fitted to Dundalk Works built radiators
Batteries 6 volt (each)	Exide Ireland Ltd	£3 10s 3d	2 per bus
Chassis switchboards (each)	Simms Motor Units Ltd	£3 10s 0d	
Body electrical switchboards (each)	Simms Motor Units Ltd	£1 13s 6d	
Head Lights (each)	Simms Motor Units Ltd	£1 19s 0d	
Side Light Units (each)	Simms Motor Units Ltd	5s 9d	
Stop & Tail light units (each)	Simms Motor Units Ltd	10s	
Headlight Dimmer Switches (each)	CAV Bosch Ireland Ltd	4s 6d	
Horn Units (each)	CAV Bosch Ireland Ltd	12s 6d	
Lamp Holders (each)	CAV Bosch Ireland Ltd	1s 10d	
Communication Bell Units (each)	General Electrical Corporation	9s 11d	
Bell push units (each)	General Electrical Corporation	4s 0d	
Saloon Pillar & Roof Lamps	TAW Manufacturing		
Seat Frames (2 seaters) (each)	Metal Utilities Limited	£1 12s	
Seat Frames (3 seaters) (each)	Metal Utilities Limited	£1 15s	
Seat Legs (each)	Metal Utilities Limited	7s	
Chromium Plated Handrails	Accles and Pollock Ltd	£8 17s 1d	

Gardner Omnibus Parts Suppliers			
Component or Unit Description	**Supplier**	**Cost per Unit**	**Comments**
Aluminium Sheets 18SWG	British Aluminium Ltd	1s 3d lb	
Aluminium Sheets 16 SWG	CER Brownlow Ltd	£1 11s 2d lb	
Masonite Tempered Presdwood	Masonite Ltd		Used for selected exterior panelling
ICI Dulux Paints	Haslett Clarke and Co Ltd		
African Mahogany Wood	Parkers of Ancoats Manchester		Used for body framing
African White Wood	Parkers of Ancoats Manchester		Used for body framing
Lagos Mahogany Wood	Parkers of Ancoats Manchester		Used for body framing
Teak	Slater & Birds & Co Ltd		
Rexene Covering	ICI Rexine Ltd		
Insulated Electrical Cable	Irish Driver Harris Co Ltd Dublin		
Cushion Foam pre-formed	Dunlopillo-Irish Dunlop Ltd		
Seat squab hair filling	The Hairlok Co Ltd		
Seat Moquette Red	John Holdsworth Co Ltd		
Saloon Glazing toughened Plate	Triplex Glass Northern Ltd		
Widney Stuart Patent Aero-Drop			
Saloon windows	Hallam, Sleigh & Cheston Ltd		
Driver and signal window units	William Young and Co		
Brake Cross Shafts	Ashenhurst, Williams		Leyland Part
Brake Pull Off Springs	Ashenhurst, Williams		Leyland Part
Jaw Ends	Ashenhurst, Williams		Leyland Part
Adjusting Ends (Brake)	Ashenhurst, Williams		Leyland Part
Turnbuckles	Ashenhurst, Williams		Leyland Part
Pedal operating brackets	Ashenhurst, Williams		Leyland Part
Pivot lever support brackets	Ashenhurst, Williams		Leyland Part
Hand brake shaft brackets	Ashenhurst, Williams		Leyland Part
Hand brake levers	Ashenhurst, Williams		Leyland Part
Circlip for pivot lever	Ashenhurst, Williams		Leyland Part
Nipples in catch handle	Ashenhurst, Williams		Leyland Part
Pawl for Hand Brake Levers	Ashenhurst, Williams		Leyland Part
Springs for Hand Brake Levers	Ashenhurst, Williams		Leyland Part
Hand Brake Quadrants	Ashenhurst, Williams		Leyland Part
Springs for levers	Ashenhurst, Williams		Leyland Part
Springs for Clutch pedals	Ashenhurst, Williams		Leyland Part
Radiator Support Pads top & bottom	Ashenhurst, Williams		Leyland Part
Bonnet handles	Ashenhurst, Williams		Leyland Part
Bonnet hinges top and side	Ashenhurst, Williams		Leyland Part
Support Tubes	Ashenhurst, Williams		Leyland Part
Spring clips for bonnet supports	Ashenhurst, Williams		Leyland Part
Catches for bonnet top clips	Ashenhurst, Williams		Leyland Part
Pins for links	Ashenhurst, Williams		Leyland Part
Buffers for links	Ashenhurst, Williams		Leyland Part
Bonnet Catches	Ashenhurst, Williams		Leyland Part
Silencer baffle plates	Ashenhurst, Williams		Leyland Part
Springs	Ashenhurst, Williams		Leyland Part
Rubber buffers	Ashenhurst, Williams		Leyland Part
NS front wing stays Radiator end	Ashenhurst, Williams		Leyland Part
NS front wing stays centre	Ashenhurst, Williams		Leyland Part
Buffer plates	Ashenhurst, Williams		Leyland Part
Balls for headlamp pillars	Ashenhurst, Williams		Leyland Part
Steering drop arms	Ashenhurst, Williams		Leyland Part
Steering Boxes	Ashenhurst, Williams		Leyland Part
Adjusting shims	Ashenhurst, Williams		Leyland Part
Steering shafts	Ashenhurst, Williams		Leyland Part
Marles Cam LH	Ashenhurst, Williams		Leyland Part
Rocker shafts LH	Ashenhurst, Williams		Leyland Part
Keys for arm	Ashenhurst, Williams		Leyland Part
Felt washers	Ashenhurst, Williams		Leyland Part
Welch washers	Ashenhurst, Williams		Leyland Part
Keys	Ashenhurst, Williams		Leyland Part
Serrated pins	Ashenhurst, Williams		Leyland Part
Steering shaft nuts	Ashenhurst, Williams		Leyland Part
Rocker shaft nuts & washers	Ashenhurst, Williams		Leyland Part
Serrated pin nuts & washers	Ashenhurst, Williams		Leyland Part
½" studs for steering box	Ashenhurst, Williams		Leyland Part
⅜" studs for cover plates	Ashenhurst, Williams		Leyland Part

Chapter Ten
GNR Double-Deckers

The decision to introduce double-deck vehicles to the GNR was taken at a Board Meeting in Amiens Street Station Dublin on 24th June 1936, the direct result of increased loadings on its northeast Dublin services. Dublin District Superintendent John H Scott proposed the introduction of six double-deckers on services to Howth, Skerries and Malahide. Although these areas were served by the GNR's railway from Dublin Amiens Street to Belfast and the branch to Howth, allied to the fact that there was an extensive North Dublin suburban train service to Howth serving Clontarf, Killester, Raheny, and Howth Junction, bus patronage was increasing. In conjunction with the Howth service there was a frequent train service between Dublin and Drogheda, which called at principal towns *en route*. The inland route used by GNR omnibuses to Howth, which was away from the railway line, served new high-density housing developments at Killester, Raheny and Sutton Cross.

Double-decker operation in Dublin was believed to have begun as far back as 1907. In August that year a company called the Motor Bus and Traction Company of Ireland with a registered address of 69, Victoria Street, London published a prospectus seeking capital of £250,000 in £1 shares for the purpose of operating omnibuses in all parts of Ireland. In early 1908 The Mercury Motorbus Company with its General Manager Ronald G Bachelor, a name which appeared on the share prospectus of the Motor Bus and Traction Company, began a service from Aston's Quay to Rathmines via Harcourt Street, using chain driven Orion buses which had come from the Victoria Motor Omnibus Company of London. It is believed that the Mercury acquired two or possibly three buses for their Dublin operation. The Dublin venture was short lived following a street brawl in mid-May which occurred outside the Tivoli Theatre between Mercury staff and a group of Jarvies, who resented the intrusion of buses, which they viewed as taking their revenue away. The Mercury was officially wound up on February 19th 1909. Thus ended Dublin's brief early flirtation with double-deck buses.

In January 1937 tender documents were issued for the supply of six double-deck buses. Leyland Motors were supremely confident that they would receive an order for six Titan chassis from the GNR. There was also considerable interest in this product from the Dublin United Tramways Company at the time. By March 1937 Leyland Motors agents in Ireland Messrs Ashenhurst, Williams were reporting back to the factory in the following terms: "We should receive an order for six double-deck bus chassis from the GNR. The vehicles will arrive in Ireland in an incomplete state and will be finished by the railway themselves". The Leyland product was £215 cheaper than its AEC rival at the time. However, and not surprisingly, the problems encountered between the GNR and Leyland in relation to the LT5A single-deck buses and their disastrous performance swung the order to AEC. In April 1937 GNR Company Secretary FC Wallace signed a contract with AEC for six AEC Regent 0661 double-deckers for its fleet. These chassis were bought at a cost of £1,650 plus £200 import duty per vehicle. The first two (Nos. 62/3, ZC 2576/7) were delivered to Dundalk in September. The vehicles were very similar in external appearance to a batch of Regents with the same Park Royal metal-framed body delivered to Salford Corporation in the mid 1930s. One of the Salford vehicles (No. 235) is currently preserved at the Greater Manchester Museum of Transport, Boyle Street Manchester.

The GNR vehicles had 56-seat Park Royal framed bodywork (each frame cost £192) finished at Dundalk works, complete with high-backed dual-purpose seats supplied by Chrom Furnishings in England. The staircase, mouldings, seat fittings, cowls etc. were supplied in kit form from Park Royal at a cost of £149 10s 0d for each bus. The new double-deckers, as stated, were 0661 AEC Regents with A173 7.7 litre oil engines which developed 90bhp at 1750rpm and were the latest version with direct injection (AEC had previously been great advocates of indirect injection) and two separate cylinder heads. Other refinements incorporated in the engine included a new type of piston top face as dictated by the direct injection method, where fuel is sprayed into the space above the piston instead of into, or towards, a separate small combustion chamber, as on the earlier AEC indirect injection oil engines. The vehicles were fitted with four speed crash gearboxes. Following a period of driver training, fleet Nos. 62/3 commenced work on the Dublin to Howth service on Monday 18th October 1937.

There was an unofficial race between the GNR and the DUTC to determine which company could introduce them to Dubliners first. The DUTC began using deckers on 20th December 1937 with service 50 to Crumlin and as such lost the race. On the first day of GNR double-deck operations officials from the *Garda* Carriage Department joined Jonathan Stephens on the first trip. All were said to be impressed with the new vehicles. Trial runs had been made the previous Saturday and these were regarded as satisfactory.

Double-decker introduction did cause industrial unrest, as the Federation of Irish Rail and Road Workers demanded significant increases in pay for Motormen and Conductors who operated double-deckers. The company was steadfast in rejecting the claim of the staff. At midnight on 10th June 1938 all Motormen and Conductors staged a wildcat strike. They did not return to work until 6.00am on 13th June, after the company agreed to consider the matter. The company did not give into the demands of the staff and the issue

Brand new AEC Regent No. 62 alongside AEC Reliance No. 23 at Sheriff Street Garage on 16th October 1937, two days before double-deck operation commenced. *(AS)*

dissipated. The success of the double-deck service to Howth was all the more astonishing given that the Dublin United Tramways Company ran their No. 31 service using trams to Howth. The first two AECs continued to perform very successfully for some six years, during which period they had clocked up some 400,000 miles and were by 1942 due a works overhaul. Richard Meredith, in line with his policy of adopting a standard diesel engine, decided to fit 62 and 63 with Gardner 5LW engines at overhaul from a stockpile of engines built up before the war. They were returned to traffic and gave many more years satisfactory service. These two pioneers of double-deck working were given their final overhaul at Dundalk in December 1950 when £1,000 was spent on each. They spent their final summers from 1954-56 working at Pettigo, conveying pilgrims from the station to Lough Derg Mainland Shore, before enjoying an honourable retirement.

Following the successful introduction of the first two deckers, early in 1938 an arrangement was reached with the Dublin United Tramways Company for the loan of a new Leyland TD4 56-seat double-deck vehicle for evaluation. The DUTC vehicle R6 (ZC 719) operated on a variety of GNR Dublin services for a number of weeks before being returned to its owner. The *quid pro quo* for the DUTC was realised when AEC Regent No. 63 was loaned to the Dublin Company for evaluation on service number 50 to Crumlin. In the light of the evaluation of the Leyland, the GNR continued its policy of purchasing AEC vehicles to meet its requirements and the remaining four identical machines (Nos. 64-7, ZC 6981-4) entered service from Dublin Garage between May and July 1939. The chassis were purchased at the reduced price of £1,116. The GNR managed to obtain agreement from the Irish Free State government to waive the import duty, which was an important concession during those years of economic warfare with Britain. These buses were in fact the first double-deckers to receive Gardner 5 LW engines in 1941, a full year before their older stable mates. Fleet No. 64 was prematurely withdrawn in 1948 following a serious road traffic accident. Numbers 65 and 67 were withdrawn from service in 1954 as they had very high mileage.

The Company's experience with double-deckers was not always so positive. In the early days of double-deck operations several mishaps occurred. On 4th December 1939 at 8.30pm bus No. 64 overturned between Raheny and Sutton after colliding with a stationary motorcycle combination. It appears that the Motorman lost control of the vehicle after the collision and many passengers on board were injured. After being repaired at Dundalk costing £210 No. 64 got into trouble again when it struck an overhead bridge in late 1942, causing £33 damage. On Christmas Day 1939 GNR double-deck bus No. 62 had an unusual drive. In the early hours a man called Campbell got into the cab of the bus, which was lined up with others outside the Sheriff Street garage, and drove off. He took the route directly towards Amiens Street, ordinarily barred to GNR drivers of double-deckers on account of the low railway bridge. GNR buses usually reached the city via Commons Street and North Wall. As the bus passed under the bridge its roof was slightly damaged, to the tune of £19. Campbell continued along Amiens Street and North Strand. Meanwhile the nightshift cleaner at the

A nocturnal 1942 view inside the GNR's Abercorn Road Garage of four AEC Regents, 66, 64, 62 and 63. Minor differences in livery and destination displays are apparent in this view. *(RP)*

AEC Regent No. 66 began operating in Drogheda on 22nd March 1948. It is seen here at the GNR Bus Office in the City at South Quay about to depart for Ardee. *(WM)*

garage informed the *Gardai*, having seen from some distance the bus being driven off. They got in touch with the Guards at Coolock who set up a roadblock and Campbell was detained. Following a court appearance he received two months in jail. A year later a Motorman lost control of the same vehicle, striking a wall, causing £162 damage.

World War Two interrupted the GNR plans to expand double-deck operations. The company did however place an order with AEC on 24th November 1943 for delivery of four additional AEC Regent chassis as soon as these could be delivered to Dundalk. There was a suggestion that the company try to obtain second hand vehicles, but this suggestion was thwarted by the scarcity of such vehicles at this period in time.

Military vehicle production now became AEC's main activity, with nearly 13,000 such units being produced for the war effort. When war ended the bus industry in the UK and Ireland was in dire straits due to extreme vehicle shortages, further exacerbated by the lack of materials and skilled labour. Operators were desperate to obtain new vehicles, the GNR among them. The November 1943 order of four AEC Regent II 0661 vehicles was fulfilled when No. 285 entered service from Dublin garage on 23rd December 1946, followed by 286 on 24th January 1947, 287 on 6th March and 288 on 29th of that month. The specification of these four Regents differed little from the pre-war versions as development activity had been directed to the war effort by AEC. They had the AEC (A173) 7.7 Oil engine and D124 crash gearbox, a triple-servo vacuum brake system was fitted in lieu of the pre-war vacuum hydraulic system. The acute foreign currency situation in post war Britain ensured that the GNR as export customers enjoyed early fulfilment of its order. The vehicles were delivered with Park Royal framing, which was completed at Dundalk Works. They were delivered without platform-doors; however these were fitted to the vehicles in 1949 in addition to saloon heating, thus making the vehicles suitable for longer distance work.

The arrival of new double-deckers allowed the GNR management yet again to demonstrate a pioneering spirit with their introduction on longer distance work outside the greater Dublin area. Numbers 65 and 67 were transferred to Dundalk garage and fitted with platform doors, upper and lower saloon heating. On Monday 15th February 1948 they commenced work on the Dundalk to Newry service, which had been enjoying particularly heavy traffic. Double-deck workings were further expanded with the allocation of three new vehicles to Dundalk on the 28th September 1948; they were fleet Nos. 435/6/8. Double-deckers were, for the first time, allocated to Newry Garage the previous day when Nos. 67 and 439 took up workings on the Dundalk service. Drogheda gained its first double-decker on 22nd March 1948 with No. 66 commencing work on the Togher service; it was followed by Nos. 285/6/7 on 28th September 1948. Ardee garage commenced double-decker operations on the same day with workings to Dundalk and Drogheda. The

The rear of AEC Regent No. 285 seen loading up for the trip to Skerries in 1947, at the O'Connell Street end of Eden Quay. *(MC)*

latter town had a major impediment in relation to double-deck operation in the form of overhead railway bridge No. 52 which carried the Navan Branch of the GNR across the main Drogheda to Dublin road. Double-deck vehicles could not pass under without striking it. On 6th April 1953 a Motorman attempted to drive bus No. 285 under this bridge, causing extensive damage to the vehicle, which cost £415 to repair. The company made several applications to the council for the lowering of the roadway, thus permitting double-deck vehicles to negotiate the obsticle.

District Superintendent Tommy Carton told Council officials on 16th April 1955 that the diversion for double-deck vehicles via Beamore was costing the company dearly in terms of resources. The council said they would only lower the road if the GNR paid for this to be carried out and a sum of £5,000 was sought for work to be undertaken. It was not carried out until after the GNR had ceased to exist. The bridge claimed the upper saloon of a CIE double-decker (R446) when it was stolen from outside Conyngham Road bus garage by a John Kirwan of Cabra at about 11.30pm on 13th January 1957. At 1.10am the next day the Drogheda GNR signalman reported hearing the crash of the bus striking the railway bridge and immediately contacted the *Gardai* who arrested the driver. The vehicle was quickly recovered to the GNR garage at Scarlet Street from where it was removed by CIE officials to Spa Road in Dublin for repairs.

Ten new 8ft wide 58 seat Regent III double-deckers (Nos. 289-98, IY 5391 – IY 5400) were delivered between March and October 1948 with bodies completed at GNR Dundalk on Park Royal framing. Later additions included the fitting of platform doors to Nos. 293/5/7 in 1952. The last built of these vehicles, No. 298, was the first bus in Ireland to be fitted with fluorescent interior lighting supplied by Park Royal from parts delivered from the German company Siemens. Four light units were fitted in each saloon two on each side with a fifth unit fitted in the upper saloon above the rear emergency exit as well as a unit mounted above the conductor's area on the platform. Tungsten lighting was additionally provided for use in an emergency. Seven additional 7ft 6in wide AEC Regent IIIs completed the order (Nos. 433-9, ZH 3932-7 & MZ 2529) in July 1948. They came complete from Park Royal Coachworks in London unlike all of their predecessors. Many GNR staff referred to these as the 'British' buses. There were minor differences of detail in the interior finish. The reason for this change of policy was the inability of the GNR works at Dundalk to complete the vehicles due to railway rolling stock commitments. They were delivered without platform doors but gained these by 1952. From new they were fitted with front semaphore trafficators.

These Regents represented the latest contemporary versions available. They incorporated the larger AEC 9.6 litre direct-injection A204 engine that at 1800rpm produced 125bhp with the Wilson designed and AEC produced pre-selective epicyclic gearbox driven through a fluid flywheel. The vehicles were fitted with a compressed air system, which was employed to apply the brakes on all wheels, and for the actuation of the gear-changing mechanism from a lever working through a gate mounted on the steering column, in conjunction with the 'gear change pedal' located in the traditional position normally occupied by a clutch pedal. Major WG Wilson, who had been a military engineer, had developed the epicyclic gearbox in 1927. This represented significant advantages over a conventional layshaft gear train

AEC Regent No. 298, the last of the 1948 batch of 8ft wide machines and the one fitted with fluorescent saloon lighting, seen at Eden Quay shortly after entering service. *(JG)*

AEC Regent No. 439, a Northern Ireland registered bus, captured in this 1958 view at the Crescent Dundalk adjacent to the GNR Bus Office. *(JG)*

in that changes from one ratio to another could be effected without interruption to the drive due to the permanently meshed gear train engaged by friction elements. The gearbox was more compact for a given torque capacity, because its members rotate about a common axis, in addition there are a greater number of teeth in contact to share the load. It was particularly popular in bus applications because of the high frequency of gear changes. GNR Motormen loved the pre-selector buses, particularly in the stop start environment of Dublin, although problems very quickly materialised. Second gear brake bands started to break prematurely. Dundalk gave the problem to Bobby Pelissier to solve. A brake band is provided for each gear train so that each time a brake is applied a gear change is made with the gears always in mesh. When a change into top gear is made, none of the brake bands is applied, but instead a multiplate clutch is engaged to lock together the gear trains to provide a direct drive. Bobby quickly discovered that Motormen were complaining that there was a fierce kick from the gear pedal when they changed from first into second gear. This provided the clue to solve the mystery, as there was nothing wrong mechanically with any of the pressures or settings on the gearbox. This was a training issue for Motormen who were changing from first into second without releasing the throttle. An instruction went out to start off in second gear on the flat and release the throttle between changes. This resolved a problem, which had irritated GNR engineers.

Dundalk to Newry operations were, by 1949, completely dominated by double-deckers. Numbers 438/9 were almost permanently based at Newry and No. 441 was a regular car based at Greenore depot. Three GNR buses were garaged overnight at Newry during this time in order to facilitate early morning duties from Newry to Dundalk, Carlingford and Greenore. The closure of the Dundalk Newry and Greenore Railway a little later ensured the success of double-deck operations in this part of the GNR's territory. Contemporary Northern Ireland Public Service Vehicle legislation prevented the GNR from operating any of the 8ft wide double-deckers into the Province and as a result these vehicles worked mainly in the Dublin area. This arrangement outlived the GNR itself and was perpetuated right through until the mid 1970s when CIE R class Leyland OPD2/10 vehicles and C Class Leyland Leopards were often garaged at Newry Edward Street.

Donegal Deckers

A north-western outpost of double-deck working had been established by the GNR, which was to continue into CIE days. Selected workings on the Sligo to Ballyshannon service were operated by double-decker 437 which began work on 1st October 1948 based at the GNR outstation of Cliffoney a small town fourteen miles north of Sligo on the Bundoran road. Motorman Austin Foley and conductor Jimmy McGloan both of whom lived in the town worked this bus. The machine was

AEC Regent No. 436, one of the double-deckers based in Donegal, seen at Ballyshannon Garage in 1955. *(JG)*

left overnight on the main street adjacent to the post office. Another bus, No. 434, started operations from Ballyshannon garage, working on the Sligo service on the same day. During the fifties bus No. 287 was a regular performer, working from Cliffoney, Ballyshannon and Grange until 1957 when 285 took over. This Donegal outpost of GNR double-deck operation has never been credibly explained until now. The decision to introduce these high capacity vehicles into one of the most sparsely populated counties in Ireland seemed strange. The Erne hydro-electric scheme aimed to conquer the majesty of the river whose every ripple signified the soul incarnate of Ballyshannon. Work commenced in 1945 to construct the massive hydro-electric scheme, which gave employment to hundreds of men. During the construction phase 80,000 cubic yards of rock, about 170,000 tons, was excavated. A tidal wall constructed at Assaroe Falls held back the Erne waters in an artificial lake further down river, near the GNR bus garage where another set of sluice gates was situated – the power contained in the velocity of the water was evident. The GNR decided to dispatch the double-deckers to Donegal to cater for the large demand in recreational weekend and evening trips to Sligo and to facilitate the Bundoran holiday traffic. Many students of GNR bus operation of the period believed that the double-decker worked right through between Sligo and Londonderry as it was often seen and photographed at Sligo with Donegal or Londonderry on its destination scroll. The truth of the matter is that on Londonderry bound double-deck workings from Sligo passengers had to change buses at Ballyshannon into a single-deck vehicle to continue their northbound journey. A low bridge at Laghey crossed the main Ballyshannon to Donegal road carrying the County Donegal Railways narrow gauge line, thus preventing double-deckers going any farther north. The road was lowered in 1957 and this allowed deckers to reach Donegal Town. Prior to 1957 the double-decker was maintained at Ballyshannon Garage, which became quite a bastion of double-deck working, as a special Lough Derg summer allocation of two additional deckers catered for large volumes of pilgrims between Pettigo Station and Lough Derg. The Lough Derg vehicles were garaged in the yard at Pettigo railway station. After the bridge obstruction was overcome another impediment had to be addressed by the GNR. The garage at Donegal could not accommodate a double-deck vehicle, as the doors were not high enough. The middle doors were extended in height to facilitate double-deckers getting into the garage for maintenance purposes. This allocation survived until replaced by a CIE Leyland OPD2/10 No. R796 in September 1959, then garaged at Sligo.

In 1953 the last new double-deck vehicles were purchased by the GNR, again 12 AEC Regent III vehicles in two batches. The first batch of AEC Regent IIIs was to a 9613E specification. This version of the Regent was introduced in 1950; it was a 26ft long chassis with the AEC 9.6 litre (A218 unit see below) engine, 7ft 6 in wide with pre-selector gearbox etc. The 'E' designation in the AEC nomenclature denotes that the vehicle was built to a 'standard provincial' with pre-selector gearbox *ie* non-London specification. Fleet numbers were 440-2, IY 8391/4/7 respectively; they were on Park Royal frames completed by the GNR at Dundalk and from new were fitted with platform doors with seats for 56. They were also fitted with front semaphore trafficators, a new innovation for buses at the time. These three vehicles were ordered specifically to replace trams on the Hill of Howth system, which would have

(Above) CIE Leyland OPD2/10 R796 on the former Great Northern service from Sligo to Londonderry is seen at Grange in 1959. *(RG)*

(Below) AEC Regent No. 440, seen when new at the Crescent, Dundalk, in an official GNR photograph, on 19th December 1952. *(DN)*

(Right) AEC Regent No. 302 is pictured at Eden Quay, Dublin. These larger 8ft wide by 30ft long machines were 66-seaters and were delivered in 1953 to cater for increased North Dublin suburban loadings. It should be noted that this length for a double-deck vehicle on two axles was not legal in the UK at the time. *(JG)*

UBLIN I
302
ZO-9840
GREAT NORTHERN

Left: **Interior view of lower saloon of AEC Regent No. 440 in this official GNR photo dated 19th December 1952.** *(DN)*

Lower: **Interior view of the upper saloon of GNR double -deck bus No. 440.** *(DN)*

closed later that year if Percy Reynolds had had his way. This small batch of AEC Regents incorporated the Neate multi-pull hand brake control levers. This device, which provides for safer parking on any type of hill, also aids the stopping of a vehicle in a run-away situation as well as permitting a gradual release of the hand brake. The incorporation of this feature further illustrates the ingenuity of the mechanical engineers in the GNR. Fortunately the closure of the Howth tramway required for essential maintenance was temporary and the good burghers of Dublin were to enjoy its delights for a few more years.

The remaining nine vehicles were AEC Regent IIIs to an 9612E specification and were 8ft wide 30ft-long chassis, with the 9.6 litre engine, which by now was known as the A218 unit with modifications to the water circulation system designed to improve cooling. They had an increased carrying capacity of 66 seats with platform doors. They followed the convention in respect of most GNR double-deckers in having Park Royal frames completed by the GNR works. They were fleet numbers 299-307, with registrations marks ZO 8643, IY 8593/6, ZO 9840, ZU 3142 and ZU 4879/80/78/7 respectively. Resulting from the deliveries of the last 12 new vehicles the GNR introduced a new double-deck service on 28th February 1955 from Eden Quay to St Anne's Estate at Raheny. The pioneer GNR double-deckers Nos. 62/3 remained in service until 1956. This was partly attributable to the catastrophic

Former DUTC/CIE Leyland TD5s at Eden Quay in 1957. The difference between the front vehicle (No. 280) with its original DUTC body, contrasts with that of the upper saloon of the vehicle behind (No. 284) with its transplanted upper saloon from a scrapped TD4 following a collision with a low bridge at Drogheda. *(MC)*

fire at the GNR Dundalk Works on 7th September 1955 when double-deck vehicles 300, which was barely 2½ years old, and 305, which was only 20 months old, were totally destroyed. Thirty-one AEC Regents passed into ownership of *Córas Iompair Éireann* on 1st October 1958 (Nos. 286-299/301-4/6/7, 433-42) when the original GNR fleet numbers were prefaced with the CIE type code AR. Withdrawals of the AEC Regents started in December 1960, the last being finally withdrawn in 1971. Bus No. 297 served for several years as the CIE skidpan bus at the Broadstone driver-training department. They were all painted into CIE livery; some went into the olive and eau-de-nil scheme, whilst many went into the monastral blue and cream colour scheme. Because CIE sprayed their vehicles they had the annoying feature on many vehicles of having the chrome radiator surround painted green.

One GNR AEC Regent III, No. 435, which was based at Drogheda garage stubbornly refused to adopt the CIE livery scheme until late 1961. Up to that time it still appeared in full GNR livery of Oxford Blue and cream including the historic GNR Crest on both sides of the vehicle surmounted by the GREAT NORTHERN lettering just below the window line. The only concession to its new owners was the legal lettering which identified its then owner as CIE, all of this a full three years after the GNR was subsumed into CIE. Regent No. 442 that numerically had the highest fleet number, and one of the last deckers delivered to the GNR, spent its final days in Drogheda before being scrapped in 1971. An illustration of GNR defiance at being taken over by CIE is that Dundalk Works were repainting vehicles into the Oxford Blue GNR livery right up to the very end. The unfortunate reality for many GNR men was that CIE were in effective control of the bus and lorry fleet from early September 1958. The first AEC Regent to be painted into CIE livery was No. 286, which was out shopped from the works on 9th September 1958, three weeks before the official ending of the Great Northern. GNR staff decided that in repainting their vehicles into the CIE livery that they would adopt their own form of that scheme. The dark green of the CIE livery was applied to the blue areas and the light green to the cream sections. The result was that former GNR buses in CIE service were highly distinctive – its as if the GNR employees were saying "you might have taken over but we're still different to you lot". The story of the GNR double-deck operations would not be complete without reference to events which took place in 1956 when the GNRB purchased six former CIE Leyland Titan TD's for £474 each. Five vehicles, which entered service in June and July 1956, became fleet Nos. 280-284. A sixth vehicle R109, was purchased at the same time for spare parts, having been involved in an earlier accident, but it did not enter service at any time with the GNR. All five operational vehicles were sent to Dundalk works where they were overhauled and repainted into GNR livery before being returned to Abercorn Road garage for work on the Dublin suburban services. These vehicles required a great deal of work to get them to a standard acceptable to the GNR before entry into service. An interesting story concerns fleet No. 284, which was on its way back to Dublin following overhaul and repaint at Dundalk. The vehicle, being driven by a shunter from Dublin garage, hit the notorious overhead railway bridge at Drogheda, causing extensive damage to the upper saloon of the vehicle. It was recovered back to Dundalk for repairs, whereupon the GNR purchased the upper saloon of an older and squarer former DUTC Leyland TD4 bus R18 from its new owner the Wicklow County Council. The body had been removed from the chassis to facilitate its conversion to a tar tanker. Thus the square top deck of R18 was married to the more stylish lower saloon of 284, making quite a conversation piece for enthusiasts of the time. Just two years later CIE acquired the Leyland double-deckers for the second time and Nos. 280-4 reverted to their original CIE fleet numbers for the year in which they were retained by CIE. One vehicle, No. 280 even regained its cast iron fleet number plate R111 that happened to be in a store somewhere.

GNR garages or depots that operated double-deck vehicles during the period 1937-1958 were:–

Dublin	Skerries Dormer Shed	Rush	Donabate
Drogheda	Ardee	Dundalk	Greenore
Newry	Carlingford	Ballyshannon	Grange
Cliffoney	Pettigo Summer Only		

Right through into the 1970s CIE continued to operate a former GNR double-decker from its Carlingford out-station, replacing it with a Leyland OPD2/10 fleet number R746 specially fitted with platform doors for the purpose. The Transport Museum Society of Ireland has splendidly preserved one GNR double-deck vehicle, fleet No. 438.

(Right) A GNR Conductor's Journal sheet. GNR conductors had to produce a journal recording passenger numbers and timings which were analysed in the road motor offices in Belfast and Dublin.

(Below) A Park Royal bodybuilders general arrangement drawing of the GNR Regent III buses supplied in 1948.

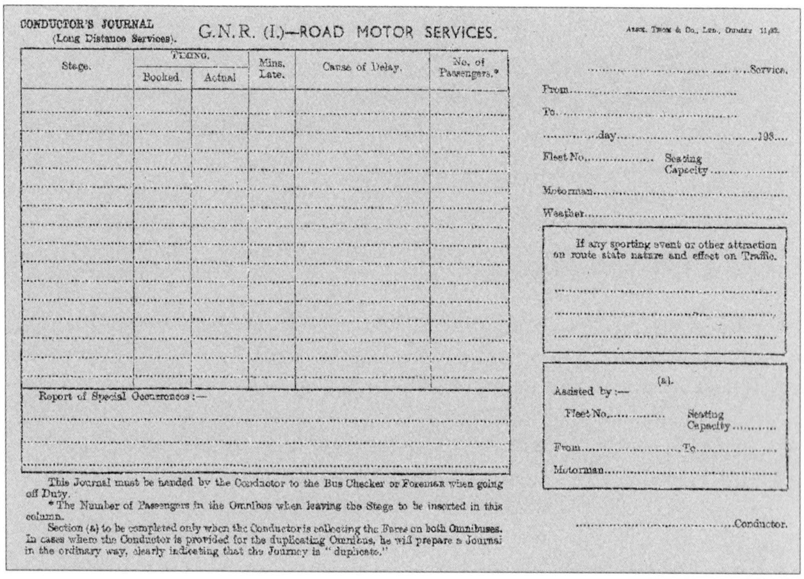
CONDUCTOR'S JOURNAL (Long Distance Services). G.N.R. (I.)—ROAD MOTOR SERVICES. Alex. Thom & Co., Ltd., Dublin 11,82.

Stage.	Timing. Booked.	Actual.	Mins. Late.	Cause of Delay.	No. of Passengers.*

Report of Special Occurrences:—

This Journal must be handed by the Conductor to the Bus Checker or Foreman when going off Duty.

*The Number of Passengers in the Omnibus when leaving the Stage to be inserted in this column.

Section (a) to be completed only when the Conductor is collecting the Fares on both Omnibuses. In cases where the Conductor is provided for the duplicating Omnibus, he will prepare a Journal in the ordinary way, clearly indicating that the Journey is "duplicate."

..........Service.

From..........

To..........

..........day..........193....

Fleet No.......... Seating Capacity..........

Motorman..........

Weather..........

If any sporting event or other attraction on route state nature and effect on Traffic.

(a).

Assisted by:—

Fleet No.......... Seating Capacity..........

From.......... To..........

Motorman..........

..........Conductor.

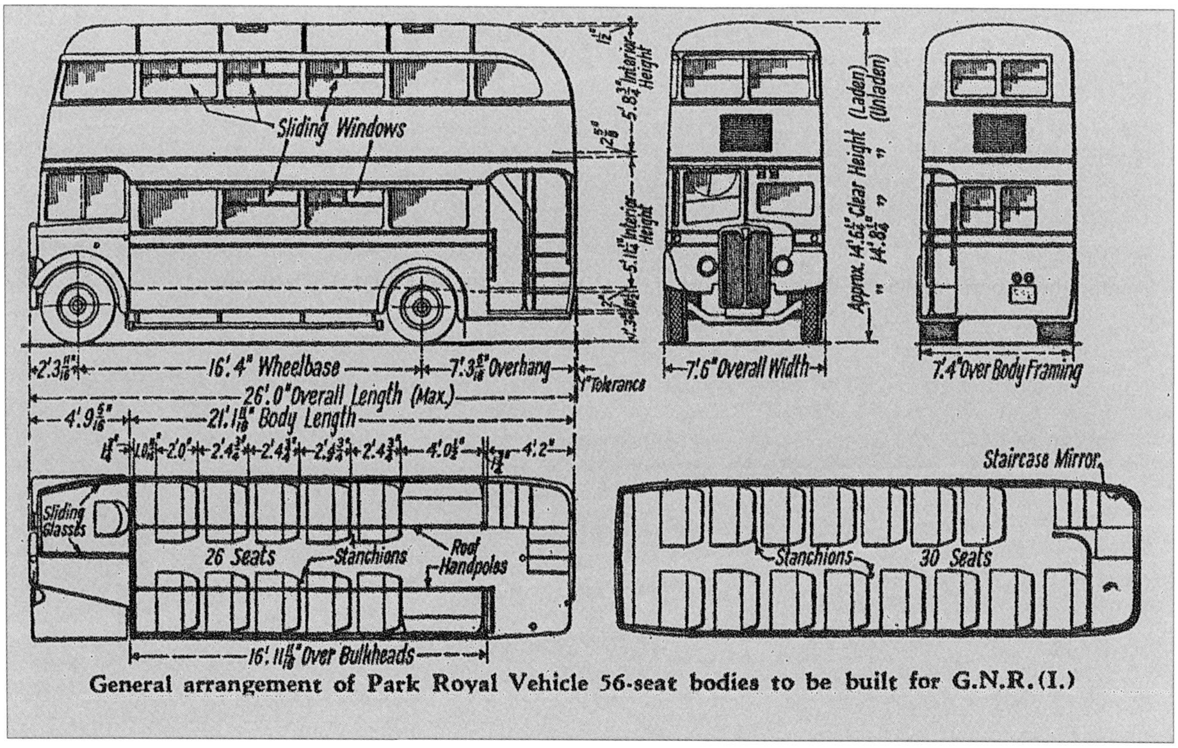

General arrangement of Park Royal Vehicle 56-seat bodies to be built for G.N.R.(I.)

Chapter Eleven
Keeping the Wheels Rolling

Premises

With the Road Motor Services being run as a department of the railway this often led to peculiar arrangements for its management. It was necessary for Road Motor Superintendent Joe Mackle to build an organisation from scratch to ensure effective control of the railway's bus services. Mackle initially ran the service from his office at Amiens Street Station in Dublin, with a branch office in Belfast where his deputy Tom Hutcheson looked after Northern Ireland operations. Mackle was anxious at the outset to ensure he attained compelling supervision. Writing to his Chief Inspector Albert Switzer on 3rd January 1930 he said, "You will, no doubt, appreciate that the unexpected element in inspection is most effective and I am especially anxious regarding the Dublin-Howth, Dublin-Malahide and Belfast-Lurgan services. The timekeeping, cleanliness and courteousness and mechanical efficiency of the vehicles are all important points". In October 1930 the Company decided to take advantage of an offer made by the Great Southern Railway for an examination of the organisation's Road Motor Services by the English Great Western Railway's Road Motor Superintendent Mr FCA Coventry.

Fulwar Cecil Ashton Coventry was born in 1874 and educated at Winchester. In 1893 he entered Swindon Works of the GWR as a pupil. Following a period in the drawing office he was appointed Inspector of Materials. In 1904 he was transferred to the Traffic Department engaged on road motorcar work, which became a well-known branch of the Great Western Railway at that time. In 1912 Coventry was transferred to Paddington as an assistant to the Superintendent of the line. At the end of 1915 he was seconded to the Ministry of Munitions during the Great War for which work he was awarded the Order of the British Empire. In 1922 he was appointed the Superintendent of Road Transport of the GWR and as such was ideally experienced to examine the GNR operation.

Mackle's running of the Road Motor Department was criticised in the report, which suggested that he spend more time in the field. The GNR quickly bought him a car to enable him to travel to rural garages. The report also recommended the establishment of the post of Chief Inspector together with mobile inspectors on motorcycles. In December 1930 Mackle started to introduce many of the recommendations contained in the Coventry document. The control of terminal points in Northern Ireland, especially Belfast and Lurgan, was almost non-existent, leaving the GNR open to the ravages of competition from the Belfast Omnibus Company and others. Various changes were enacted from 15th of December. Albert Switzer was transferred from Dundalk to Belfast and replaced by Inspector J Mulcahy from Dublin. Switzer was appointed Northern Ireland supremo with all Inspectors and Controllers in a subordinate role. Motorman J Tate was appointed temporary Assistant Controller at Belfast. Acting Controller T Walker was transferred from Belfast to Lurgan to assist Controller Henderson. Controller A McCormick was moved from Portadown to Belfast to supervise bus operations from the recently opened Smithfield Bus Station from which the LMS (NCC) permitted the GNR to operate its buses. A mechanic called Quinn at Portadown fulfilled the dual role of mechanic and Controller. Albert Switzer improved the engineering operating co-operation with regular meetings with the Belfast Garage Foreman Mr Jordan, which resulted in a higher standard of efficiency with regard to the mechanical condition of the vehicles.

Joe Mackle resigned from the company on 30th June 1933. He subsequently joined Belfast Corporation Tramways in September 1933 as Superintendent of the Coachbuilding and Motor Omnibus Department. He was made Deputy Acting General Manager during the Second World War. He was appointed General Manager in September 1951, a position held until his retirement in April 1963. After Mackle's departure the GNR decided that the Belfast Traffic Manager James Lockhart would assume ultimate responsibility for the Road Motor Services, with Tom Hutcheson in support. Hutcheson was rewarded with a salary increase to £500 per annum from 14th June 1933 in lieu of being passed over for the Superintendents job.

This arrangement continued until October 1935 when Hutcheson became an employee of the NIRTB. Lockhart continued to manage the Road Motor Services until he suddenly resigned with effect from 31st December 1944. James Lockhart joined the GNR on 1st March 1931 as Traffic Manager in Belfast in succession to WJ Baillie, who retired on 4th June 1931. His retirement was a brief affair as he died a short time afterwards on 31st July 1933.

Lockhart had entered the service of the Caledonian Railway in February 1896 where he gained experience as a booking clerk. He later served in various departments of the District Superintendent's Office in Glasgow. From June 1909 to September 1918 Lockhart was in the service of the Peking – Mukden Railway where he was in charge of passenger audit. In September 1918 he was transferred to the Chinese Ministry of Communications, Peking, as Chief Accountant of the Railway Clearing House. On the collapse of the Peking Government in 1928 Lockhart was transferred to Nanking as an advisor to the 'Through Traffic Administration' attached to the new Chinese Nationalist government, where he was appointed to take charge of the Traffic Department. GNR men regarded Lockhart as somewhat of a 'control freak' as he quickly sought to immerse himself in every aspect of the Company's operations, rail and road.

In 1938 Lockhart was the author of a very comprehensive rulebook containing 254 clauses for the regulation of Road Motor Services in which he coined its motto – 'Courtesy and Comfort with Safety and Service'. Harold Stanley Knott, who was appointed as assistant to Lockhart on 1st August 1944, became the new Traffic Manager later that year following Lockhart's sudden resignation on 31st December 1944. The Great Northern was truly an international railway, operating in the Irish Free State and Northern Ireland. With it came the complexities of operating an integrated bus service whilst operating in accordance with different road transport legislation North and South. Once the Northern Ireland operation passed to the NIRTB it was only a matter of time until the control was passed from Belfast to Dublin.

Initially the bus fleet was maintained at Sheriff Street Garage in Dublin and Grosvenor Street in Belfast with overhauls being carried out at the Dundalk Works. Belfast Garage overhauled buses and lorries in the Northern Ireland fleet until 30th August 1933 when additional space became available at Dundalk to facilitate this. As the services expanded, more and more depots opened to support the operation where mechanics carried out running repairs, mainly at night. By the end of 1930 the Dublin and Belfast facilities were joined by depots in Lurgan (twelve cars), Drogheda (six cars) and Tanderagee (eight cars). Where bus garages were located in railway towns, for example Drogheda, Dundalk, Keady etc, (except Dublin), the Railway Agent exercised nominal supervisory control, but the road motor supervisor received instructions directly from the Head Office in Belfast or Dublin. At smaller garages, which were not controlled directly by Road Motor Supervisory staff, the Railway Agent controlled the working and corresponded directly with Head Office. In the pioneering days of Joe Mackle he set about the task of building and equipping the bus garages and the appointment and training of inexperienced traffic and maintenance staff.

The table below illustrates the growth of GNR Road Motor Service operations during those early Mackle years:–

Date	No. of Buses	No. of Lorries	Bus Route Miles	Annual Route Miles
1 January 1920	Nil	Nil	Nil	Nil
31 December 1929	60	8	535	1508872
31 December 1930	104	33	1021	3639628
31 December 1931	128	49	1406	4079898

Dublin – City Office

During September 1929 the GNR held discussions with Palmolive to lease premises at 9 Eden Quay, two doors up from the well-known temperance Rothesay Hotel at an annual rent of £250. Catherwood's were also intent in leasing this property and finally agreed terms resulting in the GNR being gazumped. Undeterred, the GNR purchased premises at 2 Lower O'Connell Street (then Sackville Street), on 8th January 1930 from John Elliott Scott and William Scott for £7,000. The Office was opened on Monday 28th July 1930, following

The GNR(I) Dublin City Office at 2A Lower O'Connell Street in this 1957 image. The building is now a branch of the Ulster Bank. *(SS)*

renovations to create a general enquiry and passenger booking office for both rail and road services together with an omnibus waiting and cloak room and parcels receiving office, accessed from the rear of the building. The rear entrance was also used by Inspectors and bus crew for access and egress. The property on the corner of O'Connell Street and Eden Quay from where most of the GNR buses departed was known officially as the 'City Office'. It was sandwiched between the Abbey Factory, a frock manufacturing company, who occupied No. 3, and the Ulster Bank still in existence today. The GNR rail terminus of Amiens Street Station could not handle bus departures and was quite a walk from the city centre anyway. Parts of the GNR City Office were periodically leased to other companies. The earliest tenant was the famous Dublin pipe makers Kapp and Peterson, who signed a lease with the GNR for £300 per year. They were still there in 1960. The GNR omnibus advertising contractor WE Magill also rented offices on the first floor of the building. The Company appointed TH Algeo as Controller of Road Motor Services for the Dublin area in 1929; he had his office at the Bureau. Algeo did not enjoy a positive working relationship with his boss Paddy Foley, who was determined to remove him. George Howden, who knew and liked Algeo, intervened despite James Lockhart's objections (Algeo had always been a busman) and appointed him to the position of Stationmaster at Ballinamallard in late 1940.

Dublin Corporation decided to reorganise and regulate bus stands on Eden and Aston Quay. For the first time it imposed restrictions on the number of buses and placed a waiting time limit of 10 minutes for buses to dwell on stands. The new regime came into effect on Monday 22nd May 1939 and was reorganised thus:–

- Eden Quay – (at rear entrance to City Bureau) – Skerries; Drogheda; Dundalk; Monaghan.
- along River Liffey Wall from opposite No. 15 to No. 28 Malahide.
- Opposite Butt Bar/Rothesay Hotel Howth & Portmarnock/ Strand Road.
- Aston Quay – along River Liffey river wall from opposite Bedford Row to Aston Place Kells and Cavan services departed from the GSR stance.

The stands, which were along the River Liffey wall, exemplified a method of working buses that would never be permitted in this day and age. Boarding passengers entered the vehicle not from the footpath but from the roadside, a dangerous endeavour given today's level of traffic, although in 1940 traffic consisted of a few cars, lorries and a large number of bicycles and was considered quite safe. The Corporation again intervened with new arrangements on Monday 28th October 1940, compelling GNR in-bound buses to drop passengers at the Grand Central Cinema in Lower O'Connell Street. Buses were not permitted to pick up passengers from there on the outbound services although this was more convenient than the Eden Quay departure points.

Dublin Garage

The original GNR bus garage in Dublin, established in 1929, was located at the company's Goods Depot on the north side of Sheriff Street adjacent to Amiens Street Station. Sheriff Street so named the result of the building of a prison where French prisoners of war were confined during the period between the Revolution and the fall of Napoleon.

At first buses were parked in the open yard; the only other facility was a Conductors Office, which had been converted from a bicycle storage room in the railway station in May 1929. During July 1930 work began on a long galvanised iron shed, which formed the workshops and was erected at a cost of £3,148. There was a yard and bus wash pad in front of the workshops; opposite were to be found the stables which catered for the cartage horses. Unfortunately due to space constraints, many buses had to be parked overnight on Sheriff Street, a situation the company was to regret given that buses were often stolen. In February 1930 a 3,000-gallon

Another nocturnal view of a GNR garage – this time a 1939 view of Sheriff Street garage with the engineering staff posing for the photographer in the midst of preparing buses for service the following day. The motorcar in this shot was a Dublin Morris 8 staff car, fleet number SC2. *(MC)*

fuel storage tank was installed which allowed deliveries of fuel by rail truck. At the Board meeting in Dublin on 22nd September 1937 the imminent arrival of double-decker buses and the lack of civilised facilities in Sheriff Street prompted them to take up the offer from the LMS Railway for the lease of 1¾ acres of land at Upper Sheriff Street on the corner of Abercorn Road for £150 per annum. Nearly five years later Sheriff Street was closed as a road motor service garage, on the 2nd February 1942, although it remained in use as the base for the Dublin Cartage operations, necessitating conversion funding of £1,500. Johnny Owens, the GNR Clerk of Works on the project to build the new garage, had a budget of £17,599. Wartime premiums for material resulted in an overspend of £3,331 once the final accounts were received by the middle of February 1942.

The new garage, situated at Abercorn Road, opened on 18th October 1941. It was the largest running garage on the system. It consisted of a large concrete yard surrounded by three storage sheds (total capacity 42 vehicles), and a three vehicle washing bay which was equipped with a Hydraforce washing plant supplied by the Dublin firm of Joyce and Brady. The workshops had pit accommodation for 11 vehicles. The latter was of the sunken workshop type. All benching and equipment was at pit level with the exception of the chargehand's, electrician and bodybuilder's shops. The Foreman's office, Motorman's rest room and lavatories were housed in a separate building at one side of the yard. The workshops and storage sheds were constructed in vitreous enamelled corrugated iron and a two-storied spare parts and timber store was housed in one end of one of these sheds, as was a bodybuilder's shop for dealing with British Railways' vehicles.

Dublin garage dealt with a total of between 239 to 261 vehicles (including 27 lorries and 130 trailers belonging to British Railways). A total of 28 lorries and 19 trailers owned by the GNR operated from this garage. The funding of Abercorn Road garage is an interesting tale as the land on which it was built belonged to the LMS Railway. They also provided all of the funding and this was agreed with the GNR as far back as May 1938. A sinking fund charge of £1 15s at 8% for 30 years was agreed. Abercorn Road garage still exists today in the property portfolio of CIE. It does not function as a bus garage and was closed in early 1959 by that company. It enjoyed another use in the early sixties when it was used by CIE as a base to carry out a programme of trafficator fitment on its bus fleet.

Paddy Dillon, the garage charge hand at both Sheriff Street and Abercorn Road garage, lamented the passing of the GNRB more than most employees at the time. When CIE took over they soon discovered that Paddy was then 72 years of age but looked and acted 50 and would have carried on working until he dropped. He was quickly retired by CIE and took up new employment as a fitter in a car garage in Dublin the following day.

Outside of Dublin the GNR could boast several other 'town offices' and garages not all of which were located at or near the local GNR railway station. The first GNR bus garage Joe Mackle had opened was at Skerries on 18th April 1929 when A & J Main Ltd completed the erection at a cost of £266 of a garage measuring 40ft by 29ft designed to accommodate two omnibuses in the railway station yard. It was operated as a sub-depot of Dublin garage and is still in daily use today by Dublin Bus as a 'Dormy Shed' of Summerhill garage.

A trio of GNR Gardners undergoing washing at Abercorn Road Garage before service in 1942. *(RP)*

This view of the interior of the then newly opened Abercorn Road Garage was taken in 1942 with a mixture of Fordson lorries, Leyland LT5A and GNR Gardner buses. *(RP)*

Ballyshannon – Market Yard

This garage was the main focus of GNR operations in County Donegal from 1932 until 1936. An agreement was signed between the company and Michael Cassidy and Robert Sweeney who were collectively known as Ballyshannon Market Yard Trustees, for £50 per annum rent. A garage, waiting room and bus enquiry/parcels office was built in 1933, all of which were of concrete construction. The decision to build this facility followed the acquisition of HMS Catherwood. However in 1936 the GNR garage at Donegal Town became the centre their operations. Three Ballyshannon maintenance staff, Percy Johnston, Jimmy Dixon and Joe McCann were transferred to Donegal Town garage. Ballyshannon garage was retained for routine maintenance purposes and could accommodate four vehicles and there was an inspection pit and wash. Double-deckers stood in the open. Maintenance staff had to travel to Ballyshannon by road from Donegal. The garage was on the north side of the Erne River away from the town's GNR railway station. It was demolished in 1998 to provide a public car park.

Cavan – Farnham Street

This property was leased from AW Gordon (the local Ford Main Agent and original owner of the Magnet Bus Service) on 14th December 1932 and consisted of a small office with a waiting room and parcels office at a weekly rental of £1. Located behind this was a corrugated iron garage with two pits and a total omnibus accommodation for five, opened on 23rd April 1931, over a year before the company took over the tenancy of the bus office. A total of approximately six lorries stationed at Cavan, Ballybay, Cootehill and Clones were maintained at Cavan, together with approximately eight buses that operated the following services:–

- Dublin/Cavan (partly)
- Dundalk/Cavan (partly)
- Cavan/Cootehill
- Cavan/Enniskillen
- Cavan/Ballybay
- Cavan/Oldcastle
- Cavan/Monaghan

During the 1950s Farnham Street became Roger Casement Street, reverting to its original name again about 1960. The bus depot and garage was a quarter of a mile away from the town's railway station, which was on St Patrick's Terrace and was a joint GNR and Midland and Great Western Railway station (later GSR and CIE). The passenger station was the property of the GSR who allowed the GNR to use it. They ran a goods depot and signal cabin at the north side of Railway

This 1956 view at Ballyshannon Garage of AEC Regal IV No. 271, which was based at St Johnson, portrays how it was kept in pristine condition by its regular Motorman and Conductor. *(RG)*

Road. There was not sufficient space available for a bus garage. The GNR bus garage at Farnham Street is still in daily use today by Bus Éireann and has recently been extensively modernised.

Donegal Town

Traver's Commercial Hotel in the Diamond served as the GNR bus departure and arrival point. It serves this purpose today, although it is now known as the Abbey Hotel. The GNR bus garage, which was situated at the County Donegal railway station, was built in 1934 one mile away from the Diamond. Materials began arriving on site from Lambhill Ironworks on 4th April 1934 at a cost of £370 4s 4d. It is a galvanised structure with two pits and a total omnibus accommodation of six. The GNR used some offices in the CDR station building which was in fact owned by a company called Donegal Station Limited, to support the omnibus and road freight operations. The garage itself was rented from the CDR at a peppercorn rent of £1 per annum from the date of opening, which was 4th July 1934. A total of three lorries and a trailer were stationed at Ballyshannon, together with up to eight buses. Seasonal variations saw 17 to 32 buses operated in the Donegal Area from Drumshanbo, Cliffoney, Malinmore, Glenties, Portnoo, Stranorlar, Letterkenny, Grange, Londonderry, St Johnston, Sligo and Pettigo.

Services operated from Donegal Area included:–

- Sligo/Londonderry
- Ballyshannon/Portnoo
- Carrick-on-Shannon/Bundoran
- Ballyshannon/Rosnowlagh
- Killybegs/Malinmore
- Pettigo/Lough Derg
- Ballybofey/Letterkenny
- Sligo/Ballintrillick
- Glenties/Dungloe
- Ardara/Portnoo

The garage still exists today and is largely unchanged except for the fact that all Bus Éireann maintenance is now centred on a new garage at Stranorlar.

Drogheda

Moorland Café West Street was converted in 1933 to a bus office. All services had previously operated from premises at 96/7 West Street, rented from Paddy Callan, which consisted of a small bus office and waiting room for £35 per year effective from 12th February 1930. On 30th April 1937 a parcel office, waiting room and office was rented from a man called Jordan in St George's Square, from where all bus operations were centred, at an annual rent of £10. On 3rd May 1939 the GNR entered into an agreement with Drogheda Harbour Commissioners to lease some land at South Quay, which backed onto the Boyne River. T McDonald & Sons were contracted to build a Bus Office, waiting room and Parcels Office. This facility served Drogheda until the opening of a new Bus Éireann facility on 25th May 1998, at the bottom of the Donore Road. Buses and lorries were initially garaged in the goods yard adjacent to the railway station even after the BAM Bus Service belonging to CM Markey was bought in March 1930. Following the compulsory purchase of Paddy McCloskey's road haulage business on 23rd January 1935, the GNR also took over tenancy of McCloskey's garage from Drogheda Corporation at a rental of £65 per year. At the same

Leyland Royal Tiger PSU1/9 with Saunders Roe Rivaloy body No. 227 seen in 1958 at South Quay Drogheda just after the CIE takeover. *(WM)*

time the road haulage fleet of Thomas Cooney was bought and with it came a lease to a yard in West Street, which was used for a short time to park buses whilst crews were on meal relief. The former McCluskey premises in Scarlet Street were once the town jail and boasted several cells and a horizontal steel rail, which protruded from the front wall, from which convicts were publicly hanged. The garage consisted of a yard and two Garages, the larger of which had two single pits and a total bus capacity of five, but due to the low entrance gates was inaccessible to double-deck machines. The second workshop, having a higher entrance was used for double-deck vehicles (from 25th April 1945), and was provided with one pit, the total bus accommodation being two. A two-bus covered washing bay was situated in the yard, as were the Foreman's office (which was a converted GNR rail carriage) and Motorman's rest room. Accommodation was very limited at Drogheda, as a result a major portion of the lorry fleet lay in the open at the Railway Station.

In the mid-1950s the GNR resisted a consultant's recommendation to close Drogheda garage. The long-serving garage foreman at Drogheda, an Englishman called Charlie Yardley, was the incumbent from the 1930s right through to the 1960s. Charlie, a contemporary of Johnny Owens, was well travelled and a frequent visitor to the Owens house where he would entertain both families with his latest holiday photographs. Charlie, an enthusiastic amateur photographer, claimed that he had a photo of every bus and lorry that worked from the garage during his time there.

Drogheda outstations where lorries and buses were stationed include Navan, Kells, Oldcastle and Ardee. Principal bus services from Drogheda include:–

- Drogheda Town and Local Services
- Drogheda/Mullingar
- Drogheda/Baltray/Togher
- Drogheda/Tenure
- Drogheda/Ardee (partly)
- Dublin/Newry (partly)
- Drogheda/Duleek
- Drogheda/Dromin
- Drogheda/Slane
- Drogheda/Laytown
- Drogheda/Bellewstown

The Scarlet Street bus garage was still in use by Bus Éireann up to October 1999 when it became builder's merchants. Bus Éireann moved to a purpose built facility on the Donore Road Industrial Estate Drogheda about one mile from the current modern bus interchange.

Dundalk– Market Square

The GNR acquired a wooden hut opposite the Courthouse, which backed onto the Market Square. It served as an enquiry and parcels office. Buses departed from either side of Clanbrassil Street, depending on which direction they were headed. HMS Catherwood used an adjacent hut to control their services from Dundalk. In October 1937 the GNR proposed building a new bus station at Douglas Place, however the deal with the property company fell through. In 1938 the Company signed an agreement with R&G Gray to lease some land at Market Square for 90 years at £140 per annum. A purpose built bus station was constructed at a cost of £1,500 with a waiting room, parcels/enquiry office and a six-bus bay, which was opened on 23rd November 1938. The Bus Office required rebuilding following a fire, which

This 1930 postcard view of Market Square Dundalk shows GNR buses on the left parked outside their bus office. The Leyland PLSC vehicles on the right belonged to the competing Catherwood service. *(CMc)*

occurred on 18th January 1954. The centre of Dundalk was redeveloped with EEC funds about ten years ago. The former GNR bus station was demolished and Bus Éireann were relocated to nearby Longwalk. Dundalk garage, situated on Ardee Road and adjacent to the Dundalk Works, general stores, etc, consists of a yard with a main workshop, three vehicle storage sheds, and a single washing bay. The former had a sunken workshop and pit accommodation for seven vehicles, with a bodybuilder's workshop at ground level, the total omnibus accommodation being 31. The original maintenance garage, which also opens onto the main yard and had an accommodation for nine buses, including four pits, was for a period used by the works as a body overhaul shop with the exception of one pitted bay which was used for greasing. Dundalk garage, including bus and lorry out stations at Carrickmacross, Castleblaney, Carlingford, Omeath, Monaghan, and Greenore, maintained 38 vehicles. The main services operated from Dundalk garages were:

- Dundalk Town and Local services
- Dundalk/Ardee (partly)
- Dublin/Newry (partly)
- Dundalk/Drumbilla
- Dundalk/Monaghan and surroundings
- Dundalk/Cavan (partly)
- Dundalk/Omeath

Kilkeel – The Square

This office was taken over from HA Matier's Bus Service on a rental of £1 per week. The one bus, which was allocated to the town, was parked in a small yard about 250 yards away, which had also belonged to Matier.

Londonderry – Lorne Street

This was the first arrival and departure point for GNR buses in the maiden city until 1st May 1934. The office and waiting room was rented from John N Wilkinson from July 1931 at a cost of £31 per year. Lorne Street was short – 67 yards in length; it joined Foyle Street and Princes Quay and was not considered very suitable for buses. Following the closure of the Lorne Street office, buses departed from the front of Foyle Road Railway Station. Arriving buses disgorged their passengers at the side of the station in Foyle Road itself. Buses were garaged in the goods yard adjacent to the station until 1953, when they were housed in the UTA garage.

Monaghan – North Road

This small office, located above the Ulster Bar and accessed from a separate entrance adjacent to the pub, was established in the 1930s and lasted there until 1st March 1954, when it was closed. From the same date operations were relocated to the railway station, although buses continued to serve the existing stands in North Road. A local baronial colonial who owned large tracts of land in County Monaghan and most of the town, the 6th Lord Rossmore, offered to build a new

Unique to the GNR was this AEC Regal II No. 61, purchased new in 1936 and with a body constructed in Dundalk. It was used for evaluation purposes prior to the decision being take to build the GNR Gardners. It is seen in 1950 at South Quay Drogheda. *(JG)*

AEC Regal III No. 416 captured on film on 2nd August 1950 outside the GNR Garage in Armagh Road Monaghan, a structure still standing today. *(JG)*

bus station at Monaghan at his expense, renting the facility back to the GNR on favourable terms. The GNR declined this offer in June 1949 as operations were under review, given the parlous state of the Company's finances. The buses were garaged adjacent to Monaghan railway station goods yard with a separate entrance on the Armagh Road. The garage, a corrugated structure with materials supplied by Smith and Pearson at a cost of £630, was opened on 12th March 1930. In the lock-up garage provision was made for three single-deckers, complete with an inspection pit and wash. During the forties and fifties a Posts and Telegraphs Departmental lorry was garaged in the GNR yard. When CIE moved the buses up to the former railway station in the early sixties the Posts and Telegraphs bought the GNR bus garage. The Garage still exists today almost exactly as it did in the forties in spite of the fact that it is now disused.

Sligo – 14 Quay Street

These premises, which included a small waiting room together with an enquiry and parcels office were formerly the Sligo office of HMS Catherwood. Catherwoods had rented the property for ten years from 1st December 1931. The GNR took over the unexpired lease from Michael O'Hara at a rental of £50 per annum.

This office had an impressive bus departures board mounted on the outside wall of the building and clearly visible from the footpath. A female clerk called Mrs Moore (a former Catherwood employee), and a parcels boy staffed the Bus Office. The premises were bought on 28th April 1943 at auction for £850. The building is still there today although it does not serve any bus-related purposes. The GNR initially commenced bus operations in Sligo around the corner in Wine Street. The company used the IOC garage on the corner of Lord Edward Street and Adelaide Street for overnight parking where its buses invariably stood in an open yard, an arrangement that lasted into CIE days.

Tandragee – Market Yard

A small bus parcels office existed here in the early 1930s which came as a result of the GNR's purchase of the United Motor Service, although this was closed when the NIRTB took over GNR operations. A single bus was also out-stationed at the Banbridge, Lisburn and Markethill Railway Stations.

Bundoran – Main Street

This small office existed for a period of time located beside a building known locally as the 'White House'. It existed in the thirties and was a seasonal (summer only) facility to cater for the inevitable influx of holidaymakers, which the tourist resort enjoyed annually. It is described as being very basic and did not even have a telephone installed. Staff from the nearby railway station manned it. On the 23rd June 1948 the refreshment pavilion at the station was converted into a bus waiting room, parcels office and tea room at a cost of £805.

Rear view of Leyland Lion LT2 No. 150 with 31-seat Stewart bodywork at Grosvenor Street garage Belfast. This bus was written off in a serious collision in 1940. *(WM)*

This view was taken in the dying days of the GNR at Edward Street Newry, showing AEC Regal IV No. 261 with the engine shed providing an interesting backdrop. *(JG)*

Belfast – Queen Street

This was the first pavement terminus for GNR omnibuses in Belfast from 28th March 1929 when the initial Northern Ireland services to and from Lurgan commenced. An omnibus waiting room was established shortly afterwards which lasted until operations were moved. On 1st November 1930 the LMS (NCC) opened a new central bus station at Smithfield in Belfast, which could accommodate 40 plus buses under its main canopy. The GNR had by this time an interavailability ticketing arrangement with the NCC and further negotiated a deal permitting GNR omnibuses to operate from Smithfield bus station in 1931, at an annual cost of £800. This was the earliest manifestation in Ireland of a central bus station. From this date all GNR omnibuses from and to Belfast started and arrived at Smithfield. The outward route from Smithfield was via College Square (North) and Carlisle Street where there were boarding stops. Passengers arriving by GNR omnibuses in Belfast were permitted to alight from them in College Square (East) or Carlisle Street or Smithfield bus station. Buses were not allowed to set down passengers between College Square (East) or Carlisle Street and Smithfield. The GNR garage and works overhaul facility for buses and lorries was established on 23rd October 1929 when a portion of number five railway goods shed at Grosvenor Street was converted at a cost of £520. Specialist tools and equipment to the value of £368 were purchased to establish the operation. In November 1934 the Belfast garage was extended, necessitated by the volume of the road freight and cartage operation in the city. Ironically, less than a year later it was closed and by 8th January 1936 it had been converted to a railway Permanent Way and Electrical Workshops.

Newry Edward Street

A garage was established in Newry on 11th July 1934 when agreement was reached from the Bessbrook and Newry Tramway Company to lease a shed (160ft by 25ft) adjoining Newry Edward Street Goods Yard at a rental of £35 per annum for a bus and lorry garage. Road Motor Services operations were by the middle of 1935 carried out from the following towns and villages (all figures for rent are annual) :–

- Armagh Railway Station
- Aughnacloy – Garage let from George Wright effective from 15th November 1932 for £12.
- Castlederg – Railway Station
- Crumlin Railway Station
- Dungannon – Garage let from Lylburn & Co cost £90, effective from 14th June 1932.
- Enniskillen – premises rented from Mr J McLoughlin effective 28th March 1934 for £25.
- Keady Victoria Street garage let by Mrs Margaret Nugent effective from 23rd March 1933 for £104.
- Kilnaleck – Garage let from Mr PJ Sheridan effective from 22nd December 1932 rental £13.
- Lurgan Railway Goods yard – on the down side of the railway line a 4,000-gallon fuel tank installed in February 1930. An outstation was established at Maghery in 1930.
- Omagh – Corn Market Store converted to a garage in September 1931 at a cost of £1,120.
- Omeath – parking rented from P&M Maguire for £10.
- Portadown Goods Station access from Woodhouse Street.
- Strabane – Railway Station
- Swanlinbar – premises rented from Felix J McGovern effective from 28th March 1934 for £15.
- Warrenpoint Railway Station

The term 'Garage' as used by the GNR was for locations where bus/lorry maintenance was carried out. Each garage inevitably had a number of what were termed depots where buses were parked for traffic reasons, often one bus parked in the street. These subsidiary depots were always tied to a specific garage for maintenance and administrative purposes.

In 1932 such was the proliferation of Garages and Depots that Joe Mackle introduced a Garage coding system for easy identification of Garage or Depot from where buses operated. The code letter was applied to the vehicle just above the fleet number as recorded in official documentation which I have in my possession. The Company also divided the fleet into two distinct operating areas as under:–

Garage Codes Summer 1933

Southern Area & Cross Border Services	Northern Ireland Area
A – Dublin	Q – Newry
B – Portrane	R – Kilkeel
C – Rush	S – Markethill
D – Skerries	T – Tanderagee
E – Drogheda	U – Portadown
F – Kells	V – Lurgan
G – Kilnaleck	W – Belfast
H – Dundalk	X – Diamond
I – Ballybay	Y – Dungannon
J – Cootehill	Z – Omagh
K – Ardee	AA – Castlederg
L – Cavan	AB – Strabane
M – Belturbet	AJ – Maghery
N – Carrickmacross	AN – Lisburn
O – Monaghan	AO – Banbridge
P – Keady	AR – Ballybofey
AC – Londonderry	
AD – Donegal	
AE – Ballyshannon	
AF – Bundoran Great Northern Hotel	
AG – Pettigo	
AH – Sligo	
AI – Enniskillen	
AL – Aughnacloy	
AM – Omeath	

People

GNR drivers were called 'Motormen' and staff always referred to buses as 'cars', designations grafted from the Hill of Howth Tramway, which persisted right to the very end. New traffic staff were invariably taken on as bus cleaners, thereafter progressing to a Motorman/Cleaner a sort of relief person before becoming an established Motorman or Conductor. Motormen were responsible for filling their vehicles with fuel, oil and water. They also changed their own wheels if a puncture or other tyre failure occurred whilst the vehicle was *en route*. A spare wheel, jack and handle was carried on every vehicle. A basic tool kit, which was contained in a leather roll up pouch for minor running repairs, tyre changes etc. was kept on each vehicle in a locked box, a key being kept in another smaller box with a glass front. This was wired with a lead seal and the Motorman was instructed to break the glass to obtain access to his tools. There was a nightly check on all seals. These tool kits were bought in June 1931 at a cost of £1 2s each.

Each Motorman had to complete a daily report card on the mechanical condition of every vehicle driven. This report was kept in a specially fitted holder on the door of the driver's cab. The Motorman was also responsible for filling in details of each day's mileage, fuel taken and tyres changed. The completed card was handed into the agent at the nearest station for forwarding to the Road Motor Superintendent's Office. In garages and the works great care was taken to ensure that each job performed on a bus was correctly costed. Every job, whether it was a repair, dock or overhaul was given a job number, and two loose leaf sheets were kept, one for the work done and the other for the materials used.

From 1st November 1934, the responsibility for Motormen passed from the Traffic Department to the Mechanical Engineer's Department as a result of Joe Mackle's departure. Conductors continued under the control of the Traffic Department. The company started to issue uniforms to its entire road motor service traffic staff from October 1929. The costs of the uniforms were recovered by weekly deductions from employee's wages. The uniform issue consisted of a double-breasted navy blue tunic with chrome buttons, and pants each year. A navy blue greatcoat was issued every two years, as was a peaked cap. The lapel of the tunic and greatcoat bore the legend 'GNRI' in embroidered silver lettering. The grade of the uniform wearer was displayed on the cap, again embroidered silver lettering, eg 'Motorman' 'Conductor' or 'Inspector', whichever was applicable. Motormen and Conductors worked a 48-hour week. Overtime and Sunday working attracted a premium payment of time and a quarter, meal breaks were unpaid. The Federation of Irish Rail and Road Workers Trade Union, which was recognised by the GNR, continually pressed for improvements in working conditions throughout the years. Eventually double-deck drivers enjoyed a premium of one shilling and sixpence a week by 1948. Parity of pay and conditions with comparable grades in CIE was initially achieved at the formation of the GNRB but was quickly eroded. Motorman and Conductor's rosters were compiled and produced for all staff on the system by Road Motor Assistant Jack Lambert, a full-time job given that these had to be revised and reissued with each new timetable or service revision. The head office received daily reports of all the work of each vehicle in the fleet through Inspectors located at principal garages. These reports gave the arrival and departure of every service showing the appointed and actual times. Appended to this document Inspectors also attached their daily reports showing the condition of 'cars' arriving during the day, an explanation of late departures and arrivals, and particulars of any overcrowding. Inspectors also carried out a wide variety of other duties including mobile revenue protection, supervising special events and carrying out garage supervision tasks.

Inspectors used motor-cycle and sidecar combinations from 1929 through to the mid 1930s for mobile work. Rudge/Whitworth 4hp combinations were bought by the company for about £95 each. They were an effective and efficient method of getting Inspectors to the more remote areas of the operation. On Monday 9th June 1930 one such combination, registration number ZI 3802, driven by Motorcyclist P O'Hagan, with Acting Controller T Algeo in the sidecar, was involved in an accident at Lisdoonan Cross, resulting in the machine being written off. The work of every vehicle was graphically shown by two charts, which were kept by the District Manager in Dublin (and the Traffic Manager Belfast prior to 1935). One showed the progressive weekly mileage of each car and when it was docked and overhauled, while the other showed the fuel and oil consumption. In this way the senior management knew exactly what each vehicle was doing on each day.

In the Road Motor Office at Amiens Street Station Joe Robinson prepared highly detailed and complex car workings covering all the garages and depots on the GNR system. Joe enjoyed a reputation as a meticulous and diligent member of staff who took a particular interest in ensuring that garages operated a full service, all day everyday. His encyclopaedic knowledge of the car rosters ensured that he was able to suggest ingenious permutations of the rosters, thus ensuring that garages operated at maximum efficiency. Within the car working rosters buses often interworked with others. An example of this kind of working is roster number 128 from Belturbet garage. This bus would work the 08.10am service to Dublin, arriving there at noon, leaving the capital again at 1.40pm, arriving back at Belturbet at 5.15pm. It would then work a service back to Dublin again at 6.05pm, arriving at 9.50pm. Crew changes would take place on the road at crossing points with vehicles coming in the opposite direction. Dublin garage bus on roster number 15 would operate the balancing working ending up at Belturbet at 10.10pm. These cars were often referred to as 'rotating cars' and a special watch had to be kept on them, to ensure they were made available for the engineering department to carry out essential maintenance.

Chief Inspector Albert Switzer

Albert Leonard Switzer re-joined the GNR at Dundalk (he had been previously employed as a messenger before 1914), in 1929 as a Road Motor Inspector on a weekly salary of £3 per week. He had previously worked for the Imperial Bus Service, as an Inspector, which had its Head Office at 15-23 Cuba Street, Belfast. During his time at the Imperial he was remembered for his establishment of a bus conductor's training school, the introduction of conductors' waybills and a ticketing system for the Imperial's Belfast City Services. He played a prominent role in the management of the Imperial's Belfast service which ran from Balmoral in the south of the city to Strandtown in the east end competing with Belfast City Tramways. This was at a time when the Belfast bus war was at its height and eventually ended on 17th December 1928. Albert Switzer was descendent from Palatine stock that came to Ireland in 1709 from the Rheinland Pfalz (the Palatinate) in Southwestern Germany. The Palatines, as they became known, fled religious persecution (they were in the main Methodists, although Albert was a Presbyterian) and hardship. They established roots in Counties Kerry, Limerick, Tipperary and Wexford but mainly in the Rathkeale area of County Limerick. Albert was born in Milltown, a quaint mill village near Shaws Bridge on the southern outskirts of Belfast on 30th January 1898. He first donned a uniform whilst in the Boys Brigade in 1908 as a member of 1st Drumbo Presbyterian Church Company. At the age of 16 young Albert put on another uniform, as he went to serve King and Country in the battlefields of Europe. He was awarded the Military Medal in October 1916. Albert's wartime service is remembered even today by the presence of his name on the war memorial of Great Victoria Street Presbyterian Church, Belfast where he was a member.

Chief Inspector Albert Switzer. *(AS)*

He was a protégé of Joe Mackle, with whom he shared a common army background. Although Albert did not take up his appointment until Monday 13th May 1929, he travelled to Dublin with Mackle on the 7.45am train from Belfast the previous Friday to familiarise himself with the GNR's Dublin operations. He booked in to lodgings at 61 Lower Gardner Street, owned by a Mrs Powderley. On Wednesday 15th May Mackle and Switzer were in Howth monitoring the activities of two independent bus operators, who were jointly affecting railway revenues on the Howth branch. They retired to the St Lawrence Hotel opposite Howth Station to consider how they could best combat the effects of the independents. Following the departure of Mackle, Albert reported directly to the James Lockhart, Traffic Manager in Belfast and in later years to the Dublin based District Superintendent.

Albert Switzer was recognised for three distinct contributions to the development of the Road Motor Services. Firstly he effectively diminished the detrimental effects of competition from the Belfast Omnibus Company, by the deployment of anti-competition buses in the Lurgan/Banbridge/Dromore areas until the arrival of the GNR railcar for the Scarva Branch. He also put in place the arrangements at Pettigo for the large volumes of pilgrims who came by rail to be transferred to Lough Derg by GNR bus, making his first visit to the frontier village on 31st May 1929. Again, during the Second World War emergency he was in charge of all the GNR's Air Raid Precautions. He carried out staff training, travelling throughout the GNR system in his specially adapted railway coach. George Howden, writing to Albert Switzer on 25th May 1939 informed him that he had obtained a First Class Certificate in an ARP Instructor's Course.

Thirdly, he was often sent out on 'cloak and dagger' missions to gather intelligence on the activities of independent bus operators. I have many such reports in front of me as I write this. The value of such reports can be realised when one appreciates that but for Albert's intensive investigations having been committed to paper between the thirties and fifties, there would be a considerable void in our knowledge of the period.

After the wartime emergency Albert assumed the important function of co-ordinator for all service planning. The GNR operated two timetables each year, one summer, one winter. Prior to the introduction of a new timetable or when a public holiday was due, representative Inspectors from each garage would be invited to Albert's office in Amiens Street. They would discuss and agree service levels, car workings, tours, school workings and specials. The Road Motor Assistants would then produce and distribute the workings to the garages for implementation. New services were planned from Amiens Street with input from local Superintendents, Inspectors and Station Masters, the final authority to proceed coming from the District Superintendent. Albert was the archetypical embodiment of someone with a very strong work ethic. He was the epitome of a bygone era in the conduct of affairs with his subordinates. His reputation for ensuring safe, reliable and efficient bus operations by the GNR was acclaimed the length and breadth of its territory. He saw out his time with the GNR, continuing to serve his new master in the form of CIE until finally retiring on 31st August 1959 when he returned to his native Belfast; not to retire though!

Albert was firstly employed as a Temporary Ship Inspector by the Northern Ireland Ministry of Agriculture between August 1959 and January 1963. His final job was that of an Inspector with the Ulster Society for the Prevention of Cruelty to Animals, serving in this capacity until the day he passed away. He suffered a fatal heart attack on May 25th 1977, after which he was buried in Roselawn Cemetery aged 79. His loyal co-operation with the strategy devised by the GNR and his extensive knowledge of road passenger working on the ground was second to none. By common acclaim he was one of the great GNR Officials and a real hero of the struggle to keep the company alive.

General

Destination displays

The GNR standard in respect of destination displays was a single line display at the front, replicated on the nearside, mounted at the high point of the window bay immediately forward of the entrance doors (or on the roof cantrail on the AEC Regal IVs) single-deckers. Buses did not have a rear display. Provincial double-deck vehicles had a single line display at the front and rear, whilst vehicles used in the Dublin area exhibited an ultimate destination with characters 4in high and a three line intermediate display with 3in high characters. The only deckers with a side display were the 'British' buses 433-9. The GNR did not use route or service numbers. Destination blinds were produced using alphabetical listing of displays for the Dublin, Louth, Meath, and Cavan areas; separate blinds were fitted to the buses in the Sligo/Donegal area. Motormen and Conductors complained about this practice, citing the example of the Cavan to Virginia service, where at either end of the route staff had to rewind to almost the opposite end of the blind, which could have been 40ft long. Destination slip boards were utilised on all the early vehicles right up to and including the first four GNR Gardners produced in 1937. The practice ceased thereafter and died out progressively from about 1940.

Timetables

Omnibus timetables were first issued from 1929 and consisted initially of double-sided card showing details of a particular service or group of services. Composite timetables, of which there were four distinctive versions, were issued from February 1931 until October 1958 as described below:–

February 1931-July 1932 – a plain turquoise cover bearing the motto 'GNR Omnibus Time Table' the issue date and General Manager's name contained details of all road services. Each service was given a number (discontinued at the end of 1931) despite the fact that this detail never appeared on the buses themselves. Advertising by a wide range of companies assisted with production costs.

July 1932-January 1933 – the same style of cover now received the Oxford Blue treatment, as more advertisements were strategically placed adjacent to a local traders neighbourhood bus timetable on the opposite page.

January 1933-September 1947 – the Oxford Blue cover now received a makeover as the attractive GNR crest was incorporated. The timetable layout improved dramatically with the inclusion of table numbers for easy reference and most importantly train/bus through connections were for the first time shown thus providing passengers with co-ordinated information.

May 1948-October 1958 – a completely new cover blended a photograph of GNR AEC Regent bus number 286 superimposed over GNR in large lettering surmounted by a sketch of a rural scene and represented the final version of GNR bus timetable. From September 1952 a comprehensive bus and rail map was attached to the inside back cover.

Sunday services were printed in red ink to distinguish them from weekday times from 13th April 1947 – the practice ceasing with the issue of the timetable dated 20th June 1955.

Non-GNR advertising in timetables ceased in August 1941 as a result of emergency strictures; a year later a charge of one (old) penny was applied each bus timetable and by 1958 this had increased to 3d.

Advertising

The buses themselves carried adverts internally and externally. The internal adverts were normally bill posted on the side windows in the uppermost portion of the glass. Double-deck vehicles often had bills posted on the upper saloon front windows, again in the uppermost part of the glass. An advertising contractor Messrs International Services was first appointed in 1929 sharing profits with the GNR on a 50/50 basis until the contract was terminated on the 30th April 1932. Advertising was an important source of additional revenue for the company and as such every inch of available vehicle space was utilised for this purpose. One early advertiser who caused more than his fair share of controversy was Victor Fiorentini, who advertised his Strand Road Londonderry ice cream parlour in the GNR bus timetable. Mr Fiorentini was the Italian born secretary of the Fascist Party in Derry. He became embroiled in damaging publicity when he met Benito Mussolini on New Year's Day 1934, following which he was not permitted to advertise in GNR publications.

On 4th August 1932 WE Magill was appointed as the Company's advertising contractor for a two-year period, on the basis that he kept 20% of all the net revenue. Magill operated from the third floor GNR offices at 2, Lower O'Connell Street Dublin. Unfortunately for Magill and the GNR, he went bankrupt in June 1937, leaving a trail of debts behind him including large sums owed to the Great Northern. Robert Y Slaughter & Co, who had offices in Howard Street Belfast and St Andrew's Square Edinburgh, were appointed to take over this contract, which they held until 1958.

The GNR made prodigious use of the handbill to publicise special services or excursions or for purposes of announcing new services etc. The handbills were often on display in bus offices and railway stations. Invariably, conductors would carry supplies of current handbills to give to interested passengers. Timetables, farecharts and other information posters were applied in the lower saloon of GNR buses on the centre of the front bulkhead in accordance with legislation. The GNR Williamson bus tickets also carried advertising on the reverse side. A noted bus enthusiast and the son of a GNR conductor, John Curran, recalls his Dublin childhood memories of GNR bus advertising thus: "Mention of advertisements reminds me that GNR buses normally carried different ads to CIE buses with certain exceptions, such as the larger companies like the cigarette, food and drink manufacturers. Some advertisers, such as Kennedy's Bread and C&C (Club Orange) had different ads for both GNR and CIE. I was always fascinated by the ads for strange products such as McCann's Bread of Dundalk and other 'parochial' ads on GNR double-deckers, which travelled long distances into Dublin, unlike CIE's double-deckers, which were confined to that geographic area. The rear ads on double-deckers were positioned centrally on certain classes of buses across the lower saloon rear emergency door and on others to the extreme right, not cut in half by the door. Another common feature of GNR buses was the small oval ads on each rear upper deck corner panel. This was a rare feature on CIE buses"

Tickets and Fares

Joe Mackle established the Road Motor Services ticketing arrangements through the Ashton-Under-Lyne supplier Williamsons, which produced 5,237,000 omnibus tickets and 5460 monthly tickets as well as 4,200 parcels tickets on 10th April 10th 1929 at 11½d per 1,000. Mackle also hired 85 Williamson Punch machines at 12s 6d per annum and bought 92 ticket boxes, ticket holders and 45 ticket nippers to get things up and running.

There was a vast array of the Williamson pre-printed tickets in 1d stages to about 8s 0d cancelled by conductors using the Williamson Punch machines. Return tickets were over printed with a red 'R' with the value underneath. The proliferation and complexity of the GNR tickets resulted in the innovative character of the company coming to the fore in 1948 when it was decided to adopt a new ticketing system.

The Setright Company of Hackney Wick London had introduced a new ticket machine, which used a continuous ticket roll and was capable of printing tickets of multiple value and type. On 10th September 1948 the first 30 of the new machines were delivered to Dundalk. The model, known as the 'Setright Speed', were the first of a total of 170

Adverts were hand painted, as illustrated by this 1934 view of Leyland LT5A 301 having the Switzers department store advert applied to the roof luggage rack at Sheriff Street garage. This bus was rebodied in 1936 following a severe accident in Dublin. *(MC)*

such machines leased from Setright for the annual sum of £9 7s 8d, the order being completed at the end of January 1950. They were serially numbered 001-170 and were the very first such machines to see service with any bus operator in Ireland. One machine delivered to the GNR on 25th October 1948, number 027 was used at Finaghy Station near Belfast on the busy Lisburn commuter line. Due to the intensity of boarding passengers in the morning peak into Belfast the company needed a machine capable of issuing tickets at high speed. This machine was returned to CIE by the UTA on 24th February 1959. The Setright Speed machine was introduced by CIE in January/February 1957, some nine years after the GNR introduced theirs. During mid-May to the end of August 1958 twelve TIM ticket machines were hired from CIE by the GNR for Dublin based services. The GNRB went to the trouble and expense of having 12 printing plates for these machines manufactured by TIM at Cirencester England. The Donabate bus continued to be worked by Conductors using the Williamson pre-printed tickets right up to the take over by CIE. During 1959 CIE replaced the ex-GNR machines with new CIE machines and returned the hired GNR machines to Setright Registers. Bus conductors could pay in at any GNR railway station, thus eliminating the need to have dedicated staff for this purpose at bus garages. The Road Motor Services also had a very healthy parcels business and lucrative newspaper distribution contracts with the Irish Times, Independent and Press newspapers, all of which were printed in Dublin and distributed by GNR buses throughout the operating area.

A surprising development occurred during November 1939 in the Donegal area. The GNR issued bi-lingual fare charts for the Sligo/Londonderry service, which were displayed on buses and notice boards. Undoubtedly the large number of Irish speakers in the Gaeltacht area of West Donegal, many of whom would have been natural GNR customers, influenced this laudable development. The significance of this advancement is underscored by the fact that the 1924 Railways Act, which established the Great Southern Railway through amalgamation, imposed upon it a requirement for bilingual signage and tickets. There was no such legal requirement imposed upon the GNR or any of the other cross-border companies such as the CDR, Lough Swilly, DNGR and SL&NCR. Neither was there any such requirement imposed upon bus operators under the Road Transport Act 1932. However, one of the standard conditions of a passenger road service licence under that Act stipulated that 'where the route, or any stage of the route, of the service in respect of which this licence is granted is situated within the Gaeltacht the conductors employed shall be capable of discharging their duties in the Irish language'. The following year section 120 of the Road Transport Act mandated that bus operators had to adopt a policy of bilingualism, which apart from the GSR was universally ignored. The GNR translations into the Irish language were according to the noted Irish language scholar CB Mac tSaoir rather 'school boyish' and were merely a token effort in adapting to the realities of modern Irish life, for example the 'Great Northern Railway of (Ireland) Road Motor Services Londonderry-Sligo Route: Fares List' became *'bothar iarainn Tuaisceart Éireann – Cursai Bus Doire – Sligeach : Tailli'*, to which General Manager George Howden appended his Irish name and title as *Seoirse B Howden Bainisteoir I Gcoiteinne (Seoirse B Howden Bainisteoir I Gcoiteinne).*

GNR Vehicle Engineering

Vehicle engineering standards in the GNR were widely acknowledged to be among the best in the country, far superior to that of any of its contemporaries The Chief Mechanical Engineer, based at Dundalk, controlled the engineering arrangements for the Road Motor Services. He did this through Jack Rogers, a native of Antrim town who became the Road Motor Superintendent in charge of engineering, who monitored the overhaul and docking programme throughout the company. His colleague Bobby Pelissier was responsible for visiting garages to carry out maintenance audits, and offer technical assistance, such was the attention to detail that was paid to vehicle engineering. Each vehicle allocated to a garage was docked on a mileage basis to a programme drawn up in the Road Motor Office in Dundalk by Chief Clerk Harold Ritchie in accordance with the under noted schedule:–

Description	Single-deck Vehicles	Double-deck Vehicles
First dock overhaul	30,000 miles	45,000 miles
Second dock overhaul	60,000 miles	-
Complete overhaul (Loco)	90-100,000 miles	90-100,000 miles

Dock and complete overhauls to lorries were carried out at 30,000 and 60,000 miles respectively. Each garage foreman submitted a weekly mileage return in respect of each vehicle so that Dundalk's records and planning boards could be updated and thereby monitored. Some garages carried out overhauls and repaints of vehicles locally such as Donegal, Drogheda (both of whom had very good garage painters) Dublin (Abercorn Road) and Dundalk Garage. Full repaints were generally carried out in 5-year cycles with half repaints every 2 – 3 years. Donegal buses were invariably distinguished by the application of additional cream flashing on the vehicle sides which resulted in them standing out among buses from other garages and were always in first class paint condition. Overhauls at Dundalk works, which usually took four weeks per vehicle, were carried out at intervals of between 90,000 and 100,000 miles. This was referred to as a 'loco overhaul' and normally consisted of an engine top end reconditioning; axles, suspension, steering, chassis and body were all inspected and overhauled as necessary. Any damaged trim was repaired or replaced and paintwork refreshed. In the 1930s and 40s buses undergoing loco overhaul were often rebodied or received transplanted bodies from other buses, a system the GNR christened 'body interchange'. When a bus left Dundalk to return to a garage after loco overhaul it was like a new vehicle, along similar lines to London Transport's Aldenham 'Works Annual Service Programme', albeit on a much smaller scale. The GNR entered into a contract with Simms Motor Units Ltd on the 26th March 1931 for the maintenance of all magnetos on buses and lorries. For some reason vehicles in Northern Ireland were charged £2 10s 0d per year, 5s 0d less

AEC Regent No. 67 undergoing maintenance at Abercorn Road garage soon after it was opened in 1942. *(RP)*

than vehicles based in the Irish Free State. Irish Dunlop also entered into a contract with the company for the provision of all pneumatic tyres from the 2nd April 1931; this lasted right up to end of the GNR.

The company had two six wheeled flat wagons, Nos. 8503/4, which were used to convey single-deck buses by rail to and from garages and the works for overhaul and repair. Further explanation for the introduction of these wagons, that entered service on 9th May 1934, was the policy of circumventing the imposition of temporary import duty when transferring buses from Dundalk to the Donegal area through Northern Ireland. Buses were loaded onto the rail wagons at Traffic Place Dundalk, just across the road from the bus garage, where they were conveyed by train to Ballyshannon. This journey by rail entailed crossing into Northern Ireland, where the authorities regarded the cargo as being 'Free to Free' (from one part of the Irish Free State to another) and as such exempt from duty. To conform to loading gauge restrictions roof mounted luggage racks were designed to fold down flat. Bodybuilders would remove the four retaining bolts from the front and rear sections and these would be stored inside the vehicle. The two side sections, which were hinged, would be folded inwards flush with the roof.

Garage Tenders

Garages had staff cars attached to them, which they were responsible for maintaining. Additionally each had Garage Tenders allocated for attending to breakdowns. The company had serious concerns about the condition of the roads in counties Monaghan, Cavan and Donegal from the commencement of bus and lorry operation, right through until the CIE take-over. They lobbied the county councils heavily to make improvements in the standards, with very limited success. Adverse cambers, potholes and poor road surfaces, together with inadequate vehicle headlamps for night driving gave rise to the high level of vehicles that ran off the road. The Garage Tender was very much a feature of GNR engineering operations, as can be seen from the table below. In 1957 the company had no less than nine such tenders. Most of these vehicles originated as GNR service buses – after withdrawal they were taken into Dundalk works where they had their bodies cut down and were fitted with a gantry for recovery purposes.

It is worth mentioning here tender No. 6, which was based in Dundalk. It began its career with the GNR as a Leyland Lion LT2 fleet No. 110, entering service in 1930. It was one of the vehicles that went to Northern Ireland in 1941 to assist the NIRTB. In 1945 it was renumbered 271 and fitted with a Gardner 4LW engine and converted to a lorry for the road freight department, gaining another new number, 150. In 1949 it was converted to a garage tender No. 6 and was unique in GNR history by virtue of having a de-mountable wooden container, which housed 'tick tock' winch equipment, hydraulic jacks and cables, designed to aid recovery of

vehicles which had left the road. By the time CIE took over it had been officially scrapped by the GNR in 1958 and was parked up inside the Road Motor Garage on the Ardee Road at the very back of the shed. In 1971 I recall seeing this vehicle in Dundalk Garage in its dust laden Oxford Blue GNR livery. Garage Foreman Paddy Hardy told me that it had been forgotten about after the GNR was taken over by CIE; in that same year it went to the National Transport Museum collection where it is today.

The extract below shows the disposition of staff cars, garage tenders and trade plates for January 1957:–

Staff Cars, Garage Tenders & Trade Plates			
Garage	Staff Cars Fleet numbers	Garage Tenders Fleet numbers	Trade Plates
Dublin	6, 9, 15	1, 4	Dublin Garage : 068 IY
Drogheda	11	11	Drogheda Garage: 050 IY
Dundalk	8, 10, 14	2, 3, 6, 12	Dundalk Garage: 022 IY
Donegal	4	5	Dundalk Works: 021 IY
Cavan		9	Donegal Garage: 028 IY
Untaxed	1, 2, 3, 5, 7		

On 11th March 1948 Road Merchandise Superintendent Ivor McCullough bought a Linn Catruk C5 tractor manufactured in Morris, New York from a dealer called George Hamill of Portadown, for £987. The vehicle had been left in Northern Ireland by the United States Navy following the end of the Second World War. This vehicle, unique in Ireland, was powered by a six-cylinder 45hp Cadillac side-valve petrol engine, the drive being taken through a gearbox

In this 1930 view of the interior of Sheriff Street Garage it should be noted that the Leyland Tiger TS2 (No. 87) nearest the camera was the first bus with GNR Dundalk Works Body. *(MC)*

having five forward and two reverse ratios. The Linn was capable of driving in a variety of combinations on the front wheels and/or caterpillar half-tracks and coupled to a tandem axle of moderate loading height. There was conventional semi-elliptic springing on the front axle, but the rear tractor axle was unsprung. It was held in position by means of two swinging shackles attached to the chassis ahead of the axle, and two elbow type arms attached directly above the centre line, the position of the latter being controlled by a hydraulic ram driven off the power take off. Under ordinary conditions the vehicle was capable of hauling loads of 30-40 tons with ease while utilising the normal drive and in cases where it was found necessary to travel over soft ground such as fields, lanes and building sites it was only necessary for the driver to raise the rear wheels (which did not drive) and engage a suitable track ratio. The half-track 'Linn' was allocated fleet No. 169 and was the ideal 'off road' recovery vehicle and heavy machinery mover. The Linn was kept inside the Road Motor Garage at Drogheda under the control of Paddy McCloskey. It was particularly useful for recovering GNR vehicles that had ended up in a field or ditch and on a few occasions was used to pull buses out of rivers. The vehicle was scrapped by CIE in 1959.

New GNR Gardner No. 326 loaded onto railtruck 8504 in January 1942 for conveyance to Ballyshannon where it will be used in the Donegal area. *(DN)*

Garage Tender No. 1 based at Abercorn Road had been converted in 1949 from a Leyland Tiger TS2 (No. 276), which started life with HMS Catherwood. *(RG)*

Livery

The GNR livery originally started life as a lighter shade of blue for the vehicle sides with a cream roof. The AEC Reliance vehicles were delivered in 1929 bearing the lettering 'Great Northern Railway (I) ' below the window line, this was later shortened to 'Great Northern'. A *'GNRI'* monogram was applied to both vehicle sides at a mid point along the lower body, a practice shared with the Hill of Howth Tramcars. Early GNR Reliances, Lions, Albions and Dennis buses had slip boards fitted to their sides giving principal stopping points *en route*. It was in 1934 that the Oxford Blue and Cream became firmly established as the definitive livery. By now the GNRI Coat of Arms started to appear in an 18in transfer affixed to each side of the body. The 'Great Northern' lettering in red with black shadow was applied to all vehicles up to 1948. The AEC Regal III and IV vehicles and the four Royal Tigers never had this lettering applied. Conversely in 1956 when the GNRB bought the six former CIE Leyland TD5 double-deckers all five that entered service had the 'Great Northern' lettering applied. Many AEC Regal IV vehicles entered service with no coat of arms applied, due to a shortage experienced in the mid 1950s.

Another aberration of the official GNR livery occurred in the Donegal area which began as a result of a wartime livery instruction, which saw all single-deck buses having white paint applied to the edges of the front and rear wheel arches and mudguards. White lines were painted along the front of mudguards and included the dumb irons. The rear skirt panels also had the same white line treatment, designed to improve all round visibility. Danny O'Donnell, the Donegal garage painter, perpetuated a variation of the wartime livery, adding a thin cream coach line around the waistrail and a shadow cream line below the cream flashes applied to the vehicle sides. This unofficial Donegal livery applied to all vehicles maintained in the area, and lasted right into CIE days – as long as Danny O'Donnell continued as the Donegal painter in fact. This caused many observers to claim that buses seen after the war ended were still in wartime livery. Of course this was not true they were simply seeing the enigmatic Donegal livery. As soon as the Great Northern Railway Board was established in 1953 a modified coat of arms was applied to vehicles.

Accidents

By May 1934 the costs of providing insurance for the omnibus fleet, which had been steadily escalating, resulted in the company taking its business from the Ocean Accident and Guarantee Corporation to the Eagle Star with effect from 1st June. The relative cost of insuring a 32-seat bus on a third party and passenger basis was:–

- Irish Free State – £36 13s 4d pa with a £25 excess
- Northern Ireland – £13 5s 2d pa with a £10 excess

George Howden was concerned at the increasing costs of insuring the fleet and the level of accidents. During the summer of 1935 whilst on holiday in Scotland he contacted the Manager of Glasgow Corporation Tramways, which then operated about 400 buses. The Glasgow Manager put Howden in touch with his Claims Superintendent who in turn explained to him the bonus scheme that they operated. The scheme entailed each driver receiving a bonus of 1s 0d per week for every 26 weeks of accident free driving with an additional bonus of £2 for every two consecutive 26-week clear periods.

Howden laid before the GNR Board on 15th February 1936 a proposal to introduce an accident free bonus scheme, along the lines of the Glasgow system. The board, having considered Howden's proposals, introduced the scheme with effect from 1st March 1936. Initially it applied only to the 79 permanent and 88 temporary Omnibus Motormen. The success of the scheme was such that by April 1937 Howden obtained Board approval to extend the scheme to cover lorry drivers and the issuing of safe driving badges to omnibus drivers who had successfully completed three 26-week accident free periods. By 1939 accidents had decreased by 27% and the costs thereof had declined by 51% since 1936.

A catastrophe visited the GNR in the early hours of Sunday 14th July 1940 at Rowans, three miles from Balbriggan. Motorman Patrick McGuinness from Drogheda garage was driving an eleven-year-old AEC Reliance, bus No. 32, from Dublin to Gormanstown with 21 soldiers from the 11th Infantry Battalion Irish Army on board. At a foggy Balrothery straight McGuinness saw the headlights of an approaching car. As the car got closer McGuinness realised

Unique in Ireland, this ex-United States Navy Linn Catruck C5 (No. 169) half-track and trailer used by GNR for specialist recovery and machinery moving. ***(SS)***

that it was heading straight towards him on the wrong side of the road. Unable to take avoiding action he braked sharply bracing himself for the inevitable collision. In the aftermath of the collision the scene was described as appalling. The groans of the injured brought crowds to the spot. Sergeant PJ Walsh of Balbriggan told how he arrived about 20 minutes after the accident to find that only one of the six occupants of the car, 20-year old Nora O'Donoghue was alive, but she died minutes later. Twenty soldiers were taken to St Brecin's Military Hospital in army ambulances, ten of whom were detained for treatment. Motorman McGuinness was taken to the Mater Hospital suffering from leg and back injuries. The six people killed in the car, which was returning from a 'scavenger hunt'; organised by the Gormanstown Junior Aviation Club, which began at 6.00pm, had concluded with a dance in a Bettystown Hotel. The car was owned by the President of the Irish Rugby Football Union, Mr John Warren, and was being driven by his 23-year old son of the

A close-up of the Caterpillar tracks on the Linn recovery vehicle. *(SS)*

The Linn in action – an unidentified AEC Regal III ran off the road near Virginia Road Co Cavan and the specialist recovery crane was called for which was conveyed by Linn hauled trailer. The crane can be seen on the trailer parked on the road. The Linn tractor is in the field to the right of the picture conveying heavy steel cables which will be attached to the bus by engineering staff – there is no danger of the half-track Linn being bogged down in the field. Once the cables have been attached the crane will lift the bus back onto the road for recovery back to Dundalk Works. The Linn was an indispensable aid to GNR engineering. *(SS)*

Leyland Tiger TS2 No. 95 was involved in a serious frontal collision in 1933 near Aughnacloy Co Tyrone as can be seen from this photo taken at Dundalk Works. *(RP)*

same name, at the time of the accident. Warren junior, along with two young girls and three males, all in their teens and twenties, died almost instantaneously as a result of horrific injuries. The car was completely wrecked, whilst the front axle of the bus was ripped out as it telescoped over the car. John Warren Senior later claimed in the Dublin High Court that the Motorman in charge of the GNR bus was to blame for the accident. The Motorman was exonerated, however, and Mr Warren's insurers paid out £471 12s 9d to the company in respect of costs of the bus.

A selection of other significant incidents involving GNR buses is listed below:–

14th September 1930 – bus No. 42 damaged with three passengers injured when the bus ran into a ditch to avoid a collision with a car, which pulled out from a side road at Churchlonan Cross about a mile from Portadown;

18th September 1933 – bus collided with a motor cyclist (Arnold Hawkins) who was killed on the Drumcondra Road, Dublin;

29th September 1932 – bus No. 112 badly damaged. Motorman and a number of passengers injured when the bus skidded and overturned near Finglas;

26th December 1933 – bus No. 90 wrecked when it ran into a wall during fog at Balrath Co Meath causing slight injuries to several passengers;

8th March 1934 – bus No. 29 ran into the wall of a house in Finglas Co Dublin;

20th September 1936 – bus No. 279 collided with a DUTC bus at Westland Row causing injuries to passengers on both vehicles;

18th August 1940 – bus No. 79 collided with a car killing the driver (Phillip Howard) on the Howth Road, Dublin;

16th May 1943 – bus No. 207 collided with a USA vehicle near Londonderry the driver of which, an American sailor, received fatal injuries;

30th January 1949 – nine years after the earlier GNR disaster at Balrothery Bridge a car swerved into the wrong side of the road and struck a GNR bus then overturned. The elderly lady driver of the car died from her injuries;

9th September 1951 – near Balbriggan a car struck the wheel of a bus, which swerved and struck another car killing two passengers in the second car;

2nd August 1952 – Kilgarry near Cavan, an AEC Regal III bus (No. 420) driven by temporary Motorman James Donohue struck the side of an oncoming car, then swerved and collided with another private car, killing the driver.

Ireland endured particularly harsh weather during March and April of 1947 when arctic snowstorms and blizzards, which severely disrupted GNR Road Motor Services, gripped the country. During this period four people died in three motor accidents. Bus accidents rose from 289 in the year ended 28th February 1947 to 345 (an increase of 56) during the corresponding period ending on 29th February 1948. Almost all of these were attributable to the dire weather conditions. This statistic is ameliorated somewhat by the fact that bus mileage increased by 17% in 1947/8 as the company reintroduced services curtailed during the war. In 1952 the accident bonus scheme was expanded to include Conductors and for the first time incorporated attendance at work as an element of the bonus calculations.

A measure of the Company's contribution to safety is that the GNR were the first bus operator in Ireland to fit electric windscreen wiper units to all its buses. On 19th November 1930 approval was given for the purchase of 92 Bosch WN Type wiper motors at just under £1 4s 0d each for progressive fitting to the omnibus fleet. This development represented a positive contribution to road safety. GNR engineers were attempting to improve vehicle headlights, where on early buses the front rim carried the glass, and sealing was achieved with cork or rubber gaskets. The glass usually had a simple fluted pattern. The sealing of this type of headlight was very inefficient so that the reflector was prone to tarnishing resulting in insufficient illumination on narrow dark Irish roads. Many of the accidents involving the company vehicles occurred on dark, wet nights, as a result there was a determination to improve the situation.

The company thus became among the first major fleet operators in Ireland to fit headlights with pre-focus bulbs in light units in which the reflector and glass are permanently sealed together. Depositing aluminium using a high vacuum process produced the reflecting surface. The rear of the reflector cup was formed to take the pre-focus bulb. This type of headlight ensured that the filament was held in the correct position relative to the reflector, and minimised the problem of reflector tarnishing as well as producing improved illumination of the road ahead.

Changes to GNR operations in the Dublin area took place on Tuesday 20th October 1953 with the opening by CIE of the new central bus station (known as Busaras) in Store Street, almost opposite the GNR's Dublin rail terminal in Amiens Street. The futuristic Michael Scott-designed building enjoyed wide acclaim when opened. The co ordinated (or jointly operated) Dublin-Navan-Kells-Cavan services of the GNR and CIE were from this date transferred to operate from Busarus. Buses leaving Dublin first called at Eden Quay to pick up any parcels or newspapers at the GNR City Office, before going on to Busarus. Inbound GNR buses deposited parcels etc. at Amiens Street Railway Station.

As well as maintaining the road motor fleet, garage staff also turned their hands to other activities. In the Donegal area, for example, they also looked after railcars (mainly C1 and C2) at Bundoran. They maintained the staff car attached to the Great Northern Hotel also in Bundoran. During the months of July and August a temporary garage was set up at Pettigo with a fitter working there maintaining the additional Lough Derg season buses. One such fitter who spent several summers at Pettigo was Leonard Switzer the son of Chief Inspector Albert. Donegal Garage engineering staff also carried out maintenance on railcars operated by the County Donegal Railways. The Management of the GNR demonstrated remarkable ingenuity immaculate preparation and meticulous planning, these ingredients all combined to keep the wheels of the road fleet moving.

Q 18

Great Northern Railway Co. (Ireland)

REFERENCE TO

YOUR LETTER

Road Motor Superintendent's Office.

IN YOUR REPLY

B H 30/
2228

GIVE THIS REFERENCE

Amiens Street Station

TELEGRAPHIC ADDRESS
C/O "LINE." DUBLIN.
TELEPHONE 44703.

Dublin 26th September 1930

Dear Sir,

Garage Accommodation
Donegal.

Three of the Company's Machines require to be stabled over night in Donegal, and I shall be glad to know if suitable accommodation can be made available on the County Donegal Railway premises.

Yours faithfully,

J. Mackle,
per

H. Forbes, Esq.,
County Donegal Rly. J.C.
Stranorlar.

Chapter Twelve
New vehicles, new opportunities

The selection of buses and lorries for use by the Road Motor Services was the responsibility of Richard (Dick) Meredith the Dundalk Works Manager. Meredith was an enthusiastic proponent of diesel power and he was determined to ensure the company exploited the technology to its fullest extent. He knew of the relative advantages and disadvantages in adopting diesel-engined vehicles, which can be described thus: – the thermal efficiency of a diesel engine, 30-36% as opposed to petrol at 22-25% and steam at 11-12%, meant that diesel offered better fuel economy, thermal efficiency being the ratio of useful work performed by the engine to the internal energy it receives from its fuel. Diesels generally prove to be more reliable, require less maintenance due principally to their cooler running and more rugged construction. In spite of the fact that the petrol engine develops its maximum power at higher rotational speed than a diesel, the latter can provide improved pulling power because of the maximum turning effort or torque exerted by the crankshaft, which is greater and is better maintained over a wider band of engine speeds. Petrol engines do have some advantages; they tend to be lighter in relation to their power output. Diesel engines are noisier and generate more vibration than petrol engines, especially under idling and low speed operation. The diesel engine is criticised for having poor exhaust emissions, although it is the invisible products of combustion gases in a petrol engine that are more harmful to the environment. Petrol, because of its flammability is infinitely more dangerous, especially when stored in bulk tanks in bus garages. Overall the diesel engine is better suited to transport operations.

Meredith began by ordering three new Leyland Lion PLSC buses from Ashenhurst, Williams & Co of 15 Talbot Place, the Dublin based Leyland dealer, in November 1928. They were all delivered in early 1929 and became fleet Nos. 1-3. Fleet No. 1, an all Leyland chassis and bodied front entrance Lion PLSC1 costing £1505, was shipped from the factory on 10th January 1929. It was initially allocated to Drogheda. The remainder were of the longer PLSC3 model, with chassis costing £955 each, bodied by City Wheel Works of Dublin, to a Leyland design before being allocated to that City. The following year later all three were transferred to the Donegal area running the Sligo to Londonderry service. Following on from the Leylands, Meredith decided to purchase 19 AEC Reliance buses, all of which were delivered between April and July 1929. They were purchased in two batches. The first seven were ordered in September 1928, followed by a further 12 in December 1928. The chassis were ordered direct from AEC and were bodied by J Potter of North Wall; City Wheel Works of Pearse Street and Alesbury Brothers of Edenderry.

In February 1929 AEC sent a Reliance demonstrator with 32-seat Hall Lewis bodywork to the GNR for evaluation. This vehicle had previously been on demonstration with the Ribble Bus Company in England. The GNR purchased this vehicle on 11th April that year; it became fleet number 46 and spent most of its 8-year career allocated to Tandragee garage. The AEC Reliances, with their 6-cylinder petrol A130 engines were marketed to the GNR as fast reliable vehicles specially designed for coaching and long distance work. AEC only built 484 Reliance chassis; GNR got the fifteenth such unit produced, which became fleet No. 14. The GNR experience with the Reliance was that it suffered from the problem of shearing prop-shafts and premature gearbox failures; there were accusations at the time that this was caused by Motormen dropping the clutch.

Richard Meredith's purchase of the AEC Reliance vehicles immediately brought him into an almighty conflict with Joe Mackle who bitterly opposed the purchase of the AECs. He particularly objected to their front entrance bodywork. Mackle contended that they were wholly unsuitable for the services he was developing for the company. After some acrimonious exchanges between the two it was agreed that the next batch of new vehicles would be Leylands and that Mackle would work with Meredith on the body specifications, which was a deal brokered by Jonathan Stephens, the GNR General Manager. Many of the AEC Reliance vehicles were rebodied by the GNR between 1935 and 1937, at which point they received rear entrance bodywork featuring a 'cutaway' roof, which owed its origins to the pioneering railbus conversions completed at Dundalk some years earlier. In the main the Reliances worked out of Dublin and Dundalk garages on Monaghan, Newry and Cavan workings. Four worked out of Belfast on services to Omagh and Lurgan as well as the Portadown to Newry service.

Meredith set about the drawing up of designs and specifications for new chassis and bodies together with stores contracts to support their maintenance. In co-operation with Mackle many of these new purchases had opening roofs and were designated 'sun saloons', a specification which in the early thirties enjoyed great popularity. This consisted of a concertina-rubberised fabric, carried on a number of hoops, which ran in longitudinal side guides incorporating a rack and pinion drive. During fine weather the conductor could open the sunroof. The fashion for sunroofs died out later in the decade as a result of passenger injuries caused by some of them standing up on seats and peering out over the roofline. Quite a number of passengers had been struck by overhanging trees; this ensured its discontinuance. Meredith and Mackle tried various different types of vehicle to ascertain which best suited the operational needs of the company at the time. Mackle had obtained Board authority in December 1929 for an improved type of passenger seat to be fitted to the 20 Leylands that were due for delivery in 1930 and an improved type of 'sun-saloon' roof at a total additional cost of £490. All new GNR buses were fitted with Clayton heating systems, which was a further Joe Mackle refinement in the days when saloon heating was a rarity. Mackle was busy developing an important tour business for the company for which the sun-saloons were required. During the summer months, on Wednesdays and Saturdays a North Dublin Coastal Tour operated. The London Midland & Scottish Railway contracted the GNR to operate a special North Dublin Coastal Tour for special parties arriving from Holyhead by ship at Dun Laoghaire, who then boarded special trains to Dublin's Westland Row Station. GNR buses waited for the British day-trippers at the road adjacent to the No. 1 Bay Platform before whisking them off for their day's outing in Dublin returning them in time to catch the boat train back.

Another factor, which had to be borne in mind at that period in relation to vehicle purchases, was the poor condition of many roads throughout Ireland. In essence the GNR was trying to source a universal or multi-purpose vehicle, which could be used on long, distance, commuter and inter town workings. The early AEC and Leyland buses introduced had differentials with reduction ratios of 5.25: 1 instead of the standard ratio of 6.25: 1 given the relatively flat roads traversed by GNR buses. The 20 Leyland Tiger TS2 chassis cost £1050 each, supplemented by six Leyland Lion LT2 vehicles costing £948 each. Out of the 20 Tiger chassis bodied by two firms, ten were by J Potter & Co of Mayor Street Upper, Dublin. Nine buses were bodied by City Wheel & Carriage Works of 104-7 Pearse Street Dublin. The twentieth Tiger became the very first omnibus bodied by the GNR at Dundalk works. It compared very favourably with other contemporary bodies. There was considerable pride among the workforce and management at the works. This was exemplified by the decision to parade the new bus, which was given the fleet No. 87 in the very first Dundalk Maytime festival along with a road freight department lorry (fleet No. 120), the body of which was also built in the works. The 20 Tiger TS2's were registered in the Irish Free State, where they operated in the main from Dublin garage. One of their number (86) was for a period garaged in Armagh, working the Ballybay service, during 1931. Again the vehicles were bought through Ashenhurst, Williams & Co. They bought many of the exotic second hand vehicles the GNR inherited from private operators they took over. The GNR were only too willing to rid themselves of many poorly maintained buses. Meredith was a keen advocate of the principle of standardisation and all the advantages it brought to the company for example both AEC and Leyland vehicles used a GNR standard sized piston, by using appropriate cylinder liners to achieve this.

The six new Leyland Lion LT2s all received Northern Ireland registrations and were bodied by two Belfast concerns. The East Belfast firm of Service Motor Works was responsible for four, the remaining two were bodied by McKeown and McClaughan who had premises at 11 Templemore Street, also in the east side of the River Lagan. Two worked the Belfast/Lurgan service. Another vehicle (118) was garaged at Crumlin Railway station. It worked the Belfast/Diamond service, displacing a smaller 26-seat Gilford that had belonged to the independent operator W Dow who had been bought out by the GNR. The Gilford was transferred to Omagh to work a service to Londonderry. The remaining three, Nos. 109-11, were garaged at Tandragee whilst working services between Portadown/Newry and Keady.

Leyland Tiger TS2 No. 87 with the first Dundalk built body seen at Brook Street together with a GNR Leyland Beaver lorry with a Dundalk built body being prepared for participation in the 1930 Dundalk Maytime Festival parade through the town. *(CM)*

In 1931 the critical financial situation in the GNR ensured that it was a lean year for new bus purchases, with only four Leyland LT2s ordered in March, which were delivered in July, at a chassis cost of £942 each. All four were bodied by John Stewart and Co (Wishaw) in Scotland with 31-seat bodies to a 'sun saloon' specification, at a cost of £450 each. They were registered in Northern Ireland and worked from Belfast garage on the Lurgan and Markethill services until July 1932, when all four were allocated to Irish Free State garages.

In 1932 four of the newly launched Dennis Lancets with 30hp 4-cylinder petrol engines and four speed crash boxes with vacuum servo hydraulic brakes, were placed in service. The Dennis buses were bought through the Belfast dealer Issac Agnew, a name that will be familiar to people who live in Northern Ireland as a still thriving Belfast motor dealer. The Lancets quickly gained an unpopular reputation with crews who complained that they were underpowered. At the same time a much larger order for 24 Albion PT65 Valkyrie buses, the designation indicating the application of a 60hp five litre four-cylinder engine, was placed with Leslie Porter, the Belfast agent. The English manufacturer Weymann provided bodywork for the Albion and Dennis vehicles; all bodies were of composite construction save for one vehicle, fleet No. 262. the final bus of the batch. This vehicle was built to the Weymann patented flexible construction, used also on Weymann motor car bodies, whereby the bodywork was able to flex without damaging pillars. It would have had clear appeal on the very poor road surfaces but since it remained a 'one-off' we may assume it fared no better than its more conventional compatriots. The Dennis and Albion vehicles spent all of their working life in Northern Ireland as they were only 26ft long in conformity with the prevailing Northern Ireland Construction and Use regulations working services all over the Province. At no stage in their career did they venture into the Irish Free State other than on private hire working. They eventually passed to the NIRTB in 1935.

James Lockhart, the Belfast Traffic Manager, submitted a proposal to the Board on 27th January 1932 for ten Leyland and five AEC buses, which had been operating in Northern Ireland, to be transferred to the Irish Free State following the arrival of the Dennis and Albion buses. The proposal, which was endorsed by the Board on 10th February, was the only mass transfer of vehicles between Northern Ireland and the Irish Free State or vice versa during the company's history. The transfer of these vehicles, which took place in July, enabled the GNR to circumvent the exorbitant Irish Free State import duty introduced by the newly elected *Fianna Fail* government and also to comply with new Northern Ireland legislation restricting the overall length of buses. Given that the GNR had taken over a large number of companies during the thirties and inherited a wide range of diverse vehicles that came with the independents, they soon built up considerable experience with vehicles by Reo, Ford, Gilford, Morris, Dennis, Karrier and Lancia, none of which were considered as reliable as the Leylands or AECs.

In 1932 the GNR and LMS (NCC) jointly purchased four Leyland TS3 vehicles, two for each administration. They had 6.8 litre petrol engines with 24-seat sun-saloon (described as all weather coaches) bodywork by Short Brothers, completed to a high standard featuring carpets, heaters, luxury seats and for improved viewing quarter light observation glass. They were an interesting purchase because the TS3 had a very limited production run with Leyland as there was not much call for 26ft long vehicles, except in Northern Ireland, though Premier Line of London had some magnificent

A Weymann-bodied Dennis Lancet seen when new at the Addlestone factory and which shared the fleet number 235 with a Leyland Tiger TS3 NCC coach. *(WM)*

This interior view of one of the four All-Ireland Tour coaches jointly purchased by the GNR and LMS (NCC) in 1932 in which can be clearly seen the sun saloon roof, observation glasses and the comfortable two and one seating. *(SS)*

examples which passed to Western SMT after Premier's demise. The coaches were the first vehicles in the GNR fleet with 'all metal' bodies, which was being pioneered by Short Brothers at their Seaplane Works in Rochester, Kent. The address confirms that Short Brothers core business was that of aircraft manufacture. In the early 1920s they diversified into bus bodybuilding embodying many of the engineering principles – including the use of aluminium – which they had applied to aircraft production.

The legacy of the Short Brothers aircraft production lives on in Northern Ireland today, albeit now owned by the French Canadian Bombardier Group. Although they were delivered as 24-seaters the LMS (NCC) down seated them to 21, providing additional legroom for tourists. The vehicles were somewhat troublesome from the outset as dust entered the under floor luggage compartments and the saloons of the vehicles. Complaints were received from passengers about being covered in dust and upon arrival at their hotel finding their luggage dust laden to boot! Concern was expressed by the LMS (NCC) Loco engineer Mr HP Stewart that there was a danger of overhanging trees smashing the quarter light observation glass, although this proved to be unfounded.

The GNR undertook to investigate the most cost efficient place to register the vehicles. They found that road taxes in Northern Ireland and the Irish Free State were £2 10s 0d and £5 0s 0d per seat respectively. It was therefore decided to register all the vehicles in Northern Ireland and pay the Irish Free State import duty, as on tour the machines would be in the Free State for longer than the 48 hours allowed without import duty being paid. Import duty in 1932 was rated at 22 2/9%; accordingly the vehicles were presented to the Irish Free State Collector of Customs in Dundalk for inspection where Triptyques were issued for display on the drivers side window denoting that duty had been paid. The vehicles carried the GNR legal address as the Company operated on both sides of the border and was able to provide superior legal protection. The first two (Nos. 223/4) were delivered during March in good time for the summer tour season. The remaining two (235/6) came in the middle of June just as the tour programme was beginning. To the student of GNR affairs in the thirties a very confusing situation arose with the NCC numbered 235/6. The GNR had two Dennis Lancet buses, which also bore the numbers 235/6. This confusing position was resolved in 1935 when the two Lancets went to the NIRTB whilst the GNR bought the two LMS (NCC) vehicles on 25th September 1935.

The Leyland tour coaches were bought by the two administrations to service a joint 'All-Ireland' tour programme and operated from Belfast. The vehicles were bonded for operation on either side of the border. They carried the blue and cream GNR livery with coach lines in cream and bore the legend 'Great Northern & LMS NCC' in brown script

A Leyland Lion LT5A No. 310 was exhibited at the 1935 Industries Fair in Dublin as a static exhibit for the Howden/Meredith patent railbus wheel as can be seen here. The bus was mounted on a short piece of railway track. At the conclusion of the exhibition the vehicle was converted back to a conventional road bus. *(DN)*

painted on the cream band just below the window lines. Even after the NIRTB take-over 233/4 continued to be taxed in Northern Ireland and were allocated to Belfast during the summer months until 1939 when 233 was based in Bundoran, leaving only 234 in Belfast. The other two vehicles (235/6) worked out of Dublin garage during the summer following the introduction of the NIRTB. In May of 1940 Nos. 233/5 had their luxury seats removed and were up seated to 31, using standard bus seats from some redundant 20-seat vehicles at a cost of £10 per bus. These two vehicles were hired to the NIRTB from May 1941.

The highly damaging railway strike of 1933 ensured that funding for new buses was not available that year. The following year sixteen Leyland LT5A buses with four-cylinder oil engines (chassis cost £840 each) were delivered between September 1934 and August 1935 with Dundalk built 35-seat bodies. The first six buses (Nos. 301-6) were fitted with streamlined sloping bulkhead bodies. They represented the GNR's first attempt to improve the exterior appearance of the bodywork. The remainder of the batch resorted to bodies with a straight bulkhead. All these vehicles were allocated to Dublin garage for a wide variety of services to and from the capital.

One of the batch of Leyland LT5A vehicles has been the subject of considerable misinformation. I refer to fleet No. 310, which appeared at the 'Industries Fair' exhibition at the Royal Dublin Society from 7th to 11th May 1935. It was exhibited to publicise the patented 'Howden/Meredith' wheel. The vehicle was fitted with the new invention and appeared as a static exhibit on a length of railway track, the space for which cost the company £18. The GNR produced a leaflet entitled 'Pneumatic-Tyred Rail Omnibuses' copies of which were handed out at the Ballsbridge Show to interested parties. It had been assumed that the bus went on to commence a career with the GNR as a railbus. This is not the case. Following the end of the show the vehicle was returned to Dundalk works where it was converted back to a standard pneumatic-tyred road bus and allocated to Skerries Garage. It remained there until being transferred to Dublin in August 1944.

A Lone Leyland Lion LT7

Maurice Cassidy's Erne Bus Company loaned two of his six buses to John T McGauran, a financially ailing Ballinamore operator, who ran services from the town to Sligo and Bundoran in early 1935. As a result Cassidy ordered a new Leyland LT7 bus chassis to replace one of the vehicles on loan to McGauran. Cassidy's ultimate intention was to purchase the McGauran operation. About the same time McGauran, realising that he was merely a figurehead for an expanded Erne operation, approached John McGowan, late of the Tourist Bus Service, who had himself been bought out by the GNR in July of the previous year, to establish whether or not he was interested in buying the Ballinamore operation. The Omnibus Department of the GSR got wind of this and quickly offered to buy out McGauran the sale was completed on 23rd July 1937 for two reasons. Firstly, to stop the re-entry of McGowan to the bus industry, and secondly to prevent further expansion of the Erne Bus Service. The GSR action ensured that the two loan buses would go back to the Erne in Enniskillen. Cassidy, who earlier found out from McGauran of the impending sale of his business to the GSR, was now left with the prospect of having a Leyland LT7 chassis for which he had no work and had to pay for. A quick approach by Cassidy to GNR General Manager Jonathan Stephens resulted in its purchase for £ 845 on 24th April 1935. Approval was given on 15th May for a 32-seat Dundalk body to be constructed at a cost of £550, this vehicle became fleet No. 317 and was the only LT7 bus in the fleet. This lone Leyland was not deemed to be a success and further strengthened Dick Meredith's anti-Leyland bias.

The company required some smaller, narrower buses to serve areas where road widths were critical. In November 1934 five Dennis Ace chassis were ordered from the Dublin dealer Thomas Thompson & Co at a cost of £350 each. They were delivered to Dundalk in February of 1935; all received 20-seat Dundalk built bodies and entered service between March 1935 and March 1937 serving at Ardee (where a local bus network was introduced in 1937 for a trial period), Kilnaleck, Monaghan, Cootehill, Donegal and Dublin for service at Donabate. The Ace, with its 24.8hp side valve petrol engine and 4-speed crash gearbox, was characterised by the positioning of the front axle, which was in the rear of the bonnet. This feature ensured the vehicle had a small turning circle and gained its nickname of the 'Flying Pig' with its frontal snout. These vehicles were not popular with Motormen, as they were notoriously difficult to stop, especially when fully laden. The Dennis Ace buses were sold on 30th June 1942 to the Irish Army, the exception being fleet No. 34. From the end of March 1937 the GNR Gardner programme formed the basis of the company's new vehicle requirements. All aspects of the Gardner story are to be found in Chapter 9.

Most bus operators in Ireland faced considerable difficulties following the end of the Second World War due to spares and material shortages and many now sought to catch up on a maintenance backlog. The GNR was no exception, its railway rolling stock was literally falling apart and urgent measures were required to effect repairs and replacements. The work required to support the GNR rail passenger and freight rolling stock ensured that bus body manufacture at Dundalk Works did not enjoy a high priority. After the war the demands placed upon the GNR works were such that it was impossible to contemplate building from scratch or even finishing off imported chassis and body frames for the large number of vehicles that the company needed. The only exception was the arrival of the AEC Regent double-deckers in 1946. In that same year a maintenance crisis developed when it was realised that in September 38 machines would become overdue for overhaul. An emergency overhaul drive commenced, resulting in temporary improvement within six months. Maintenance issues raised their head again in September 1948 with steadily worsening arrears, resulting in 65 machines outstanding overhaul. Dundalk Works, in the 32 weeks of 1948 to 7th August, overhauled 25 machines. During the same period garages turned out 7 buses. This was inadequate to ensure proper maintenance of the fleet in view of the fact that it had expanded considerably, and the 'winter allocation' during that year was almost as high as many 'summer allocations' in previous years. Because of these constraints 30 AEC Regal III and seven AEC Regent III vehicles were imported from the UK, fully completed, in 1948. They were desperately needed and were quickly put to work.

By 1948 the GNR Road Motor Services urgently needed to replace worn out 19 year old AEC Reliance buses and 18 year old Leyland Tiger TS2 vehicles, together with a small number of Leyland TS3 vehicles dating from 1932, about 27 vehicles in total. The Leyland LT5A buses purchased in 1934/5, despite having been re-engined, were worn out after years of punishment on the Irish road system and were considered by the Company to be in desperate need of replacement. Dundalk Works did manage to finish ten double-deck AEC Regents between March and October 1948, at the expense of the Gardner programme, but could not cope with additional work. As a result the company decided to order 30 complete AEC Regal III vehicles of which 24 would be built as buses and six as coaches. The production costs of the GNR Gardners had increased to such an extent with the scarcity of materials in the immediate aftermath of the war that off the shelf vehicles could now be bought by the GNR cheaper than the Dundalk built machines.

Richard Meredith had been working closely with the AEC engineers on the specification and design of 20 diesel railcars, which were to be bodied by Park Royal Coachworks of London. He decided that there was considerable merit in ordering AEC buses with Park Royal bodies, given the fact that there would be some commonality of parts. In addition Dundalk works was being geared up for working on AEC engines. The first tranche of AEC Regal IIIs were delivered during June 1948 and immediately allocated to Drogheda garage. They were specifically purchased to serve the new Butlins Holiday Camp at Mosney, Co Meath, which opened its doors on 5th June. The GNR opened a Tours Office within the Butlins complex and established an intensive programme of day tours to cater specifically for the Butlins holidaymakers. They judged that this would lead to a very lucrative summer tours business and in the early years when holiday camp vacations were popular – they were not disappointed. Tours were organised to:–

- Drogheda and Clogherhead on Monday mornings
- Full Day Dundalk and Carlingford Peninsula on Tuesdays
- Afternoon tours to Slane and the Boyne Valley on Wednesdays
- Afternoon tour to Dublin Zoo on Wednesday afternoons
- Full Day Glendalough tours on Thursdays
- Full Day Dublin City tours, which included a visit to Guinness Brewery, on Fridays

The six AEC Regal III coaches (Nos. 427-432), which were the first to arrive in June 1948 from Park Royal, had 35-seat bodies of composite construction. The timber framing of the body was reinforced by steel flitches and gussets combined with 20 gauge steel interior truss panels fitted from the waist over the wheel arches. The floors were constructed from ¾in tongued and grooved softwood boards covered with 3mm brown linoleum extending up to the seat rails on radiused metal cove panels. The dual-purpose seating used throughout was covered in red and black moquette designed by Firths. The sides, ends and centres of the seat backs were covered using Connolly's red hide. Vaumel piping of seat

AEC Regal III No. 423, a representative of the twenty four vehicles built to standard bus specification, at South Quay Drogheda. *(WM)*

This interior view of one of the 1948 batch of AEC Regal coaches illustrates the level of appointment provided by Park Royal. *(SS)*

edges was used extensively. Interior luggage racks were provided and saloon heating was facilitated by a bulkhead mounted Clayton heater. The impressive interior finish was complemented by extensive use of polished walnut, which looked very smart. Externally these 8ft wide and 30ft long vehicles, the maximum dimensions permitted at the time, were panelled using 18-gauge aluminium sheet, incorporating vertical joints covered with flat aluminium strips. Concave mouldings of polished alloy were fitted at the waistrail in a streamlined pattern on the vehicle sides. These features gave the vehicles a very attractive clean appearance, even allowing for the roof-mounted luggage rack, whose access was by means of a rear mounted stainless steel ladder with handrails on either side, positioned between the two rear windows. A full-fronted canopy incorporated a centrally mounted single line destination display. The appearance of the vehicles was likened to coaches supplied at the time to the Southdown company. These six coaches served as the premier tour vehicles for six years until they were ousted from these duties by the arrival of the underfloor AEC Regal IV machines.

Two dozen AEC Regal IIIs (Nos. 403-26), with 39-seat bodies, followed up the coaches by Park Royal on Metal Sections frames, which entered revenue earning service between July and October 1948. In general appearance they were similar to the first six, except for the cut away front canopy resulting in the front destination unit being located on the nearside. The rear skirt panels on the coach versions were raked upwards to give an improved angle of departure. This was deemed necessary as those vehicles would be required to traverse roads and tracks not normally used by buses and coaches where ground clearances could be critical. Similarly the coach version had Widney Aero half-drop side windows finished in stainless steel whereas the dual purpose type was fitted with sliding vent type windows. The vehicles were purchased to improve reliability on longer distance services, where better roads permitted their operation. Mechanically all of Regal IIIs were to an identical specification, which featured the AEC (A208) 9.6 litre engine with fluid flywheel, pre-selector gearbox and air braking system.

These vehicles were very popular with all the GNR staff that operated them. This may account for the fact that the majority of the vehicles worked from Dublin, Drogheda and Dundalk areas with one or two allocated to Cavan garage for most of their time in service. Donegal, Leitrim and North Cavan areas could not operate them, as the roads were considered too narrow for them. When Abercorn Road garage closed, most of the Regal IIIs were transferred to the Dundalk/ Drogheda area. Monaghan was a regular user of Regal IIIs where they were a popular car on the Dublin service as they could achieve speeds of 55mph. Some Regal III vehicles lasted long enough in CIE ownership to operate for a brief period as school buses in the Dundalk/Drogheda area in 1971/72. This was a period in CIE's history when severe bus shortages occurred as a result of the Irish Government's decision to provide free school transport at relatively short notice. I remember seeing a number of these vehicles performing school bus duties at Cavan garage. They were in a very down at heel condition with torn panels, faded paintwork and filthy interior as they prepared to be pensioned off. The last Regal III vehicles ended their days dumped at Dundalk, lined up against the wall between the Dundalk Grammar School and the GNR yard. Their condition deteriorated rapidly through a combination of exposure to the elements and vandalism by kids who enjoyed almost unrestricted access to them from the Dublin Road. Fleet Nos. 427 and 438 have thankfully been preserved in the National Transport Collection of the Transport Museum Society of Ireland.

Number 423 is seen here again, this time in company with a coach version, No. 432, seen on the left. Note the contrasting body styling of the two types. *(GL)*

The year 1952 proved to be an interesting one for the GNR as far as new vehicles was concerned. The Company had been loyal AEC bus purchasers since 1946 and were generally satisfied with the products supplied by Southall. The Dundalk engineers knew the AEC product, which they regarded as tried and tested for both road and rail vehicles. Richard Meredith, now the Chief Mechanical Engineer, required further new buses urgently. He consulted the Londonderry and Lough Swilly Railway Company who had placed four new Royal Tiger vehicles in service during 1951. A novel method of importation in respect of these vehicles was enacted to reduce the importation tariff liability, as the bodies were built on the chassis by Saunders-Roe works at Beaumaris, Anglesey and then separated with the chassis returned to Leyland for shipment in CKD form to Ashenhurst, Williams. Anticipating the completion of the chassis the body shell was then shipped to Dublin where it was remarried to the chassis at Dublin docks and then taken to Dublin Vehicle Builders of Summerhill for completion. The Swilly Engineer James Armstrong gave the buses a glowing report. Based on that information Meredith ordered four at the beginning of 1952.

Leyland put a grey and blue liveried Royal Tiger demonstrator into the GNR on 12th April 1952 with a 41-seat centre entrance coach bodywork by Leyland themselves. The vehicle, (registration MTD 235), had been on extended trial with CIE for some four months beforehand and was delivered to the GNR Garage at Abercorn Road by a CIE official. The company used the vehicle for six weeks mainly on the Dublin to Dundalk service; it also managed to visit Carrickmacross and Cavan for evaluation purposes. They were suitably impressed with the 9.8 litre O600 engine, with its ample 125bhp.

On Friday 20th June 1952 the Depot Superintendent of CIE's Donnybrook Garage, John O'Byrne-Gregan, a 'colourful' character known locally as 'Johno' and John Carroll, a CIE Customs Official, were required to take the vehicle to the port of Larne in Northern Ireland for the ferry back to Preston. Their journey north from Dublin turned into a drama. A strange calamity occurred at a bend near Monasterboice called Kiernan's Cross. This still unexplained accident resulted in the vehicle running off the road and overturning, ending up in the ditch on its offside. Accident investigators were at a loss to determine the cause of the accident. Furthermore they were totally dumbfounded at the fact that when the bus came to rest it was facing in the direction from which it had just come. The location of the mishap was a notorious accident black spot known to Louth County Council who had closed the road for some weeks on 8th February 1939 between Kiernan's Cross and Woodland Three Roads in an attempt to effect improvements.

An extract from the Leyland Motors General Manager's report to his Board of January 1952 is revealing. 'We have been successful in obtaining an order for four PSU1/9 Royal Tigers with Saunders-Roe 'Rivaloy' bodies. Whether or not we get further orders from the GNR, who for some years have standardised on AEC and with whom we were on bad

Leyland Royal Tiger demonstrator MTD235 lying on its side 20th June 1952 near Monasterboice. This vehicle is still in existence with Pennine of Gargrave. *(MC)*

terms, will probably depend very largely on our ability to meet their delivery requirements in this instance'.

The Saunders-Roe Rivaloy body featured centre entrance 44-seat bodywork to a bus specification. They became fleet Nos. 225-8. The vehicles were late in arriving; 225 was delivered to Dublin Abercorn Road Garage in July 1952, 226 joined it in August, followed by 227 going to Drogheda in September. The last vehicle, 228, entered service at Ballyshannon on New Year's Day 1953. By 1954 three of the Royal Tigers, 226/7/8 had been allocated to Drogheda. The Royal Tigers were not popular with conductors because of the centre entrance and the narrow aisles between seats as result of the 7ft 6in body. They did enjoy some tangible use after CIE took over when in 1964 they were transferred to the Dublin Garage at Donnybrook, working the 44B service from College Street to Glencullen, which was a weekday only service operating from about 7.00am to 7.00pm so they were not overworked. This service had to traverse some very narrow and winding roads to which 7ft 6in wide vehicles were better suited.

In August 1952 a further entry in the Leyland General Manager's Board report provides evidence of the desire of the company to win GNR business. 'An enquiry has been received from the GNR for 17 underfloor-engined type chassis. We quoted a Royal Tiger OPSU3/3 model, as air brakes were required. It will be recalled that the GNR recently purchased four Royal Tiger chassis with Saunders-Roe bodywork. Unfortunately the delivery of these machines was very late and might have an adverse effect on our quotation. We are meeting competition on this enquiry from AEC and we have asked Ashenhurst, Williams (Leyland agent in Dublin) to keep their commission at the minimum.'

Leyland also demonstrated a red liveried Tiger Cub PSUC1/1 (registration OTC 738) vehicle with a 44-seat lightweight Saunders-Roe bodywork, which the GNR used from 1st January 1953 for a month before handing this over to CIE who used it until 25th March. The GNR engineers were not impressed with the 5.76 litre 90bhp engine in spite of the obvious advantages in having the Eaton two-speed rear axle. Donald Stokes (later Sir Donald) of Leyland visited George Howden in October 1952 in his dual role of General Manager of both CIE and the GNR in a determined attempt to persuade the GNR to resume buying Leyland products. A high-powered Leyland delegation consisting of the Home Sales Manager, Mr S Cartmell and the Northern Ireland Regional Manager Mr CR Clutsom, tried to persuade Dick Meredith of the merits of Leyland vehicles. They were spectacularly unsuccessful, as the GNR never bought anything else from Leyland.

The AEC company maintained a sales office in Middle Abbey Street, Dublin to cater for its business in the Irish Republic of which the GNR probably constituted its largest customer given that after the war they were buying large numbers of AEC buses and lorries. In December 1952 AEC decided to relocate the Dublin based Sales Manager, integrating its Irish Republic sales effort with that of Scotland. It was a decision taken in the belief that AEC could not obtain large-scale business with CIE given that company's strong relationship with Leyland. The decision was partly reached as a result of a perception that the newly formed GNRB would transfer its allegiance from AEC to Leyland. Events would prove this to be a mistaken assumption. In 1952 the GNR ordered the last new double-deckers in the company's history with twelve AEC Regent III vehicles. They entered service between January 1953 and January 1954.

Mindful of Leyland's courtship of the GNR in 1952, AEC decided to send its latest product for trials. An AEC Monocoach 44 seat demonstrator (Registration No. 210 AMP), which had been built for and displayed at the Scottish Motor Show at the Kelvin Hall in Glasgow during November 1953. The bus arrived at North Wall, Dublin on 10th August 1954 and was used by CIE until it was delivered to the GNR Dublin garage on 9th November. The GNR used the vehicle on the Dublin/Dundalk service for two months. It had front entrance Park Royal bodywork and was of integral construction, which did not suit the GNR's requirements. In retrospect this was a wise choice by GNR as later Monocoach vehicles suffered from structural weaknesses near the spring mountings and did not sell well being overtaken by the underfloor-engined Reliance. The AEC Company offered to supply new chassis to the GNR, complete with body framing which could be finished in Dundalk works and which the Company was keen to accept. In early 1954 an initial order for 17 AEC Regal IV vehicles with Park Royal body frames to be completed at Dundalk works received Board approval

The Regal IV product had enjoyed considerable success, particularly in London, where 700 entered service there between 1951-53, becoming London Transport's RF class. The GNR Regal IVs, all designated 9822E, were 7ft 6in wide and 30ft in length. The AEC A219 horizontal 9.6-litre engine, developing 120bhp at 1800rpm, supplied engine power. A Wilson four speed pre-selector gearbox, which was mounted separately from the engine, was fitted. Drive was transmitted from the engine through a fluid flywheel and intermediate carden shaft to the gearbox. A further carden shaft from the gearbox output flange to the rear axle completed the driveline arrangement.

Air brakes were fitted as standard, which together with the air actuation required for gearbox operation necessitated a belt driven compressor being fitted. A Westinghouse low air pressure warning flag unit was fitted above the driver's windscreen which when air pressure fell below 20lbs dropped into the driver's view, bearing the legend 'STOP'. As soon as the air pressure reached its operational level the warning flag rose into its housing. Trico-Folberth air driven wiper motors were fitted to the vehicles, the first such occasion the company used this method of drive. The engine output of the AEC A219 unit was claimed as being 125bhp. However it was discovered that because of the unequal lengths of the fuel injection pipes this was in fact never achieved. Officially a bhp of 120 was conceded by AEC. The engines were noted for their quiet and smooth operation – they were also renowned for their poor fuel consumption at about 8.5mpg, illustrating that the Regal IVs were no lightweights.

The first two Regal IVs were allocated to the Donegal area for the Sligo/Londonderry service on 4th June 1954. Number 268 went to Sligo whilst No. 269 went to Ballyshannon. A further four vehicles entered service on 1st July 1954.

Another view of the St Johnston based AEC Regal IV No. 271 loading in Grange *en route* to Sligo – compare the body detail with views of other machines of this type. A close examination of windows, driver's cab door and exterior mouldings reveal the unit distinctiveness of these vehicles. *(RG)*

Numbers 260/1 went to Dundalk, No. 262 was allocated to Dublin and No. 270 was sent to St Johnston. The next tranche started work on 1st October 1954 with 271, which bore the Northern Ireland registration T987, going to Londonderry. 272 was sent to Dublin and its sister vehicle 273 was allocated to Swanlinbar. Number 274 was next to enter service from Dublin on 1st December 1954. On New Year's Day 1955 a further four vehicles entered service; Nos. 263/275 went to Dundalk, 264 became Drogheda's first Regal IV and 265 went to Dublin Garage. On 1st March 1955 bus No. 276 entered service from Dundalk.

Whilst working a mystery tour from Dublin on 6th May 1955 No. 265 was involved in a serious accident when it struck the railway bridge at Albert Avenue, Bray, smashing the roof mounted luggage rack to bits. This was an unusual accident as the route taken by the bus followed that of the normal CIE bus route. Mechanical Inspector Bill Supple, Road Motor Supervisor John Duffy and Joe Robinson from the Traffic Manager's Office visited the scene on 19th May for the purposes of investigating the accident. From their on-site observations it was clear that the CIE single-deckers using Albert Avenue were Leyland OPS3/1 Tigers, which had sunken roof racks and lower floor lines, thus permitting them to clear the bridge. An alternate route along Quinsborough Road passing over the railway level crossing at the north end of the Esplanade was proposed as the solution. Finally, on 1st May 1955 the last two (Nos. 266/7) of the initial order of 17 commenced work at Dublin Garage.

George Howden's Secret

George Howden performed the official launch of the Regal IV's on Thursday 13th January 1955 at Dundalk Bus Depot where five vehicles were neatly lined up for a photo-call. He was quick to point out that the vehicles had cost between £6,146 and £6,310 each depending on seating configuration, stressing the investment by the GNRB in new vehicles. At the same time he announced officially the purchase of a further batch of 16 vehicles. In fact these had been ordered in late 1954 and the first of these vehicles entered service from Dublin (Nos. 331/2) on 1st June 1955. George Howden did not reveal the coup just achieved by Dick Meredith and Harry Wilson in relation to the second batch of 16 AEC Regal IVs.

Dick Meredith and Harry Wilson had successfully negotiated a deal with Mr Molloy of the Irish Department of Industry and Commerce to import 16 Regal IV chassis and Park Royal body frames duty free. The chassis/body frames were imported in what was known as 'pre-assembled' condition as opposed to CKD or completely knocked down. It is generally assumed in the automotive industry that CKD applies to vehicles shipped from one country to another in the form of a kit for local assembly in the country of destination. In this context 'pre-assembled,' meant that the parts had at no stage been assembled into a chassis prior to their importation and assembly in Ireland combined with some locally manufactured components. The licence to import free of the 12½% duty was granted on 28th June 1954. The chassis and body frames arrived at Greenore in crates and were conveyed by road to Dundalk for assembly. The GNR's secret deal did not leak out until 1957. When CIE heard of this, the Rolling Stock Engineer at Broadstone, Mr JJ Alexander and the Stores Superintendent at Inchicore, Mr TJ Murphy met with Meredith and Wilson on 4th January

Seen in 1958, this AEC Regal IV No. 266 is loading a private hire party, probably off a GNR train, at Amiens Street Station, side entrance, which was at the top of the ramp leading up to this position from the roadway. This has all disappeared now thanks to the introduction of the new LUAS Light Rapid Transit system. *(RG)*

1957 at Dundalk, anxious to find out how the GNR had saved themselves £3,040 on the 16 new buses! Deliveries continued with No. 333 entering service on 1st July 1955 from Dublin working tours in the company of its stable mates 331 and 332. By the beginning of September all three buses were de-licensed and put in store at Abercorn Road garage. Number 334 also joined the fleet at Dublin on 27th July 1955, working the Newry service. Drogheda got three more Regal IVs when 337 started work on 8th October 1955, followed by 335 on 27th October 1955 and 336 on 1st December. Number 338 went to Dublin and 339 started work from Dundalk on 13th December 1955; 340/1 were joined in Dundalk Garage on New Year's Day 1956. On 1st May 1956 a further three vehicles entered service, with Nos. 342/3 going to Drogheda and 344 allocated to Dublin. The last two machines joined the Dublin Abercorn Road fleet on 1st June 1956.

The Park Royal body framing produced a most pleasing looking vehicle with a roof-mounted luggage rack. The rear of the vehicle was very similar in appearance to the Regal III vehicles with some notable additions including the provision of a small rear boot, which was used to convey bus parcels whilst the rear corners were fitted with stylish bumpers. All the vehicles were delivered in a rear entrance configuration, surprising many as the contemporary trend was towards front entrances. The front styling was very similar to a batch of export vehicles supplied by AEC to the municipal transport undertaking in Montevideo in South America. The frontal design of these vehicles was in fact a Crossley Motors Ltd of Stockport creation. Crossley was part of the then ACV group and specialising in the export market. All Crossley derived products for the home market were built as Park Royal products. A full width bumper was fitted at low level just below the twin front towing eyes. A separate offside driver's door and half height fixed interior partition to the nearside of the drivers cab was a feature of these vehicles as was the fitting of flashing front and rear trafficators. The radiator filler cap, which was located on the front of the vehicle in a central position, was hidden by a flush fitting bottom-hinged flap just below the front windscreens.

In June and July 1955 fleet Nos. 331-4 emerged from Dundalk works, built to a high standard as 38-seat luxury coaches. Number 334 was a 40-seater by fitting an additional twin seat at the nearside front of the vehicle alongside the drivers cab. Having cream rear wheel flashing and a frontal cream flash in the form of a 'V' just below the front windscreens distinguished these vehicles. Other vehicles did have the rear wheel flashing although the special frontal treatment was reserved for these particular vehicles. They were fitted with a very hardwearing brown rubber backed carpet supplied by the Yorkshire company TF Firth of Heckmondwycke, which was laid under the seats along the full length of the vehicle. These machines had narrower driver's cab door compensated for by the fitting of a quarter light forward of the door, which improved offside vision for the driver. Sixteen vehicles (Nos. 331-46) in the class were fitted at build with internal loudspeakers for tour work. The amplification equipment was housed in a key-controlled box mounted adjacent to the side destination equipment on the interior luggage rack. The Conductor always provided tour commentary from notes compiled by the Commercial Department and issued prior to every tour. The Regal IVs were as close as the GNR got to individual unit distinctiveness

AEC Regal IV No. 335, in yet another different GNR livery, is seen in this 1957 view, taken under the Boyne Viaduct at Drogheda, probably for the front cover of a tours brochure. *(WM)*

exemplified by the varying different types of windows fitted which altered the external appearance. Some vehicles had droplights; others had sliding vents as can be seen in some of the illustrations in this book. Seating varied greatly a number were fitted with dual-purpose seats whilst other members of the class had bus seats all of which were supplied by Chrom Furnishings. Seat moquette differed in that the majority of vehicles had a London Transport geometric pattern of horizontal lines of brown, green and black broken by vertical red stripes as fitted to RT and RF vehicles. The later vehicles in the collection 340-6 were adorned with seat moquette in the same brown and yellow striped pattern as the 1957 batch of Dundalk built British United Traction railcars. The reason for the two differing patterns of moquette was that Park Royal Vehicles could only supply 504 yards of the London Transport style. The remainder of the moquette, some 120yds of it, was supplied by Messrs B Wood & Sons (Ireland). Two different types of brown leather cloth supplied by Arlington Plastics and Bernard Wardle (Everflex) Ltd were applied to the vehicle interiors from the bottom seat rail up the inner sidewall of the bus to a point just below the window line to complete the soft interior appearance.

Taking the heat out of the situation

In 1956 some problems developed with certain members of the Regal IV class in that the radiator was mounted centrally to the rear of the number two cross member, putting it just forward of the front axle with a shaft driven fan. The frontal body design of the GNR Regal IVs, with their absence of coolant grilles, meant that the airflow through the radiator was insufficient. A number of vehicles, although not all,

AEC Regal IV No. 340 loading at Eden Quay for Dundalk on 25th September 1958, just days before the GNRB ceased to exist. Similar bus No. 332 can just be seen in rear. *(JG)*

persistently overheated; many could be seen with the radiator filler cap access panel open in service as motormen attempted to improve airflow to the radiator. There were two ventilation grills located at low level at either side on the front of the vehicle for cooling purposes; the front bumper, which covered them, obscured these. The problem was passed to Bobby Pelissier to provide a solution. The result was that buses which had displayed engine-overheating problems had a modification carried out to the offside underfloor engine access panels. The two access panels just to the rear of the front offside wheel were remodelled, incorporating a frame within which was contained a mesh arrangement. The forward panel also incorporated an oil filler access flap. This arrangement solved the airflow problem and as such lasted up until the respective vehicles were scrapped by CIE. The GNR could not carry out a similar arrangement on the nearside panels for fear of a person (particularly a child) poking their fingers through the mesh and possibly causing injury. From the initial allocation detailed in this chapter the Regal IVs were the maid of all work for the GNR as they were quickly allocated all over the system and were probably the most popular car ever to see service.

Fleet No. 271 (TZ 987) was allocated to Londonderry for many years and was always kept in pristine condition by Motorman Willie Carson and his Conductor Daniel Doherty. Just across the border in nearby St Johnston No. 270 was allocated there for many years. When parked at the railway station Motorman Samuel Guthrie and his Conductor Frank Flood were often seen polishing the vehicle as evidenced by its condition. When CIE took over, 271 was sent to Sligo garage to join its stable mate 268, both of which were used on the Derry service. Number 271 deteriorated fast through neglect, ending up in Dundalk before scrapping in 1972. Regal IVs were popular with passengers and crew alike for their comfort, speed, ride quality and low noise particularly on long journeys. In 1957 Nos. 265/6, which were built as 40-seaters, were up seated to 45 in December to be similarly followed twelve months later by 345/6 as the need for higher capacity buses, grew. They were the very last new buses purchased by the GNR and at the time of the take-over by CIE they were only three or four years old and as such spent most of their life under that administration.

All 33 members of the family were transferred to CIE ownership and continued to see service in a front line role for many years to come. They were given the type prefix by CIE of 'AU' for AEC underfloor. The attractiveness of the vehicles for CIE ensured that some were quickly repainted into the very drab two-tone green livery. A broad yellow band was added to the vehicles, applied just below the front windscreen right around the vehicle in response to complaints from passengers about not being able to see the approaching bus as its livery camouflaged it rather successfully. Many AEC Regal IVs went straight into the CIE red/white livery.

In 1959 CIE was enjoying a dramatic increase in foreign tourists visiting Ireland, particularly from the United States, as transatlantic air travel became more commonplace. It could not obtain suitable new vehicles with which it could operate the tours programme and so twelve of the former GNR Regals were fully overhauled at Broadstone, which included the body and chassis. Each vehicle was upgraded to full CIE tours specification. CIE knew that the vehicles were a mere four years old and were highly reliable. Bobby Pelissier, by now based at Broadstone, co-ordinated the programme of conversion, which began on 2nd January 1959 when bus No. 331 entered Spa Road Works from its storage at Abercorn Road.

AEC Regal IV No. 263 waiting at Belturbet Station on 30th September 1958, the last day of GNRB operation, on a rail substitution service to Monaghan following closure of the railway in September 1957 Note the offside ventilation grilles to assist with engine cooling. *(JG)*

AEC Regal IV No. 344, now in CIE ownership and in sunflower and lavender livery and renumbered AU344 in the Tours fleet is seen in this 1959 view at Bundoran Station with the Sligo/Londonderry CIE R796 double-deck bus in the rear. *(RG)*

In this 1956 view we see from left to right the rear of AEC Regal IV 261, a side view of an unidentified GNR Gardner, a front view of another Regal IV 272 and a rear view of preserved AEC Regent double decker 438 waiting their next duties at the Crescent Dundalk. The large building in the background is the Adelphi Cinema and restaurant, a popular haunt for Dundalk folk. *(MC)*

The mechanical overhauls were carried out in Broadstone whilst the body refurbishment was completed at Spa Road. The result of this was that Nos. 260-6, 331/4/8 and 342-4 were all re-seated with 34 full luxury seats removed from CIE's River Class coaches, re-trimmed complete with white plastic antimacassars with the CIE monogram embroidered in red, and fitted to the headrolls. For aesthetic reasons additional mouldings were applied to the front of the vehicles in a 'V' design which continued along both sides of the body in a rear wheel-flashing outline. Where the side valence panels had grille openings, which were provided earlier by the GNR to assist with engine ventilation, these were closed up. A single top opening 'Weathershield' rooflight was fitted to each vehicle just forward of the roof luggage rack for additional ventilation purposes. Bus Nos. 342-4 were retrofitted with Widney Ace Mk VII droplite windows to improve sightseeing potential in line with the remaining nine vehicles. All twelve coaches were completed by 30th May when the last (343) left Spa Road painted in the CIE tour bus livery of sunflower and lavender, serving faithfully in this role until 1962.

In 1963 a programme was instituted to convert all of the rear entrance Regal IVs to front entrance in preparation for imminent one-person operation. The work was carried out at Spa Road Works in Dublin. It was completed by 1964 and involved upseating the whole class to 45-seaters for bus work. The vehicles were fitted with air operated twinleaf entrance doors, the half height driver's partition was removed and a Setright ticket machine and coin dispenser stand fitted. A fluorescent step/ticket machine light was fitted on the roof just above the throat area, which operated when the sidelights were on and the entrance doors were open. These proved to be very troublesome, as the inverters could not cope with the succession of switching cycles when doors were opened at stops. On the offside the driver's door was blanked off, as access to the driver's cab was now through the front entrance.

By 1967 CIE had put large numbers of Leyland Leopards (C Class) into service and this provided much needed relief for the provincial bus fleet. The result of this was that all of the Regal IV fleet was repatriated to the Dundalk/Drogheda area and were dispersed throughout that zone to sub depots as diverse as Monaghan, Cavan, Ballybay, Cootehill, Carlingford, Ardee, Castleblaney and Carrickmacross. The swansong of the Regal IVs occurred when CIE deployed about half of their number to the schools fleet in 1972. Many vehicles after retirement lay wasting in Dundalk, Cavan and Drogheda garages, the last serviceable vehicles being scrapped in 1973 aged 18 years. Fortunately one Regal IV survives (fleet No. 274) and is currently undergoing restoration at the Transport Museum Society of Ireland at Howth.

The AEC story does not quite end there because new bus purchases were still on the mind of Richard Meredith. He submitted a proposal to purchase 15 new double-deckers. In October 1956 an AEC Regent Mk V vehicle with Park Royal 61-seat bodywork was demonstrated, after having been on trial with CIE during the preceding two months. Authority was sought for the purchase of two Regent V vehicles to replace the two double-deckers lost in the Dundalk Works fire in 1955. The authority for these and for the purchase of 15 more AEC Regent Mk V vehicles was withheld as the whole future of the GNRB was in doubt. At the time even CIE was having great difficulty in obtaining permission from government for capital purchases, the GNR was in a far weaker position overall.

The GNR management then attempted to obtain agreement to buy 12 new Leyland Tiger Cub PSUC1/4 vehicles with semi-automatic transmission to a 30ft long, 7ft 6in wide chassis configuration for delivery in December 1957, through Ashenhurst, Williams & Co. Financial difficulties encountered by the Dublin Government again prevented the company from obtaining these new buses. Appendix D of this book details all the new vehicles purchased or built by the GNR during the period 1929-58. The numerical fleet number sequence of GNR vehicles also included lorries from the road merchandise department; new vehicles were allocated fleet numbers wherever suitable gaps existed. The highest allocated fleet number either bus or lorry was 442. During its history the company often renumbered vehicles making life confusing to many students of the GNR story.

The Saunders Roe-bodied Leyland Tiger Cub which spent some time with GNR and CIE on demonstration in 1953 *(SA)*

Chapter Thirteen
Road Merchandise Service

The 'Road Merchandise Service' was the title given to the lorry and cartage department of the railway. The earliest manifestation of this service was in Northern Ireland. An agreement was reached with Hugh Bennett on 25th April 1928 for the provision of cartage services from Ballyroney Railway Station to the County Down town of Rathfriland four miles away which had previously been undertaken by horse and cart belonging to the railway. Shortly afterwards Michael O'Neill provided a comparable service on a brief contract at Stewartstown County Tyrone, to be succeeded by Ross Henderson the following year. Early policy in this aspect of operations seems to have been to rely solely on contractors although this was soon to change. In late 1928 a decision was taken to purchase the first of what was to become a large fleet of railway lorries, as an order was placed with AEC for three 2½-ton vehicles for £450 each. The lorries, fleet Nos 53-5, were allocated to Omagh, Dundalk and Lisburn respectively, entering service in February 1929. Three more AEC lorries started work in May from Banbridge (36) Ballyroney (37) and Lurgan (38), thus ending the Bennett contract.

The short-lived Bennett agreement was followed in 1931 by contracting out much of the Cartage service to the well-known Glasgow haulier William Wordie to their Irish operation. Wordie's provided this service at Ballybay, Belfast, Castleblaney, Cootehill, Dromore, Londonderry, Monaghan and Trew and Moy railway stations. Cartage activities at Monaghan were later contracted to Humphrey Graham of Tullyherim who used horse drawn carts for many years. Cartage operations at Lurgan were, following the NIRTB take over of the GNR's Northern Ireland Road operations, undertaken by J Gallery and Sons in a move widely interpreted at the time as a snub to the Road Transport Board.

Railhead Collection and Delivery System

In 1931 further road merchandise developments were taking place as the recently appointed Traffic Manager James Lockhart presented a new strategy to the Board. It was well received and approved, resulting in the establishment of a system of railhead collection and delivery services an important element of which was the reduction of goods rates to secure traffic, which the GNR was losing, to independent road freight carriers. The Lockhart plan established regular road services operated by the company, serving specific towns and villages on nominated days, which did not have a direct railway connection and brought in some semblance of a co-ordinated approach after a couple of years of organised chaos. Lockhart obtained GNR Board authority for the purchase of 43 lorries to establish the network in both Northern Ireland and the Irish Free State. He set about changing the old policy which had been to use a mixture of contractors and the company's own vehicles between 1929 and 1931. Lockhart adopted the policy of contracting out much of the cartage services where possible whilst retaining the regular railhead services operated with GNR lorries.

As soon as new lorries became available they were quickly pressed into service and soon the GNR's fleet of Leyland Badger, AEC, Morris Commercial and Albion lorries became ubiquitous throughout the territory on both sides of the border. The Badger, with its 2½-ton payload, was a particular favourite of the GNR with 30 entering service up to August 1931. A number of these hardy machines were still operating well into the 1950s. As late as 1957 many examples could still be seen in the vehicle graveyard at Drogheda Railway Station, some of which were still in very good condition after years of loving care being lavished on them by their dedicated drivers and helpers over the years. Other popular marques purchased in the thirties were the Ford 2-ton and 2½-ton models and the very attractive Albion lorries, which were bought by the company in the 1½ and 4-ton payload capacity. On 2nd May 1930 Dundalk works constructed a single dropside body on a Leyland Badger lorry (fleet No. 120), at the same time as the first bus body was completed. In Northern Ireland Messrs Harkness and McKeown and McClaughan of Belfast built bodies on a variety of lorries. The Dublin firm of Michael Gray bodied a mixture of twelve Ford and Albion lorries during April and May 1932 after the contract had been declined by the well-known Clonmel firm of O'Gorman Brothers. Serious construction of lorry bodies at Dundalk Works did not commence until 1937 when suitable space became available.

By the end of 1932 the GNR had a very comprehensive system of railhead road services, which provided door-to-door transport for goods. The basic concept of running road services from railheads is one which the Great Western Railway in England successfully pioneered. The railhead scheme was the principal recommendation of the 1930 report of the Great Western Railway Road Motor Superintendent Mr FCA Coventry into Road Motor Services, which confirmed the GNR's earlier 1928 conclusions. The GNR refined the concept by ensuring that the lorries operated on definite time schedules. The importance of this was to establish the services on a sound and lasting basis, and enabling them to secure a regular flow of traffic. Each day the lorries set out on their rounds, and regularly made their calls at the appointed times. Within three years of its inception in 1929 a total of 38 GNR railheads had a regular lorry service in both Northern Ireland and the Irish Free State. From these railheads over 470 towns and villages in the GNR area enjoyed a daily service, enabling customers to avail themselves of both collection and delivery services by lorry. A tangible illustration of the service the GNR provided can be gleaned by the fact that traffic collected in Belfast at 5.00pm on one day was delivered in Enniskillen, 80 miles away, the next morning at 9.00am, or in villages eight or ten miles from Enniskillen before noon. A number of joint agreements for the provision of lorry services were concluded. From Navan, Kells and Belturbet there were joint services with the Great Southern Railways and from Cookstown there was a joint service with the LMS (NCC). There was also the GNR lorry service from Ballyshannon and Bundoran linking that with the Great Southern Railway at Sligo.

For each railhead service a special booklet was prepared which included a route map, and lorry timetable showing principal places. Great emphasis was placed upon timekeeping and each driver had to provide a daily report on which he recorded the actual times of his calls. In the event of a delay occurring the local GNR agent investigated the circumstances with a view to obviating a recurrence. This shows how much attention to detail was afforded to the service in order that confidence in the services was maintained. Each booklet also contained details of the rates charged which were calculated on a mileage basis. As far as the GNR was concerned a bag is a bag and a box is a box and there were no bewildering rate classifications; the only exception was grass seed, on account of its light loading and, of course exceptional traffic such as explosives. The GNR set out from the beginning to keep the railhead scheme as simple as possible in operation and was a very early example of a highly customer focused service which undoubtedly contributed to its success. Such a comprehensive system of railhead services did not materialise overnight although by June 1932 most of the network was in place. Despite the depressed state of industry worldwide, and in both parts of Ireland, the utilisation of system was profitable although it was felt that some damage was continuing as a result of the private carrier. The system was successful in winning back an appreciable chunk of revenue which otherwise would have remained with the small carrier. The reliability and regularity of the service enabled the GNR to obtain a number of important contracts, notably in the carriage of leading daily newspapers. In the Irish Free State contracts were secured for the carriage of mails and parcels. The fact that the GNR system straddled the border between Northern Ireland and the Irish Free State meant that the services were organised in two distinctive groups for operational and maintenance purposes. Those in the Free State were based in Dundalk while those in Northern Ireland had their headquarters in Belfast. The fleet of vehicles engaged on the railhead services were painted in the standard Great Northern Oxford Blue livery and carried specially lettered sideboards indicating the service on which they were mainly employed. They were kept in very good condition, as it was realised that appearance counted for a great deal when creating confidence in the services.

Irish Free State – Road Transport Act 1933

In 1933 *Fianna Fail* introduced a significant restraint on road competition. The Road Transport Act, 1933, restricted the operation of road freight for reward, outside small exempted areas adjoining the main towns (cartage operations), to persons operating prior to the passing of the Act. The existing carriers were restricted in their areas of operation, classes of merchandise carried, weight and numbers of vehicles. The Act provided for the acquisition of hauliers, by compulsory

This 1931 view of Leyland Badger open platform lorry No. 122 taken in Sheriff Street Garage illustrates a well respected type which remained in service for 23 years. *(MC)*

This Dennis Parcels Van No. 269, seen at Dundalk Works on 9th May 1938, worked from Drogheda Garage delivering railway merchandise in the local area. *(RP)*

purchase if necessary, by the railways. Through the Act Sean Lemass, the Minister of Industry and Commerce, hoped to make it possible for the Great Southern Railway in its area, and other railway companies in their areas, to establish themselves in what is described as a monopoly position. The Great Southern Railways and Great Northern Railway established a Joint Road Transport Conference in 1934 specifically to pool their resources for the coordinated purchase of private hauliers. A special joint account was set up by both administrations to fund acquisitions. Agreement was reached between both railways on general policy principles, foremost among which was the determination that there was no intention of continuing to operate Road Merchandise Services running parallel with the railway services or where equally satisfactory service could be delivered by a combination of rail and road. The Conference chaired alternatively by James Lockhart (GNR) and Robert Stewart (GSR) also agreed a territorial delineation in respect of both companies. Joint territory, often contentious, was also agreed upon and also that of the Dublin and city suburban areas. The split here was purely related to the proximity of a railway from either company. The joint territory agreement applied only in respect of purely road services and did not relate to railhead services, already established by either company. The joint territory provided for in the agreement was as set out as follows:–

- As between Dublin and Navan, to be bounded on one side by the Dublin – Dunshaughlin Road and on the other by the Dublin, Ashbourne, Balrath Cross and Navan Road, with the Navan Joint Railhead included.
- The Road from Navan to Cavan via Kells and Virginia. Belturbet Town.
- The road between Sligo and Ballyshannon as agreed previously on 10th October 1933.

The table below, correct at 22nd March 1937, illustrates the number of Road Merchandise Licences acquired by both companies both jointly and separately.

Category	No. of Licences Acquired
Road Merchandise Licences acquired by the GNR	71
Road Merchandise Licences acquired by the GSR	191
Road Merchandise Licences acquired by the GNR & GSR	50

A full list of all sole GNR and joint acquisitions with the GSR appears in Appendix C. The GNR obtained ministerial authority for the purchase of eleven licences held by companies who transported their own goods not for reward in the Dublin, Rush and Skerries area in April 1935. The clamour to buy up the small independent carriers continued resulting in a near monopoly in the provision of road transport in the GNR area by 1937.

In Northern Ireland up to 1935 road freight business was conducted using 58 lorries through the local agent at railway stations and centrally by James Lockhart the Traffic Manager in Belfast.

The Northern Ireland Government adopted a quite different approach in matters of road freight transport in contrast to the position south of the border. Nationalisation and co-ordination of all road freight and passenger activities was the objective of the government consequent with the formation of the Northern Ireland Road Transport Board. Surprisingly even after the nationalisation of all road transport in Northern Ireland during October 1935, GNR road freight activity within the Province continued right up to 1958. Under a specially agreed consent, firstly with the NIRTB and latterly with the UTA, the GNR operated three lorries from Portadown railway goods yard. Additionally the GNR had a 'lift van' based at Grosvenor Street goods for loading and unloading containers from rail wagons. A number of tractors were also used from Dundalk garage to haul Cross Channel trailers from the port of Newry back into the Irish Republic. This traffic was considered very important continuing right into CIE days. On 13th October 1937 a lorry working agreement was reached with the County Donegal and Londonderry and Lough Swilly Railway Companies, which saw the GNR taking over responsibility for lorry services in the South Donegal Area on behalf of the CDR. The Company further agreed not to operate any lorry services within the Lough Swilly operating area.

Drogheda features prominently in the road transport history of the GNR where the premises of acquired freight operator Paddy McCloskey in Scarlet Street became the GNR Road Motor Garage. On 23rd January 1935 the GNR appointed Paddy McCloskey to the position of Freight Controller at Drogheda. He held this position until 1st October 1946 when he was promoted to the position of Controller of Road Merchandise Services on an annual salary of £550.

On the same day of the McCloskey take-over the GNR paid £3,000 for the substantial Drogheda carrier Thomas Cooney. His ten lorries, one tractor and trailer were soon assimilated into the fleet at Drogheda where road merchandise activities were carried out from the railway station. One of the former Cooney lorries was sold to the County Donegal Railways three weeks after purchase for the sum of £110.

The developing business soon required more specialised vehicles and turned to the products of William Beardmore, a well renowned Glasgow engineer, who started his own company in 1919 producing a range of light commercial engines and taxis. The company later developed a range of diesel engines of which the GNR were early customers. Beardmore started to produce its own range of commercial vehicles and provided the GNR with their first tractor units. A ten-ton tractor 'Python' (No. 173), built in 1930 and inherited from the McCloskey acquisition, together with two twelve-ton 'Python' units (Nos. 170/1) gave the GNR volume load capacity. The GNR, impressed with the Beardmore tractors, purchased a new 12-ton tractor (No. 172) in 1938, which replaced an earlier 10-ton unit, which bore the same fleet number and was scrapped after a road accident. They gave excellent service on a wide variety of work as tractor units living up to the Beardmore slogan 'It is cheaper to pull than carry' right through until the late forties and early fifties after which they were converted to trailers for continued use.

Ivor McCullough, based at Dundalk, was the Road Motor Superintendent in charge of the Merchandise service. His principal function was responsibility for the maintenance of the lorry fleet and the conduct of negotiations to acquire independents. Paddy McCloskey reported directly to McCullough and exercised general supervision over all lorry working at stations and depots. McCloskey had his headquarters at Drogheda railway station, where he acted as required for the company in commercial matters, advising Ivor McCullough where awkward traffic necessitated the provision of special equipment. As far back as 1924 the company had purchased two Aveling & Porter type F steam road rollers complete with awning, scarifer and water lifter (YI 6778, YI 6827), which were used by the Civil Engineer's department to lay tarmac on station approach roads and goods yards, to facilitate the smooth passage of lorries serving the railway. The vast majority of the road merchandise haulage performed during the 1940s and 1950s by the company was

This unusual scene shows Beardmore Tractor No. 171 with trailer attached having been loaded with a GNR works manufactured boiler for a hospital in Mullingar. The GNR official in the hat to the right of the Beardmore Tractor is Jack Webster, then foreman of the Road Motor Shop, who supervised the loading operation. *(MC)*

A 1938 Albion M550 6 ton lorry (No. 10) seen at Dundalk Barrack street goods depot. It was later fitted with a Gardner engine. *(RP)*

lorry load traffic. These trips were worked to meet the special requirements of the hirer, who nominated places of collection and delivery and stipulated the times.

Dillon's Decision

On 9th July 1948 James Mathew Dillon, Minister of Agriculture in the recently elected Inter-Party Government in Dublin, presented his first estimates to the *Dail*. In the Land Bill of 1949 Dillon promised a scheme to reclaim four-and-a-half million acres of land by draining, liming and fertilising fields and improving fencing together with the removal of scrub and boulders. The Government provided two thirds of the costs which included the supply and delivery of ground limestone and phosphates. The scheme began in County Mayo on 16th August 1949 and was eventually rolled out across the country. The spin off benefit for the GNR was that a number of Bedford, Ford V8 and Albion tipper lorries were employed on the delivery of ground limestone to farms in the Cavan, Monaghan and Donegal areas in pursuance of Dillon's decision to revitalise the land.

Cementing a relationship

Trading under the name 'Cement', FL Smith obtained *Dail* approval under the Cement (Amendment) Act, 1938 to construct, maintain and operate a cement works in the townland of Newtownstalaban, just north of Drogheda. The Cement works provided colossal opportunities for the conveyance of bulk cement traffic by rail and road for the GNR. A number of significant events in relation to the establishment of the cement works quickly brought innovative new designs for the movement of bulk cement by road, introduced by GNR engineers working in co-operation with FL Smith. In April 1947 Cement Limited awarded the GNR the contract to transport 5,000 tons per year of product by road lorry from Drogheda to Lucan, where a factory producing concrete blocks, bricks and tiles was situated. Three new AEC Matador lorries were purchased in late 1947 with eight-ton de-mountable containers, manufactured to a GNR design by the Drogheda company C Morgan and Sons, to undertake the work. In September 1950 a further large Cement Limited contract was gained for the conveyance of bulk cement by road from Drogheda to Messrs Weatherwell's factory at Clondalkin. Arrangements were put in hand to purchase two AEC Mammoth Major lorries

However, events forced the pace somewhat when in July 1951 a new contract was announced. The GNR was now required to provide additional lorries and specialist bulk cement containers to move 15,000 tons per week. The massive new contract entailed the movement of cement between Drogheda and Dublin Docks, required for the construction of a new graving dock. The rethink by GNR Officials, particularly Ivor McCullough, resulted in the purchase of five AEC Mammoth Major 15-ton lorries each of which carried three five ton de-mountable containers

AEC Mammoth Major oil tanker No. 190, which was assembled in Dundalk Works is seen in this 1954 GNR photograph on the Ardee Road. *(DN)*

AEC Matador No. 178, the chassis of which was assembled at Dundalk Works, had the body built by C Morgan of Drogheda and is seen here carrying the GNR Bulk cement containers associated with this important traffic in this 1948 view. *(DN)*

specially designed and constructed at the Dundalk Works. In October 1954 the GNR proposed to CIE and the London based proprietors of the Cement Works, Messrs FL Smith that they jointly develop an aerated bulk cement semi-trailer. CIE contributed £500 which represented a half share of the development and drawing costs of the tankers of which the GNR obtained three, together with a corresponding number of AEC Mandator tractors in the first half of 1956. The 15-ton load was capable of being discharged in just 20 minutes.

The GNR was very successful in obtaining contracts for the conveyance of livestock (including bloodstock), furniture, fish, meat (in insulated containers), bulk liquids and heavy indivisible loads. By mid-1951 markets were being developed for chilled meat, destined to land on the dining tables of England and frozen meats consigned to the USA. This traffic originated in Monaghan and Dundalk, right in the heart of GNR territory and resulted in two furniture lift vans being converted at Dundalk works into insulated containers at a cost of £320 for this merchandise. Ivor McCullough designed and built at Dundalk Works many special vehicles and trailers to convey this traffic. The company even had an Albion 6-ton explosives lorry (fleet No. 41) with a specially constructed security body built by C Morgan and Sons of Drogheda. The vehicle was used to transport gelignite from the factory at Enfield Co Meath to service the quarries, working from Dublin garage. One interesting feature of the GNR's furniture removal business was that after the nationalisation of the company's road freight activities in Northern Ireland, it was permitted to continue with cross border removals in either direction under consent from the NIRTB. Furniture removal services were advertised in publicity material with this slogan:

Good vans
No worries
Reliable service
Inquiries invited

In June 1952 the GNR negotiated a six-year contract with the Drogheda Margarine factory of W&C McDonnell for the bulk conveyance of edible oils from Drogheda to Dublin, for a fixed annual payment of £2,760 per annum. Three ten-ton Scammell built semi-trailers with heater units were purchased. A Bedford Tractor (fleet No. 77) hauled the trailers, operated by a driver and helper. The tractor and trailers were painted in a special livery, bearing the legend 'Stork Margarine' on the vehicle sides. The W&C McDonnell contract initially called for two trailers; this was increased in 1954 with the addition of a third for which the GNR obtained a further £366 per annum in respect of the additional volumes being moved. The size of cement and McDonnell's traffic ensured that Drogheda had twice the lorry and trailer fleet of any other in the GNR territory.

In common with the road passenger side of the business the company had inherited a wide variety of lorries and trailers as a result of the take-overs, and others were bought to supplement the fleet. Due to emergency restrictions and the complete unavailability of new vehicles the GNR was forced to buy two 6-ton lorries (one of which was a 1916 Maudslay lorry) and two trailers from McCalden's of Monaghan on 16th May 1939. Continual efforts were made at standardising lorry types particularly in the late forties and fifties. A couple of 1930 vintage Leyland Badger lorries (fleet Nos. 136/7) were converted into tractors in 1948 for the purpose of carting the contents of heavily-laden goods trains loaded with wheat. The bags of wheat which came from farms in the Meath, Louth and North Dublin area were loaded onto the lorries and trailers at the GNR Goods Depot in Sheriff Street and taken to the Dublin Port Milling Company at Alexandra Quay ultimately ending up in the nation's bakeries. There was an eighteen-year gap between the arrival of the first AEC lorries and the next batch of AEC Matador diesel tractors, which arrived in 1947, replacing the Beardmore machines. The company imported all the AEC and Albion lorries bought after the Second World War in a completely knocked down condition with assembly taking place in Dundalk Works. At least one AEC Mammoth Major (fleet No. 184) was re-engined

This vehicle began life as a Leyland Tiger TS2 bus number 97 in 1930. It was converted to a horse box in 1945 at the GNR works and could accommodate 4 horses. *(DN)*

using a Gardner 5LW unit, giving an additional 30hp. Additionally, new forward control Bedford lorries with the distinctive bulbous bull-nosed cabs and tipping bodies were purchased in some numbers, principally from the Dundalk agent Byrne and Maguire. Two brand new AEC Mercury and three Mandator lorries, purchased by the GNR at the end of 1956, were put into storage at Drogheda and never saw service with the company until after CIE took over. These vehicles were part of a batch of AECs assembled in Dundalk Works and fitted with lightweight aluminium alloy bodies constructed by the Dublin firm of JH Moore and at the time the weight savings were regarded as revolutionary.

The Dundalk Works assembled AEC Matador No. 174 tractor and trailer, which had a capacity of 15 tons of bulk cement, is seen in this 1956 view. *(DN)*

AEC Mercury No. 117 with its 8 ton payload, assembled at Dundalk Works in 1956, has a full load of bagged merchandise and is seen at Drogheda station ready to depart. *(DN)*

UTA/GNRB Freight Co-ordination

In October 1953 the GNRB and the UTA agreed to co-ordinate their freight activities in Northern Ireland, which resulted in elimination of wasteful duplication. Even after the establishment of the NIRTB in 1935 the GNR continued to employ contractors to deliver sundries traffic from railway stations throughout the Province. The GNR now agreed to use UTA lorries at all its railway stations with the exception of Coalisland, Fintona, Lisbellaw, Newcastle, Pomeroy and Sixmilecross, all points where the volume of traffic did not warrant such a step. The sum of £43,100 was spent by the GNR during 1952 with William Wordie's who operated from Belfast's Waring Street for cartage services in Northern Ireland, a contract that was quickly withdrawn. Wordie's had lost all its road freight business to the NIRTB on 5th June 1937, leaving it to concentrate on railway cartage. Three smaller contractors employed by the GNR, who used horse drawn lorries for the delivery of the sundries traffic had their business withdrawn.They were:

- Dromore County Down-Carlisle worth £200 per annum
- Irvinestown County Fermanagh-McGuire worth £150 per annum
- Lisnaskea County Fermanagh-McGinley worth £250 per annum.

Despite the creation of the NIRTB and its successor Ulster Transport Authority, the GNR continued to employ freight drivers in Northern Ireland right up to 1958. At Portadown goods station three 5-ton Ulster Transport lorries were hired to and driven by GNR personnel. Similarly at Banbridge one Ulster Transport lorry was on long term hire and was periodically joined by a second hired to deal with seasonal grass seed traffic, both driven by GNR road merchandise drivers.

William Wagner Kennedy

Belfast road freight operator WW Kennedy & Co, with offices at 22-28 Academy Street had extensive cross-border haulage, furniture removal and horse drawn cartage interests. They maintained a Dublin depot at 122 Upper Dorset Street from where about one fifth of their business was generated. A large volume of inaccurate information has appeared in various publications with regard to the Kennedy operations and in order to correct these erroneous accounts I have prepared the following narrative using contemporary documentation within my GNR archive.

On 5th June 1935 the Irish Free State Ministry of Industry and Commerce issued an Order under Section 51 of the Road Transport Act, 1933 approving an application by the GNR to have the Kennedy Licence number 396 restricted to furniture removal only. Prior to this order the Kennedy business was allowed to convey all classes of general goods. This development effectively obliterated the Kennedy cross-border traffic at the stroke of a pen. Events in Northern Ireland were to add further pressure on the Kennedy operation. With the 1935 Act, which set up the Northern Ireland Road Transport Board, came a statutory responsibility conferred upon the NIRTB. This statutory position declared:–

'The Board shall ... acquire every road motor undertaking operated for hire or reward in Northern Ireland ... but not including (certain local specialised and ancillary transport services)'.

The business was liable to be taken over by the NIRTB except for furniture removing and city haulage, which were exempt from acquisition, together with general haulage and furniture removing between Belfast and Dublin.

James Lockhart, representing the GNR, met the Kennedy family together with the NIRTB on 18th May 1937 to discuss acquisition terms. The Kennedys informed the NIRTB and GNR that they were not prepared to voluntarily agree to the NIRTB taking over part of their business but wished to press for the acquisition of the whole business. In July 1937 the GNR obtained certified accounts for the Kennedy business, with a view to making an application jointly with the GSR for its compulsory acquisition. The GSR was not enthusiastic about this proposal and it did not proceed past the informal discussion stage. On 22nd September 1937 the NIRTB proposed to the Board of the GNR the joint purchase of the Kennedy cross-border furniture removal and haulage business. The entreaties of the NIRTB were rejected by the GNR who had obtained previous sight of the accounts. The NIRTB then issued a vesting order on the Kennedy business, but the effect of it was the subject of litigation between the parties, going as far as the Court of Appeal; no small part of the trouble concerned the difficulty of trying to sever the transferable road motor haulage from the exempt furniture removal, city horse haulage and cross-border work.

Eventually it was agreed between Messrs Kennedy and the NIRTB not to attempt to sever the undertaking into its parts, as contemplated by the 1935 Act. This being well nigh impossible in any event, but that all haulage, exempt or not, in Northern Ireland should be taken over by the NIRTB and that all cross-border haulage, whether acquirable or not, should be retained by Messrs Kennedy. A price was agreed on this basis, part of it, namely £37,000, being statutory compensation under the Act and £12,500 being an agreed contractual sum for the voluntary acquisition, the undertaking transferred for this compensation under the Act. Messrs Kennedy transferred 23 lorries, 6 trailers, 18 containers and two valuable Belfast city centre properties, together with the goodwill to the NIRTB. This left the Kennedys with one lorry and one trailer for cross-border work, which was excluded from the compensation.

A working arrangement and agreement was entered into with the NIRTB and approved by the government for the continuance of the Kennedy cross-border business, which had a six month termination clause that could be invoked by either party, although if the NIRTB terminated it the Kennedys would be entitled to compensation. The Kennedy cross-border business continued to grow, with four lorries plying between Belfast and Dublin by the mid-1950s, with the potential for further expansion. The Transport Act (Northern Ireland) 1948 which merged the Northern Ireland Road Transport Board with the LMS (NCC) and the Belfast & County Down Railway to form the Ulster Transport Authority continued the Kennedy agreement. The Kennedys claimed that their agreement now applied to rail haulage or cross-channel consignments as the UTA was a combined rail and road authority. Kennedys laid claim to first refusal of all load hauls between Larne and the border and to the first refusal of all consignments from Northern Ireland to Eire, or vice versa, unless by its nature it can only go by rail, or the customer has expressly stated that it is to go by rail. The position of the Kennedys outraged the GNR, who had enjoyed consents from the NIRTB, which continued under its successor UTA in respect of cross-border road freight traffic. The consents obtained by the GNR from the NIRTB were issued before the Kennedy/NIRTB agreement. Kennedys now alleged that they enjoyed a monopoly on all cross-border road haulage and were pressing the UTA to award any road traffic for Eire to them. The UTA resisted the Kennedy claim and continued to pass any Eire road haulage traffic to the GNR providing that the consignment was destined for delivery within the GNR territory south of the border.

With the formation of the Great Northern Railway Board in 1953 the Kennedys declared to the UTA that any rights to road haulage now pass to them. The UTA repudiated this contention and towards the end of 1954, following the UTA/GNRB freight co-ordination agreement, the Boards of both undertakings decided to initiate talks with Messrs Kennedy & Company yet again, which proceeded satisfactorily until the statutory basis of compensation came to be discussed. In Northern Ireland this was fixed by Act of Parliament and by the Courts at ten years purchase of super profits, but in the Republic it was very much less than this and Messrs Kennedy indicated that they were not prepared to continue negotiations unless they obtained a guarantee from both parties that ten years purchase would be applied in both jurisdictions. The GNRB and UTA quite rightly indicated that they were not prepared to part from the statutory basis in either territory and thereupon Kennedys promptly called off the negotiations. Relations between the parties became demonstrably strained with the Kennedys issuing threats of further litigation against the GNRB and UTA. The Kennedys continued to be a thorn in the side of both transport undertakings up to and after the demise of the GNRB. In 1959 the UTA proposed to CIE the joint acquisition of the Kennedy cross border business – yet another failed attempt to remove the Kennedys from the road haulage scene.

Horse Power

Right up to the take-over by CIE and subsequently, cartage collection and delivery services at Dublin Goods and Barrack Street, Dundalk were performed by horse drawn lorries. As late as February 1941 four motor lorries, which were used on Dundalk Cartage activities, were withdrawn and replaced by four horse drawn vehicles saving the company £600 per annum, a move forced upon the company by the stringent fuel restrictions imposed by the government during the wartime emergency. Horses were purchased from Mr A Munro of Wordie & Co, who had been supplying the company for many years, with prices ranging from £50 in 1929 to £60 in 1949 for a respectable animal. Provisions for the horses were always sourced from local farmers in the Louth/Meath area, the principal suppliers for hay were J Lawlor of Donore and R Hughes of Drogheda, with Mr PJ Halpenny of Ardee the main supplier of oats. In November 1940 the Company appointed Mr GS Farrelly, who had previously been a Traffic Representative, to the position of Supervisor Dublin Cartage (Horse and Lorry) at a salary of £300 per year. This event coincided with the decision in October 1941 to spend £1,500 to concentrate all Dublin cartage activity in the old omnibus garage in Sheriff Street, which had recently been vacated following the move to the new garage at Abercorn Road. Even in 1953, when mechanisation was the order of the day, the company purchased 20 second-hand horse-drawn lorries from British Railways (Dublin) for £10 each. In 1958, at the time of amalgamation with CIE, fifteen horses in Dublin and a further eight in Dundalk, giving a total of 39 horse-drawn lorries, were in daily service. These quaint vehicles were progressively withdrawn in early 1968 by CIE.

British Railways Contract

The GNR had a contract with the British Railways Board to service and maintain a fleet of 27 lorries and 130 trailers, which were based in Dublin and used for cartage operations in the city. The maintenance was carried out at Abercorn Road Garage in Dublin and was an exceptionally lucrative commercial proposition for the Company. The contract awarded in the early 1950s was linked to the funding by the London Midland Scottish Railway of the building of the GNR Dublin garage. This intense activity ensured that Henry Bowie, the Garage Foreman, and his maintenance staff were kept particularly busy in addition to dealing with his own fleet of vehicles.

Horse drawn lorry number No. 24 photographed at Dundalk Works after overhaul on April 7th 1943 before being returned to cartage duties in Dublin. *(DN)*

Chapter Fourteen
Buses into Railbuses, Tramway Troubles

In early 1926 one of the first tasks Richard Meredith embarked upon was to travel to Donegal to meet Henry Forbes, the General Manager of the CDR. The CDR was suffering from declining revenues and Forbes found himself under considerable pressure to reduce his operating costs. Richard Meredith proposed the development of a number of railbuses for the Donegal Railway, thus providing the necessary savings. Forbes, quickly realising the advantages to be gained with the introduction of these vehicles, readily agreed to fund development in conjunction with the GNR. Richard Meredith quickly and eagerly set to work at Dundalk. Meredith thus began the pioneering work in converting buses into railbuses. He was years ahead of any other railway company – including the Great Western Railway in England.

In 1928 the GNR produced a railbus based upon a Ford 30cwt chassis, suitably converted at Dundalk to run on the narrow gauge Donegal Railway. The body was constructed by O'Doherty's coachbuilders in Station Road Strabane, who's premises were in close proximity to the CDR Railway, to a design developed by the CDR workshops in Stranorlar. The GNR had of course not yet entered the business of building bus bodies. The railbus became CDR No. 4, a 21-seater, which saw 19 years of Donegal service.

The Koppel Industrial Car & Equipment Company of the United States was asked on 29th January 1930 to supply one rail motor car chassis, with a 40hp Ford engine, at a cost of £385. This vehicle was intended for use by the central permanent way gang on the Oldcastle branch line. Koppel declined to supply the vehicle, and as a result Dundalk Works was authorised to build an alternative at a cost of £450. The outcome was that two Ford 30cwt chassis were obtained and converted to run on the 5ft 3in Irish standard gauge. They were allocated fleet Nos. 8177/8 with a seating capacity of 20. On 2nd April 1930 the company approached the Buda Company with a request to quote on the supply of three petrol driven railcars with trailers and portable turntables, for track maintenance gangs on the Antrim, Cookstown and Armagh branch lines. The Buda Company quoted £585 per vehicle, which was considered too expensive, and no further action was taken.

The railbus developments began at the GNR a full year before the company started to run road buses themselves, although the potential to convert road buses to railbuses was quickly realised. Conveniently for the company the little modification that was required to transform a road bus into a railbus of 5ft 3in gauge meant that each vehicle cost little over £100 to convert. One of the vehicles acquired with the United Motor Services business, a Reo 20-seater bus, registration No. IA 5629, which became No. 72 in the GNR fleet, was sold to the CDR in July 1930. Dundalk works converted this vehicle for use as railbus and body modifications were carried out at O'Doherty's of Strabane. It became CDR railbus No. 6, entering service in 1930 as a 31-seater and lasting in this form until 1945, when it was rebuilt as a trailer for further use right up to 1958. In 1931 the GNR designed and built two further railbuses for the CDR. They were the first diesel-engined railbuses in the British Isles with their Gardner 6L2 engines and O'Doherty built bodies. They were CDR Nos. 7 and 8 and were regulars on the Ballyshannon Branch until 1949.

In 1934 Richard Meredith invented a special wheel specifically designed by him for railbus operation, known as the 'Howden-Meredith' wheel. The patent wheel was, like all good inventions, simply practical with all the necessary safety

A close up photograph of the patent Howden/Meredith Railbus wheel as illustrated on Railbus F. *(DN)*

features built in. Meredith realised that pneumatic tyres fitted to road omnibuses contributed to the overall improvement of the ride characteristics of the vehicle. He set about combining the pneumatic tyre with the flanged steel tyre necessary to operate the railbuses. The invention consisted of a steel rim rail tyre with a normal outer-flanged profile, the inside being machined in a manner which accepted the tread profile of the pneumatic tyre, which was fitted inside. The inside diameter of the steel tyre was made slightly smaller than the outside diameter of the fully inflated pneumatic. This ensured that the two distinctly different tyres were firmly held together. In the event of an unplanned deflation of the pneumatic inner tyre a brake block was positioned above the wheel, which would apply braking power and also ensure that the rim was held in a vertical plane.

The rear of the donor bus body was modified to permit passengers to enter or leave from platforms on either side. The body was cut away at each side to provide room for swing doors to open outwards on each side where platform extensions were added to increase the overall width from 7ft to 9ft, thereby reducing the gap between the bus and station platforms. Two steps were also provided to enable

The Gardner/Edwards Railcar sent to Colombia used GNR expertise from Richard Meredith in order to build this machine in 1934. *(GL)*

Railbus D at Dundalk Works was the pioneer vehicle of September 1934 and despite the radiator it was not an AEC Reliance. *(GL)*

Railbus No. 4 (formerly DNGR No. 2) about to depart from Banbridge Station to Scarva providing an economic connection to the GNR main line. *(GL)*

passengers to join the railbus at level crossings. Two of the second-hand Leyland SG7 buses purchased from England for the Lough Derg Pilgrimage traffic were converted at Dundalk into replacement permanent way gang railbuses. They were converted in June 1934 and gained the departmental fleet Nos. 8188 and 8190. Richard Meredith used number 8188 in connection with early experimentation of the patent 'Howden-Meredith' wheel between Londonderry and Omagh. As a result of these experiments some refinements were introduced, resulting in a squatter profile of pneumatic being adopted.

On 17th October 1934 the GNR granted permission to the Gardner-Edward's Diesel Railcar Company Limited of 3, Brunswick Street, Belfast to incorporate the company's patent tyre in a tender for railcars to be supplied to a South American railway company, on payment of a royalty fee to the GNR. RW Meredith was a Director of this company, in addition to being the GNR Works Manager. A railcar with a Gardner 74bhp engine was exported to Peru with a body built by Service Motor Works Belfast after first being tested on the 3ft Ballymena-Larne line with its 1 in 26 gradients.

A number of the omnibuses acquired by the GNR made ideal vehicles for conversion to railbuses. Not all such conversions were successful however. Former Gordon's Motor Services ADC omnibus (GNR fleet No. 186) after conversion was not deemed suitable due to an earlier break in the chassis frame. On 23rd May 1934 the GNR board was asked to consider its fate – the proposal was to recondition the chassis and fit a new body for continued service as a road omnibus. The matter was left in the hands of Sir Lingard Goulding, the acting Chairman, who eventually decided that the vehicle be cannibalised for spares. The body of omnibus 186 was thus transplanted onto the chassis of bus No. 5 which was converted into Railbus D.

The pioneer railbus entered service between Dundalk and Clones on 17th September 1934. Number 5 was replaced as D in 1935 when sold to the Sligo Leitrim & Northern Counties by No. 4. Number 7 allowed the company to re-open the Scarva Branch to passengers on 15th October 1934. This vehicle was renumbered again in 1947 to railbus No. 1. In 1957 the railbus was allocated to the Civil Engineer and it was renumbered 8178 and was based at Portadown. It passed to the UTA in 1958 and was saved for preservation and has been fully restored to front line railbus condition and is on proud display at the Ulster Folk and Transport Museum. In January 1935, railbus F appeared, becoming F3 in 1938. It was destroyed in an accident at Dundalk Square Crossing on 26th April 1944. A replacement, also numbered F3, went into service later in the same year. Renumbered 2 in 1947, it went to CIE in 1958. Bus Nos. 35 and 185, both ADC 416 vehicles, were converted to railbuses for the Dundalk Newry and Greenore Railway and became Nos. 1 & 2 in that company's

Omnibus to Railbus Conversions

GNR Bus Fleet No.	Bus Type	Reg. No.	Original Owner	Converted	Railbus Designation	Notes
5	AEC 413	IY 9432	Duffy	Sept 1934	D became D1 in 1936	Sold to SLNCR in 1939
7	AEC 426	ZI 2452	Duffy	Oct 1934	E then became E2 in 1936 then renumbered 1 in 1947	Renumbered 8178 in 1957. Preserved at Cultra Transport Museum Body from Bus 186
6	AEC 426	ZI 2451	Duffy	Jan 1935	F became F3 in 1938	Destroyed in accident 26.4.44
4	AEC 413	YI 9431	Duffy	April 1935	SLNCR A	
34	ADC 416	ZI 1704	Fairways	May 1944	Replacement F3	GNR No. 2 – to CIE rebuilt at Inchicore
33	ADC 416	ZI 1693	Fairways	Jan 1938	SLNCR 2A	
35	ADC 416	ZI 2089	Fairways	June 1935	DNGR No. 1	Bought by GNR became No. 3 Scrapped 1955
185	ADC 416	ZI 960	Gordon's	July 1935	DNGR No. 2	Bought by GNR became No. 4 Became 8177
186	ADC 416	ZI 996	Gordon's			Unsuitable as a railbus scrapped 1934 body used on Railbus E

Two official views of railbus E following its rebuilding and transformation into a rail vehicle in lieu of a road one. *(GL both)*

stock. Both were taken back into GNR stock in 1947 after being overhauled at Dundalk works and were renumbered 3 and 4. Number 3 was scrapped in 1955; No. 4 was transferred to the Civil Engineer at Drogheda and numbered 8177 in 1957, ultimately being taken into CIE stock in 1958.

Hill of Howth Tramway

The Hill of Howth tramway was technically part of the Road Motor Services. In reality though, it was managed as an integral part of the railway and the 1933 railway strike resulted in the suspension of services on the Hill of Howth tramway. Once the strike had been settled on April 7th 1933 railway services recommenced progressively within a few days. The Hill of Howth tramway did not resume immediately. There was a proposal to operate the services using railbuses although this was not adopted. A Vulcan Duke 20-seat bus (fleet No. 171) from Dublin garage manned by a Road Motor Service Motorman and tram Conductor from Sutton provided a substitute service from 18th April to 14th May 1933 inclusive between Sutton Railway Station and Bailey Post Office. This action raised a storm of protests by residents on the hill. The Tramway was under threat again when on 5th October 1938 a proposal was given consideration to operating the services with a Gardner bus. A time and suitability trial was carried out on Friday 21st October 1938. History records the proposal was not implemented and time moved on.

The Irish summer of 1944 was uncharacteristically long and hot, resulting in drought conditions throughout the country. The Electricity Supply Board was unable to generate enough current for traction purposes and asked the government to enact emergency legislation to conserve power supplies. The government issued an order on the GNR in terms of the Emergency Regulations to prohibit of the use of electricity for traction purposes on the Hill of Howth tramway. This order was effective from 10.30pm on Sunday 11th June 1944. On Monday 13th June a GNR Gardner from Dublin garage operated a substitute road service over the south side of the Howth peninsula between Sutton Station and Bailey Post Office making a connection with trains. A test was carried out using a GNR Gardner bus from Drogheda garage on the section from Howth Station to Howth Summit on Tuesday 14th June 1944. The restricted road widths over this section resulted in the trials being declared a failure.

Matters returned to normal until November 1953 witnessed the closure of the Hill of Howth tramway temporarily to permit urgent track maintenance to be undertaken together with a road-widening project, which was to be carried out by Dublin Corporation. A substitute omnibus was based at Sutton Station during this interruption. Percy Reynolds (the Senior GNRB member from the Irish Republic) wanted a permanent closure of the tramway at the time, as it had never made any money. However, Dubliners held the tramway in great affection. This, together with the GNR's plans to introduce a permanent substitute bus service, was not given the approval of the Department of Local Government. Reynolds and Howden, by now the senior representative nominated by the Northern Ireland government on the GNRB and a professional railwayman clashed over this issue. Howden won the day and the tramway enjoyed a reprieve in early 1954 before being finally closed in May 1959 following the road widening by Dublin Corporation between Sutton Cross and Howth via the Summit.

Tramcars 1, 2 and 6 on a busy summer's day at the Hill of Howth. *(GL)*

Teak car No. 9 on route to Sutton. *(RB)*

Tram No. 8 seen close to the depot in September 1956. *(JAS)*

There are four surviving Hill of Howth trams out of the fleet of ten and these are listed below:

Car No. 2 is preserved in California USA.

Car No. 4 is preserved in the Oxford Blue and Cream livery at the Ulster Folk and Transport Museum, Cultra, Co Down.

Car No. 9 is exquisitely preserved by the National Transport Museum, Howth, Co Dublin in the teak livery under the direction of Jim Kilroy. This was the last car in service on the 31st May 1959.

Car No. 10 which was re-gauged from the Irish Standard of 5ft 3in to 4ft 8½in and is currently on display at the National Tramway Museum, Crich, Derbyshire having operated in Blackpool, England, in connection with the Centenary of tramways in that town in 1985. It also carries the teak livery seen on No. 9.

In addition, a pair of bogies was purchased and re-gauged for use in the restoration of Manchester 'California Car' 765 which operates in Manchester's Heaton Park and which also operated in Blackpool in 1985.

Chapter Fifteen
A fond farewell

The year 1929 observed the birth of the first Great Northern Railway Road Motor Services bus in Drogheda. It was not without a sense of irony that it should also end there with the arrival in the Bull Ring at 12.25am on 1st October 1958 of the last bus, which had departed from Eden Quay Dublin at 11.10pm the previous evening. The arrival of this bus brought to an end 29 years of GNR buses. New owners CIE were in effective control of the Road Motor Services of the GNR from about September 1958 as arrangements were being made for the integration of the company's operations. Bobby Pelissier was given the responsibility of amalgamating the GNR depot and engineering functions into that of CIE. Tommy Carton assumed responsibility for the integration of the operations side whilst former GNR Publicity Officer Max Beaton dealt with the complex industrial and staff relations issues.

The integration of the GNRB with CIE was not without complication, particularly as far as the Road Motor Services was concerned. There were four GNR Road Motor Service staff based in the Irish Republic but who actually lived in Northern Ireland, paying income tax and National Insurance there. Whilst this arrangement was acceptable to the GNRB, which operated on both sides of the border, it would be problematical once the GNR interest was split. Similarly there were six Road Motor Staff based in Londonderry and Newry, all of whom lived in Northern Ireland paying tax there. Special arrangements were made by CIE to continue the arrangement. Most of the senior officials of the company retired or pursued independent careers outside CIE, notable exceptions were Tommy Carton, Johnny Owens, Bobby Pelissier, Joe Robinson and Albert Switzer, all of whom have featured in this story and saw out their time with CIE.

The marriage between the GNR and CIE was for the 'former GN men' as they were known, not a happy one. The talk was of 'dissolution' of the GNR but the reality was the 'disillusionment' of many of its former staff. This despite the laudable sentiments expressed by the Chairman of *Córas Iompair Éireann* CS (Todd) Andrews, who in a written address to all staff on 1st October 1958 declared:–

'To-day the part of the undertaking of the Great Northern Railway Board within the State vests in Córas Iompair Éireann. This creates a new situation in Public Transport in Ireland. I feel honoured at being given the task of heading this great concern and on behalf of the Board I offer a welcome to all employees and good wishes for the future. The Board feels sure that the highest traditions of the two undertakings will be fused in the new organisation and will help to create an efficient and economic public transport system of which Ireland will be proud. Such a system can be created only by a belief in success and high endeavour on the part of all employees. It will be the aim of the Board to promote conditions in the organisation where initiative will be encouraged and where merit will be recognised and rewarded.'

Actions speak louder than words , however; of the GNR Chief Officers, not a single one was offered employment by CIE, despite years of transport experience.

George Bruce Howden went on to serve as Chairman of the Ulster Transport Authority, retiring from that position in 1963. He had become Ireland's greatest transport authority of the 20th Century. He passed away peacefully on Saturday 22nd January 1966 after a short illness in the Musgrave and Clark Clinic in Belfast, aged 75 years. His funeral, which was a massive affair, was conducted from Glencraig Church of Ireland Church Craigavad on Tuesday 25th January. Howden's wife Cathryn, his son Harry who had travelled from Northern Rhodesia (now Zambia), and his daughter Helen, who came from Cardiff, led the large contingent of former GNR mourners who, with officials from other railway companies and governments North and South, paid their respects to this great man of Irish Transport. Traffic Manager Campbell Baillie also joined the UTA as did experienced and well-respected railway men such as Norman and Joyce Topley. Conversely, Civil Engineer William Henry Copeland Stone, Company Secretary Plunkett Henry Mumford Carey and Chief Accountant Patrick Henry Patterson all ended their working lives upon the demise of the GNR.

At first there were not too many changes in operations other than the fact that the garages were instructed to change all the legal lettering and apply the type code prefixes whilst retaining the GNR fleet numbers on the buses and lorries. The GNR uniforms for Motormen, Conductors and Inspectors remained for about 18 months until existing stocks at the stores in Dundalk were exhausted. On 1st October 1958 the Dublin City office of the GNR at 2, Lower O'Connell Street was closed. Its functions were now dealt with by the CIE office at 33, Bachelors Walk. The Eden Quay departure points for buses to Howth, Portmarnock, Malahide, Strand Road, St Anne's, Hole in the Wall and Skerries continued for some time. Other former GNR bus services from Dublin were moved to Busaras.

On day one of CIE operation of the GNR the Sligo, Quay Street, parcels and enquiry office was closed with all bus operations being moved up to the railway station. The Cavan/ Enniskillen bus service now used the premises of the Ulster Transport Authority in Eden Street, Enniskillen as an arrival and departure point replacing the recently closed former GNR railway station. Motormen suddenly became known as Omnibus Drivers and now fell under the control of the CIE Traffic Department. Some garages even continued to paint buses in the blue and cream, notably Dundalk and Donegal in a clear act of defiance, until instructed to cease this practice by angry CIE officials in Dublin. Resistance to the imposition of the CIE corporate culture on the fiercely independent 'Great Northern' men was widespread. Many GNR buses went straight from the blue and cream into the CIE livery of the eau-de-nil green livery; some went into an all green scheme and others straight into the cherry red and broken white circa 1959-60. One change that did affect all the staff on the take-over by CIE was that they all got a pay rise, bringing their wages into line with those enjoyed by CIE staff. Parity of pay and conditions between the GNR and CIE was eroded during the GNRB period from 1953-58. Welcome though this was for all concerned, the universal feeling among staff was still one of sadness that the old order was no more.

All services operated by the GNR, which CIE considered were within the Dublin City Area, were given route numbers and some double-deckers were allocated to Clontarf and Summerhill Garages.

These services were:–

- City Centre-St Anne's Estate became service number 29 operated from Clontarf Garage;
- City Centre-Hole-in-the-Wall became 29A and was extended to Grange Road Cross operated from Clontarf Garage;
- City Centre-Howth became service 31 operated from Clontarf Garage;
- City Centre-Strand Road became service 31A operated by Clontarf Garage;
- City Centre-Portmarnock and Malahide became service 32 operated by Clontarf Garage;
- City Centre-Malahide became service 32A operated by Clontarf Garage;
- City Centre-Balbriggan became service 33 operated by Summerhill Garage.

CIE also continued to operate the less frequent GNR services although they did not always allocate them service numbers:

- Skerries Station-Skerries Town;
- Donabate-Portrane eventually became service number 33c from Summerhill Garage;
- Portrane-Swords – no service number operated, from Summerhill Garage;
- Rush Railway Station – Rush Town – no service number, operated from Skerries Dormer Shed;
- Vernon Avenue – Howth via Raheny – the GNR discontinued this service before 1958, however, CIE re-introduced it again in 1959. It operated weekdays only during school terms.

The residents of the St Anne's Estate on the Dublin – Howth Road at Raheny were delighted at the passing of the GNR. CIE increased the frequency of services serving the estate and immediately ousted the few GNR single-deck machines with double-deckers. Conversely CIE infuriated the Dublin populous by closing the Hill of Howth tramway on 31st May 1959, which was technically part of the Road Motor Services. As part of the post-tramway closure arrangements in 1958 CIE ordered three AEC Regent V double-decker buses (AA1-3 HZA 278-80) which were 8ft wide and 30ft long models with semi-automatic transmission. The buses were originally intended to replace the Howth trams but were diverted to Waterford City to operate a rail replacement service between Waterford and Tramore. The bodies were a modification of contemporary CIE style giving accommodation for 69 seated passengers. They were, however, unique in having a luggage compartment at the rear of the vehicle. The staircase was located several feet forward of conventional vehicles as was the rear entrance complete with platform doors. Upon closure of the Hill of Howth tramway CIE introduced two substitute bus services:

- Service 87 – Sutton Station to Baily Post Office; .
- Service 88 – Howth Station to Stella Maris via The Summit.

The two services did not cover the whole route of the tramway – as a result stops between Baily Post Office and Stella Maris (Earlscliffe; Maxwell's Corner; Convent Gate) were not served by any form of public transport.

Abercorn Road bus garage of the GNR was closed as an operational centre on 15th December 1958, although it continued for some time as the base for road freight vehicles. In November 1958 former GNR buses in the Dublin area were allocated as under:

- Clontarf:- 280, 281, 282, 283, 284, 288, 289, 290, 291, 294, 296, 298, 301, 303, 304, 436, 266, 338, 418.
- Summerhill – Sub Depot Allocations as under:-
- Donabate:- 287
- Rush:- 293
- Skerries:- 295,297,302

The single-deck fleet at Abercorn Road was dispatched to the Provincial bus garage at Broadstone; they were:-

- 225, 267, 334, 414, 420, 329, 421, 422.

Engineering and Traffic staffs were redeployed to various CIE Garages in Dublin. A number of surplus former GNR buses and lorries were stored for a short time at Abercorn Road garage pending disposal as was the case at Dundalk Works. The central administration staff of CIE Road Passenger Provincial Services moved from 59 Upper O'Connell Street to the former GNR premises at Amiens Street station in 1959, to make room for a central passenger sales bureau and tours office. The Road Control Office (Passenger) as it was officially known dealt with mainly route licensing, timetables, fares, fleet allocation and vehicle taxation.

Joe Robinson (ex-GNRI Road Motor Services) and Bill Weymes (ex-IOC/GSR) were the senior staff, reporting to Jim Purcell who was also ex-IOC from the pioneering days of that company. They were a splendid team who put into practice the best of both GNR and CIE methods in their work. When Jim Purcell retired in 1970, Dan Kelly who brought with him his own School Transport section replaced him. The combined unit then moved to Conyngham Road in 1971 and became the Road Passenger Planning Group in 1972. There appeared to be indecent haste on the part of senior CIE officials to eradicate any reference to the Great Northern Railway on any item of property or vehicle. Soon after the take-over many former GNR bus stations such as those in Dundalk, Cavan, Drogheda were all quickly repainted in the eau-de-nil colour scheme. Garage and bus depot signage was immediately changed to obliterate the GNR name, replacing it with the new owner's CIE initials. A new 6d CIE provincial bus timetable was issued before the take-over incorporating all the GNR omnibus services the timings of which were largely unaltered. It appeared oddly enough with the front cover in blue and cream. It came as a bit of a shock to most people to find Ardee, Carlingford, Collon, Castlebellingham and all the other areas of Monaghan, Cavan, Donegal, Meath listed under any other title but GNR. The timetable noted under each former GNR service 'The above services will be operated by Great Northern Railway Board until 30th September 1958'.

Most of the former GNR bus fleet was concentrated in its former operating territory although notable exceptions are detailed in chapters dealing with the Gardners, Regal III & IV. At Dundalk most of the records, which the company had archived, were incinerated indiscriminately at the behest of CIE officials who were not interested in keeping any records of the GNR. Some did survive only through the foresight of enthusiasts and employees who were appalled at the way company documents and records were being discarded. Apparently CIE officials were not even interested in retaining works drawings or spare parts books for buses and lorries. The recommendations contained in the 1955 Urwick, Orr and Partners report into the GNRB with its proposal to make the Road Motor Services a highly autonomous company within a company with its own senior management accountable to the Board may have ensured its survival as an independent element of the railway. After all the Londonderry and Lough Swilly Railway have not run trains since 1953 and they are still in existence to this day.

It is the source of great pleasure to me that so many former GNR men and women are still living healthy lives with razor sharp memories of those halcyon days of the mysterious and enigmatic Great Northern Railway. I am happy to report that regular GNR staff reunions take place from Belfast to Dublin, Donegal to Sligo. A Great Northern Railway Clerk from the Traffic Manager's office in Belfast penned the poem below, lamenting the demise of the Great Northern.

The GNR Line

Oh! my darling, Oh! my darling
Oh! My darling, GN Line
Thou art merged and gone forever
Dreadful sorry, railway line.

Like she was and like no other,
But the finest of her kind
Now, alas she is divided,
What an end for such a line.

Eighty years of faithful service,
Generations yet unborn,
Will remember that she once served
Enniskillen and the Boyne.

Directors pleased well with debentures,
Handsome profits from the line,
Basking in the ten per centum,
This could go on for all time.

Came the motors, horrid motors,
And they cut the rates so fine,
Will they even last the month out?
That they did in twenty-nine.

We will save you, pool the traffic,
Said the Gov'ment of the day,
But the pool is now an ocean
Of indecision and delay.

Try one Board and then another,
But, och sure, they're all the same
People want their own wee motors
And they sometimes go by plane.

North and South she's now divided
In new colours she'll be seen,
But to us she'll be the same lads'
Tho' in different shades of green.

And so this was it – the end of the GNR, which had been formed 77 years earlier, which began life as a revenue earner opening up parts of the Irish countryside to a rural folk, who in the early days knew little of life outside their local district. It quickly became a household friend and when buses and lorries came along the railway, which began to take the appearance of an integrated transport, network was no more. Into the mists of history disappeared this most 'Mysterious and Enigmatic' railway.

Appendix A (1) – Bus and Lorry Fleet								
Fleet No.	Reg'n	Type	Chassis Number	Body	Date New	Seats	Payload	Comments
1	ZI 2583	Leyland PLSC1	47791	Leyland	15.1.29	31		Became Garage Tender GT1 in 1938 – Scrapped 1950
1	ZA 933	Morris CS	173 05241		18.11.33		3 ton	Purchased from T Cooney & Sons, Drogheda 29.3.44 – Scrapped 7.4.49
1	IY 4413	Ford	T 279659		1940		2.5 ton	Became Garage Tender GT5 in 1954 – Scrapped 1955
1	IH 6154	Ford	799AF1723852	V8 Station Wagon	12.2.47	6	1 ton	Former SC21 renumbered newspaper van No. 1 (Jan '53) renumbered SC17 baggage van (Mar '55)
1	IY 9922	Bedford A5L	A5L CO34185	Newspaper Van	1.10.54		4 tons	Passed to CIE as B100
2	ZI 2725	Leyland PLSC3	47515	City Wheel Works	22.2.29	32		Scrapped 1.10.37
2	IY 3157	Morris CS	649C21727		3.2.36		3 tons	Purchased from T Cooney & Sons, Drogheda 29.3.44 – Scrapped Dec 1948
2	ZY 2	Bedford A5LCO	A5L CO36666	Tipper	25.10.54		5 tons	Passed to CIE as BT 60
3	ZI 2741	Leyland PLSC3	47516	City Wheel Works	4.3.29	32		
3	IY 3558	Morris Leader	1054C31921		1.9.37		4 tons	Purchased from T Cooney & Sons, Drogheda – Scrapped 4.8.51
3	ZY 3	Bedford A5LCO	A5L CO36665	Tipper	25.10.54		5 tons	Passed to CIE as BT61
4	IY 9431	AEC 413	413131		4.11.26	32		Converted to a railbus SLNCR A
4	ZA 4432	Morris Leader	365PB1269		18.4.35		4 tons	Purchased from freight operator J Reilly, Navan 25.2.35 – Scrapped 13.6.53
4	ZY 4	Bedford A5LCO	A5L CO36659	Tipper	1.11.54		5 tons	Passed to CIE as BT62
5	YI 9432	AEC 413	413119		4.11.26	32		Converted to a railbus
5	AI 4095	Morris C	56/C 3615		24.7.33		3 tons	Purchased from freight operator J Hughes 25.2.35 – Scrapped 1938
5	MI 3047	Morris Leader	133 - AI/02/260		1.5.45		3 ton	Built from spare parts – Scrapped 23.2.48
5	ZY 5	Bedford A5LCO	A5L CO36661	Tipper	1.12.54		5 tons	Passed to CIE as BT63
6	ZI 2451	AEC 426	426161		20.12.28	30		Converted to railbus F – Destroyed 1944
6	AI 4122	Morris C	56/C 3491		22.7.33		3 tons	Acquired from freight operator J Reilly, Navan 25.2.35 – Scrapped 7.4.49
7	ZI 2452	AEC 426	426179		20.12.28	30		Converted to railbus E using body from bus 186
7	ZI 338	ADC	506169	Open Platform	22.7.27		6 tons	From freight operator J Reilly, Navan 25.2.35 tractor/trailer combination – Scrapped 1938
7	IY 3081	Morris Leader	AI/13/2199		2.10.35		4 tons	Purchased from freight operator S Lockington Ltd 31.1.45 – Scrapped 7.4.49
8	ZI 1164	Leyland PLSC3	46493	Leyland	4.2.28	B32F		
8	IY 3167	Morris Leader	AI/27/2210		8.2.36		4 tons	Purchased from freight operators S Lockington Ltd 31.1.45 – Scrapped 3.3.50
9	ZI 1429	Leyland PLSC3	46339		17.5.28	B35		Scrapped 1.10.37
9	ZC 3442	Albion M550	17744I	GNR Body	4.3.38		6 tons	Scrapped 5.9.56
10	ZI 2226	Leyland PLSC3	47549	Leyland	12.10.28	B35F		Scrapped 1.10.37
10	ZC 3443	Albion M550	17744J	GNR Body	25.3.38		6 tons	Fitted with Gardner Engine – Scrapped 30.10.56
11	Z 1916	Leyland PLSC3	47510	Leyland	18.12.28	B36F		Scrapped 1.10.37
11	ZC 5566	Albion CXIN	54006K	GNR Body	1.1.39		6 tons	Fitted with Gardner 5LW engine.Sold to Sheiling & Sons 24.6.57
12	Z 1310	Morris T	16254		25.5.28	14		Became the Bundoran Hotel Bus 1930 later converted to mechanics van
12	IY 4930	Albion CXIL	54049D		22.4.47		6 tons	Became CIE fleet No. AP12
13	ZI 5503	Ford A	A3731542	Mail Van Body	1930		0.5 ton	Purchased from freight operator J Reilly of Navan 25.2.35 mail van body – Scrapped 1940
13	IY 4931	Albion CXIL	54049E	Furniture Van	11.4.47		6 tons	Became CIE fleet No. AP13
14	ZI 2985	AEC Reliance	660015	City Wheel Works	17.4.29	31		Fitted with new body 21.12.35 with 'cutaway' rear entrance door
14	IY 4732	Albion FT3L	70560B	GNR Open Platform	21.6.46		5 tons	Chassis assembled in Dundalk Works Became CIE Fleet No. AP14
15	AZ 94	Dennis G	70118		5.3.28	20	2 tons	Converted to an open platform lorry 1930 – Scrapped 25.5.39
15	IY 4733	Albion FT3L	70560C	GNR Open Platform	1.7.46		5 tons	Chassis assembled in Dundalk Works Became CIE Fleet No. AP 15
16	AZ 301	Dennis G	70190		28.3.28	20		To NIRTB October 1935

Appendix A (1) – Bus and Lorry Fleet								
Fleet No.	Reg'n	Type	Chassis Number	Body	Date New	Seats	Payload	Comments
16	IY 4822	Albion AZ7N	50265F	GNR Open Platform	9.12.46		3 tons	Chassis assembled in Dundalk Works Became CIE Fleet No AP 16
17	AZ 402	Dennis G	70199		7.4.28	20	2 tons	Converted to an open platform lorry 1929 – Scrapped 1938
17	IY 4823	Albion AZ7N	50266F	GNR Furniture Van	20.12.46		3 tons	Chassis assembled in Dundalk Works Became CIE Fleet No. AP 17
18	AZ 724	Dennis G	70225		25.5.28	20	2 tons	Converted to a lorry
18	IY 2695	Fordson	B5150404	Open Platform	27.3.33		2 tons	Purchased from freight operator JJ O'Hare, Dundalk 3.5.35 – Scrapped June 1949
19	AZ 1039	Dennis G	70185		30.6.28	20		To NIRTB October 1935
19	IY 4853	Albion AZ7N	50267E	GNR Open Platform	13.1.47		3 tons	Chassis assembled in Dundalk Works Became CIE Fleet No. AP 19
20	AZ 1054	Dennis G	70293		7.7.28	20	2 tons	Converted to a lorry 1929
20	IY 2695	Fordson	AA4481354	Open Platform	9.5.32		1.5 tons	Purchased from freight operator JJ O'Hare, Dundalk 3.5.35 – Scrapped 1938
20	IY 4852	Albion AZ7N	50265H	GNR Open Platform	5.2.47		3 tons	Chassis assembled in Dundalk Works Became CIE Fleet No. AP20
21	IB 3981	Dennis E	17576		3.9.28	31		To NIRTB October 1935
21	IY 4906	Albion AZ7N	50267F	GNR Open Platform	10.3.47		3 tons	Chassis assembled in Dundalk Works Became CIE Fleet No AP 21
22	ZI 3185	AEC Reliance	660266	City Wheel Works	7.5.29	31		Rebodied to rear entrance 9.5.36
22	IY 5829	Albion FT7N	71502D	C Morgan & Son Drogheda	15.10.48		3 tons	Chassis assembled in Dundalk Works Became CIE Fleet No. AP22
23	ZI 3264	AEC Reliance	660267	City Wheel Works	7.5.29	31		Rebodied to rear entrance 6.7.35
23	IY 5830	Albion FT7N	71502C	C Morgan & Son Drogheda	15.10.48		3 tons	Chassis assembled in Dundalk Works Became CIE Fleet No. AP 23
24	ZI 3265	AEC Reliance	660269	City Wheel Works	5.8.29	31		Rebodied to rear entrance 24.6.36
24	IY 5831	Albion FT7N	71502J	C Morgan & Son Drogheda	15.10.48		3 tons	Chassis assembled in Dundalk Works Became CIE Fleet No. AP 24
25	ZI 3263	AEC Reliance	660268	City Wheel Works	17.5.29	31	6 tons	Fitted with 'streamline' body 16.2.35 then converted to a lorry 1941 cost £215 renumbered 69 in 1947
25	IY 5832	Albion FT7N	71502F	C Morgan & Son Drogheda	12.10.48		3 tons	Chassis assembled in Dundalk Works Became CIE Fleet No AP 25
26	ZI 3354	AEC Reliance	660274	Aylesbury Brothers	3.6.29	34		Scrapped 1.10.37
26	IY 5833	Albion FT7N	71502E	C Morgan & Son Drogheda	11.10.48		3 tons	Chassis assembled in Dundalk Works Became CIE Fleet No. AP 26
27	ZI 3461	AEC Reliance	660270	J Potter	22.6.29	32		Scrapped 1.3.37
27	IY 5834	Albion FT7N	71502H	C Morgan & Son Drogheda	11.10.48		3 tons	Chassis assembled in Dundalk Works Became CIE Fleet No. AP 27
28	ZI 3483	AEC Reliance	660281	Aylesbury Brothers	27.6.29	31		Fitted with new body 23.11.35 with rear entrance
29	ZI 3512	AEC Reliance	660144	J Potter	29.6.29	32		Scrapped 1.10.37
29	IY 5152	Albion FT3L	70633F	C Morgan & Son Drogheda	20.10.47		5 tons	Chassis assembled in Dundalk Works Became CIE Fleet No. AP 29
30	ZI 3513	AEC Reliance	660145	J Potter	29.6.29	32		Fitted with new body 12.10.35 with rear entrance
30	IY 5153	Albion FT3L	70633E	C Morgan & Son Drogheda	17.11.47		5 tons	Chassis assembled in Dundalk Works Became CIE Fleet No. AP30
31	ZI 3533	AEC Reliance	660282	Aylesbury Brothers	3.7.29	31		Fitted with new body 25.1.36
31	IY 5154	Albion FT3L	70640H	C Morgan & Son Drogheda	1.2.48		5 tons	Chassis assembled in Dundalk Works Became CIE Fleet No. AP31
32	ZI 3545	AEC Reliance	660146	City Wheel Works	6.7.29	31		Fitted with new body 11.2.36
32	IY 5155	Albion FT3L	70644H	C Morgan & Son Drogheda	1.2.48		5 tons	Chassis assembled in Dundalk Works Became CIE Fleet No. AP 32
33	ZI 1693	ADC 416	416629		9.6.28	30		Converted to a Railbus DNGR No. 1
33	ZA 3827	Dennis Ace	200376N116	GNR	6.3.35	20		Sold to Irish Army June 1942
33	IY 5156	Albion FT3L	70644J	C Morgan & Son Drogheda	18.3.48		5 tons	Chassis assembled in Dundalk Works Became CIE Fleet No AP 33
34	ZI 1704	ADC 416	416631		4.6.28	30		Converted to a railbus DNGR No. 2
34	ZA 3827	Dennis Ace	200385N116	GNR	31.5.35	20		Converted to ARP Ambulance – restored to bus renumbered 225 in 1946

Appendix A (1) – Bus and Lorry Fleet								
Fleet No.	Reg'n	Type	Chassis Number	Body	Date New	Seats	Payload	Comments
34	IY 5960	Albion FT35L	72808E	C Morgan & Son Drogheda	21.1.49		5 tons	Chassis assembled in Dundalk Works Became CIE Fleet No. AD34
35	ZI 2089	ADC 416	416491		31.8.28	34		Converted to a Railbus
35	ZA 3829	Dennis Ace	200386N116	GNR	6.3.35	20		Sold to Irish Army June 1942
35	IY 5961	Albion FT35L	72808D	C Morgan & Son Drogheda	26.1.49		5 tons	Chassis assembled in Dundalk Works Became CIE Fleet No. AD 35
36	AZ 2754	AEC	204436		6.5.29		2.5 tons	Allocated to Banbridge – To NIRTB October 1935
36	ZA 7154	Dennis Ace	200492F116	GNR	1.3.37	20		Sold to Eire Army 1942
36	IY 5962	Albion FT35L	72812K	C Morgan & Son Drogheda	15.3.49		5 tons	Chassis assembled in Dundalk Works Became CIE Fleet No AD 36
37	AZ 2839	AEC	204434		6.5.29		2.5 tons	Allocated to Ballyroney – To NIRTB October 1935
37	ZA 7155	Dennis Ace	200493F116	GNR	1.3.37	20		Sold to Eire Army 1942
37	IY 5963	Albion FT35L	72812J	C Morgan & Son Drogheda	1.4.49		5 tons	Chassis assembled in Dundalk Works Became CIE Fleet No AD 37
38	AZ 2838	AEC	204413		6.5.29		2.5 tons	Allocated to Lurgan – To NIRTB October 1935
38	IH 3196	Dennis 4 ton	160043		25.4.32	25	4 tons	Acquired from Nawn Ballyshannon converted to bus 1936, to lorry 24.7.42 renumbered 70
38	IY 5964	Albion FT35L	72812L	C Morgan & Son Drogheda	1.4.49		5 tons	Chassis assembled in Dundalk Works Became CIE Fleet No. AD 38
39	ZI 3552	AEC Reliance	660363	J Potter	9.7.29	32		Fitted with new body 21.9.35
39	IY 5965	Albion FT35L	72826J	C Morgan & Son Drogheda	1.5.49		5 tons	Chassis assembled in Dundalk Works Became CIE Fleet No AD 39
40	ZI 3553	AEC Reliance	660364	J Potter	13.7.29	32		Fitted with new body 7.11.35
40	IY 5966	Albion FT35L	72826L	C Morgan & Son Drogheda	1.5.49		5 tons	Chassis assembled in Dundalk Works Became CIE Fleet No AD 40
41	ZI 3554	AEC Reliance	660300	J Potter	19.7.29	31		Fitted with new body 25.2.36
41	IY 5967	Albion FT35L	72826H	C Morgan & Son Drogheda	1.5.49		5 tons	Chassis assembled in Dundalk Works Body designed for conveyance of Explosives Became CIE Fleet No. AD 41
42	IB 4249	AEC Reliance	660273	Vickers	17.6.29	32		Fitted with new body 27.6.35
42	IY 5968	Albion FT35L	72826K	C Morgan & Son Drogheda	1.6.49		5 tons	Chassis assembled in Dundalk Works Became CIE Fleet No. AD 42
43	IB 4251	AEC Reliance	660272	Service Motor Works	8.7.29	32		Scrapped 1.10.37 following a fire.
43	IY 8057	Albion FT37	73201E	GNR	1.6.52		5 tons	Chassis assembled in Dundalk Works Became CIE Fleet No. AD 43
44	IB 4250	AEC Reliance	660271	Service Motor Works	4.7.29	31		Fitted with new body 30.5.36
45	AZ 2962	AEC Reliance	660013	Service Motor Works	17.5.29	32		AEC Demonstrator purchased for £1, 300 – Destroyed by fire following collision with lorry near Cavan 20.8.32
45	ZI 3511	AEC Reliance	660232	O'Gorman	12.7.29	32		Very low roof – Sun Saloon purchased from Furey's Motor Coaches – Scrapped 1.10.37
45	BM 5601	Maudslay	1429		1916		6 ton	Purchased from McCalden Monaghan 16.5.39
45	IY 5032	Ford V8	799TF1567549	Tipper	5.7.47		5 tons	Scrapped 29.11.54
46	MT 3228	AEC Reliance	660009	Hall Lewis	11.4.29	32		AEC Demonstrator bought by GNR in September 1929 for £1, 275 – Scrapped 1.10.37
46	IB 3740	ADC 506	506293		3.12.27		6 tons	Purchased from McCalden Monaghan 16.5.39 – Scrapped 3.3.50
47	BI 1514	Reo	147021		1.10.27	20		Sold to Ashenhurst, Williams
47	AI 4171	Bedford WL	127195	Open Platform	5.12.33		2 tons	Purchased from freight operator Peter Geraghty 25.2.35 – Scrapped 1937
47	IY 4889	Ford V8	699TF11215949	Tipper	26.2.47		5 tons	Scrapped 25.10.54
48	BI 1524	Reo	147247		14.11.27	20		Sold to Ashenhurst, Williams
48	AI 4092	Bedford WL	123394	Open Platform	13.4.33		2 tons	Purchased from freight operator Peter Geraghty 25.2.35 – Scrapped June 1946
48	IY 4907	Ford V8	699TF11216002	Tipper	10.3.47		5 tons	Scrapped 29.11.54
49	BI 1535	Dennis G	70153		1928	20		Scrapped 1.10.36
49	IY 2672	Bedford WL	106408		12.12.32		2 tons	Purchased from freight operator Daly Bros 31.10.35 – Scrapped June 1946
49	IY 4814	Ford V8	669TF11997873	Tipper	11.11.46		5 tons	Scrapped 29.4.55
50	BI 1567	ADC 416	416681		15.7.28	32		Rebodied at Dundalk March 1933

Appendix A (1) – Bus and Lorry Fleet								
Fleet No.	Reg'n	Type	Chassis Number	Body	Date New	Seats	Payload	Comments
50	IY 4782	Austin	K4/VF/97459	Tipper	10.10.46		4 tons	Scrapped 30.10.56
51	BI 1574	Dennis F	45507		11.7.28	26		Converted to Dundalk Garage Tender 18.10.30 open platform fitted with crane, toolbox, searchlight.
51	IY 4811	Austin	K4/VF/99367	Tipper	11.11.46		4 tons	Scrapped 30.10.56
52	BI 1589	Dennis G	70324		1.9.28	20		To Bundoran Hotel bus in 1934 – Scrapped 1.10.36
52	ZH 37	Austin	K4/VF/107803	Tipper	14.6.47		4 tons	Scrapped 5.9.56
53	AZ 3574	AEC 204	204387		22.2.29		2.5 tons	Allocated to Omagh To NIRTB October 1935
53	YI 5743	Karrier	20458		13.8.24		3 tons	From freight operator HJ Boylan 23.12.35 became Garage Tender – Scrapped 1938
53	ZH 38	Austin	K4/VF/107953	Tipper	14.6.47		4 tons	Scrapped 30.10.56
54	ZI 3766	AEC	204395	Open Platform	2.9.29		2.5 tons	Allocated to Dundalk Barrack Street – Scrapped December 1938
55	AZ 3575	AEC 204	204403		22.2.29		1.5 tons	Allocated to Lisburn – Destroyed by accident October 1929
55	IY 2451	Morris Commercial	5801		13.12.30		1.5 tons	Purchased from freight operator S Lockington 22.10.35 – Scrapped 1940
55	IY 5045	Austin	K2/VV/108829		19.7.47		2 tons	Passed to CIE as AN55
56	XI 8777	Dennis E	17089		3.6.27	32		To NIRTB October 1935
56	IY 2615	Morris Commercial	26362		1.4.32		1.5 tons	Purchased from freight operator S Lockington 22.10.35 – Scrapped 1940
56	IY 5208	Austin	K2/VV/112823		12.11.47		2 tons	Passed to CIE as AN56
57	AZ 1119	Dennis E	17534		7.7.28	32		To NIRTB October 1935
57	IY 2642	Morris Commercial	296	6 wheeler	9.7.32		3 tons	Purchased from freight operator S Lockington 22.10.35 – Scrapped June 1946
57	IY 5218	Austin	K2/VV/112828		12.11.47		2 tons	Passed to CIE as AN57
58	AZ 1131	Lancia	2088		11.7.28	26		Scrapped 1.10.37
58	ZI 3510	Dennis E	17676		29.6.29	29		Purchased from Furey's Motor Tours 27.3.35 – Scrapped 1.10.37
58	IY 5417	Austin	K4/VF/113587	Tipper	21.2.48		4 tons	Scrapped 5.9.56
59	AZ 1386	Dennis E	17570		10.9.28	30		To NIRTB October 1935
59	IY 5418	Austin	K4/VF/113590	Tipper	21.2.48		4 tons	Withdrawn and converted to Garage Tender No. 3 16.1.57
60	AZ 2110	Graham/Dodge	A659586		5.4.26	20		Sold to Ashenhurst & Williams
60	ZA 2421	AEC Regal	6621535		29.6.34	32		Purchased from Furey's Motor Tours 27.3.35 had a sliding roof – Scrapped 20.5.54
61	AZ 2023	Dennis E	17002		11.5.29	31		
61	ZA 7156	AEC Regal MKII	862052	GNR	2.7.36	35		Purchased new from Dublin AEC dealer Thomas Thompson – Scrapped 8.5.53
62	IK 4580	Karrier CX	CX 20003		25.1.27	20		Converted to Garage Tender for Dublin Garage 1930
62	ZI 502	ADC 417	417054		4.7.27	29		Purchased from Furey's Motor Tours 27.3.35 – Scrapped 1.10.37
62	ZC 2756	AEC Regent	6615342	PRV/GNR	16.10.37	56		Scrapped 2.7.56
63	AZ 3918	Morris	3923		6.12.29		1.5 tons	Allocated to Dromore Road – To NIRTB October 1935
63	ZC 2577	AEC Regent	6615342	PRV/GNR	18.10.37	56		Scrapped 2.7.56
64	AZ 3919	Morris	3847		6.12.29		1.5 tons	Allocated to Banbridge – To NIRTB October 1935
64	ZC 6981	AEC Regent	6616374	PRV/GNR	23.5.39	56		Scrapped 16.10.48 following a Road Traffic Accident
64	ZY 2017	Bedford SA	SAO48620		12.10.56		10 tons	Passed to CIE as BS64
65	AZ 3920	Morris	3242		1.1.30		1.5 tons	Allocated to Ballyroney To NIRTB October 1935
65	ZC 6982	AEC Regent	6616375	PRV/GNR	22.7.39	56		Scrapped 20.5.54
65	ZY 2018	Bedford SA	SAO48623		24.10.56		10 tons	Passed to CIE as BS65
66	AZ 3921	Leyland Badger	TA1 65714		3.1.30		2.5 tons	Allocated to Dungannon – To NIRTB October 1935
66	ZC 6983	AEC Regent	6616379	PRV/GNR	17.6.39	56		Scrapped 2.7.56
66	ZY 2023	Bedford SA	SAO48617		7.10.56		10 tons	Passed to CIE as BS66
67	AZ 3922	Leyland Badger	TA1 65713		3.1.30		2.5 tons	Allocated to Lurgan – To NIRTB October 1935

Appendix A (1) – Bus and Lorry Fleet								
Fleet No.	Reg'n	Type	Chassis Number	Body	Date New	Seats	Payload	Comments
67	ZC 6984	AEC Regent	6616376	PRV/GNR	1.5.39	56		Scrapped 20.5.54
67	ZY 1485	Bedford SA	SAO43215	Tractor	1.3.56		10 tons	Passed to CIE as BS67
68	ZI 4110	Leyland Badger	TA1 65715		3.1.30		2.5 tons	Allocated to Dublin Goods – Scrapped 1956
68	ZY 1487	Bedford SA	SAO43216	Tractor	1.3.56		10 tons	Passed to CIE as BS68
69	IB 3572	Reo	142533		16.4.27	20		Sold to County Donegal Railways July 1930
69	BI 1760	Chevrolet	L 061085	Open Platform	12.12.29		1.5 tons	Purchased from freight operator R Chambers, Dundalk 1.7.35 – Scrapped 1936
69	ZI 3263	AEC Reliance	660268		17.5.29		6 tons	Converted from bus to lorry – Scrapped 29.11.54
69	ZY 1488	Bedford SA	SAO45686	Tractor	1.5.56		10 tons	Passed to CIE as BS69
70	IB 3841	Dennis G	70209		7.4.28	20		
70	BI 1879	Chevrolet	68590	Box Van	1.11.30		1.5 tons	Purchased from freight operator J Kiernan, Inniskeen 9.5.35 – Scrapped 1936
70	IH 3196	Dennis 4 ton	160043		25.4.32	25	4 tons	Purchased from R Nawn, Ballyshannon formerly lorry 38, reconverted to lorry (333) 1942 renumbered 70 in 9/1948 – Scrapped 7.4.49
70	IY 9158	Bedford A4SSG	A4SSG.16461	Scammell	1.1.54		8 tons	Passed to CIE as BS70
71	IB 3527	AEC 414	414095		19.3.27	26		Converted to Garage Tender Belfast – to NIRTB October 1935
71	AI 4305	Bedford	135242	Open Platform	1.9.35		2 tons	Acquired from J Barnes freight operator Drogheda 14.11.35 – Scrapped 2.9.48
71	IY 9159	Bedford A4SSG	A4SSG16551	Scammell	1.1.54		8 tons	Passed to CIE as BS71
72	IA 5629	Reo	119157		11.8.25	20		Sold to County Donegal Railways July 1930
72	ZA 4112	Bedford WTL	873203	Open Platform	26.3.35		3 tons	Purchased from freight operator Peter Geraghty 25.2.35 – Scrapped 4.8.51
72	IY 9161	Bedford A4SSG	A4SSG16640	Scammell	1.1.54		8 tons	Passed to CIE as BS72
73	IA 5773	Reo	119399		10.7.25	14		Sold to County Donegal Railways July 1930
73	IY 2735	Bedford WL	125887	Open Platform	7.10.33		2 tons	Purchased from freight operator P McCloskey, Drogheda 8.1.35 – Scrapped 23.5.45
73	IY 6117	Bedford OSS	OSS60662	Scammell	13.4.49		8 tons	Passed to CIE as BS73
74	XI 9530	Reo	147247		31.10.27	21		Sold To H McAnulty Warrenpoint 29.4.32
74	IY 2753	Bedford	125887	Open Platform/Sheep rails	7.12.33		2 tons	Purchased from freight operator P McCloskey, Drogheda 8.1.35 – Scrapped 1938
74	IY 6861	Bedford OSS	OSS62645	Scammell	1.7.50		8 tons	Passed to CIE as BS74
75	XI 5587	Reo	123879		2.11.23	14		Sold to County Donegal Railways July 1930
75	IY 2835	Federal	15B 162119	Platform Truck	5.7.34		2 tons	Purchased from freight operator P McCloskey, Drogheda 8.1.35 – Scrapped 12.48
75	IY 7525	Bedford OSS	OSS213923	Scammell	17.7.51		8 tons	Passed to CIE as BS75
76	ZI 4331	Morris Commercial	3485/2	Open Platform	18.1.30		1.5 tons	Allocated to Castleblaney – Scrapped 12.38
76	IY 3202	Federal	86013	Open Platform	14.4.36		2 tons	Purchased from freight operator CF Bellew Ltd 26.8.44 – Scrapped 7.4.49
76	IY 7836	Bedford OSS	OSS223005	Scammell	1.2.52		8 tons	Passed to CIE as BS76
77	ZI 4332	Morris Commercial	4730K	Open Platform	27.1.30		1.5 tons	Allocated to Dundalk Works – Scrapped June 1946
77	IY 8339	Bedford	OSS244941	Scammell Tractor	15.12.52		8 tons	Purchased for W & C McDonnell Stork Margarine Contract Passed to CIE as BS77
78	ZI 4333	Morris Commercial	4741R	Open Platform	31.1.30		1.5 tons	Allocated to Cavan – Scrapped 1941
78	IY 8819	Bedford OSS	OSS244933	Scammell	1.7.53		8 tons	Passed to CIE as BS78
79	ZI 4262	Leyland Tiger TS2	60641	CWW	31.1.30	31		Scrapped February 1949
79	IY 8822	Bedford OSS	OSS260704	Scammell	1.8.53		8 tons	Passed to CIE as BS79
80	ZI 4263	Leyland Tiger TS2	60825	Potter Sun Saloon	1.2.30	31		Fitted with new GNR body 8.1.36 with cutaway rear door then converted to Garage Tender GT2
80	IY 7983	Bedford SST	SSC6318	Tipper	1.5.52		7 tons	Passed to CIE as BT46
81	ZI 4264	Leyland Tiger TS2	60872	Potter Sun Saloon	8.2.30	30		Fitted with new GNR body 8.3.37 with folding doors – Scrapped 5.12.49
81	IY 7984	Bedford SST	SSC8632	Tipper	1.5.52		7 tons	Cab replaced following severe accident Inniskeen 21.12.55 £170 Passed to CIE as BT47

Appendix A (1) – Bus and Lorry Fleet								
Fleet No.	Reg'n	Type	Chassis Number	Body	Date New	Seats	Payload	Comments
82	ZI 4265	Leyland Tiger TS2	60873	CWW	14.2.30	31		New GNR body 4.3.36 – Scrapped 9.6.48
82	IY 7985	Bedford SST	SSC8634	Tipper	1.5.52		7 tons	Passed to CIE as BT48
83	ZI 4266	Leyland Tiger TS2	60874	Potter Sun Saloon	28.2.30	31		Fitted with new GNR body 23.11.35 with cutaway rear door – Scrapped 5.12.49
83	IY 7986	Bedford SST	SSC8631	Tipper	1.5.52		7 tons	Passed to CIE as BT49
84	ZI 4267	Leyland Tiger TS2	60875	CWW	3.3.30	31		Scrapped 28.4.47
84	IY 7987	Bedford SST	SSC8636	Tipper	1.5.52		7 tons	Passed to CIE as BT50
85	ZI 4268	Leyland Tiger TS2	60876	Potter Sun Saloon	28.2.30	31		Fitted with new GNR body with cutaway rear door 16.10.36 – Scrapped 28.4.47
85	IY 7988	Bedford SST	SSC 8633	Tipper	1.5.52		7 tons	Passed to CIE as BT51
86	ZI 4269	Leyland Tiger TS2	60877	CWW	14.3.30	31		Converted to a Horse Box No. 127
86	IY 7989	Bedford SST	SSC8635	Tipper	19.9.52		7 tons	Passed to CIE as BT52
87	ZI 4270	Leyland Tiger TS2	60878	GNR	20.5.30	31		First GNR built bus body built at Dundalk – Scrapped February 1949
87	ZY 1772	Bedford SST	74284	GNR Van Body	7.6.56		5 tons	Long wheel base Dundalk built body Passed to CIE as B101
88	ZI 4271	Leyland Tiger TS2	60879	Potter Sun Saloon	14.3.30	31		Fitted with new GNR body 30.5.36 – renumbered 279 in 1945
88	IY 4642	Ford V8	BB 18F7164565	Platform Truck	10.12.45		5 tons	Scrapped 4.8.51
88	ZY 1773	Bedford SST	72426	GNR Van Body	1.7.56		5 tons	Long wheel base Dundalk built body Passed to CIE as B102
89	ZI 4272	Leyland Tiger TS2	60880	CWW	24.3.30	31		Fitted with new GNR body 13.6.36 – renumbered 280 in 1945
89	IY 4643	Ford V8	BB 18F7164928	Platform Truck	10.12.45		5 tons	Scrapped 30.10.56
90	ZI 4273	Leyland Tiger TS2	60881	Potter Sun Saloon	24.3.30	31		Written off at Balrath 26.12.33
90	IY 4644	Ford V8	BB 18F7164966	Platform Truck	10.12.45		5 tons	Scrapped 1.9.45
91	ZI 4274	Leyland Tiger TS2	60882	Potter Sun Saloon	9.4.30	31		Fitted with new GNR body with cutaway rear doors 21.11.36 – renumbered 281 in 1945
91	IY 4645	Ford V8	BB 18F7165193	Platform Truck	10.12.45		5 tons	Scrapped 1.1.56
92	ZI 4275	Leyland Tiger TS2	60883	CWW	24.3.30	31		Fitted with new GNR body with cutaway rear doors 9.10.36 – renumbered 282 in 1945
92	IY 4646	Ford V8	BB 18F7165212	Platform Truck	10.12.45		5 tons	Scrapped 27.9.55
93	ZI 4276	Leyland Tiger TS2	60884	CWW	9.4.30	31		Fitted with new GNR body with rear door 14.12.35 converted to Lorry 128 Horsebox 17.9.45
93	IY 4647	Ford V8	BB 18F7164890	Platform Truck	10.12.45		5 tons	Scrapped 1.1.56
93	ZY 1982	Bedford A5L	A51CO 85232	GNR Tipper Body	1.1.57		5 tons	Passed to CIE as B103
94	ZI 4277	Leyland Tiger TS2	60885	Potter Sun Saloon	17.4.30	31		Fitted with new GNR body cutaway rear door 13.11.36 – renumbered 283 in 1945
94	IY 4648	Ford V8	7166593	Tipper	26.8.46		4 tons	Scrapped 7.8.53
94	ZY 1376	Bedford A5L	A51CO 74282	GNR Tipper Body	1.1.56		5 tons	Passed to CIE as BT64
95	ZI 4278	Leyland Tiger TS2	60886	CWW	17.4.30	31		Fitted with new GNR body 22.6.35
95	IY 4649	Ford V8	7166649	Tipper	16.3.46		4 tons	Scrapped 8.4.54
95	ZY 1377	Bedford A5L	A51CO 72427	GNR Tipper Body	1.1.56		5 tons	Passed to CIE as BT65
96	ZI 4279	Leyland Tiger TS2	60887	Potter Sun Saloon	5.5.30	31		New GNR body fitted 20.11.37 sold to Sligo Leitrim & Northern Counties Railway 20.3.45
96	IY 4650	Ford V8	7166597	Tipper	16.3.46		4 tons	Scrapped 2.12.53
96	ZY 1378	Bedford A5L	A51CO 74275	GNR Tipper Body	1.1.56		5 tons	Passed to CIE as BT66
97	ZI 4280	Leyland Tiger TS2	60893	CWW	16.5.30	31		Fitted with new GNR body 12.12.36 – converted to Lorry 129 (Horsebox) 17.9.45
97	IY 4651	Ford V8	7166634	Tipper	26.8.46		4 tons	Scrapped 25.10.54
97	ZY 1379	Bedford A5L	A51CO 74276	GNR Tipper Body	1.1.56		5 tons	Passed to CIE as BT67
98	ZI 4281	Leyland Tiger TS2	60894	Potter Sun Saloon	8.5.30	31		New GNR body 30.5.36 renumbered 284 in 1945
98	IY 4652	Ford V8	7166608	Tipper	19.8.46		4 tons	Scrapped 25.10.54
98	ZY 1983	Bedford A5L	A51CO 74279	GNR Tipper Body	8.10.56		5 tons	Passed to CIE as BT68
99	AZ 1961	Gilford 15 SD	10607		7.2.29	26		To NIRTB October 1935
99	IY 4653	Ford V8	7165585	Tipper	10.8.46		4 tons	Scrapped 29.11.54
99	ZY 1984	Bedford A5L	A51CO 87256	GNR Tipper Body	12.10.56		5 tons	Passed to CIE as BT69
100	IY 1973	Dennis G	70037		6.10.27	19	2 tons	Converted to a lorry 1.9.32
100	IY 4592	Ford V8	BB 18F7151942	Tipper	4.5.45		5 tons	Scrapped 25.10.54

Appendix A (1) – Bus and Lorry Fleet								
Fleet No.	**Reg'n**	**Type**	**Chassis Number**	**Body**	**Date New**	**Seats**	**Payload**	**Comments**
100	ZY 1985	Bedford A5L	A51CO 87250	GNR Tipper Body	1.11.56		5 tons	Passed to CIE as BT70
101	IY 1989	Dennis G	70020		10.12.27	20	2 tons	Converted to a lorry
101	IY 4593	Ford V8	BB 18F7152028	Tipper	4.5.45		5 tons	Scrapped 25.10.54
101	ZY 1986	Bedford A5L	A51CO 87255	GNR Tipper Body	1.1.57		5 tons	Passed to CIE as BT 71
102	IY 2001	Dennis G	70033		4.1.28	20	2 tons	Converted to a lorry – Scrapped 25.5.39
102	IY 4594	Ford V8	BB 18F7151607	Tipper	8.8.45		5 tons	Scrapped 30.10.56
102	ZY 1987	Bedford A5L	A51CO 87249	GNR Tipper Body	19.10.56		5 tons	Passed to CIE as BT72
103	IJ 5228	Ford	794828		3.1.24	14		Sold in 1932
103	IY 2770	Bedford	128425	Open Platform	26.1.34		2 tons	Purchased from freight operator L Muckian, Dundalk 7.5.35 – Scrapped 1937
103	IY 4595	Ford V8	BB 18F7155632	Tipper	5.7.45		5 tons	Scrapped 8.4.54
103	ZY 1988	Bedford A5L	A51CO 87253	GNR Tipper Body	12.10.56		5 tons	Passed to CIE as BT73
104	IJ 7518	Ford	12976587		27.5.26	14		Sold in 1931
104	IY 2250	Morris Commercial	20279	Open Platform	1.10.29		1.5 tons	Purchased from freight operator Maher Bros. Dundalk 1.7.35 – Scrapped 1936
104	IY 4596	Ford V8	BB 18F7154884	Tipper	5.7.45		5 tons	Scrapped 29.11.54
105	IA 7372	Dennis G	70182		26.3.28	20		To NIRTB October 1935
105	IY 4597	Ford V8	BB 18F7155105	Tipper	5.7.45		5 tons	Scrapped 1.1.56
106	IA 6983	Overland	BMT 5382		15.6.27	14	2 tons	Converted to a lorry 4.5.31 – Scrapped June 1933 Allocated to Belfast Goods
106	BI 2023	Ford	4794664	Open Platform	14.1.32		2 tons	Purchased from freight operator J Joyce, Castleblaney 7.5.35 – Scrapped 1938
106	IY 4598	Ford V8	BB 18F7155630	Tipper	1.10.45		5 tons	Scrapped 2.7.56
107	AZ 5075	Leyland Badger	TA1 66063		3.6.30		2.5 tons	Allocated to Newry – To NIRTB October 1935
107	IY 4599	Ford V8	BB 18F7150350	Covered Van	20.4.45		5 tons	Scrapped 2.7.56
108	AZ 5076	Leyland Badger	TA1 66165		25.7.30		2.5 tons	Allocated to Belfast Garage – To NIRTB October 1935
108	IY 4600	Ford V8	BB 18F7149816	Platform Truck	20.4.45		5 tons	Scrapped 29.4.55
109	AZ 5082	Leyland Lion LT2	51114	SMW	14.6.30	31		Fitted with new GNR body December 1937 following accident Coolock – maliciously destroyed by fire near Keady 1940
109	IY 4601	Ford V8	BB 18F7150200	Platform Truck	20.4.45		5 tons	Scrapped 1.1.56
110	AZ 5078	Leyland Lion LT2	51113	SMW	2.6.30	31		New GNR body fitted (normal door) renumbered 271 in 1945 then lorry 150 (1946) & finally GT6
110	IY 4602	Ford V8	BB 18F7150401	Platform Truck	20.4.45		5 tons	Scrapped 29.4.55
111	AZ 5081	Leyland Lion LT2	51112	SMW	13.6.30	31		Renumbered 272 in March 1945
111	IY 4603	Ford V8	BB 18F7150027	Platform Truck	20.4.45		5 tons	Scrapped 5.9.56
112	AZ 5077	Leyland Lion LT2	51110	McKeown & McClughan	14.6.30	31		
112	IY 4604	Ford V8	BB 18F7150449	Tipper	20.4.45		5 tons	Scrapped 31.12.54
112	ZY 1845	AEC Mercury	GM4RA936		24.8.56		8 tons	Passed to CIE as AY112
113	IB 4446	Guy OND	9390		28.1.30	20		To NIRTB October 1935
113	IY 4605	Ford V8	BB 18F7152088	Tipper	23.5.45		5 tons	Scrapped 31.12.54
113	ZY 1940	AEC Mercury	GM4RA933		13.9.56		8 tons	Passed to CIE as AY113
114	IB 4534	Guy OND	9477		3.8.30	20		
114	IY 4606	Ford V8	BB 18F7152270	Tipper	1.6.45		5 tons	Scrapped 29.8.55
114	ZY 1941	AEC Mercury	GM4RA935		17.9.56		8 tons	Castrol Van Became CIE Fleet No. AY 114
115	AZ 4922	Leyland Badger	TA1 66080		17.4.30		2.5 tons	Allocated to Portadown Goods – To NIRTB 10.35
115	IY 4697	Ford V8	BB 18F7152160	Tipper	1.6.45		5 tons	Scrapped 8.4.54
115	ZY 1942	AEC Mercury	GM4RA937		1.1.57		8 tons	Passed to CIE as AY 115
116	AZ 4920	Morris Commercial	6030		17.4.30		1.5 tons	To NIRTB October 1935
116	IY 4608	Ford V8	BB 18F7151932	Tipper	1.6.45		5 tons	Scrapped 2.12.53
116	ZY 1943	AEC Mercury	GM4RA934		1.10.56		8 tons	Passed to CIE as AY116
117	AZ 4921	Morris Commercial	6061		17.4.30		1.5 tons	Allocated to Pomeroy – To NIRTB October 1935
117	IY 4609	Ford V8	BB 18F7151496	Tipper	1.6.45		5 tons	Scrapped 2.12.53
117	ZY 1944	AEC Mercury	GM4RA938		15.10.56		8 tons	Passed to CIE as AY 117

Appendix A (1) – Bus and Lorry Fleet								
Fleet No.	Reg'n	Type	Chassis Number	Body	Date New	Seats	Payload	Comments
118	AZ 5079	Leyland Lion LT2	51111	McKeown & McClughan Sun Saloon	18.6.30	31		Fitted with new GNR body 6.3.37 – renumbered 273 in 1945
118	IY 4610	Ford V8	BB 18F7151778	Tipper	23.6.45		5 tons	Scrapped 29.8.55
118	ZY 1945	AEC Mercury	GM4RA932		1.11.56		8 tons	Passed to CIE as AY 118
119	AZ 5080	Leyland Lion LT2	51115	McKeown & McClughan	4.7.30	31		Renumbered 274 in 1945
119	IY 4611	Ford V8	BB 18F7151622	Tipper	23.6.45		5 tons	Scrapped 30.10.56
119	ZY 1946	AEC Mercury	GM4RA766	JH Moore Dropside			8 tons	Chassis assembled Dundalk Works Passed to CIE as AY119
120	ZI 4811	Leyland Badger	TA1 66078	Open Platform	2.5.30		2.5 tons	Allocated to Navan – Scrapped 1.9.56
120	ZY 1947	AEC Mercury	GM4RA767	JH Moore Dropside			8 tons	Chassis assembled Dundalk Works Passed to CIE as AY120
121	ZI 4812	Leyland Badger	TA1 66079	Open Platform	13.5.30		2.5 tons	Allocated to Carrickmacross – Scrapped 1940
121	IY 2530	Leyland Bison	67475		10.7.31		5 tons	Purchased from freight operator CF Bellew Ltd 26.8.44 – Scrapped 30.10.56
122	ZI 5057	Leyland Badger	TA1 65909	Open Platform	3.5.30		2.5 tons	Allocated to Dublin Goods – Scrapped 2.12.53
123	ZI 5058	Leyland Badger	TA1 66102	Tipper	4.6.30		2.5 tons	Allocated to Drogheda – Scrapped 1.1.56
124	AZ 5442	Leyland Badger	TA1 66166		22.7.30		2.5 tons	Allocated to Armagh – To NIRTB October 1935
125	ZI 5400	Leyland Badger	TA1 66326	Tipper	28.7.30		2.5 tons	Allocated to Oldcastle – Scrapped 1.1.56
126	ZI 5401	Leyland Badger	TA1 66327	Tipper	31.7.30		2.5 tons	Allocated to Oldcastle – Scrapped 5.9.56
127	UI 2194	Dennis G	70525		2.12.29	20		To NIRTB October 1935
127	ZI 4280	Leyland Tiger TS2	60893	Horsebox	16.5.30		4 horses	Formerly bus number 97 converted to horse box (30.10.46) – Scrapped 1.7.54
128	UI 2154	Gilford 166 OT	10949		11.7.29	32		Scrapped 1.10.36
128	ZI 4276	Leyland Tiger TS2	60884	Horsebox	9.4.30		4 horses	Formerly bus number 93 converted to horse box by Dublin Vehicle Builders 6.2.48 – Scrapped 12.11.57
129	UI 2029	Dennis G	70216		11.6.28	20		Scrapped 1.10.36
129	AZ 1514	Leyland Tiger TS2	60088		1928	31		Was bus 296 renumbered 1942. Sold to SLNCR in 1946
129	IY 5969	Austin	134400	Horsebox	14.3.49		2 horses	Became CIE Fleet No. AN 129
130	UI 2082	Chevrolet	LP48143		11.2.29	14		Sold in 1930
130	IY 1121	Leyland	12459	Open Platform	24.11.22		6 tons	Purchased from freight operator Thomas Cooney, Drogheda 8.1.35 – Scrapped 1939
131	AZ 5443	Leyland Badger	TA1 66328		18.8.30		2.5 tons	Allocated to Belfast Goods – To NIRTB 10.35
132	AZ 5444	Leyland Badger	TA1 66329		18.8.30		2.5 tons	Allocated to Portadown Goods – To NIRTB 10.35
133	ZI 3426	Leyland Badger	TA1 65294		11.6.29		2.5 tons	Purchased from freight operator S Greene 27.1.31 allocated to Belturbet – Scrapped 1.1.56
134	AZ 5932	Leyland Badger	TA1 66574		3.10.30		2.5 tons	Allocated to Ballyroney – To NIRTB 10.35
135	AZ 5933	Leyland Badger	TA1 66576		20.10.30		2.5 tons	Allocated to Newry – To NIRTB 10.35
136	ZI 5569	Leyland Badger	TA1 66575		26.9.30		2.5 tons	Allocated to Cootehill – Scrapped 2.10.53
137	ZI 5570	Leyland Badger	TA1 66577	Cattle Lorry	26.9.30		2.5 tons	Allocated to Dundalk Works – Scrapped 5.9.56
138	CK 3558	Leyland SG7	12866	Leyland	29.3.24	B38D		Purchased from Blakes of Salford became engineers car 8188 Ex Ribble No 76
138	IY 2883	Fordson	BB 55273929	Platform	17.9.34		2 tons	Purchased from freight operator Thomas Cooney, Drogheda 8.1.35 – allocated to Dundalk Garage – Scrap Dec 1951
138	IY 9528	Albion FT37CL	74007L	GNR Body	13.5.54		5 tons	Chassis assembled Dundalk Works Became CIE Fleet No AD 138
139	CK 3559	Leyland SG7	12867	Leyland	29.3.24	B38D		Purchased from Blakes of Salford – Scrapped in 1934 Ex Ribble No. 77
139	IY 2675	Fordson	AAB5107430	Covered Van	1932		2 tons	Acquired from Cooney 9.1.35 – Scrapped 28.4.47 Allocated to Dundalk Garage
139	IY 9713	Albion FT37CL	74008H	GNR Body	11.8.54		5 tons	Chassis assembled Dundalk Works Became CIE Fleet No. AD 139
140	CK 3576	Leyland SG7	12966	Leyland	2.6.24	B38D		Purchased from Blakes of Salford became engineers r/car 8190 Ex.Ribble No. 79
140	IY 2802	Fordson	BB5259556	Open Platform	1934		2 tons	Acquired from Cooney Drogheda 9.1.35 – Scrapped 4.8.51 Allocated to Dundalk
140	IY 9945	Albion FT37CL	74011E	GNR Body	1.10.54		5 tons	Chassis assembled Dundalk Works Became CIE Fleet No. AD 140

Appendix A (1) – Bus and Lorry Fleet								
Fleet No.	**Reg'n**	**Type**	**Chassis Number**	**Body**	**Date New**	**Seats**	**Payload**	**Comments**
141	CK 3607	Leyland SG9	13057	Leyland	1.10.24	B38D		Purchased from Blakes of Salford – Scrapped in 1934 Ex.Ribble No. 94
141	IY 2834	Morris Commercial	233C/10834	Platform canvas sided	5.7.34		3 tons	Purchased from freight operator P McCloskey 8.1.35 – Scrapped 3.3.50 Allocated to Drogheda
141	IY 9946	Albion FT37CL	74016F	GNR Body	1.10.54		5 tons	Chassis assembled Dundalk Works Became CIE Fleet No. AD 141
142	CK 3609	Leyland SG9	13059		1.10.24	B36D		Purchased from Blakes of Salford – Scrapped in June 1934 Ex.Ribble No. 96
142	IY 2890	Morris Commercial	310C/12830	Covered Van	5.10.34		3 tons	Purchased from freight operator Thomas Cooney Drogheda 8.1.35 – Scrapped 14.6.46 Allocated to Drogheda
142	ZY 35	Albion FT37CL	74023J	GNR Body	1.11.54		5 tons	Chassis assembled Dundalk Works Became CIE Fleet No. AD142
143	CK 3610	Leyland SG9	13060		1.10.24	36		Purchased from Blakes of Salford – Scrapped in June 1934 Ex.Ribble No. 97
143	IY 2905	Morris Commercial	350C/13231	Open Platform	3.11.34		3 tons	Purchased from freight operator Thomas Cooney Drogheda 8.1.35 – Scrapped 28.4.47 Allocated to Dublin Garage
143	IY 9315	Albion FT37ANT	73291L	GNR Tipper Body	9.3.54		5 tons	Chassis assembled Dundalk Works Became CIE Fleet No. AD 143
144	BI 1591	International	15BR634E		17.8.28	20		Scrapped in 1931
144	IY 2915	Morris Commercial	350C/14028	Open Platform	5.12.34		3 tons	Purchased from freight operator Thomas Cooney Drogheda 8.1.35 – Scrapped 2.9.48 Allocated to Drogheda
144	IY 9316	Albion FT37ANT	73296B	GNR Tipper Body	25.3.54		5 tons	Chassis assembled Dundalk Works Became CIE Fleet No. AD 144
145	BI 1599	International	15BR630E		7.9.28	20		Scrapped in 1931
145	IY 2747	Morris Commercial	149C/5809		9.11.33		3 tons	Purchased from freight operator Thomas Cooney Drogheda 8.1.35 – Scrapped 7.4.49
145	IY 9947	Albion FT37 HNT	74515E	GNR Tipper Body	1.10.54		5 tons	Chassis assembled Dundalk Works Became CIE Fleet No AD 145
146	IP 1935	International	15BR597E		1928	20		Dismantled 1931 parts used for 144 Body sold for £10
146	IY 2911	Morris Commercial	350C/14025		2.4.35		3 tons	Purchased new from freight operator Peter McCloskey Drogheda 8.1.35 – Scrapped 28.4.47
146	ZY 810	Albion FT37 HNT	74515F	GNR Tipper Body	16.7.55		5 tons	Chassis assembled Dundalk Works Became CIE Fleet No AD 146
147	JI 3978	Morris T	4583Z		1.11.27	14		Reconditioned 1931 – Scrapped June 1934
147	ZI 2767	Morris Commercial	TX2170	Van	4.3.29		2 tons	Purchased from freight operator Peter McCloskey Drogheda 8.1.35 – Scrapped 1937
147	ZY 994	Albion FT37HNT	74515D	GNR Tipper Body	1.9.55		5 tons	Became CIE Fleet No. AD 147
148	AZ 7641	Leyland Lion LT2	51593	Stewart Wishaw	1.7.31	31		Scrapped 19.12.51
149	AZ 7642	Leyland Lion LT2	51594	Stewart Wishaw	3.7.31	31	6 tons	Converted to lorry (18.4.46) same fleet number – Scrapped 25.10.54
150	AZ 7643	Leyland Lion LT2	51595	Stewart Wishaw	3.7.31	31		Scrapped after accident at Carrigans 30.11.40
150	AZ 5078	Leyland Lion LT2	51113	SMW	2.6.30	31	6 tons	Started life as bus 110 renumbered 271 then became lorry 150 (24.1.47) and finally Garage Tender 6
151	AZ 7644	Leyland Lion LT2	51596	Stewart Wishaw	1.7.31	31	6 tons	Converted to a lorry same number (7.10.46) – Scrapped 29.8.55
152	ZI 6851	Leyland Badger	TA1 67377		2.7.31		2.5 tons	Allocated to Balbriggan – Scrapped 1.9.56
153	ZI 6852	Leyland Badger	TA1 67378		6.7.31		2.5 tons	Allocated to Dublin Goods – Scrapped 8.4.54
154	ZI 6853	Leyland Badger	TA1 67379		6.7.31		2.5 tons	Allocated to Kells – Scrapped 30.10.56
155	AZ 7645	Leyland Badger	TA1 67380		3.7.31		2.5 tons	Allocated to Enniskillen – To NIRTB October 1935
155	ZI 6854	Leyland Beaver	TC1 67383		2.7.31		4 tons	Started life as lorry 158 renumbered 155 in 1937 – Scrapped 24.6.57
156	AZ 7646	Leyland Badger	TA1 67381		16.7.31		2.5 tons	Allocated to Belfast – To NIRTB October 1935
156	IY 3826	Fordson V8	BB 18F4151273	GNR Body	2.4.38		3 tons	New chassis bought from Byrne & Maguire, Dundalk – Scrapped 3.3.50
156	ZY 423	Albion FT37CL	74040A		12.4.55		5 tons	Became CIE Fleet No AD 156

Appendix A (1) – Bus and Lorry Fleet								
Fleet No.	Reg'n	Type	Chassis Number	Body	Date New	Seats	Payload	Comments
157	AZ 7647	Leyland Badger	TA1 67382		11.7.31		2.5 tons	Allocated to Banbridge – To NIRTB October 1935
157	ZC 3441	Fordson V8	BB 18F4151569	GNR Body	10.3.38		3 tons	New chassis bought from Byrne & Maguire, Dundalk – Scrapped 28.4.47
157	ZY 211	Albion FT37CL	74040B	JH Moore Body	22.1.55		5 tons	Chassis assembled Dundalk Works Became CIE Fleet No. AD 157
158	ZI 6854	Leyland Beaver	TC1 67383		2.7.31		4 tons	Allocated to Dublin Goods – renumbered 155 in 1937
158	ZC 3440	Fordson V8	BB 18F4151430	GNR Body	24.9.38		3 tons	New chassis bought from Byrne & Maguire, Dundalk – Scrapped 2.9.48
158	ZY 688	Albion FT37CL	74043F	JH Moore Body	16.6.55		5 tons	Chassis assembled Dundalk Works Became CIE Fleet No AD 158
159	AZ 7648	Leyland Beaver	TC1 67384		3.7.31		2.5 tons	Allocated to Lurgan – To NIRTB October 1935
159	ZC 3827	Fordson V8	BB 18F4151398	GNR Body	26.3.38		3 tons	New chassis bought from Byrne & Maguire, Dundalk – Scrapped 2.9.48
159	ZY 510	Albion FT37CL	74044B	JH Moore Body	1.5.55		5 tons	Chassis assembled Dundalk Works Became CIE Fleet No AD 159
160	AZ 7649	Leyland Beaver	TC1 67385		3.7.31		4 tons	Allocated to Portadown Goods – To NIRTB 10.35
160	ZC 3828	Fordson V8	BB 18F4151519	GNR Body	26.2.38		3 tons	New chassis bought from Byrne & Maguire, Dundalk – Scrapped 23.2.48
160	ZY 710	Albion FT37CL	74054F	JH Moore Body	1.7.55		5 tons	Chassis assembled Dundalk Works Became CIE Fleet No. AD 160
161	AZ 7650	Leyland Beaver	TC1 67386		3.7.31		4 tons	Allocated to Belfast – To NIRTB October 1935
161	IY 3829	Fordson V8	BB 18F4151748	GNR Body	26.3.38		3 tons	New chassis bought from Byrne & Maguire, Dundalk – Scrapped 2.9.48
161	ZY 995	Albion FT37CL	74054H	JH Moore Body	1.9.55		5 tons	Chassis assembled Dundalk Works Became CIE Fleet No. AD 161
162	AZ 343	Gilford LL 15	10330	Unknown	2.4.28	28		To NIRTB October 1935
162	IY 3830	Fordson V8	BB 18F4151612	GNR Body	26.3.38		3 tons	New chassis bought from Byrne & Maguire, Dundalk – Scrapped 3.3.50
162	ZY 623	Albion FT37CL	74054L	JH Moore Body	1.6.55		5 tons	Chassis assembled Dundalk Works Became CIE Fleet No. AD 162
163	JI 4305	Gilford 166 OT	10473	Unknown	17.12.28	32		To NIRTB October 1935
163	IY 3831	Fordson V8	BB 18F4151532	GNR Body	26.3.38		3 tons	New chassis bought from McGee's, Drogheda – Scrapped 7.4.49
163	ZY 1108	Albion FT37CL	74054K	JH Moore Body	1.10.55		5 tons	Chassis assembled Dundalk Works Became CIE Fleet No. AD 163
164	JI 4630	Gilford 168 OT	11133	Unknown	21.12.29	32		To NIRTB October 1935
164	IY 3832	Fordson V8	BB 18F4151669	GNR Body	25.3.38		3 tons	New chassis bought from McGee's, Drogheda – Scrapped 2.9.48
164	ZY 529	Albion FT37CL	74054J	JH Moore Body	1.5.55		5 tons	Chassis assembled Dundalk Works Became CIE Fleet No. AD 164
165	JI 4720	Gilford 166 OT	11011	Unknown	25.3.30	32		To NIRTB October 1935
165	IY 3833	Fordson V8	BB 18F4151448	GNR Body	25.3.38		3 tons	New chassis bought from McGee's, Drogheda – Scrapped 7.4.49
166	JI 5048	Commer Avenger	36017		28.3.31	32		To NIRTB October 1935
166	IY 3834	Fordson V8	BB 18F4151908	GNR Body	2.7.38		3 tons	New chassis bought from McGee's, Drogheda – Scrapped 3.3.50
167	JI 5049	Commer Invader	C28237		4.4.31	20		To NIRTB October 1935
167	ZA 3344	Fordson V8	BB 18F1513814		11.6.35		3 tons	Purchased from T Cooney & Sons, Drogheda 29.3.44 – Scrapped 3.3.50
168	XI 9770	Dennis G	70022		20.12.27	20	2 tons	Converted to a lorry – Scrapped 25.5.39
168	ZC 5809	Fordson V8	BB 18F4594073		1939		3 tons	From Eire Army 2.10.45 – Scrapped 4.8.51
169	AZ 1282	Dennis G	70329		29.8.28	20	2 tons	Converted to a lorry – Scrapped in 1938
169	IY 5448	Linn Catruk C5	4419	GNR Body	11.3.48		20 tons	Purchased from G Hamill Portadown 12.2.48 Ex US Navy – Specialist half track recovery vehicle Became CIE Fleet No. CT 169
170	VA 4595	Dennis G	70320		1928	20	2 tons	Former Nugent Bus converted to lorry – Scrapped 38
170	GT 9983	Beardmore Tractor	72118		19.12.31		12 tons	Purchased from CF Bellew Ltd 26.8.44 – Scrapped 13.6.53 converted to a trailer T21
171	IB 4078	Vulcan Duke	3XS35	Vulcan	6.2.29	20		Scrapped 1931

Appendix A (1) – Bus and Lorry Fleet								
Fleet No.	Reg'n	Type	Chassis Number	Body	Date New	Seats	Payload	Comments
171	IY 2570	Beardmore Tractor	72205		20.10.31		12 tons	From Peter McCloskey (8.1.35) – Scrapped (7.4.49) converted to trailer T17 June 1949
171	ZY 3208	AEC Mandator	34751091	Tractor	1.7.58		16 tons	Did not enter GNR service became CIE AO 311
172	IB 4082	Vulcan Duke	3XS29	Vulcan	21.2.29	20		Scrapped 1931
172	IX 1128	Beardmore Tractor	WT 72294		15.4.32		10 tons	Acquired from McCloskey 9.1.35 – Scrapped following road accident 1937
172	ZC 5567	Beardmore Tractor	85306	Python	2.11.38		12 tons	Fitted with a Gardner 4LW engine 1940 – Scrapped 25.10.54 converted into trailer T18
172	ZY 1824	AEC Mandator	3472963	Tractor	1.7.56		15 tons	Chassis assembled Dundalk Works became CIE AO 312
173	IB 4222	Vulcan Duke	3XS30	Vulcan	11.6.29	20		Scrapped 1931
173	IP 2429	Beardmore Tractor	UT 51962	Cobra Tractor	1.1.31		10 tons	Purchased from McCloskey Drogheda 8.1.35 – Scrapped 28.4.47 converted to Trailer T19
173	ZY 1545	AEC Mandator	3472961	Tractor	25.3.56		15 tons	Chassis assembled Dundalk Works became CIE AO 313
174	IB 4405	Vulcan Duke	3XS37	Vulcan	12.12.29	20		Scrapped 1934
174	IY2285	Chevrolet	835501	Open Platform	1.9.28		1.5 tons	Purchased from McCloskey Drogheda 8.1.35 – Scrapped 1936
174	IY 4014	Fordson V8	BB 18F4435773	Tractor	1.12.38		5 tons	Scrapped 13.6.53 converted to a Tank Trailer T20.
174	ZY 1440	AEC Mandator	3472962	Tractor	1.3.56		15 tons	Chassis assembled Dundalk Works became CIE AO 314
175	IB 4406	Vulcan Duke	3XS54	Vulcan	12.12.29	20		Scrapped after serious accident Armagh 22.2.34
175	ZH 1704	AEC Matador	34651224	C Morgan & Son Drogheda	15.10.47		8 tons	Chassis assembled at Dundalk Works Became CIE Fleet No. AO 300
176	IB 4404	Vulcan Duchess	D35	Vulcan	12.12.29	26		To NIRTB October 1935
176	ZH 1705	AEC Matador	34651225	C Morgan & Son Drogheda	15.11.47		8 tons	Chassis assembled at Dundalk Works Became CIE Fleet No. AO 301
177	BI 1871	Vulcan Duchess	D46	Vulcan	11.10.30	26		Scrapped 1934
177	IY 2506	Ford A	AA 4473084		1.4.31		1.5 tons	Purchased from freight operator J Crilly, Dundalk 4.5.35 – Scrapped 1936
177	ZH 9502	AEC Matador	3471147	C Morgan & Son Drogheda	15.12.48		8 tons	Chassis assembled at Dundalk Works Became CIE Fleet No. AO 302
178	IB 4689	Vulcan Duchess	D48	Vulcan	31.10.30	26		To NIRTB October 1935
178	IY 2606	Bedford	115736		4.3.32		2 tons	Purchased from freight operator EM Murphy, Dundalk 23.3.36 – Scrapped 1941
178	ZH 9503	AEC Matador	3471148	C Morgan & Son Drogheda	15.12.48		8 tons	Chassis assembled at Dundalk Works – Used for furniture removals Northern Ireland to Northern Ireland Became CIE Fleet No. AO303
179	BI 1872	Vulcan Duchess	D47	Vulcan	11.10.30	26		Scrapped 1934
179	AI 4100	Bedford	124072	Open Platform	25.5.33		2 tons	Purchased from freight operator Sweeney & Swan, Kells 30.7.35 – Scrapped 25.5.39
179	IY 7531	AEC Matador	3472488	Tractor	1.8.51		8 tons	Chassis assembled Dundalk Works Became CIE Fleet No. AO 315
180	TE 2039	Vulcan Duchess	VWBL28	Vulcan	30.11.27	31		To NIRTB October 1935
180	ZI 6056	Bedford	6136640		23.4.35		2 tons	Purchased from freight operator TJ McNally Skerries 27.2.36 – Scrapped 21.4.44
180	IY 8182	AEC Matador	3472804		9.8.52		8 tons	Chassis assembled Dundalk Works passed to CIE as AO 304
181	GD 5184	Vulcan VWBL	VWBL12	Vulcan	29.1.27	31		To NIRTB October 1935
181	IY 2658	Bedford	105606		3.8.32		2 tons	Purchased from freight operator H McKeown Dundalk 24.1.36 – Scrapped 30.9.45
181	IY 8236	AEC Matador	3472803		16.9.52		8 tons	Chassis assembled Dundalk Works passed to CIE as AO 305
182	ID 1614	Morris T	11275T	Morris Motor	1.12.26	14		Acquired with Magnet Bus Co Gordon Motor Services Converted to a lorry 1932 – Scrapped 1934
183	ID 1620	ADC 413	413105	Strahan & Brown	1.12.26	32		Acquired from Magnet Bus Co – Scrapped 1933
183	ID 2261	Morris Commercial C	656/C2207	Open Platform	1.6.33		3 tons	Purchased from freight operator JB King, Virginia 7.5.35 – Scrapped 7.4.49
184	ID 1733	ADC 415	415A218	Strahan & Brown	6.12.27	32		Converted to SL & NCR Railbus

Appendix A (1) – Bus and Lorry Fleet								
Fleet No.	Reg'n	Type	Chassis Number	Body	Date New	Seats	Payload	Comments
184	ZA 5612	Morris Commercial C	4556.172	Open Platform	2.9.35		3 tons	Purchased new from freight operator TJ Duffy, Castleblaney 7.5.35 fitted with body from Lorry 6 in 1936 – Scrapped 2.9.48
184	IY 9317	AEC Mammoth Major	3671H.329	Tractor	25.3.54		20 tons	Chassis assembled Dundalk Works became CIE AO 316 six wheeler, heavy haulage with winch
185	ZI 960	ADC 416	416D466	Strahan & Brown	16.11.27	30		Withdrawn 1933 converted to a railbus
185	MI 3047	Morris Leader		Open Platform	13.10.30		2 tons	Purchased from freight operator Maher Bros. Dundalk 6.5.35 – Scrapped 1938
185	IY 2920	Fordson	BB5300177		1934		2 tons	Scrapped 16.12.48 originally numbered 325 changed in 1941
185	IY 7555	AEC Mammoth Major	3871H.804		26.7.51		15 tons	Chassis assembled Dundalk Works became AM 185
186	ZI 996	ADC 416	416D465	Strahan & Brown	2.12.27	30		Body used to convert bus number 7 to railbus – chassis damaged and scrapped in 1934
186	BI 2223	Fordson	BB5259534		1934		2 tons	Scrapped 23.2.48 originally numbered 326 changed in 1941
186	IY 7919	AEC Mammoth Major	3871H.1209		15.3.52		15 tons	Chassis assembled Dundalk Works became CIE AM 186
187	ZI 4427	GMC T 30	T30/3235	Potter	1.2.30	20		
187	BI 2126	Fordson	BB5194106		1933		2 tons	Scrapped 1949 originally numbered 327 changed in 1941
187	IY 7990	AEC Mammoth Major	3871H.1210		1.5.52		15 tons	Chassis assembled Dundalk Works became CIE AM 187
188	ZI 4915	GMC T 30	T30/3308	Potter	16.5.30	20		Scrapped following collision with a lorry at Baldoyle 14.5.32
188	BI 2090	Fordson	BB 5152799	Open Platform	24.3.33		2 tons	Purchased from freight operator J Gray, Castleblaney 20.5.35 – Scrapped 1938
188	BI 2087	Fordson	BB5152766	Open Platform	1933		2 tons	Scrapped 16.12.48 originally numbered 328 changed in 1941
188	IY 8270	AEC Mammoth Major	3871H.1361		18.10.52		15 tons	Chassis assembled Dundalk Works became CIE AM 188
189	Z 1510	Reo GB	GB554	Eaton	15.7.27	26		Sold to Halpenny Dundalk 11.8.32
189	BI 2176	Fordson	BB5252762	Open Platform	10.1.34		2 tons	Purchased from freight operator J Gray, Castleblaney 20.5.35 – Scrapped 16.12.48
189	IY 8323	AEC Mammoth Major	3871H.1362		14.11.52		15 tons	Chassis assembled Dundalk Works became CIE AM 189
190	AZ 9280	Albion LB41	14113I	Harkness Open Box	1.6.32		1.5 tons	To NIRTB October 1935
190	IY 2842	Fordson	BB5274389	Platform	9.7.34		2 tons	Purchased from freight operator McDonald Bros Riverstown 29.11.35 – Scrapped 4.8.51
190	IY 9318	AEC Mammoth Major	3871H.1204	Oil Tanker	1.7.54		15 tons	Chassis and body assembled Dundalk Works became AM 190
191	AZ 9281	Albion LB41	14113J	Harkness Open Box	1.6.32		1.5 tons	To NIRTB October 1935
191	IY 2798	Fordson	BB525278	Platform	4.4.34		2 tons	Purchased from M Sheilds of Irish Grange 18.1.36 – Scrapped 7.4.49 converted to Garage Tender GT3
191	ZY 460	AEC Mammoth Major	3871H.1794	JH Moore Body	1.5.55		15 tons	Chassis assembled Dundalk Works became CIE AM 191
192	AZ 9282	Albion LB41	14113K	Harkness Open Box	1.11.32		1.5 tons	To NIRTB October 1935
192	IY 2837	Fordson	BB5271390	Platform	3.11.34		2 tons	Purchased from freight operator J Barry of Dundalk 22.1.36 – Scrapped 2.12.53
193	AZ 9283	Albion LB41	14113L	Harkness Open Box	1.6.32		1.5 tons	To NIRTB October 1935
193	BI 2198	Fordson	BB5271412	Platform	4.4.34		2 tons	From freight operator E & F McMahon of Clones 1.10.35 – Scrapped 14.6.46
193	ZY 1842	AEC Mandator	3473957	JH Moore Tipper	1.8.56		10 tons	Chassis assembled Dundalk Works became CIE AO 317
194	AZ 9284	Albion LB41	14114A	Harkness Open Box	1.6.32		1.5 tons	To NIRTB October 1935
194	BI 2083	Fordson	AAB5107429	Platform	13.2.33		2 tons	From freight operator J McGeough of Castleblaney 19.12.35 – Scrapped 23.2.48
194	ZY 1843	AEC Mandator	3473956	JH Moore Tipper	10.9.56		10 tons	Chassis assembled Dundalk Works became CIE AO 318
195	AZ 9285	Albion LB41	14114B	Harkness Open Box	10.12.32		1.5 tons	To NIRTB October 1935
195	ZY 1645	AEC Mandator	3473958	JH Moore Goods Body	1.5.56		10 tons	Chassis assembled Dundalk Works became CIE AO 306

Appendix A (1) – Bus and Lorry Fleet								
Fleet No.	**Reg'n**	**Type**	**Chassis Number**	**Body**	**Date New**	**Seats**	**Payload**	**Comments**
196	AZ 9286	Albion LB41	14114C	Harkness Open Box	3.1.33		1.5 tons	To NIRTB October 1935
196	IY 2689	Fordson	AAB5150412	Platform	7.3.33		2 tons	Purchased from freight operator TL McDonald of Dundalk 15.1.36 – Scrapped 16.12.48
196	ZY 1844	AEC Mandator	3473959	JH Moore Goods Body	1.7.56		10 tons	Chassis assembled Dundalk Works became CIE AO 307
197	AZ 9287	Albion LB41	14114I	Harkness Open Box	3.1.33		1.5 tons	To NIRTB October 1935
197	ZY 2827	AEC Mandator	34741085	JH Moore Goods Body			10 tons	Chassis assembled Dundalk Works – entered service after GNRB ceased to exist was in storage at Drogheda became CIE AO 308
198	AZ 9288	Albion LB41	14515G	McKeown & McClaughan	1.12.32		1.5 tons	To NIRTB October 1935
198	ZY 2828	AEC Mandator	34741086	JH Moore Goods Body			10 tons	Chassis assembled Dundalk Works – entered service after GNRB ceased to exist was in storage at Drogheda became CIE AO 309
199	AZ 9289	Albion LB41	14515H	McKeown & McClaughan	16.12.32		1.5 tons	To NIRTB October 1935
199	ZY 2829	AEC Mandator	34741087	JH Moore Goods Body			10 tons	Chassis assembled Dundalk Works – entered service after GNRB ceased to exist was in storage at Drogheda became CIE AO 310
200	AZ 9290	Albion LB41	14515I	McKeown & McClaughan	31.1.33		1.5 tons	To NIRTB October 1935
200	ZC 197	GNR Gardner	3/37/200	GNR	25.3.37	27		Scrapped 30.10.56
201	AZ 9291	Albion LB41	14515K	McKeown & McClaughan	31.1.33		1.5 tons	To NIRTB October 1935
201	ZC 198	GNR Gardner	4/37/201	GNR	1.6.37	27		Scrapped 23.4.53
202	AZ 9292	Albion LB41	14515J	McKeown & McClaughan	31.1.33		1.5 tons	To NIRTB October 1935
202	ZC 199	GNR Gardner	4/37/202	GNR	1.6.37	27		Scrapped 20.5.54
203	AZ 9293	Albion LB41	14515L	McKeown & McClaughan	31.1.33		1.5 tons	To NIRTB October 1935
203	ZC 200	GNR Gardner	4/37/203	GNR	1.6.37	27		Scrapped 11.6.54
204	AZ 9294	Albion LK50	17101I	McKeown & McClaughan	1.2.33		3 tons	To NIRTB October 1935
204	ZC 1289	GNR Gardner	5/37/204	GNR	2.7.37	35		Scrapped 1.1.54
205	AZ 9295	Albion LK50	17101J	McKeown & McClaughan	31.1.33		3 tons	To NIRTB October 1935
205	ZC 1290	GNR Gardner	5/37/205	GNR	2.7.37	35		Scrapped 20.5.54
206	AZ 9296	Albion LK50	17101K	McKeown & McClaughan	1.2.33		3 tons	To NIRTB October 1935
206	ZC 1291	GNR Gardner	6/37/206	GNR	8.6.37	35		Scrapped 20.5.54
207	AZ 9297	Ford	AA4794992	Harkness Open Box	30.3.32		1 ton	To NIRTB October 1935
207	ZC 1292	GNR Gardner	6/37/207	GNR	18.6.37	35		Scrapped 9.5.53
208	AZ 9298	Ford	AA4835204	Harkness Open Box	30.3.32		1 ton	To NIRTB October 1935
208	ZC 1576	GNR Gardner	6/37/208	GNR	3.7.37	35		Scrapped 30.10.56
209	AZ 9299	Ford	AA4835236	Harkness Open Box	30.3.32		1 ton	To NIRTB October 1935
209	ZC 1577	GNR Gardner	6/37/209	GNR	10.7.37	32		Scrapped 29.8.55
210	AZ 9300	Ford	AA4835188	Harkness Open Box	30.3.32		1 ton	To NIRTB October 1935
210	ZC 1578	GNR Gardner	6/37/210	GNR	11.7.37	32		Scrapped 2.12.53
211	AZ 9301	Ford	AA4835180	Harkness Open Box	19.5.32		1 ton	To NIRTB October 1935
211	ZC 1579	GNR Gardner	7/37/211	GNR	17.7.37	32		Scrapped 23.4.53
212	AZ 9302	Ford	AA4835183	Harkness Open Box	30.3.32		1 ton	To NIRTB October 1935
212	ZC 1848	GNR Gardner	7/37/212	GNR	31.7.37	35		Rebuilt 31.3.49
213	AZ 9303	Ford	AA4835282	Harkness Open Box	1.6.32		1 ton	To NIRTB October 1935
213	ZC 1849	GNR Gardner	7/37/213	GNR	13.8.37	35		Scrapped 2.12.53
214	AZ 9304	Ford	AA4835291	Harkness Open Box	19.5.32		1 ton	To NIRTB October 1935
214	ZC 1850	GNR Gardner	7/37/214	GNR	4.9.37	35		Scrapped 23.4.53
215	AZ 9305	Ford	AA4795266	McKeown & McClaughan	30.3.32		1.5 tons	To NIRTB October 1935
215	ZC 1851	GNR Gardner	9/37/215	GNR	1.11.37	31		Scrapped 30.10.56
216	AZ 9306	Ford	AA4794535	McKeown & McClaughan	30.3.32		1.5 tons	To NIRTB October 1935
216	ZC 2267	GNR Gardner	8/37/216	GNR	10.1.38	35		Scrapped 23.4.53

Appendix A (1) – Bus and Lorry Fleet								
Fleet No.	Reg'n	Type	Chassis Number	Body	Date New	Seats	Payload	Comments
217	AZ 9307	Ford	AA4835295	McKeown & McClaughan	1.12.32		1.5 tons	To NIRTB October 1935
217	ZC 2268	GNR Gardner	8/37/217	GNR	1.11.37	35		Scrapped 23.4.53
218	AZ 9308	Ford	AA4835296	McKeown & McClaughan	30.3.32		1.5 tons	To NIRTB October 1935
218	ZC 2269	GNR Gardner	9/37/218	GNR	1.11.37	35		Scrapped 9.5.53
219	AZ 9309	Ford	AA4835193	McKeown & McClaughan	19.5.32		1.5 tons	To NIRTB October 1935
219	ZC 2270	GNR Gardner	8/37/219	GNR	1.11.37	35		Scrapped 30.10.56
220	AZ 9310	Ford	AA4835194	McKeown & McClaughan	19.5.32		1.5 tons	To NIRTB October 1935
220	FZ 831	GNR Gardner	11/37/220	GNR	5.4.38	35		Scrapped 1.10.55
221	ZI 8366	Albion LK50	17101E	Michael Gray Box Van	18.5.32		3.5 tons	Scrapped 1.1.56
222	ZI 8367	Albion LK50	17101G	Michael Gray Box Van	11.5.32		3.5 tons	Scrapped 13.6.53
223	ZI 8368	Albion LK50	17101F	Michael Gray Box Van	7.5.32		3.5 tons	Scrapped 1.1.56
224	ZI 8369	Albion LK50	17101H	Michael Gray Box Van	5.5.32		3.5 tons	Scrapped 1.7.54
225	ZI 8370	Ford	AA4831610	Michael Gray Box Van	19.5.32		1.5 tons	
225	ZA 3828	Dennis Ace	200385N116	GNR	31.5.35	20		Former bus 34 converted to ARP ambulance then back to bus 225
225	ZO 3762	Leyland Royal Tiger PSU1/9	521182	Saunders-Roe	5.7.52	44		Withdrawn 1972
226	ZI 8371	Ford	AA4831599	Michael Gray Box Van	5.5.32		1.5 tons	
226	JI 4837	Reo Speedwagon	7312		28.6.30	14		Re-bodied 1945 sent to Londonderry as spare then scrapped 2.49
226	ZO 4076	Leyland Royal Tiger PSU1/9	521183	Saunders-Roe	1.8.52	44		Withdrawn 1972
227	ZI 8372	Ford	AA4831652	Michael Gray Box Van	30.4.32		1.5 tons	
227	ZO 4401	Leyland Royal Tiger PSU1/9	521184	Saunders-Roe	1.9.52	44		Withdrawn 1972
228	ZI 8373	Ford	AA4831564	Michael Gray Box Van	19.5.32		1.5 tons	
228	IY 8390	Leyland Royal Tiger PSU1/9	521181	Saunders-Roe	1.1.53	44		Withdrawn 1972
229	ZI 8374	Ford	AA4831585	Michael Gray Box Van	2.4.32		1.5 tons	
230	ZI 8375	Ford	AA4831589	Michael Gray Box Van	2.4.32		1.5 tons	
231	ZI 8376	Ford	AA4831638	Michael Gray Box Van	12.4.32		1.5 tons	
232	ZI 8377	Ford	AA4831590	Michael Gray Box Van	22.4.32		1.5 tons	
233	AZ 9134	Leyland Tiger TS3	636	Short Bros	26.3.32	24		Purchased from Leyland dealer Belfast Alister Kirk – All Ireland Tour Coach – Scrapped 28.8.47
234	AZ 9135	Leyland Tiger TS3	635	Short Bros	26.3.32	24		Purchased from Leyland dealer Belfast Alister Kirk – All Ireland Tour Coach – Scrapped 5.12.49
235	AZ 9533	Dennis Lancet	170065	Weymann	28.3.32	30		To NIRTB October 1935
235	AZ 9136	Leyland Tiger TS3	638	Short Bros	13.6.32	24		All Ireland Tour Coach – Scrapped 28.4.47 bought from LMS (NCC) 1.10.35
236	AZ 9534	Dennis Lancet	170066	Weymann	28.3.32	30		To NIRTB October 1935
236	AZ 9137	Leyland Tiger TS3	637	Short Bros	13.6.32	24		All Ireland Tour Coach – Scrapped 19.12.51 bought from LMS (NCC) 1.10.35
237	AZ 9535	Dennis Lancet	170067	Weymann	28.3.32	30		To NIRTB October 1935
238	AZ 9536	Dennis Lancet	170068	Weymann	28.3.32	30		To NIRTB October 1935
239	AZ 9537	Albion PT 65	16012D	Weymann	29.3.32	30		To NIRTB October 1935
240	AZ 9538	Albion PT 65	16012E	Weymann	10.4.32	30		To NIRTB October 1935
241	AZ 9539	Albion PT 65	16012F	Weymann	10.4.32	30		To NIRTB October 1935
241	ZC 3823	GNR Gardner	4/38/241	GNR	14.4.38	35		Scrapped 23.4.53
242	AZ 9540	Albion PT 65	16012G	Weymann	10.4.32	30		To NIRTB October 1935
242	ZC 4102	GNR Gardner	4/38/242	GNR	14.4.38	35		Scrapped 31.12.54
243	AZ 9541	Albion PT 65	16012H	Weymann	10.4.32	30		To NIRTB October 1935
243	ZC 4396	GNR Gardner	4/38/243	GNR	13.5.38	35		
244	AZ 9542	Albion PT 65	16012I	Weymann	11.4.32	30		To NIRTB October 1935
244	ZC 4103	GNR Gardner	4/38/244	GNR	30.4.38	35		Scrapped 30.10.56 – converted to Garage Tender No. 2
245	AZ 9543	Albion PT 65	16012J	Weymann	11.4.32	30		To NIRTB October 1935

Appendix A (1) – Bus and Lorry Fleet								
Fleet No.	Reg'n	Type	Chassis Number	Body	Date New	Seats	Payload	Comments
245	ZC 4104	GNR Gardner	4/38/245	GNR	30.4.38	35		Scrapped 31.12.54
246	AZ 9544	Albion PT 65	16012K	Weymann	16.4.32	30		To NIRTB October 1935
246	ZC 4397	GNR Gardner	4/38/246	GNR	30.5.38	35		Scrapped 1.6.55
247	AZ 9545	Albion PT 65	16012L	Weymann	16.4.32	30		To NIRTB October 1935
247	ZC 4398	GNR Gardner	5/38/247	GNR	30.5.38	31		Scrapped 31.12.54
248	AZ 9546	Albion PT 65	16013A	Weymann	16.4.32	30		To NIRTB October 1935
248	ZC 4399	GNR Gardner	5/38/248	GNR	30.5.38	31		Scrapped 2.7.56
249	AZ 9547	Albion PT 65	16013B	Weymann	16.4.32	30		To NIRTB October 1935
249	ZC 4572	GNR Gardner	5/38/249	GNR	30.5.38	31		Scrapped 29.4.55
250	AZ 9548	Albion PT 65	16013C	Weymann	16.4.32	30		To NIRTB October 1935
250	ZC 4573	GNR Gardner	5/38/250	GNR	30.5.38	31		Scrapped 1.1.54
251	AZ 9549	Albion PT 65	16013D	Weymann	16.4.32	30		To NIRTB October 1935
251	ZC 4574	GNR Gardner	5/38/251	GNR	30.5.38	35		Scrapped 1.12.55
252	AZ 9550	Albion PT 65	16013E	Weymann	16.4.32	30		To NIRTB October 1935
252	ZC 4575	GNR Gardner	5/38/252	GNR	30.5.38	35		Scrapped 29.11.54
253	AZ 9551	Albion PT 65	16013F	Weymann	21.4.32	30		To NIRTB October 1935
253	ZC 4731	GNR Gardner	6/38/253	GNR	17.6.38	35		Scrapped 31.12.54
254	AZ 9552	Albion PT 65	16013G	Weymann	21.4.32	30		To NIRTB October 1935
254	ZC 4732	GNR Gardner	6/38/254	GNR	1.7.38	35		Scrapped 29.4.55
255	AZ 9553	Albion PT 65	16013H	Weymann	21.4.32	30		To NIRTB October 1935
255	ZC 4733	GNR Gardner	6/38/255	GNR	1.7.38	35		Scrapped 1.7.54
256	AZ 9554	Albion PT 65	16013I	Weymann	21.4.32	30		To NIRTB October 1935
256	ZC 4734	GNR Gardner	6/38/256	GNR	15.7.38	35		Scrapped 1.7.54
257	AZ 9555	Albion PT 65	16013J	Weymann	21.4.32	30		To NIRTB October 1935
257	ZC 4735	GNR Gardner	7/38/257	GNR	15.7.38	35		Scrapped 29.4.55
258	AZ 9556	Albion PT 65	16013K	Weymann	21.4.32	30		To NIRTB October 1935
258	ZC 5472	GNR Gardner	7/38/258	GNR	30.11.38	35		Scrapped 29.4.55
259	AZ 9557	Albion PT 65	16013L	Weymann	21.4.32	30		To NIRTB October 1935
259	ZC 5473	GNR Gardner	7/38/259	GNR	30.11.38	35		Scrapped 23.4.53
260	AZ 9558	Albion PT 65	16014A	Weymann	21.4.32	30		To NIRTB October 1935
260	IY 9559	AEC Regal IV	9822E1537	PRV/GNR	1.7.54	40		Converted to 34 seat 'Yellow Coach' by CIE Summer 1959 Withdrawn 1973
261	AZ 9559	Albion PT 65	16014B	Weymann	21.4.32	30		To NIRTB October 1935
261	IY 9560	AEC Regal IV	9822E1529	PRV/GNR	1.7.54	40		Converted to 34 seat 'Yellow Coach' by CIE Summer 1959 Withdrawn 1972
262	AZ 9560	Albion PT 65	16014C	Weymann	21.4.32	30		To NIRTB October 1935 This vehicle was the only timber framed Weymann body delivered to the GNR Body No. W906
262	IY 9561	AEC Regal IV	9822E1536	PRV/GNR	1.7.54	40		Converted to 34 seat 'Yellow Coach' by CIE Summer 1959 Withdrawn 1972
263	ZI 8544	Leyland Tiger TS4	1171	GNR	17.6.32	30		Sun saloon – Scrapped 19.12.51
263	ZY 126	AEC Regal IV	9822E1542	PRV/GNR	1.1.55	40		Converted to 34 seat 'Yellow Coach' by CIE Summer 1959 Withdrawn 1972
264	ZI 8545	Leyland Tiger TS4	1172	GNR	17.6.32	30		Sun Saloon – Scrapped 19.12.51
264	ZY 127	AEC Regal IV	9822E1531	PRV/GNR	1.1.55	40		Converted to 34 seat 'Yellow Coach' by CIE Summer 1959
265	TI 1478	AEC 414	414021		1926	26		Scrapped June 1933
265	IY 2445	Dennis	6933	Cattle Truck	8.31		6 tons	Acquired McCloskey 8.1.35 allocated to Dublin Garage towed a cattle trailer No. 377 – Scrapped 23.2.48
265	ZY 128	AEC Regal IV	9822E1538	PRV/GNR	1.1.55	40		Converted to 34 seat 'Yellow Coach' by CIE Summer 1959
266	ML 7421	Chevrolet	16360		1927	14		Scrapped June 1933
266	AZ 325	Dennis	6490	Platform Truck	1928		6 tons	Purchased from Peter McCloskey, Drogheda 8.1.35 – Scrapped June 1946
266	ZY 489	AEC Regal IV	9822E1545	PRV/GNR	1.5.55	40		Converted to 45 seater (1.12.57) then converted to 34 seat 'Yellow Coach' by CIE Summer 1959 Withdrawn 1972
267	ID 1724	International	3LR6780		1925	20		Scrapped June 1933

Appendix A (1) – Bus and Lorry Fleet								
Fleet No.	Reg'n	Type	Chassis Number	Body	Date New	Seats	Payload	Comments
267	IY 2091	Dennis	6493	Platform Truck	28.7.28		6 tons	Purchased from Peter McCloskey, Drogheda 8.1.35 – Scrapped 25.5.39 Allocated to Drogheda
267	ZY 490	AEC Regal IV	9822E1544	PRV/GNR	1.5.55	40		Converted to 45 seater (1.12.57) then converted to 34 seat 'Yellow Coach' by CIE Summer 1959 Withdrawn 1972
268	ZI 1534	International	4888E		8.5.28	20		Scrapped June 1935
268	IH 3050	Dennis	35736	Platform Truck	19.6.31		4 tons	Purchased from Peter McCloskey, Drogheda 8.1.35 – Scrapped 14.8.46 Allocated to Drogheda
268	IY 9562	AEC Regal IV	9822E1539	PRV/GNR	4.6.54	45		Withdrawn 1973
269	ID 1346	Studebaker	22003		1928	6		Scrapped June 1933
269	IY 2637	Dennis	135203	Parcels Van	8.7.32		2 tons	Purchased from Peter McCloskey, Drogheda 8.1.35 – Scrapped 12.38 Allocated to Drogheda
269	IY 9563	AEC Regal IV	9822E1532	PRV/GNR	4.6.54	45		Withdrawn 1972
270	ZI 1793	Dennis G	70268		30.6.28	20		Scrapped 1.10.37
270	IY 9673	AEC Regal IV	9822E1533	PRV/GNR	1.7.54	45		Withdrawn 1972
271	JI 4753	Dennis GL	70637		15.5.30	20		Scrapped 1.10.37 converted to Garage Tender No 4 in 1941
271	AZ 5078	Leyland Lion LT2	51113	SMW	2.6.30	31		Was bus 110 then became 271 shortly afterwards lorry 150 finally GT6
271	TZ 987	AEC Regal IV	9822E1535	PRV/GNR	1.10.54	45		
272	IY 2182	Guy OND	9240	Guy	23.5.29	20		Scrapped June 1936
272	AZ 5081	Leyland Lion LT2	51112	SMW	13.6.30	31		Formerly bus No. 111 renumbered 271 (1945) – Scrapped 2.49
272	IY 9920	AEC Regal IV	9822E1534	PRV/GNR	1.10.54	45		Withdrawn 1973
273	IY 2488	Guy B	23710	Guy	14.4.31	24		
273	AZ 5079	Leyland Lion LT2	51111	McKeown & Claughan	18.6.30	31		Formerly bus No. 118 renumbered 273 (1945) – Scrapped 2.49
273	IY 9921	AEC Regal IV	9822E1540	PRV/GNR	1.10.54	45		Withdrawn 1973
274	AZ 1358	Leyland Tiger TS2	60086	Leyland	6.9.28	31		Ex HMS Catherwood – Scrapped 12.38
274	AZ 5080	Leyland Lion LT2	51115	SMW	4.7.30	31		Formerly bus No. 119 renumbered 274 (1945) – Scrapped 2.49
274	ZY 79	AEC Regal IV	9822E1543	PRV/GNR	1.12.54	45		Withdrawn 1973 – Preserved TMSI
275	AZ 1553	Leyland Tiger TS2	60089	Leyland	20.10.28	31		Ex HMS Catherwood – Scrapped 12.38 Converted to Pole Perch Trailer 6.6.39 (T11)
275	ZY 130	AEC Regal IV	9822E1530	PRV/GNR	1.1.55	45		
276	AZ 4059	Leyland Tiger TS2	60614	Leyland	1.2.30	31		Ex HMS Catherwood fitted with new GNR body 9.2.37 became Garage Tender GT1 in 1950
276	ZY 238	AEC Regal IV	9822E1541	PRV/GNR	1.3.55	45		
277	ZI 9197	Leyland Tiger TS4	1743	Leyland	18.7.32	31		Raised roof type luggage carrier fitted ex HMS Catherwood – Scrapped 5.12.49
278	ZI 9198	Leyland Tiger TS4	1744	Leyland	19.7.32	31		Ex HMS Catherwood – Scrapped 5.12.49
279	AZ 3030	Leyland Tiger TS2	60184	Catherwood	1.7.29	26		Semi-luxury body ex HMS Catherwood – Scrapped
279	ZI 4271	Leyland Tiger TS2	60879	Potter	14.3.30	31		Former bus 88 renumbered in 1945 – Scrapped 5.12.49
280	AZ 3353	Leyland Tiger TS2	60623	Catherwood	11.7.29	26		Ex HMS Catherwood – Scrapped 19.4.38
280	ZI 4272	Leyland Tiger TS2	60880	City Wheel Works	24.3.30	31		Former bus 89 renumbered in 1945 – Scrapped 5.12.49
280	ZC 6624	Leyland Titan TD5	302812	DUTC Body	1939	30/26		Former DUTC bus bought from CIE
281	XI 8686	Leyland Lion PLSC3	45673	Leyland	31.5.27	30		Ex HMS Catherwood withdrawn 1.10.36
281	ZI 4274	Leyland Tiger TS2	60882	Potter	9.4.30	31		Former bus 91 renumbered in 1945 Scrap 5.12.49
281	ZC 6655	Leyland Titan TD5	302841	DUTC Body	1939	30/26		Former DUTC bus bought from CIE
282	XI 8794	Leyland Lion PLSC3	45675	Leyland	9.6.27	34		Ex HMS Catherwood withdrawn 25.3.36
282	ZI 4275	Leyland Tiger TS2	60883	City Wheel Works	24.4.30	31		Former bus 92 renumbered in 1945 Scrap 8.2.49
282	ZC 6663	Leyland Titan TD5	302849	DUTC Body	1939	30/26		Former DUTC bus bought from CIE

Appendix A (1) – Bus and Lorry Fleet								
Fleet No.	Reg'n	Type	Chassis Number	Body	Date New	Seats	Payload	Comments
283	XI 9226	Leyland Lion PLSC3	46583	Leyland	22.8.27	31		Ex HMS Catherwood withdrawn 1.10.36
283	ZI 4277	Leyland Tiger TS2	60885	Potter	17.4.30	31		Former bus 94 renumbered in 1945 Scrap 8.2.49
283	ZC 6665	Leyland Titan TD5	302850	DUTC Body	1939	30/26		Former DUTC bus bought from CIE
284	AZ 1394	Leyland Lion PLSC3	47490	Leyland	13.9.28	36		Ex HMS Catherwood withdrawn 1939
284	ZI 4281	Leyland Tiger TS2	60894	Potter	8.5.30	31		Former bus 98 renumbered in 1945 Scrap 8.2.49
284	ZC 6667	Leyland Titan TD5	302853	DUTC Body	1939	30/26		Former DUTC bus bought from CIE
285	AZ 1403	Leyland Lion PLSC3	47491	Leyland	13.9.28	30		Ex HMS Catherwood
285	ZD 7856	AEC Regent II	6617537	PRV/GNR	23.12.46	H30/26R		
286	AZ 1435	Leyland Lion PLSC3	47495	Leyland	22.9.28	36		EX HMS Catherwood
286	ZD 7857	AEC Regent II	6617538	PRV/GNR	1.2.47	H30/26R		
287	AZ 1529	Leyland Lion PLSC3	47503	Leyland	16.10.28	36		Ex HMS Catherwood
287	ZD 7858	AEC Regent II	6617535	PRV/GNR	1.3.47	H30/26R		
288	AZ 1530	Leyland Lion PLSC3	47509	Leyland	16.10.28	36		Ex HMS Catherwood
288	ZD 7859	AEC Regent II	6617536	PRV/GNR	28.3.47	H30/26R		
289	XI 8902	Leyland Lion PLSC3	45669	Catherwood	5.7.27	29		Ex HMS Catherwood withdrawn 1.10.37
289	IY 5391	AEC Regent III	9611694	PRV/GNR	23.3.48	H32/26R		Withdrawn 1967
290	ZI 551	Leyland Lion PLSC3	45671	Hall Lewis	15.7.27	31		Ex HMS Catherwood withdrawn 1941
290	IY 5392	AEC Regent III	9611691	PRV/GNR	25.3.48	H32/26R		Withdrawn 1967
291	XI 9124	Leyland Lion PLSC3	45670	Hall Lewis	1.8.27	31		Ex HMS Catherwood withdrawn 1937
291	IY 5393	AEC Regent III	9611693	PRV/GNR	19.4.48	H32/26R		Withdrawn 1967
292	ZI 709	Leyland Lion PLSC3	45676	Hall Lewis	2.9.27	36		Ex HMS Catherwood withdrawn 1937
292	IY 5394	AEC Regent III	9611685	PRV/GNR	1.5.48	H32/26R		
293	XI 9521	Leyland Lion PLSC3	46190	Leyland	21.10.27	35		Ex HMS Catherwood withdrawn 1937
293	IY 5395	AEC Regent III	9611689	PRV/GNR	1.6.48	H32/26RD		
294	AZ 294	Leyland Lion PLSC3	47052	Leyland	28.3.28	36		Ex HMS Catherwood withdrawn 1937
294	IY 5396	AEC Regent III	9611686	PRV/GNR	1.6.48	H32/26R		Withdrawn 1967
295	AZ 1434	Leyland Lion PLSC3	47496	Leyland	22.9.28	36		Ex HMS Catherwood withdrawn 1941
295	IY 5397	AEC Regent III	9611687	PRV/GNR	17.6.48	H32/26RD		
296	AZ 1514	Leyland Tiger TS2	60088	Leyland	15.10.28	31		Ex HMS Catherwood renumbered 129 (1942) sold to SLNCR in 1946
296	IY 5398	AEC Regent III	9611692	PRV/GNR	7.7.48	H32/26RD		
297	AZ1377	Leyland Tiger TS2	60579	Leyland	12.10.29	31		Ex HMS Catherwood withdrawn 10.2.37
297	IY 5399	AEC Regent III	9611690	PRV/GNR	10.9.48	H32/26RD		
298	ZI 1086	Leyland Lion PLSC3	46635	Leyland	3.1.28	35		Purchased second hand from General Omnibus Co, Dublin 25.7.34 – Scrapped 1938
298	IY 5400	AEC Regent III	9611688	PRV/GNR	1.10.48	H32/26R		
299	ZI 1472	Leyland Lion PLSC3	46637	Leyland	1.5.28	35		Scrapped 1.6.37 – after which spent a short period as a Garage Tender in Dublin
299	ZO 8643	AEC Regent III	9612E4720	PRV/GNR	11.4.53	H36/30RD		Withdrawn 1967
300	ZI 1684	Leyland Lion PLSC3	47491	Leyland	9.6.28	35		Purchased from General Omnibus Co, Dublin 25.7.34 – Scrapped 1938
	ZI 844	Leyland Lion PLSC3	46221					Ex GOC Dublin – Scrapped 25.7.34
	ZI 1473	Leyland Lion PLSC3	46636					Ex GOC Dublin – Scrapped by 7.8.36
300	IY 8593	AEC Regent III	9612E4718	PRV/GNR	18.4.53	H36/30RD		Destroyed in Dundalk Works Fire 7.9.55

Appendix A (1) – Bus and Lorry Fleet								
Fleet No.	Reg'n	Type	Chassis Number	Body	Date New	Seats	Payload	Comments
301	ZA 2712	Leyland Lion LT5A	5098	GNR	3.8.34	35		Body replaced following severe accident Philipsburgh Avenue Dublin 22.10.36 – Scrapped 19.12.51
301	IY 8656	AEC Regent III	9612E4717	PRV/GNR	8.5.53	H36/30RD		Withdrawn 1967
302	ZA 2723	Leyland Lion LT5A	5099	GNR	29.10.34	35		Scrapped 10.3.52
302	ZO 9840	AEC Regent III	9612E4719	PRV/GNR	1.6.53	H36/30RD		Withdrawn 1967
303	ZA 2724	Leyland Lion LT5A	5100	GNR	1.9.34	35		Scrapped 10.3.52
303	ZU 3142	AEC Regent III	9612E7756	PRV/GNR	1.10.53	H36/30RD		Withdrawn 1967
304	ZA 2725	Leyland Lion LT5A	5101	GNR	3.1.35	35		Scrapped 10.3.52
304	ZU 4879	AEC Regent III	9612E7755	PRV/GNR	1.1.54	H36/30RD		Withdrawn 1967
305	ZA 2726	Leyland Lion LT5A	5102	GNR	1.11.34	35		Scrapped 2.12.53
305	ZU 4880	AEC Regent III	9612E7754	PRV/GNR	1.1.54	H36/30RD		Destroyed in Dundalk Works Fire 7.9.55
306	ZA 2727	Leyland Lion LT5A	5103	GNR	1.12.34	35		Scrapped June 1951
306	ZU 4878	AEC Regent III	9612E7753	PRV/GNR	1.1.54	H36/30RD		
307	ZA 3830	Leyland Lion LT5A	6226	GNR	2.8.35	35		Scrapped June 1951
307	ZU 4877	AEC Regent III	9612E7757	PRV/GNR	1.1.54	H36/30RD		Withdrawn 1967
308	ZA 3831	Leyland Lion LT5A	6227	GNR	25.7.35	35		Scrapped 10.3.52
309	ZA 3832	Leyland Lion LT5A	6228	GNR	8.6.35	35		Scrapped December 1950
310	ZA 3833	Leyland Lion LT5A	6229	GNR	17.5.35	35		Scrapped June 1951
311	ZA 3834	Leyland Lion LT5A	6230	GNR	17.8.35	35		Scrapped 9.5.53
312	ZA 3835	Leyland Lion LT5A	6231	GNR	22.6.35	35		Scrapped 19.12.51
313	ZA 3836	Leyland Lion LT5A	6232	GNR	5.7.35	35		Scrapped December 1950
314	ZA 3837	Leyland Lion LT5A	6233	GNR	1.5.35	35		Scrapped 19.12.51
315	ZA 3838	Leyland Lion LT5A	6234	GNR	14.8.35	35		Scrapped 10.3.52
316	ZA 3839	Leyland Lion LT5A	6235	GNR	1.5.35	35		Scrapped 2.49
317	ZA 4584	Leyland Lion LT7	7013	GNR	5.7.35	35		Chassis bought from Erne Bus Company on 26.4.35
318	IY 2256	Ford	AA137518	Open Platform	1.10.29		1.5 tons	Purchased from freight operator SD Kearney, Dundalk 7.5.35 – Scrapped 1936
318	ZD 720	GNR Gardner	1/41/318	GNR	4.1.41	35		
319	IY 2257	Ford	AA1486269	Open Platform	1.10.29		1.5 tons	Purchased from freight operator SD Kearney, Dundalk 7.5.35 – Scrapped 1936
319	ZD 721	GNR Gardner	1/41/319	GNR	4.1.41	35		Scrapped 1.1.56
320	ZI 2712	Ford	746378	Open Platform	28.3.29		1.5 tons	Purchased from freight operator SD Kearney, Dundalk 7.5.35 – Scrapped 1936
320	ZD 722	GNR Gardner	1/41/320	GNR	4.1.41	35		Rebuilt 4.10.49
321	BI 1687	Ford	1013324	Open Platform	17.7.29		1.5 tons	Purchased from freight operator H Higginson, Dundalk 4.5.35 – Scrapped 1936
321	ZD 723	GNR Gardner	3/41/321	GNR	26.3.41	34		
322	IY 2232	Ford	1376721	Open Platform	12.8.29		1.5 tons	Purchased from freight operator H Higginson, Dundalk 4.5.35 – Scrapped 1936
322	ZD 724	GNR Gardner	3/41/322	GNR	26.3.41	35		
323	IY 2586	Ford	AA 4792131	Open Platform	1.1.32		2 tons	Purchased from freight operator J Crilly, Dundalk 4.5.35 – Scrapped 1939
323	ZD 725	GNR Gardner	3/41/323	GNR	26.3.41	35		Scrapped 1959 by CIE
324	BI 1981	Ford	AA4488745	Open Platform	5.10.31		1.5 tons	Purchased from freight operator P Martin, Carrickmacross 6.5.35 – Scrapped 1936

Appendix A (1) – Bus and Lorry Fleet								
Fleet No.	**Reg'n**	**Type**	**Chassis Number**	**Body**	**Date New**	**Seats**	**Payload**	**Comments**
324	ZD 726	GNR Gardner	3/41/324	GNR	26.3.41	35		Rebuilt 31.3.49 – Preserved
325	IY 2920	Fordson	BB5300177	Open Platform	3.12.34		2 tons	Purchased from freight operator J Breen, Knockbridge 6.5.35 – renumbered 185 (Nov 1940) – Scrapped Dec 1948
325	ZD 727	GNR Gardner	6/41/325	GNR	4.7.41	35		
326	BI 2223	Fordson	BB5259534	Open Platform	3.7.34		2 tons	Purchased from freight operator J Joyce, Castleblaney 7.5.35 – renumbered 186 (Nov 1940) Scrap June 1948
326	ZD 728	GNR Gardner	6/41/326	GNR	31.5.41	35		
327	BI 2126	Fordson	BB5194106	Open Platform	10.7.33		2 tons	Purchased from freight operator J Howell, Carrickmacross 6.5.35 – renumbered 187 (Nov 1940) Scrap June 1950
327	ZD 729	GNR Gardner	12/49/327	GNR	4.7.41	35		Rebuilt following accident (1950) re-registered ZJ 2123 chassis no.12/49/327
328	BI 2087	Fordson	BB5152766	Open Platform	13.3.33		2 tons	Purchased from freight operator TJ Duffy, Castleblaney 7.5.35 – renumbered 188 (Nov 1940) Scrap Dec 1948
328	ZD 730	GNR Gardner	6/41/328	GNR	8.1.42	35		
329	ID 1854	Ford	1153729		1929		1.5 tons	Acquired from Maher Brothers 1.7.35 freight operator Dundalk – Scrapped 1936
329	ZD 731	GNR Gardner	6/41/329	GNR	8.1.42	35		
330	AI 3997	Chevrolet	LT 76370	Low slung Timber Carrier	22.2.32		1.5 tons	Acquired from freight operator H Woodward, Navan 31.7.35 – Scrapped 1936
330	ZD 732	GNR Gardner	6/41/330	GNR	8.1.42	35		
331	AI 4220	Dodge	10511	Low slung Timber Carrier	27.7.34		2.5 tons	Acquired from freight operator H Woodward, Navan 31.7.35 – Scrapped 1938
331	ZY 625	AEC Regal IV	9822E1829	PRV/GNR	1.6.55	C38R		Converted to 34 seat 'Yellow Coach' by CIE Summer 1959 Withdrawn 8.66 following fire damage
332	IH 3136	Dennis GL	101641	Open Platform	10.12.31		2 tons	Acquired from R Nawn freight operator 5.9.35 Ballyshannon – Scrapped June 1946
332	ZY 626	AEC Regal IV	9822E1830	PRV/GNR	1.6.55	C38R		Converted to 34 seat 'Yellow Coach' by CIE Summer 1959 Withdrawn 1973
333	IH 3196	Dennis Lancet	160043	GNR	25.4.32		4 tons	Acquired from R Nawn freight operator 5.9.35 Ballyshannon converted to bus became No. 38
333	ZY 627	AEC Regal IV	9822E1831	PRV/GNR	1.7.55	C38R		
334	XI 9581	Dennis	35381	Open Platform	15.11.27		4 tons	Acquired from freight operator J Berney Cootehill 1.9.35 – Scrapped 1937
334	ZY 773	AEC Regal IV	9822E1832	PRV/GNR	27.7.55	B40R		Converted to 34 seat by CIE – Withdrawn 1973
335	AZ 3032		21025	Open Platform	3.6.29		4 tons	Acquired from freight operator McAlpine & Nixon Monaghan 2.9.35 – Scrapped 1937
335	CIK 234	AEC Regal IV	9822E1833	PRV/GNR	27.10.55	DP45R		Withdrawn 1972
336	AZ 7813	Dennis	135056	Forward Control	3.6.31		2 tons	Acquired from freight operator J Berney Cootehill 1.9.35 – Scrapped June 1946
336	ZY 1266	AEC Regal IV	9822E1834	PRV/GNR	1.2.55	DP45R		Withdrawn 1973
337	IH 2972	Dennis	135027	Forward Control	2.2.31		2 tons	Acquired from freight operator R Nawn Ballyshannon 5.9.35 – Scrapped 1937
337	ZY 1165	AEC Regal IV	9822E1835	PRV/GNR	8.10.55	DP45R		
338	ID 2426	Studebaker	TI 7128	Open Platform	16.11.34		1.5 tons	Acquired from freight operator T Gibson Cootehill 1.9.35 – Scrapped 1936
338	ZY 1322	AEC Regal IV	9822E1836	PRV/GNR	13.12.55	DP45R		Withdrawn 1973
339	IY 1022	Commer	53165	Open Platform	7.7.33		2.5 tons	Acquired from freight operator Faulkner Dunleer 9.9.35 – Scrapped 25.5.39
339	ZY 1323	AEC Regal IV	9822E1837	PRV/GNR	13.12.55	DP45R		Withdrawn 1972
340	ID 2391	Fordson	BB5274372	Open Platform	6.7.34		2 tons	Acquired from freight operator Boyd & Sons Virginia 27.8.35 – Scrapped 2.9.48
340	ZY 1380	AEC Regal IV	9822E1838	PRV/GNR	1.1.56	DP45R		
341	ID 2448	Fordson	BB5300146		18.1.35		2 tons	Acquired from freight operator PJ Moynagh, Oldcastle 12.9.35 – Scrapped 5.2.52 became Garage Tender No. 10
341	ZY 1381	AEC Regal IV	9822E1839	PRV/GNR	1.1.56	DP45R		

Appendix A (1) – Bus and Lorry Fleet								
Fleet No.	**Reg'n**	**Type**	**Chassis Number**	**Body**	**Date New**	**Seats**	**Payload**	**Comments**
342	AI 4255	Fordson	BB5311100		23.10.34		2 tons	Acquired from freight operator J Collins, Navan 27.8.35 – Scrapped 16.12.48
342	ZY 1682	AEC Regal IV	9822E1840	PRV/GNR	1.5.56	DP40R		Converted to 34 seat 'Yellow Coach' by CIE Summer 1959 Withdrawn 1972
343	ID 2335	Fordson	BB5252737	Open Platform	1.1.34		2 tons	Acquired from freight operator P McEnroe, Oldcastle 27.8.35 – Scrapped 28.4.47
343	ZY 1683	AEC Regal IV	9822E1841	PRV/GNR	1.5.56	DP40R		Converted to 34 seat 'Yellow Coach' by CIE Summer 1959 Withdrawn 1972
344	BI 2310	Fordson	BB5304685	Open Platform	25.3.35		2 tons	Acquired from freight operator McAlpine & Nixon, Monaghan 2.9.35 – Scrapped 7.4.49
344	ZY 1684	AEC Regal IV	9822E1842	PRV/GNR	1.5.56	DP40R		Converted to 34 seat 'Yellow Coach' by CIE Summer 1959 Withdrawn 1972
345	ID 2459	Fordson	A4998981	Open Platform	2.3.35		2 tons	Acquired from freight operator P McEnroe, Oldcastle 27.8.35 – Scrapped 1940
345	ZY 1715	AEC Regal IV	9822E1843	PRV/GNR	1.6.56	DP40R		Converted to 45 seat May 1958 – Body to *Bord na Móna*
346	AI 3730	Ford	AA3013469	Open Platform	13.5.31		1.5 tons	Acquired from freight operator P Heaney, Kells 28.8.35 – Scrapped 1936
346	ZY 1716	AEC Regal IV	9822E1844	PRV/GNR	1.6.56	DP40R		Converted to 45 seat May 1958
347	AI 3980	Ford	AA4792261	Open Platform	1931		2 tons	Acquired from freight operator T Stewart, Drogheda 27.8.35 – Scrapped 1936
348	IY 2906	Bedford	134104	Open Platform	2.11.34		2 tons	Acquired from freight operator Faulkner Dunleer 9.9.35 – Scrapped 1941
349	AI 3944	Bedford	411291	Open Platform	1931		2 tons	Acquired from freight operator A Carter, Navan 26.8.35 – Scrapped 1936
350	IR 1891	Bedford	114606		5.9.31		2 tons	Acquired from freight operator J Monaghan, Drogheda 13.9.35 – Scrapped June 1946
351	IY 2554	Bedford	114172		1931		2 tons	Acquired from freight operator J Wallace, Dundalk 30.8.35 – Scrapped 30.5.45
352	IH 2933	Chevrolet	69862	Open Platform	20.11.30		1.5 tons	Acquired from freight operator R Nawn Ballyshannon 5.9.35 – Scrapped 1936
353	FI 1722	Chevrolet	63792	Open Platform	1930		2 tons	Acquired from freight operator P Heaney, Kells 28.8.35 – Scrapped 1936
354	AI 3929	Chevrolet		Open Platform	6.7.31		2 tons	Acquired from freight operator P Heaney, Kells 28.8.35 – Scrapped 1936
355	IH 3453	Morris Commercial	233/C9850		26.4.34		3 tons	Acquired from freight operator R Nawn, Ballyshannon 5.9.35 – Scrapped 1937
356	ID 2146	Morris Leader	C87G 1131185		2.10.31		3.5 tons	Acquired from freight operator J Berney, Cootehill 1.9.35 – Scrapped 1937
357	AZ 87	ADC 418	418048		1928		4 tons	Acquired from freight operator McAlpine & Nixon, Monaghan 2.9.35 4 – Cyl Dorman Diesel engine – Scrapped 1938
358	ID 2245	Fordson	AAB5107440		10.3.33		2 tons	Acquired from freight operator Jas Byers, Ballyjamesduff 24.9.35 – Scrapped 4.8.51
359	BI 2299	Fordson	BB5304330		2.2.35		2 tons	Acquired from freight operator J McMorrough 8.10.35 – Scrapped 4.8.51
360	ID 2472	Fordson	BB5304493		3.4.35		2 tons	Acquired from freight operator P Daly 24.9.35 – Scrapped 28.4.47
361	BI 2034	Ford	AA4795462		5.2.32		2 tons	Acquired from freight operator J White 13.11.35 – Scrapped 1938
361	ZH 1371	GNR Gardner	9/47/361	Harkness/GNR	26.9.47	35		
362	IY 6177	GNR Gardner	11/48/362	Harkness/GNR	1.6.49	35		
363	IY 6178	GNR Gardner	5/49/363	Harkness/GNR	1.6.49	35		
364	ZH 2662	GNR Gardner	11/47/364	Harkness/GNR	22.12.47	35		
365	IY 6179	GNR Gardner	2/49/365	Harkness/GNR	1.6.49	35		
366	IY 6180	GNR Gardner	9/48/366	Harkness/GNR	1.6.49	35		
367	IY 6181	GNR Gardner	6/49/367	Harkness/GNR	1.7.49	35		
368	IY 6182	GNR Gardner	6/49/368	Harkness/GNR	16.7.49	35		
369	IY 6183	GNR Gardner	6/49/369	Harkness/GNR	1.7.49	35		
370	IY 6184	GNR Gardner	5/49/370	Harkness/GNR	1.6.49	35		
371	IY 6185	GNR Gardner	3/49/371	Harkness/GNR	1.6.49	35		
372	IY 6186	GNR Gardner	8/48/372	Harkness/GNR	1.6.49	35		

Appendix A (1) – Bus and Lorry Fleet								
Fleet No.	Reg'n	Type	Chassis Number	Body	Date New	Seats	Payload	Comments
373	ZH 1372	GNR Gardner	9/47/373	Harkness/GNR	26.9.47	35		
374	ZH 1373	GNR Gardner	10/47/374	Harkness/GNR	15.10.47	35		
375	ZH 1374	GNR Gardner	10/47/375	Harkness/GNR	15.10.47	35		
376	ZH 2660	GNR Gardner	11/47/376	Harkness/GNR	8.12.47	35		
377	ZH 2661	GNR Gardner	11/47/377	Harkness/GNR	11.12.47	35		
378	IY 6187	GNR Gardner	6/47/378	Harkness/GNR	1.6.49	35		
379	IY 6188	GNR Gardner	4/49/379	Harkness/GNR	1.6.49	35		
380	ZH 2663	GNR Gardner	11/47/380	Harkness/GNR	10.1.48	35		Destroyed at Dundalk Works fire 7.9.55
381	ZH 72	GNR Gardner	6/47/381	Harkness/GNR	21.6.47	35		
382	ZH 73	GNR Gardner	7/47/382	Harkness/GNR	5.7.47	35		
383	ZH 74	GNR Gardner	7/47/383	Harkness/GNR	26.7.47	35		
384	ZH 75	GNR Gardner	7/47/384	Harkness/GNR	28.7.47	35		
385	ZJ 7547	GNR Gardner	2/50/385	PRV/GNR	25.3.50	33		
386	ZL 1853	GNR Gardner	11/50/386	PRV/GNR	14.11.50	33		
387	ZL 2718	GNR Gardner	12/50/387	PRV/GNR	22.12.50	35		Preserved
388	IY 7382	GNR Gardner	4/51/388	PRV/GNR	1.5.51	33		
389	IY 7383	GNR Gardner	4/51/389	PRV/GNR	1.6.51	33		Preserved
390	IY 7384	GNR Gardner	5/51/390	PRV/GNR	1.6.51	33		Preserved
391	IY 7385	GNR Gardner	5/51/391	PRV/GNR	1.6.51	33		
392	IY 8040	GNR Gardner	12/51/392	PRV/GNR	1.6.52	33		
393	IY 8041	GNR Gardner	12/51/393	PRV/GNR	1.6.52	33		
394	IY 8042	GNR Gardner	2/52/394	PRV/GNR	1.6.52	33		
395	IY 8043	GNR Gardner	3/52/395	PRV/GNR	1.6.52	33		
396	IY 8044	GNR Gardner	3/52/396	PRV/GNR	1.6.52	33		Preserved
397	IY 8045	GNR Gardner	4/52/397	PRV/GNR	1.6.52	33		
398	IY 8046	GNR Gardner	5/52/398	PRV/GNR	1.6.52	33		
399	IY 8047	GNR Gardner	6/52/399	PRV/GNR	14.6.52	33		
400	IY 8048	GNR Gardner	6/52/400	PRV/GNR	1.7.52	33		
401	IY 8137	GNR Gardner	6/52/401	PRV/GNR	1.7.52	33		
402	IY 8139	GNR Gardner	6/52/402	PRV/GNR	1.8.52	33		
403	ZH 3902	AEC Regal III	962235	Park Royal	17.7.48	39		
404	ZH 3903	AEC Regal III	962242	Park Royal	17.7.48	39		
405	ZH 3904	AEC Regal III	962243	Park Royal	17.7.48	39		
406	ZH 3905	AEC Regal III	962234	Park Royal	29.7.48	39		
407	ZH 3906	AEC Regal III	962239	Park Royal	17.8.48	39		Withdrawn 1970
408	ZH 3907	AEC Regal III	962236	Park Royal	17.8.48	39		
409	ZH 3908	AEC Regal III	962237	Park Royal	1.9.48	39		
410	ZH 3909	AEC Regal III	9621E245	Park Royal	1.9.48	39		Withdrawn 1971
411	ZH 3910	AEC Regal III	9621E246	Park Royal	6.9.48	39		
412	ZH 3911	AEC Regal III	9621E247	Park Royal	6.9.48	39		
413	ZH 3912	AEC Regal III	9621E248	Park Royal	6.9.48	39		
414	ZH 3913	AEC Regal III	9621E244	Park Royal	14.9.48	39		
415	ZH 3914	AEC Regal III	9621E250	Park Royal	14.9.48	39		Withdrawn 1970
416	ZH 3915	AEC Regal III	9621E457	Park Royal	1.10.48	39		
417	ZH 3916	AEC Regal III	9621E251	Park Royal	1.10.48	39		
418	ZH 3917	AEC Regal III	9621E249	Park Royal	1.10.48	39		
419	ZH 3918	AEC Regal III	9621E252	Park Royal	1.10.48	39		Withdrawn 1970
420	ZH 3919	AEC Regal III	9621E460	Park Royal	1.10.48	39		
421	ZH 3920	AEC Regal III	9621E459	Park Royal	1.10.48	39		
422	ZH 3921	AEC Regal III	9621E461	Park Royal	1.10.48	39		
423	ZH 3922	AEC Regal III	9621E458	Park Royal	1.10.48	39		
424	ZH 3923	AEC Regal III	9621E462	Park Royal	1.10.48	39		
425	ZH 3924	AEC Regal III	9621E514	Park Royal	1.10.48	39		Withdrawn 1971
426	ZH 3925	AEC Regal III	9621E515	Park Royal	23.10.48	39		
427	ZH 3926	AEC Regal III	962231	Park Royal	1.6.48	35		Withdrawn 1971 – Preserved
428	ZH 3927	AEC Regal III	962232	Park Royal	15.6.48	35		Withdrawn 1970
429	ZH 3928	AEC Regal III	962233	Park Royal	15.6.48	35		Withdrawn 1970

Appendix A (1) – Bus and Lorry Fleet								
Fleet No.	Reg'n	Type	Chassis Number	Body	Date New	Seats	Payload	Comments
430	ZH 3929	AEC Regal III	962238	Park Royal	15.6.48	35		Withdrawn 1970
431	ZH 3930	AEC Regal III	962241	Park Royal	17.6.48	35		Withdrawn 1970
432	ZH 3931	AEC Regal III	962240	Park Royal	19.6.48	35		Withdrawn 1970
433	ZH 3932	AEC Regent III	9612E3740	Park Royal	8.7.48	H30/26RD		
434	ZH 3933	AEC Regent III	9612E3741	Park Royal	14.7.48	H30/26RD		
435	ZH 3934	AEC Regent III	9612E3742	Park Royal	6.7.48	H30/26RD		
436	ZH 3935	AEC Regent III	9612E3743	Park Royal	6.7.48	H30/26RD		
437	ZH 3936	AEC Regent III	9612E3744	Park Royal	14.7.48	H30/26RD		
438	ZH 3937	AEC Regent III	9612E3745	Park Royal	17.7.48	H30/26RD		Preserved TMSI
439	ZH 3938	AEC Regent III	9612E3746	Park Royal	30.7.48	H30/26RD		Re-registered MZ 2529 in N Ireland 9.48
440	IY 8391	AEC Regent III	9613E2699	PRV/GNR	1.1.53	H30/26RD		
441	IY 8394	AEC Regent III	9613E2697	PRV/GNR	1.1.53	H30/26RD		
442	IY 8417	AEC Regent III	9613E2698	PRV/GNR	4.2.53	H30/26RD		

Appendix A (2) – Staff Cars and Ancillary Vehicles						
Fleet No	Reg'n	Make	Chassis number	Type	Year	Comments
*	ZI 3802	Rudge/Whitworth	36528	M/Cycle & Sidecar	26.8.29	Used by Inspectors destroyed in accident at Lisdoonan Cross 9.06.30
*	ZI 5578	Rudge/Whitworth	41968	M/Cycle & Sidecar	26.9.30	Bought second hand 25.1.33 as replacement for above machine
*	AZ 6015	Rudge/Whitworth	43477	M/Cycle & Sidecar	22.9.30	Bought for NI Inspectors – Scrapped 1936
*	EK 6840	Austin 12	55359	Burnham Saloon	30.6.29	Purchased from Isaac Agnew Ltd Belfast Joe Mackle's Car – sold 1933
*	Z 5147	Austin	G17637		17.6.33	Purchased from Huet Bros dealer for £100 10.11.37 – Scrapped December 1945
*	AI 3925	Standard	116456	16bhp	1.7.31	Car purchased with acquisition of Paddy McCloskey Haulage business 1.5.35 – Scrapped June 1942
*	IY 3544	Ford	18F3455917	V8	7.5.37	Purchased from Byrne & Maguire dealer for £213
*	ZC 634	Ford	C63097	10bhp	1.4.37	Purchased from Hon P Campbell for £60 on 19.3.42 became a Garage Tender 1942
SC1	ZA 1118	Wolsley	103/116	21bhp	13.12.33	Purchased from dealer WF Poole & Co June 1937 – Mechanical Engineers Car
SC1	IY 5788	Ford	C363917	Prefect	1.9.48	Traffic Department Dundalk
SC1	ZY 929	Ford	119437	Prefect	30.7.55	Road Motor Supervisor – Drogheda
SC2	ZI 3248	Ford			1931	Dublin Road Motor Department
SC2	BI 2610	Morris	S1/E1119877	8bhp	2.1.37	Purchased from T Martin 15.3.39 – Scrapped June 1948
SC2	IY 5789	Ford	C362259	Prefect	1.9.48	Road Motor Supervisor Breslin Bundoran – Scrapped September 1955
SC2	ZY 930	Ford	122611	Prefect	1955	Dublin – Traffic Department
SC3	ZC 1678	Ford	S2/35361	V8	1.4.37	Bought from C Bailie-Gage (£160) 9.12.39 sold 19.12.51
SC3	ZO 2938	Buick	B.52.11	31bhp	7.6.52	George B Howden's Car – after formation of GNRB this became the Chairman's Car
SC4	IY 3999	Ford	54F.453931	V8	13.9.38	Bought from Drogheda Oatmeal Milling Co (27.2.42) £150 used by Chief Inspector A Switzer
SC4	TI 4228	Hudson	171628117	21bhp	14.11.47	Purchased 17.11.49
SC4	ZJ 2604	Hudson	49170519	Commodore	29.7.52	New 4.6.49 sold 15.1.53
SC4	ZY 931	Ford	68688	Prefect	24.8.55	Crashed 24.10.55 Stradone County Cavan
SC4	ZY 1503	Ford	100F190788	Prefect	1956	Road Motor Supervisor Donegal Garage
SC5	NI 3326	Morris	SI/E141766	8bhp	8.5.37	Purchased from JB Stephens former GNR General Manager 14.3.42 – used by Traffic Dept Dublin
SC5	ZH 3938	Hillman	1897364E.30	Minx	22.9.48	Lorry Supervisor McCloskey Drogheda Sold 13.6.53
SC5	ZY 932	Ford	127494	Prefect	1955	Road Motor Supervisor – Cavan Garage
SC6	EZ 5344	Humber	18/3874	18bhp	1.1.37	Traffic Manager – Belfast
SC6	XRI 885	Austin		Cambridge	1955	Mr John McCormick – General Manager Dublin
SC7	PZ 5422	Ford	978	8bhp	27.4.39	Belfast – Goods Agent
SC7	ZL 8871	Austin	616567	A40	23.11.51	Assistant General Manager's car
SC8	IY 3397	Chrysler	10103802	23bhp	5.1.37	Used by Hotels Department – Bundoran
SC8	IY 7742	Austin	623038	A40	1.12.51	Dundalk-Ticket Inspectors & Traffic Representative
SC9	ZD 2243	Hudson	9048663	21bhp	11.10.40	Sold in part exchange for SC4 had been General Manager's Car
SC9	ZL 9948	Austin	610625	A40	1.2.52	Chief Inspector Albert Switzer
SC10	GZ 4297	Austin	242823	10bhp	31.5.46	Sold in part exchange for SC4 – used by General Manager when in Belfast

Appendix A (2) – Staff Cars and Ancillary Vehicles						
Fleet No	Reg'n	Make	Chassis number	Type	Year	Comments
SC10	IY 8436	Vauxhall	NIP25579	Velox	29.1.53	Chief Mechanical Engineer – Richard Meredith
SC11	GZ 5355	Austin	249381	10bhp	17.9.46	Bought in H Ferguson Belfast for Traffic Department
SC11	IY 8685	Vauxhall	EIX28362	Wyvern	2.6.53	Paddy McCloskey Lorry Supervisor Drogheda
SC12	ZD 7394	Austin	243630	10bhp	21.10.46	District Superintendent's Car Dublin – Scrapped 1955
SC13	GZ 5817	Austin	233150	10bhp	13.11.46	Sold 2.6.54 – Omagh District Superintendent's Car
SC14	IE 2799	Ford	18F3455942	V8	24.3.37	Donegal Garage Car
SC14	ZU 208	Austin	757550	Somerset	6.53	Bobby Pelissier – Road Motor Technical Assistant Dundalk
SC15	IY 4838	Austin	228721	10bhp	5.12.46	Scrapped 13.6.53 – used by Lorry Supervisor Drogheda
SC15	ZU 209	Austin	762020	Somerset	6.53	Tommy Carton District Traffic Manager Dublin
SC16	ZD 7989	Austin	250127	10bhp	1.1.47	Sold 19.12.51- used by Commercial representative Dublin
SC16	IY 8646	Commer	D437802	Station Wagon	24.4.53	Bundoran Hotel Station Wagon
SC17	IY 4909	Austin	246736	10bhp	30.1.47	Sold 13.6.53 Used by Traffic Representative Dundalk
SC17	IH 6154	Ford	799AF1723852	V8 Station Wagon	22.10.47	Began as SC21- renumbered Lorry No. 1 (1.53) then became SC17 (3.55) as baggage van Dublin
SC18	GZ 6894	Austin	261228	10bhp	12.2.47	Used by Traffic Representative – Belfast
SC19	GZ 7329	Austin	264301	10bhp	15.4.47	Sold 2.6.54
SC19	PZ 5293	Austin	820774	Somerset	1.1.54	Belfast Traffic Department
SC20	ZH 1146	Hudson	17138372	21bhp	3.9.47	Sold in part exchange for SC3 Buick – 19.6.52
SC20	OZ 7049	Austin	676396	Somerset	2.5.52	Portadown Traffic Department
SC21	IH 6154	Ford	799AF1723852	V8 Station Wagon	22.10.47	Became a Newspaper Van Jan 1953 then a baggage van for extended tours Dublin March 1955
SC21	PZ 5294	Austin	821063	Somerset	1.1.54	Belfast Deputy Chairman's Car
SC22	IY 5459	Ford	C330027	Prefect	10.3.48	
SC23	IY 5536	Ford	C333416	Prefect	21.4.48	
SC24	MZ 3101	Austin	GZSZ331402	A40	7.10.48	Omagh Traffic Department
SC25	OZ 8501	Austin	707100	Somerset	9.52	Belfast Traffic Department
SC26	OZ 9345	Austin	725625	Somerset	11.52	Belfast Traffic Department
SC29	OZ 3333	Austin	6498	A135 Princess Deluxe	3.5.52	Belfast Traffic Department
ED 1	ZO 7742	Commer	D452279	Utility	5.3.53	Used by Civil Engineer Dublin
ED 2	PZ 986	Bedford	CAV7930		21.4.53	Used by Civil Engineer Enniskillen
ED 3	IH 6154	Ford	799AF1723852	V8	22.10.47	Formerly Staff Car 17
* denotes no fleet number allocated						

Appendix A (3) – Garage Tender Fleet					
Fleet No.	Reg'n.	Type	Chassis Number	Date New	Comments
GT1	ZI 2583	Leyland Lion PLSC1	47791	15.1.29	Converted from Bus No. 1 in 1938 – Scrapped in June 1950 replaced by new GT1
GT1	AZ 4059	Leyland Tiger TS2	15553	1930	Converted from Bus No. 276 (9.11.49) Fitted with a Gantry Crane for lifting units
GT2	ZI 4263	Leyland Tiger TS2	60825	1.2.30	Converted from Bus No. 80 in 1940 – Scrapped June 1945 fitted with mobile crane
GT2	ZC 4103	GNR Gardner	4/38/244	30.4.38	Converted from Bus No. 244 30.10.56 Fitted with a Crane
GT3	IY 2798	Fordson	BB5252728	1934	Converted from Lorry No. 191 – 7.4.49
GT3	IY 5418	Austin 4 Ton	K4VF113590	21.2.48	Converted from Lorry No. 59 – 16.1.57
GT4	JI 4753	Dennis G	70637	1930	Converted from Bus No. 271- in 1941
GT4	ZY 1039	Bedford 10cwt Van	CAV41623	2.9.55	Purchased new 1955 for Dublin Garage
GT5	IY 4413	Ford 5cwt Van	T279659	1940	Converted from Lorry No. 1 in 1954 – Scrapped 1955
GT5	ZY 984	Ford 5cwt Van	100E107020	22.8.55	Replaced earlier GT5 allocated to Donegal Garage
GT6	ZC 634	Ford 10bhp Car	C63097	1.4.37	Purchased 19.3.42 – Scrapped 1949.
GT6	AZ 5078	Leyland Lion LT2	51113	2.6.30	Started life as bus 110 converted to lorry in 1945 (150) became GT with de-mountable container used for salvage operations
GT7	ZA 6256	Jowett Bradford Van	4/6/3078	1.6.47	Scrapped June 1953
GT8	ZA 6255	Jowett Bradford Van	4/6/3064	1.10.47	Scrapped June 1953
GT9	ZH 6786	Ford 10cwt Van	C346352	1.6.48	Purchased new for Cavan Garage
GT10	ID 2448	Fordson 2 ton	BB5300146	1935	Converted from Lorry No. 341 – 5.2.52 – Scrapped 27.9.55
GT11	IY 8716	Bedford Van	CAV9510	1.7.53	Purchased new for Drogheda Garage
GT12	IY 8717	Bedford Van	CAV9511	1.7.53	Purchased new for Dundalk Garage
*	BI 1574	Dennis F	45507	1928	Converted to a Garage Tender from Bus No. 51 (18.10.30) – Scrapped 1933
*	IK 4580	Karrier CX	20003	1930	Converted to a Garage Tender from Bus No. 62 (1930) for Dublin Garage – Scrapped 1933
*	IB 3527	AEC 413	414095	1927	Converted to a Garage Tender from Bus No. 71 (1930) for Belfast Garage – Scrapped 1935

Appendix A (4) – GNR Trailer Fleet					
Fleet No	Make	Type	Year	Capacity	Comments
T1	GNR	Platform	1933	4 tons	Built at Dundalk Works November 1933 – Scrapped 1944
T1	Scammell	Low-Loading	1944	30 tons	Purchased 18.1.52
T2	Eagle	Platform	1926	4 tons	Purchased from Lockingtons Dundalk in 1934
T3	Dyson	Platform	1924	4 tons	Purchased from Murphy's Dublin Rd Dundalk 23.3.36 fitted with solid tyres – Scrapped 13.6.53
T3	Scammell	Horse-Box (Artic)	1956	6 tons	Purchased from Connolly Motors Dundalk
T4	Dyson	Platform	1933	4 tons	Acquired as a result of McCloskey, Drogheda Purchase 9.1.35
T5	Dyson	Platform	1933	4 tons	Acquired as a result of McCloskey, Drogheda Purchase 9.1.35 – Scrapped 1.1.56
T6		Platform	1931	3/4 tons	Acquired from Reilly of Navan 25.2.35
T6	DAF	Edible Oil Tank (Artic)	1951	10 tons	
T7	Eagle	Platform	1938	3/4 tons	Purchased from Eagle Engineering Co May 1938
T8	Eagle	Platform	1938	3/4 tons	Purchased from Eagle Engineering Co May 1938
T9	Eagle	Platform	1930	3/4 tons	Acquired from McCaldin, Monaghan 16.5.39 – Scrapped 30.10.56
T10	Carrimore	Platform	1924	3/4 tons	Acquired from McCaldin, Monaghan 16.5.39
T11	GNR	Pole Perch	1939		Converted from bus chassis (275) 6.6.39 capable of carrying 45' long objects
T11	Dyson	Type A	1952	5 tons	Purchased from Summerfields Dublin
T12	Beardmore	Pole Perch	1939	15 tons	Built at Dundalk works (26.9.39) from former GSR Beardmore chassis could carry 60' long objects
T13	Irish Multi Wheel	Semi-trailers	1941	6/7 tons	Bought from Irish Multi Wheeled Transport 16.8.41 – Scrapped 1.1.56
T13	Scammell		1956	10 tons	
T14	Irish Multi Wheel	Semi-trailers	1941	8/9 tons	Bought from Irish Multi Wheeled Transport 16.8.41 – Scrapped 1.1.56
T14	Scammell		1956	10 tons	
T15	Irish Multi Wheel	Semi-trailers	1941	8/9 tons	Bought from Irish Multi Wheeled Transport December 1941 – Scrapped 1.1.56
T15	Scammell		1957	10 tons	
T16	Irish Multi Wheel	Semi-trailers	1942	6/7 tons	Bought from Irish Multi Wheeled Transport 7.2.42 – Scrapped 1.1.56
T16	Scammell		1957	10 tons	
T17	Beardmore		1953	12 tons	Converted from Beardmore Tractor (171) 1953 – Scrapped 1.1.56
T18	Beardmore		1949	12 tons	Converted from Beardmore Tractor (172) 1949 – Scrapped 30.10.56
T19	Beardmore		1947	12 tons	Converted from Beardmore Tractor (173) 1947 – Scrapped 1.1.56
T20	Fordson		1953	15 tons	Converted from Fordson Tractor (174) 1953
T21	Beardmore		1953	12 tons	Converted from Beardmore Tractor (170) 1953
T22	Dyson		1947	4 tons	Purchased from Summerfields Dublin May 1947
T23	Dyson		1947	4 tons	Purchased from Summerfields Dublin May 1947
T24	Rogers		1942	30 tons	Bought from Hamill Portadown
T25	EEC		1942	8 tons	Bought from Hamill Portadown
T26	Dyson		1948	5/6 tons	Bought new from Summerfield (Dealer) Dublin.
T27	Dyson		1948	5/6 tons	Bought new from Summerfield (Dealer) Dublin.
T28	Scammell	Semi-trailers open platform	1949	8 tons	All Scammell trailers were bought new from Connolly Motors of Dundalk
T29	Scammell	Semi-trailers open platform	1949	8 tons	
T30	Scammell	Semi-trailers	1950	8 tons	
T31	Scammell	Semi-trailers	1950	8 tons	
T32	Scammell	Van/Horse Box (Artic)	1950	6 tons	
T33	Scammell	Semi-trailers	1952	8 tons	
T34	Scammell	Semi-trailers	1952	8 tons	
T35	Scammell	Margarine Trailer	9.52	10 tons	McDonnells Contract Trailer – Dublin Garage
T36	Scammell	Margarine Trailer	9.52	10 tons	McDonnells Contract Trailer – Dublin Garage
T37	Scammell	Margarine Trailer	3.54	10 tons	McDonnells Contract Trailer – Dublin Garage
T38	Scammell	Van/Horse Box (Artic)	10.52	6 tons	
T39	Scammell	Flat Trailer (Artic)	7.53	8 tons	
T40	Scammell	Flat Trailer (Artic)	7.53	8 tons	
T41	Scammell	Flat Trailer (Artic)	9.53	8 tons	
T42	Scammell	Flat Trailer (Artic)	9.54	8 tons	Used for Cross Border Traffic from Dundalk Garage
T43	Scammell	Flat Trailer (Artic)	9.54	8 tons	
T44	Scammell	Flat Trailer (Artic)	12.54	8 tons	
T45	Scammell	Flat Trailer (Artic)	12.54	8 tons	
T46	Scammell	Flat Trailer (Artic)	12.54	8 tons	Used for Cross Border Traffic from Dundalk Garage
T47	Scammell	Tipper Trailer (Artic)	3.54	10 tons	
T48	Scammell	Tipper Trailer (Artic)	3.54	10 tons	
T49	Scammell	Flat Trailer (Artic)	1956	10 tons	Used for Cross Border Traffic from Dublin Garage

Appendix A (4) – GNR Trailer Fleet					
Fleet No.	**Make**	**Type**	**Year**	**Capacity**	**Comments**
T50	Scammell	Flat Trailer (Artic)	1956	10 tons	Used for Cross Border Traffic from Dublin Garage
T51	Scammell	Flat Trailer (Artic)	1956	10 tons	Used for Cross Border Traffic from Dundalk Garage
T52	Scammell	Flat Trailer (Artic)	1956	10 tons	Used for Cross Border Traffic from Drogheda Garage
T53	Scammell	Flat Trailer (Artic)	1956	10 tons	Used for Cross Border Traffic from Dundalk Garage
T54	Scammell	Flat Trailer (Artic)	1956	10 tons	Used for Cross Border Traffic from Dundalk Garage
T55	Carrimore	Flat Trailer (Artic)	1954	8 tons	Purchased from Thompsons of Mallow (Dealer) December 1954
T56	Carrimore	Flat Trailer (Artic)	1954	8 tons	Purchased from Thompsons of Mallow (Dealer) December 1954
T57	Carrimore	Flat Trailer (Artic)	1956	8 tons	
T58	Carrimore	Flat Trailer (Artic)	1956	8 tons	
T59	Carrimore	Flat Trailer (Artic)	1956	8 tons	
T60	Carrimore	Pressurised Cement (Artic)	1956	15 tons	Worked from Drogheda Garage with Lorry No 172
T61	Carrimore	Pressurised Cement (Artic)	1956	15 tons	Worked from Drogheda Garage with Lorry No 173
T62	Carrimore	Pressurised Cement (Artic)	1956	15 tons	Worked from Drogheda Garage with Lorry No 174
T63	Carrimore	Flat Trailer (Artic)	1957	8 tons	
T64	Carrimore	Flat Trailer (Artic)	1957	8 tons	
T65	Carrimore	Flat Trailer (Artic)	1957	8 tons	

Appendix B – Bus Companies Purchased by GNRI

Vehicles Acquired

Company Name & Owners	Date Acquired	GNR Fleet No.	Reg. No.	Make	Type	Year	Seats	Comments on Vehicles	Routes Acquired	Notes
Francis Duffy General Omnibus Co Drogheda Co Louth	6.2.29	4	YI 9431	AEC	413	1926	32	Converted to a railbus cream/blue livery	Dublin Dundalk	Two Duffy buses had to be taken immediately to Dundalk Works for overhaul costing £370, such was the poor condition of the vehicles
		5	YI 9432	AEC	413	1926	32	Converted to a railbus red/black livery		
		6	ZI 2451	AEC	426	1928	30	Converted to a railbus		
		7	ZI 2452	AEC	426	1928	30	Converted to a railbus		
Thomas O'Brien Excellence Bus Service 19 Usher's Street Dublin	25.3.29	8	ZI 1164	Leyland Lion	PLSC3	1927	32	Claret and Gold Livery	Dublin/Howth via Killester/Raheny and Sutton Cross	O'Brien was instructed by Joe Mackle to bring his buses to the arrival platform Amiens Street Station at midnight for GNR service next day
		9	ZI 1429	Leyland Lion	PLSC3	1928	35	Claret and Gold Livery		
		10	ZI 2226	Leyland Lion	PLSC3	1928	35	Claret and Gold Livery		
Captain John Penrose Bon Ami Bus Service Strand Road Baldoyle Dublin	25.3.29	11	Z 1916	Leyland Lion	PLSC3	1928	36	Began O'Connell Bridge to Killester service in June 1928 using the Morris which later became the Bundoran Hotel Bus 1930	Dublin/Howth via (1) Fairview/Killester (2) Raheny/ Sutton	Penrose obtained the same delivery instructions as O'Brien from Joe Mackle.
		12	Z 1310	Morris	T	1927	14			
James & Robert Irwin Market Street Lurgan Co Armagh	30.3.29	15	AZ 94	Dennis	G	1928	20	Converted to a lorry 1929	Belfast/Lurgan via (1) Broomhedge (2) Maze/Damhead (3) Flatfield	The younger of the two Irwin Brothers RH Irwin was employed by the GNR as its Omagh Supervisor until the establishment of the NIRTB. The six Dennis G buses had to be sent to Charles Hurst Garages, Belfast for the fitting of new cylinder blocks, pistons/liners costing £168. Buses 17 and 20 required a complete overhaul costing £65 and £56 respectively. Buses 18 and 19 were sent to McKeown and McClughan for extensive body repairs and repainting costing £56 and £55 respectively
		16	AZ 301	Dennis	G	1928	20			
		17	AZ 402	Dennis	G	1928	20	Converted to a lorry 1929 Scrapped 1938		
		18	AZ 724	Dennis	G	1928	20	Converted to a lorry 1929		
		19	AZ 1039	Dennis	G	1928	20			
		20	AZ 1054	Dennis	G	1928	20	Converted to a lorry 1929		
		21	IB 3981	Dennis	E	1928	31			
Thomas Fitzpatrick & TJ Furey Fairways Ltd 55 Lower O'Connell Street Dublin	25.4.29	33	ZI 1693	ADC	416	1928	30	Converted to a railbus	Dublin/Clones via Ashbourne Monaghan/Dublin via Ashbourne Monaghan/ Dublin via Drumconrath	The Fairway livery was Blue
		34	ZI 1704	ADC	416	1928	30	Converted to a railbus		
		35	ZI 2089	ADC	416	1928	34	Converted to a railbus June 1935		
James Parkes Muckno Street Castleblaney Classic Bus Service	17.6.29	47	BI 1514	Reo		1927	20	Sold to Ashenhurst, Williams dealer	Dundalk/ Castleblaney Dundalk/Monaghan	The GNR paid £3,800 to Parkes. Parkes rented a bus stand from Castleblaney Council when he sold the business he left considerable arrears. The Council unsuccessfully attempted to get the GNR to pay this off.
		48	BI 1524	Reo		1927	20	Sold to Ashenhurst, Williams dealer		
		49	BI 1535	Dennis	G	1928	20			
		50	BI 1567	ADC	416	1928	32			
		51	BI 1574	Dennis	F	1928	26	Converted to Garage Tender 18.10.30		
		52	BI 1589	Dennis	G	1928	20	Became Bundoran Hotel Bus 1934		
Pratt Brothers Skerries Co Dublin	1.7.29	62	IK 4580	Karrier	CX	1922	20	Ex Clondalkin Motor Omnibus Co 11/26	Skerries Railway Station/ Skerries. Dublin/Skerries	Vehicle became Dublin Garage Tender

Appendix B – Bus Companies Purchased by GNRI

Vehicles Acquired

Company Name & Owners	Date Acquired	GNR Fleet No.	Reg. No.	Make	Type	Year	Seats	Comments on Vehicles	Routes Acquired	Notes
James Winter Eclipse Motor Transport College Square East Belfast	16.9.29	56	XI 8777	Dennis	E	1927	32		Belfast/Omagh via Dungannon Portadown/Maghery	The GNR paid Winter £10,000 for the business and gave him employment as Supervisor at Dungannon. He quickly fell out with Joe Mackle leaving the Company to become a property developer. On the 3rd April 1935 Winter bought 11 GNR houses in Northbrook St and Fane St close to Adelaide Loco Shed in Belfast for £700 which were then rented out.
		57	AZ 1119	Dennis	E	1928	32			
		58	AZ 1131	Lancia		1928	26	Sold to Ashenhurst, Williams dealer		
		59	AZ 1386	Dennis	E	1928	30			
		60	AZ 2110	Graham/ Dodge		1927	20	Sold to Ashenhurst, Williams dealer		
		61	AZ 2823	Dennis	E	1929	31			
John Hill & Robert Wilkinson United Motor Services Market Yard Tanderagee Co Armagh	23.12.29	69	IB 3572	Reo		1927	20	Sold to County Donegal Railway July 1930	Newry/Portadown Tanderagee/Armagh Portadown/Ahorey Portadown/Armagh	£2,800 was paid for the Company including the Garage premises in Tanderagee which the GNR continued to use. Fleet No 71 was converted to a Garage Tender by McKeown & McClaughan cost £50 for use in Belfast. The four Reo Buses sold to the CDR established that company's Road Services.
		70	IB 3841	Dennis	G	1928	20			
		71	IB 3527	AEC	413	1927	26	Became Belfast Garage Tender		
		72	IA 5629	Reo	S/Wagon	1927	20	Sold to County Donegal Railway July 1930		
		73	IA 5773	Reo		1925	14	Sold to County Donegal Railway July 1930		
		74	XI 9530	Reo		1928	20	Sold to McAnulty Warrenpoint April 1932		
		75	XI 5587	Reo		1927	14	Sold to County Donegal Railway July 1930		
			GM 749	Lancia		1927	24	Did not enter GNR Service		
Charles M Markey BAM Bus Service Drogheda Co Louth	3.1.30	100	IY 1973	Dennis	G	1927	19	Converted to a Lorry	Dundalk Local Service Drogheda/ Clougherhead Drogheda/Laytown Drogheda Local service Drogheda/Mullingar	Markey was paid £950 for the business. He operated the Boyne Valley Tour in 1928 and a Drogheda Railway Station/Town service. A Controller, 4 Drivers and Conductors and a Cleaner all joined the GNR. The Mullingar route was contracted to William McCabe on behalf of the GNR from 25th February 1931.
		101	IY 1989	Dennis	G	1927	20	Converted to a Lorry		
		102	IY 2001	Dennis	G	1928	20	Converted to a Lorry		
William Dow Diamond Bus Crumlin Co Antrim	10.1.30	99	AZ 1961	Gilford	15 SD	1929	26		Belfast/Diamond via Crumlin	GNR Paid £1,000 for this operator

Appendix B – Bus Companies Purchased by GNRI										
Vehicles Acquired										
Company Name & Owners	**Date Acquired**	**GNR Fleet No.**	**Reg. No.**	**Make**	**Type**	**Year**	**Seats**	**Comments on Vehicles**	**Routes Acquired**	**Notes**
HA Matier Norton & Co Kilkeel Co Down	6.2.30	103	IJ 5228	Ford		1926	14	Sold in 1932	Warrenpoint/Kilkeel Kilkeel/Lisnacree	The GNR paid Matier £250 and agreed to take over his office and bus parking at Kilkeel for £1 per week rent. The service linked the GN railway at Warrenpoint with Kilkeel, which relied totally on a bus connection. Round trip tickets were issued, enabling passengers to return to Belfast. The GNR gained the Postmaster General's contract to convey mails between Warrenpoint and Newcastle (a B&CDR bus provided the link between Kilkeel and Newcastle) for the sum of £420 per year.
		104	IJ 7518	Ford		1927	14	Sold in 1931		
John Lewis & HM Smith Renown Bus Service Lambeg Co Antrim	18.3.30	105	IA 7372	Dennis	G	1928	20		Belfast/Markethill via Lurgan	£1,000 paid for this operator.
		106	IA6983	Overland		1930	14	Converted to a lorry 4.5.31 – Scrap June 1933		
John McAlinden & James P McSherry Repulse Bus Service Lurgan Co Armagh	4.5.30	113	IB 4446	Guy	OND	1929	20		Lurgan/Aghalee via Whitehall	
		114	IB 4534	Guy	OND	1929	20			
Hugh Eccles Roberts Reginald Roberts Charles Roberts 42 Foyle Street Londonderry	10.7.30	127	UI 2194	Dennis	GL	1929	20		Londonderry/ Strabane/ Castlederg/ Newtownstewart. Londonderry/ Ballybofey Strabane/ Castlederg/ Aghyaran	£2,850 was paid for the Roberts business to which the CDR contributed £500 as a result of the Ballybofey service which became a joint GNR/CDR operation. On the 16th October 1930 the GNR gained the mails contract between Strabane and Aghyaran and were paid £190 annually.
		128	UI 2154	Gilford	166 OT	1929	32			
		129	UI 2029	Dennis	G	1928	20			
		130	UI 2082	Chevrolet		1928	14	Sold in 1930		
			UI 1885	Chevrolet		1928	16	Did not enter GNR Service		
			UI 1893	Chevrolet		1928	16	Did not enter GNR Service		
Mrs J Keveligan Kelvin Bus Service Rockcorry Co Monaghan	3.4.31	144	BI 1591	International		1928	20	Scrapped 1931	Monaghan/Cootehill via Ballybay Cootehill/ Cavan via Tullyvin Cavan/ Dublin	Mrs Keveligan was paid £1,500 by the GNR
		145	BI 1599	International		1928	20	Scrapped 1931		
		146	JI 1935	International		1928	20	Dismantled in 1931		
James Grew Portadown Co Armagh	27.5.31	147	JI 3978	Morris	T	1927	14	Scrapped in 1931	Portadown Railway Station/Town	£100 paid to Mr Grew by GNR
Charles H Donaghy Dreadnought Bus Service The Keep Gortmore Co Tyrone Garage located in Abbey Street, Omagh.	30.6.31	162	AZ 343	Gilford	LL 15	1928	28		Londonderry/Omagh Londonderry/ Strabane	Donaghy was paid £12,000 for his operation and then appointed a GNR Road Motor Supervisor at Omagh
		163	JI 4305	Gilford	166 OT	1928	32			
		164	JI 4630	Gilford	166 OT	1929	32			
		165	JI 4720	Gilford	166 OT	1929	32			
		166	JI 5048	Commer NF6	Avenger	1931	32			
		167	JI 5049	Commer 6TK	Invader	1931	20			
Thomas Fitzpatrick 139 St Stephens Green Dublin.	12.9.31		ZI 1335	Thornycroft	FB	1930	20	Did not enter GNR service	Dublin Eden Quay/ Killester	

Appendix B – Bus Companies Purchased by GNRI

Vehicles Acquired

Company Name & Owners	Date Acquired	GNR Fleet No.	Reg. No.	Make	Type	Year	Seats	Comments on Vehicles	Routes Acquired	Notes
Thomas Nugent Pioneer Bus Service Victoria Street Keady Co Armagh	20.11.31	168	XI 9770	Dennis	G	1927	20	Converted to a lorry	Armagh/Ballybay Armagh/Keady via (1) Tassagh (2) Drumhillery (3) Madden Ballybay/ Carrick-macross Ballybay/ Bailieborough Cavan/Dundalk Dundalk/Monaghan Newtownhamilton/ Dundalk	Nugent waged a long campaign against the GNR take over. In October 1929 he discussed running feeder services to HMS Catherwood services at Dundalk although nothing materialised. Nugent eventually sold out for the inflated price of £16,500. This allowed the GNR to close the Armagh/Keady railway to passenger traffic on 1.1.32. Many of Nugent's buses were in such poor condition that they had to be taken immediately to Dundalk Works for extensive overhaul. The GNR continued to use the Nugent Garage in Keady until 1935
		169	AZ 1282	Dennis	G	1928	20	Converted to a lorry		
		170	VA 4595	Dennis	G	1928	20	Converted to a lorry		
		171	IB 4078	Vulcan	Duke	1928	20	Scrapped 1934		
		172	IB 4082	Vulcan	Duke	1929	20	Scrapped 1931		
		173	IB 4222	Vulcan	Duke	1929	20	Scrapped 1931		
		174	IB 4405	Vulcan	Duke	1929	20	Scrapped 1934		
		175	IB 4406	Vulcan	Duke	1929	20	Scrapped 1934		
		176	IB 4404	Vulcan	Duchess	1930	26	Sold to NIRTB 1935		
		177	BI 1871	Vulcan	Duchess	1930	26	Scrapped 1934		
		178	IB 4689	Vulcan	Duchess	1930	26	Sold to NIRTB 1935		
		179	BI 1872	Vulcan	Duchess	1930	26	Scrapped 1934		
		180	TE 2039	Vulcan	Duchess	1927	31	Sold to NIRTB 1935		
		181	GD 5184	Vulcan	VWBL	1929	31	Sold to NIRTB 1935		
			CD 3158	Vulcan	VWBL	1927	31	Did not enter GNR Service		
Gordon's Motor Services (1928) Ltd Magnet 3 Aston's Quay Dublin	15.12.31	182	ID 1614	Morris	T	1926	14	Withdrawn 1932 then converted to a lorry	Dublin/Cavan	The GNR paid £6,000 for the Magnet The Magnet livery was Blue
		183	ID 1620	AEC	413	1927	32	Withdrawn 1933		
		184	ID 1733	ADC	415	1927	32	Withdrawn 1933 converted to a railbus		
		185	ZI 960	ADC	416	1927	30	Withdrawn 1933		
		186	ZI 996	ADC	416	1927	30	Turned into railbus-unsuitable scrapped 1934		
Thomas Murphy 'The Pirate' 46 St Declan's Road Marino Dublin	12.1.32	187	ZI 4427	GMC	T30	1930	20	Began service between O'Connell Bridge to Killester in May 1927 with an old 'Whiting' bus.	Dublin/Skerries via Swords	The three red and black coloured buses of the Pirate were the last remaining rivals to the GNR on the Skerries service.
		188	ZI 4915	GMC	T30	1930	20			
		189	Z 1510	Reo	GB	1927	26			
William George & Samuel Phair Main Street Belturbet Co Cavan	23.4.32	265	TI 1478	AEC	414	1926	26		Enniskillen/Cavan via Swanlinbar/ Drumcard and Five Points	The Phair Brothers were garage owners selling the bus business to the GNR for £2,300 following the earlier sale of the Magnet service. Phair buses provided a connection with Magnet buses at Cavan for destinations to Enniskillen.
		266	ML 7421	Chevrolet		1927	14			
		267	ID 1724	International		1925	20			
		268	ZI 1534	International		1928	20			
		269	ID 1346	Studebaker		1928	6			
David Davidson Aughnacloy Co Tyrone	17.6.32	270	ZI 1793	Dennis	G	1928	20		Dungannon/ Monaghan via Aughnacloy Aughnacloy/ Fintona via Derrycush Dungannon/ Greystone	Davidson received £1,250 for his bus business. Its purchase led to the establishment of a GNR depot at Aughnacloy until July 1941 when workings were transferred to Monaghan Garage.
		271	JI 4753	Dennis	G	1930	20			

Appendix B – Bus Companies Purchased by GNRI

Vehicles Acquired

Company Name & Owners	Date Acquired	GNR Fleet No.	Reg. No.	Make	Type	Year	Seats	Comments on Vehicles	Routes Acquired	Notes
Peter Maguire Omeath Motor Services Omeath Co Louth	30.12.32	272	IY 2182	Guy	OND	1929	20		Newry/Carlingford via Omeath	Maguire sold his business for £2,500 the GNR also gained the Irish Free State postal contract for mails between Omeath and Dundalk. They were paid £230 per year for this. The GNR continued to rent the bus garage in Omeath owned by Maguire for an annual rent of £10 an arrangement that lasted into the 1970's.
		273	IY 2488	Guy	B	1931	24			
HMS Catherwood 9 Eden Quay Dublin	11.12.33	274	AZ1358	Leyland	TS2	1928	31	Fitted with new GNR 32 seat body 1937	Dublin/Drogheda/Dundalk Drogheda/Collon/Ardee Drogheda/Baltray/Clogher Sligo/Derry via St Johnston Donegal/Portnoo Londonderry/Ballybofey via Lifford	HMS Catherwood's Irish Free State purchase was compulsory
		275	AZ 1553	Leyland	TS2	1928	31	Fitted with new GNR 32 seat body 1937		
		276	AZ 4059	Leyland	TS2	1930	31	Fitted with new GNR 32 seat body 1937 then GT1		
		277	ZI 9197	Leyland	TS4	1932	31	Received transplanted GNR body 1937		
		278	ZI 9198	Leyland	TS4	1932	31	Received transplanted GNR body 1937		
		279	AZ 3030	Leyland	TS2	1929	26	Re-seated to 28 in 1937		
		280	AZ 3353	Leyland	TS2	1929	26	Re-seated to 25 in 1938		
		281	XI 8686	Leyland	PLSC3	1927	30	Withdrawn in 1936		
		282	XI 8794	Leyland	PLSC3	1927	34	Withdrawn in 1936		
		283	XI 9226	Leyland	PLSC3	1927	31	Withdrawn in 1936		
		284	AZ 1394	Leyland	PLSC3	1928	36	Withdrawn in 1939		
		285	AZ 1403	Leyland	PLSC3	1928	30	Re-seated to 35		
		286	AZ 1435	Leyland	PLSC3	1928	36	Re-seated to 35		
		287	AZ 1529	Leyland	PLSC3	1928	36	Re-seated to 35		
		288	AZ 1530	Leyland	PLSC3	1928	36	Re-seated to 35		
		289	XI 8902	Leyland	PLSC3	1927	29	Withdrawn 1937		
		290	ZI 551	Leyland	PLSC3	1927	31	Withdrawn 1941		
		291	XI 9124	Leyland	PLSC3	1927	31	Withdrawn in 1937		
		292	ZI 709	Leyland	PLSC3	1927	35	Withdrawn in 1937		
		293	XI 9521	Leyland	PLSC3	1927	35	Withdrawn in 1937		
		294	AZ 294	Leyland	PLSC3	1938	36	Withdrawn in 1937		
		295	AZ 1434	Leyland	PLSC3	1928	36	Withdrawn in 1941		
		296	AZ 1514	Leyland	TS2	1928	31	Renumbered 129(1942) sold to SLNCR 1946		
		297	AZ 1377	Leyland	TS2	1929	31	Withdrawn 1937		
Charles McAllister Beverstown Donabate Co Dublin	1.1.34		ZI 918	Morris	T	1927	14	Did not enter GNR service	Donabate Railway Station Portrane	GNR paid McAllister £100
McGowan's Tourist Bus Service Wardhouse Tullaghan Co Leitrim	29.7.34							McGowan began in May 1928 using a 20 seat International Bus. No vehicles entered GNR service	Sligo/Ballyshannon	Compulsory purchase by the GNR

Appendix B – Bus Companies Purchased by GNRI										
Vehicles Acquired										
Company Name & Owners	**Date Acquired**	**GNR Fleet No.**	**Reg. No.**	**Make**	**Type**	**Year**	**Seats**	**Comments on Vehicles**	**Routes Acquired**	**Notes**
Furey's Motor Coaches Ltd 8 Upper O'Connell St Dublin.	27.3.35	45	ZI 3511	AEC	Reliance	1928	32	The three Grey liveried AEC buses one of which was less than a year old and a Dennis E passed to the GNR. The remaining Furey vehicles went to the GSR	Boyne Valley Tour Mystery Tours and Special services/ Race Meetings etc.	Joint GNR/GSR compulsory purchase £25,000 plus £1,500 for spare parts was paid by both to Furey's.
		58	ZI 3510	Dennis	E	1928	29			
		60	ZA 2421	AEC	Regal	1934	32			
		62	ZI 502	ADC	417	1925	29			
Issac & Thomas Boyd Gas Lane Clones Co Monaghan	30.12.37		IJ 9723	Reo	GE	1929	24	Did not enter GNR Service	Clones/Monaghan via Smithborough	Compulsory purchase
Johnny O'Donnell Carrick Co Donegal Bogagh Bus Company	2.10.44		IH 4310	Ford		1937	20	Converted to a lorry and became CDR No 28	Killybegs/ Glencolumbkille via Carrick	This operator was bought by the County Donegal Railway
			IH 3382	Ford		1934	14	Converted to a lorry and became CDR No 27		
Keenan Brothers Carlingford Motor Services Carlingford Co Louth	29.10.45		ZI 1012	ADC	416	1928	30	Scrapped 1945	Carlingford/Dundalk via (1) Whitestown (2) Ravensdale (3) Grange/ Greenore/ Boherboy	Final compulsory purchase by the GNR
			ZI 1014	ADC	416	1928	30	Scrapped 1945		
			ZI 1015	ADC	416	1928	30	Scrapped 1945		
		226	JI 4837	Reo	S/wagon	1930	20	Scrapped 1945 became a clothing store at Dundalk		

Appendix C GNR Road Merchandise Companies Compulsorily Acquired Irish Free State					
Operators Name	**Location**	**Acquisition Date**	**Type of Traffic**	**Comments**	**Summary of Vehicles Acquired**
P McCloskey	Drogheda	1.1.35		Joint GNR/GSR Acquisition	
T Cooney	Drogheda	1.1.35		Joint GNR/GSR Acquisition	
PS Greene		27.1.35			
J Reilly (Navan Motor Services)	Navan	25.2.35			
J Hughes	Flower Hill, Navan	25.2.35			
P Geraghty (Navan Transport)	St Finian's Terrace, Navan	25.2.35		Joint GNR/GSR Acquisition	
James McCourt	O'Brien Place, Haddington Rd, Dublin	1.5.35		Joint GNR/GSR Acquisition	
JJ O'Hare	Dundalk	3.5.35			
J Crilly	Dundalk	4.5.35			
H Higginson	Dundalk	4.5.35			
P Martin	Carrickmacross	6.5.35			
J Breen	Knockbridge	6.5.35			
J Howell	Carrickmacross	6.5.35			
Maher Bros	Dundalk	6.5.35			
JB King	Virginia	7.5.35			
TJ Duffy	Castleblaney	7.5.35			
SD Kearney	Dundalk	7.5.35			
J Joyce	Castleblaney	7.5.35			
L Muckian	Dundalk	7.5.35			
TJ Duffy	Castleblaney	7.5.35			
J Kiernan	Inniskeen	9.5.35			
J Gray	Castleblaney	20.5.35			2 Karrier
WF Cullen	6, Thomas Lane, O'Connell St, Dublin	20.5.35	Livestock, Drink, General	Joint GNR/GSR Acquisition	
Moran Brothers	Kildore Garage, Inchicore, Dublin	23.5.35		Joint GNR/GSR Acquisition	
R Chambers	Dundalk	1.7.35			
Autoways Goods Express	Ballyconnell, Co Cavan	16.7.35		Joint GNR/GSR Acquisition	
Sweeney & Swan	Kells	30.7.35		Traded as Roadwise Transport Services	
H Woodward	Ardmulchan, Navan	31.7.35	Lambs, Cattle, Coal, Bagstuffs	Joint GNR/GSR Acquisition	1 Dodge
A Carter	Brownstown, Navan	26.8.35	Pigs, Lambs, Bagstuffs, Coal	Joint GNR/GSR Acquisition	1 Ford
JH Boyd & Sons	Virginia	27.8.35			
J Collins	Navan	27.8.35	Lambs, Pigs, Hay, Bagstuff, General	Joint GNR/GSR Acquisition	1 Ford
P McEnroe	Mountnugent, Oldcastle, Co Cavan	27.8.35	Live Pigs, Bagstuffs, Coal, Drink	Joint GNR/GSR Acquisition	2 Ford
T Stewart	Littlegrange, Drogheda	27.8.35	Cattle, Sheep	Joint GNR/GSR Acquisition	1 Ford
P Heaney	Kells	28.8.35	Livestock, Drink, General	Joint GNR/GSR Acquisition	1 Chevrolet, 1 Ford
J Wallace	Dundalk	30.8.35			
M Martin	Kilcairne, Navan	1.9.35	Sheep, Lambs, Pigs	Joint GNR/GSR Acquisition	1 AEC
George Berney	Cootehill, Co Cavan	1.9.35	Coal, Bagstuffs, Iron, Pork, Livestock	Joint GNR/GSR Acquisition	2 Dennis, 1 Morris, 1 Chevrolet
T Gibson	Cootehill	1.9.35			
George J Berney	Bailieborough, Co Cavan	1.9.35	Timber, Bagstuffs, Coal	Joint GNR/GSR Acquisition	2 Ford
McAlpine & Nixon	Monaghan	2.9.35	Millstuffs	Joint GNR/GSR Acquisition	1 ADC, 1 Dennis, 1 Ford
R Nawn & Sons	Ballyshannon	5.9.35	Sheep, Lambs, Pigs	Joint GNR/GSR Acquisition	
Trim Haulage Co	Trim, Co Meath	6.9.35		Joint GNR/GSR Acquisition	2 Bedford
J&E Smyth	Trim, Co Meath	6.9.35		Joint GNR/GSR Acquisition	
J Faulkner	Dunleer	9.9.35			
Burns Brothers	Shercock, Co Cavan	9.9.35	Potatoes, Oats	Joint GNR/GSR Acquisition	1 Bedford, 1 Chevrolet, 1 AEC
J McConnell	Wesley Street, Cavan	9.9.35	Co Council & GSR work	Joint GNR/GSR Acquisition	2 Ford
Luke Lambe	Cornalaragh, Shercock, Co Cavan	9.9.35	Milk Products, Dead Pork, Bagstuffs	Joint GNR/GSR Acquisition	1 Ford
J Penrose	Strand Road, Baldoyle, Co Dublin	10.9.35	Sand	Joint GNR/GSR Acquisition	
JS Mullery	Francis Street, Cavan	10.9.35	Petrol	Joint GNR/GSR Acquisition	1 Bedford
Ballyconnell Milling Company	Ballyconnell, Co Cavan	10.9.35	Live Pigs, Bagstuffs	Joint GNR/GSR Acquisition	1 Ford

Appendix C GNR Road Merchandise Companies Compulsorily Acquired Irish Free State					
Operators Name	**Location**	**Acquisition Date**	**Type of Traffic**	**Comments**	**Summary of Vehicles Acquired**
P Smyth	Abbey Street, Cavan	10.9.35	Beer, Building materials	Joint GNR/GSR Acquisition	1 Morris Commercial
E Flood	Abbey Garage, Cavan	10.9.35	County Council work	Joint GNR/GSR Acquisition	1 Federal, 1 Chevrolet, 1 Ford
PJ Moynagh	Oldcastle	12.9.35			
P Farrell	Market Square, Bailieborough, Co Cavan	12.9.35	Coal, Foodstufs	Joint GNR/GSR Acquisition	2 Ford
P Carolan	Bailieborough, Co Cavan	12.9.35	Coal, Bagstuffs, Eggs	Joint GNR/GSR Acquisition	1 Ford
J Monaghan	Drogheda	13.9.35			
J Moore	Bailieborough, Co Cavan	13.9.35	General Merchandise	Joint GNR/GSR Acquisition	1 Ford
W & G Bell	Bailieborough, Co Cavan	13.9.35	Live Pigs, Bagstuffs General	Joint GNR/GSR Acquisition	1 Dodge, 1 Ford
M Clarke	Bailieborough, Co Cavan	13.9.35	Live Pigs, Coal, Bagstuffs	Joint GNR/GSR Acquisition	1 Ford
Larkin Bros		16.9.35			3 Lancia, 4 Crossley
JJ Sherlock	Main Street, Kingscourt, Co Cavan	16.9.35	Live Pigs, Bagstuffs, Drink	Joint GNR/GSR Acquisition	2 Ford
RH Mulligan	Nobber, Co Meath	16.9.35	Lambs, Sheep, Pigs, Cattle	Joint GNR/GSR Acquisition	1 Ford
McEntegart Brothers	Nobber, Co Meath	16.9.35	Lambs, Sheep	Joint GNR/GSR Acquisition	2, Ford
Mrs K Cummins	Pottlereagh, Virginia Road, Kells, Co Meath	23.9.35	Livestock, Drink, General	Joint GNR/GSR Acquisition	1 Federal
PJ Mullen	Mullagh, Virginia, Co Cavan	23.9.35	Pigs, Lambs	Joint GNR/GSR Acquisition	1 Ford
Jas Byers	Ballyjamesduff	24.9.35		Joint GNR/GSR Acquisition	
P Daly	Mullagh, Virginia, Co Cavan	24.9.35	Lambs, Bagstuffs, Drink	Joint GNR/GSR Acquisition	2 Ford
D Galligan	Ballyjamesduff	24.9.35	Livestock, Drink, General	Joint GNR/GSR Acquisition	1 Ford
J Leonard	Stackallen, Navan	24.9.35	Pigs, Lambs, Cattle.	Joint GNR/GSR Acquisition	1 Ford
T Ward	Navan	1.10.35			1 Morris
J Keenan	Navan	1.10.35			1 Ford
J McMorrow		8.10.35			1 Fordson
B Farrell	Mullagh, Virginia, Co Cavan	10.10.35	Lambs, Bagstuffs, Drink	Joint GNR/GSR Acquisition	2 Ford
J Gallagher		17.10.35			1 Chevrolet
S Lockington	Dundalk	22.10.35			3 Morris
Daly Bros		31.10.35			1 Bedford
Jackson Brothers	Kellykeen, Duncormick, Co Cavan	8.11.35	Building Materials, Bagstuffs	Joint GNR/GSR Acquisition	3 Ford
CJ McHenry	19, North Brunswick Street, Dublin	12.11.35		Joint GNR/GSR Acquisition	
J White		13.11.35			
J Barnes	Drogheda	14.11.35			
J Harte	1, New Street, Sligo	22.11.35		Joint GNR/GSR Acquisition	
W O'Hare		25.11.35			2 Ford
P Duff	Skerries	30.11.35			2 Commer
O'Rourke Bros	Inniskeen	30.11.35			
JP Donnelly	Ravensdale	30.11.35			
P Campbell	Ardee	11.12.35			1 Chevrolet
J McGeough	Castleblaney	19.12.35			1 Fordson
HJ Boylan		23.12.35			1 Chevrolet
N Todd		23.12.35			1 Morris
T O'Toole		23.12.35			1 Manchester
R Derham		10.1.36			2 Ford
T & L McDonald Bros	Riverstown	15.1.36			4 Lancia
M Shields	Irish Grange	18.1.36			
J Barry	Dundalk	22.1.36			
H McKeown	Dundalk	24.1.36			1 Garford
R Grimes		2.2.36			1 Caledon, 1 Albion
W Eyers		13.2.36			1 Ford
J Regan		14.2.36			1 Chevrolet
TJ McNally	Skerries	27.2.36			1 Commer
B Campbell	Ardee	27.2.36			
TJ McNally	Skerries	27.2.36			

Appendix C GNR Road Merchandise Companies Compulsorily Acquired Irish Free State					
Operators Name	**Location**	**Acquisition Date**	**Type of Traffic**	**Comments**	**Summary of Vehicles Acquired**
Mrs EM Murphy	Dundalk	23.3.36			1 AEC, 1 Dennis, 1 Karrier, 1 Straker Squire
P Caughlin		27.5.36			1 Chevrolet
E & F McMahon	Clones	1.10.36			
J McCaldin	Monaghan	16.5.39			
CF Bellew		26.8.44			
J Duffy	Shercock, Co Cavan		Live Pigs	Joint GNR/GSR Acquisition	2 Ford
PJ Smyth	Kells, Co Meath		Pigs, Drink, General	Joint GNR/GSR Acquisition	1 Ford

OCTOBER,1958 & UNTIL FURTHER NOTICE

DEPOT	FLEET NUMBERS				TOTAL
	SINGLE DECK		DOUBLE DECK		
	7' 6"	8' 0"	7' 6"	8' 0"	
Dublin	225,266,267,334 361	418,419,420 421,422	280,281 282,283 284,288	290,291,292 294,296,298 301,302,303	25
Donabate			287		1
Rush				293	1
Skerries	338			295,297,304	4
Drogheda	226,227,228,264 275,335,336,337	404,405,409 423	286,433 442	306,307	17
Navan	276				1
Oldcastle	387				1
Ardee		407	435,437		3
Dundalk	265,318,340,341 365,367,376,379	416,424,425	440	299	13
Newry	383		438,439		3
Carlingford	261,382	426	441		4
Carrickmacross	384	413,414			3
Castleblayney	272				1
Monaghan	339,363,377,378				4
Ballybay	274,364				2
Cootehill		415			1
Clones	262,263,368				3
Cavan	327,366,381,391				4
Kilnaleck	329				1
Belturbet	260				1
Swanlinbar	273,362				2
DOCK OVERHAULS					
Dublin				289	1
Drogheda		406			1
Dundalk	212				1
Loco.		403,408,410	434,436		5
Drumshanbo	369				1
Sligo	268,330				2
Ballyshannon	269,373		285		3
Donegal	320,374				2
Doneagal(Dock)	371				1
G'columbkille	372				1
Glenties	370				1
Portnoo	322				1
Stranorlar	375				1
Letterkenny	323				1
St.Johnston	270				1
Derry	271				1
Total Taxed	62	21	19	17	119
Untaxed	243,321,324,325 326,328,331,332 333,342,343,344 345,346,385,386 388,389,390,392 393,394,395,396 397,398,399,400 401,402	411,412,417 427,428,429 430,431,432			
Total Untaxed	30	9	-	-	39
Grand Total	92	30	19	17	158

The very last GNR Road Motor Service alloaction of its 158 bus fleet handed over to CIE on 1st October 1958. *(SS)*

Appendix D GNR Directory of Bus Routes		
Section 1 – Services within Irish Republic		
Route	**Start Date**	**Route & Comments**
Drogheda Railway Station-Drogheda West Street	29.1.29	via Dublin Road, James Street, Shop Street This was the GNR's first bus service
Drogheda Railway Station-Clogherhead (Port Oriel Pier)	4.2.29	via Strand Road, Queensboro, Baldoyle, Termonfeckin
Drogheda Railway Station-Laytown	4.2.29	via Mornington Tower, Donacarney, Bettystown
Dublin Eden Quay-Dundalk GNR Station	16.2.29	
Skerries The Monument-Circular Service	18.2.29	Summer only June-September
Drogheda West Street-Togher (Tavern Cross)	11.3.29	Queensboro, Baldoyle, Baltray, Termonfeckin, Clogher
Dublin Eden Quay-Howth East Pier	25.3.29	via North Strand, Howth Road, Killester, Raheny, Sutton
Dublin Eden Quay-Monaghan GNR Station	25.4.29	
Dundalk Kelly Monument-Castleblaney GNR Station	22.5.29	
Monaghan GNR Station-Castleblaney GNR Station	22.5.29	
Dublin Eden Quay-Clones GNR Station	29.5.29	
Dublin Eden Quay-Malahide Main Street	29.5.29	via Fairview, Howth Road, Killester, Raheny, Baldoyle Road
Dublin Eden Quay-Malahide Main Street	29.5.29	via Fairview, Malahide Road, Artane, Coolock, Balgriffin
Drogheda West Street-Ardee Main Street	30.5.29	Collon
Sligo-Lough Derg	30.5.29	Seasonal service 1st June-15th August
Dublin Eden Quay-Malahide Main Street	3.6.29	via North Strand, Malahide Road, Artane, Coolock
Dublin Eden Quay-Portrane Hospital Gate	3.6.29	Summer only June-September
Drogheda West Street-Laytown Railway Station	9.6.29	Mornington Tower, Donneyvarney, Bettystown
Dundalk Kelly Monument-Monaghan Railway Station	17.6.29	Essexford, Carrickmacross, Castleblaney, Clontibret
Dublin Eden Quay-Skerries The Monument	1.7.29	
Skerries Railway Station-Town (Holmpatrick)	1.7.29	Via Station Road, Dublin Road, Cross Street, Strand Street
Dublin Aston's Quay-Cavan Railway Station	2.9.29	
Sligo-Carrigans for Londonderry	3.10.29	Grange, Cliffoney, Bundoran, Ballyshannon, Donegal, Ballybofey, Raphoe
Drogheda West Street-Slane	21.10.29	
Drogheda West Street-Circular Service	3.1.30	Balbriggan, Stamullen, Naul, Clougherstown, Platten Cross
Drogheda West Street-Laytown Railway Station	3.1.30	Mornington Church – Suspended 19.4.42 – Restored 11.9.42
Dundalk Railway Station-Ardee Railway Station	3.1.30	Knockbridge, Louth, Tallanstown
Dublin Amiens Street-Eden Quay	7.1.30	Suspended 1941
Sligo-Lifford for Strabane	7.2.30	Ballyshannon, Donegal, Ballybofey, Killygordon, Castlefin, Cloghfin
Cavan Farnham Street-Ballybay Square	1.7.30	
Cavan Farnham Street-Dundalk Market Square	1.7.30	
Cavan Farnham Street-Virginia Main Street	1.7.30	
Clones Diamond-Drogheda West Street	1.7.30	
Monaghan Diamond-Cootehill Main Street	1.7.30	via Rossanore, Strancodan, Swans Cross, Rockcorry
Monaghan Diamond-Cootehill Main Street	1.7.30	via Ballybay, Lisnalong
Donegal Railway Station-Killybegs	11.12.31	Mountcharles – Suspended 1941
Carrickmacross Railway Station-Shercock Main Street	1.2.32	Revoked 3.2.36
Cavan Farnham Street-Shercock Main Street	1.2.32	Revoked 1936
Virginia Road Station-Cavan Railway Station	1.2.32	Virginia Town, Ballyjamesduff, Kilnaleck
Ballyshannon Market Yard-Rossnowlagh (Strand)	5.6.32	Direct Road – Summer only June-September
Ballinamore (Main Street)-Bundoran (Chapel Street)	25.7.32	Manorhamilton Seasonal licence only – Suspended 14.8.41
Belturbet (Town Hall)-Bundoran (East End)	25.7.32	Enniskillen Seasonal licence only – Suspended 14.8.41
Carlingford (Square)-Dundalk (Roden Place)	25.7.32	Whitestown, Rathcor, Riverstown, Rampark. Ex Keenan Bros Service
Carlingford (Square)-Dundalk (Roden Place)	25.7.32	Riverstown, Giles Quay, Rampart, Ravensdale Ex Keenan Bros service
Carlingford (Square)-Dundalk (Roden Place)	25.7.32	Grange, Riverstown, Lordship, Bellurgan, Ballymascanlon Ex Keenan Bros
Carrickmacross-Monaghan (Diamond)	25.7.32	Castleblaney – Suspended 5.11.34 – Revoked 5.2.40
Carrickmacross Railway Station-Ballybay Market Square	25.7.32	Cootehill Cross, Ballytray Cross, Tussey Cross – Suspended 27.4.42 – Restored 1946
Carrickmacross Railway Station-Cavan Railway Station	25.7.32	Shercock, Bailieboro, Grousehall, Stradone
Cavan Post Office -Belturbet Market Square	25.7.32	Butlersbridge
Clones Diamond-Monaghan Diamond	25.7.32	Stone Bridge, Smithboro – ex I&T Boyd service acquired 1.1.38
Cootehill-Bailieboro	25.7.32	Canningstown – Operated on Fair Days
Cootehill Railway Station-Cavan Railway Station	25.7.32	Tullyvin, Drung Chapel, Fairtown, Farnham Street
Donabate Railway Station-Portrane Mental Hospital	25.7.32	Direct Road – Former McAllister service
Donegal (Market Square)-Portnoo (Main Street)	25.7.32	Ardara – from 1.6.48 diverted via Frosses – Revoked 31.10.48
Donegal Railway Station-Dunkineely	25.7.32	Revoked 1941
Drogheda West Street-Baltray (Golf Links)	25.7.32	Queensboro – Suspended 27.4.42 Restored 24.11.45
Drogheda West Street-Circular Service	25.7.32	Stamullen, Greenanstown, Bellewstown, White Cross

Appendix D GNR Directory of Bus Routes		
Route	**Start Date**	**Route & Comments**
Drogheda West Street-Clogher (Village)	25.7.32	Queensboro, Baltray, Termonfeckin
Drogheda West Street-Dromin Main Street	25.7.32	Tullyallen, Collon, Phillipstown
Drogheda West Street-Laytown Railway Station	25.7.32	Colpe Cross
Dromin-Dundalk Market Square	25.7.32	Stabannon – Revoked 31.3.36 – Replaced by service shown below
Dublin Aston's Quay-Cavan Railway Station	25.7.32	via Dunshaughlin, Navan, Kells, Virginia, Stradone
Dublin Aston's Quay-Kells (John Street)	25.7.32	Clonee, Dunboyne, Dunshaughlin, Navan, Finnnegans Cross
Dublin Eden Quay-Carrickmacross	25.7.32	
Dublin Eden Quay-Drogheda (West Street)	25.7.32	Santry, Cloghran, Swords, Balbriggan, Gormanstown
Dublin Eden Quay-Dundalk Market Square	25.7.32	Santry, Drogheda, Castlebellingham, Whitehouse Cross
Dublin Eden Quay-Howth East Pier	25.7.32	Amiens Street, Nth Strand, Howth Road, Killester, Raheny
Dublin Eden Quay-Malahide	25.7.32	Suspended 1941
Dublin Eden Quay-Portmarnock (Comerfords Cross)	25.7.32	Revoked 14.9.36 – Replaced by service shown above
Dublin Eden Quay-Skerries The Monument	25.7.32	Lower Gardner Street, Mountjoy Square, Drumcondra, Santry
Dundalk-Monaghan	25.7.32	Ballincarry Bridge
Dundalk (Kelly Monument)-Ravensdale	25.7.32	via Waterworks – Revoked 22.10.40
Dundalk (Market Square)-Castleblaney	25.7.32	Carrickmacross – Suspended 16.6.41 – Restored 27.9.48 expired 31.10.57
Dundalk Market Square-Carrickmacross (McMahon Street)	25.7.32	Channockrock, Essexford
Dundalk Market Square-Castlebellingham (Main Street)	25.7.32	Lurgangreen Cross, Clarkes Cross, Dromiskin
Dundalk Market Square-Drumbilla Border	25.7.32	Lisdoo Arms, Kilcurry Post Office, Border Bar, Drumbilla Cross
Dundalk Railway Station-Market Square Lisdoo Arms	25.7.32	Suspended 9.8.42
Grange-Boherboy	25.7.32	Greenore Ex Keenan Bros service
Hole in the Wall-Kinsealy Church	25.7.32	Balgriffin Church bus – Suspended 19.4.42 – Restored in 1944
Kilnaleck (Main Street)-Virginia Road (Railway Station)	25.7.32	Ballyjamesduff, Virginia Town.
Monaghan Railway Station-Town (Diamond)	25.7.32	Suspended 1941
Monaghan Railway Station-Cootehill Railway Station	25.7.32	Red Brae, Stranooden, Swans Cross, Rockcorry
Omeath (Chapel)-Dundalk (Kelly Monument)	25.7.32	Bellurgan – Revoked 22.10.40
Pettigo Railway Station-Lough Derg Mainland Shore	25.7.32	Seasonal licence only; expired in 1958
Portmarnock (Comerfords Cross)-Baldoyle	25.7.32	Church Bus Sunday only
Portmarnock (Comerfords Cross)-Kinsealy Church	25.7.32	Church Bus Sunday only
Portmarnock Railway Station-Portmarnock (Strand)	25.7.32	Summer only, June-September – Suspended in 1941
Rush & Lusk Railway Station-Rush Village	25.7.32	Direct Road
Rush (Main Street)-Loughshinney Cross	25.7.32	Direct Road – Church bus Sunday only – Suspended 19.4.42 – Restored 1944
Skerries (The Monument)-Loughshinney Cross	25.7.32	Direct Road – Church bus Sunday – Suspended 19.4.42 – Restored 1944
Sligo (Wine Street)-Ballyshannon (Market Yard)	25.7.32	Drumcliffe, Grange, Cliffoney, Tullaghan, Bundoran – former McGowan service
Sligo GSR Station-Ballyshannon Main Street	25.7.32	Drumcliffe, Grange, Bundoran
Sligo GSR Station-Donegal Diamond	25.7.32	Drumcliffe, Grange, Bundoran, Ballyshannon, Ballintra
Sligo GSR Station-Lough Derg Mainland Shore	25.7.32	Summer only June-September – Suspended 1942 – Restored 1944 – Revoked 6.7.55
Sligo Wine Street-Grange Post Office	25.7.32	Former HMS Catherwood service to GNR 11.12.33
Bundoran GN Railway Station-GN Hotel Bundoran	21.12.32	Operated as traffic offered – expired 21.12.37
Omeath (Chapel)-Dundalk (Roden Place)	21.12.32	Ardaghy School, Ravensdale, Water Works, Thistle Cross Wednesday only
Ballyshannon Main Street-Bundoran East End	1.6.33	Summer only June-September – Revoked 31.10.48
Dundalk Market Square-McShane's Cross	20.7.33	Clanbrassil Street, Church Street Bridge, Castletown
Dundalk (Roden Place)-Giles Quay	1.8.33	Bellurgan Ex Keenan Bros
Omeath (Chapel)-Carlingford (Main Street)	1.10.33	Calvary Hill, Sloans Road, North Common – Revoked 27.4.42 – Restored 24.11.45
Dublin Burgh Quay-Baldoyle Races	6.3.34	Occasional licence for Race Day operation 1936/41
Dublin Eden Quay-Baldoyle Races	6.3.34	Occasional licence for Race Day operation 1936/41 continued to 1958
Killybegs (Railway Station)-Glencolumblille Post Office	23.4.34	Kilcar, Carrick, Malinmore Ex J O'Donnell service
Dublin Eden Quay-Sutton Cross	3.6.34	Suspended 1941
Ardee-Dunleer	4.6.34	Dromin-Ardee Fair Days only – Revoked in 1936
Ballyshannon (GN Station)-Ballyshannon Market Yard	4.6.34	Summer only June-September – Suspended 14.8.41
Cootehill Railway Station-Monaghan Road Railway Station	4.6.34	Rockcorry
Monaghan-Swan's Cross	4.6.34	Suspended 4.4.43 – Restored 1944 – Suspended again 31.12.45
Skerries (Monument)-Rush (Markey's)	25.11.34	Suspended 19.4.42
Dundalk (Market Square)-Ardee (Mental Hospital)	7.4.35	Blackrock – Revoked – Replaced by service listed below
Dundalk (Market Square)-Ardee (Mental Hospital)	7.4.35	Blackrock, Dromiskin, Castlebellingham, Dunleer.
Dublin Eden Quay-Portmarnock (Strand)	1.5.35	Raheny Summer only June-September
Ardara Post Office-Portnoo (Main Street)	1.6.35	Glenties – Seasonal licence only
Cootehill Market Street-Blackrock	1.6.35	Ballybay, Shercock, Carrickmacross – Seasonal licence only

Appendix D GNR Directory of Bus Routes		
Route	**Start Date**	**Route & Comments**
Dublin Eden Quay-Dundalk Market Square	1.6.35	Swords, Lusk, Rush, Loughshinney, Skerries
Glenties Post Office-Portnoo (Main Street)	1.6.35	Letteraney Cross, Gweebarra Cross, Maas, Clooney Post Office Seasonal licence
Kells Railway Station-Drogheda West Street	1.6.35	Seasonal licence only
Kells Railway Station-Laytown Railway Station	1.6.35	Drogheda – Seasonal licence only
Drogheda-Navan	5.6.35	Revoked 12.3.41
Dublin Eden Quay-The Hole in the Wall	15.8.35	Nth. Strand, Howth Road, Killester, Raheny, Newgrove
Howth Junction-Baldoyle (Triangle)	25.8.35	Kilbarrack Lane, Howth Road, Baldoyle Road, Church Bus – Suspended 19.4.42
Howth Junction-Baldoyle Triangle	25.8.35	Seasonal licence only
Sligo Quay Street-Finisklin Road	1.9.35	Served Ursline Convent – Suspended 13.4.42
Ballybay Railway Station-Monaghan Diamond	1.11.35	Steins Mills, Ardaghy, Greyglass, Stewart's
Monaghan (Diamond)-Tyholland IFS Border Post	1.11.35	Suspended 1941 – Restored 27.9.48 expired 31.10.57
Dundalk Railway Station-Market Square	1.12.35	Carrick Road, Ann Street, Park Street, Earl Street – Suspended 9.8.42
Dundalk Market Square-Drogheda West Street	3.2.36	Whitehouse Cross, Castlebellingham, Dunleer
Drogheda West Street-Dundalk Market Square	1.4.36	Dunleer, Dromin, Duffy's Cross, Readypenny – Sunday only – Suspended 27.4.42
Dundalk Market Square-Ardee	1.4.36	Dunmahon Cross, Castlebellingham Cross, Lurgan Green Cross – Monday only
Dunleer-Drogheda West Street	1.4.36	Main Road – expired 31.10.57
Ardee (Main Street)-Dundalk Market Square	31.5.36	Louth, Blackrock – Seasonal licence only – Revoked 30.5.51
Donabate Railway Station-Strand	31.5.36	Summer only June-September – Suspended 14.8.41
Drogheda West Street-Mornington (Tower Cross)	31.5.36	Boathouse, Glen Road, Mornington Church – Sunday only as traffic offers
Dublin Eden Quay-Gormanstown Strand	24.6.36	Skerries – Seasonal licence only
Donegal Diamond-Manorhamilton (Main Street)	1.7.36	Ballyshannon, Bundoran, Kinlough, Glenade Post Office Occasional licence
Dundalk (Market Square)-Faughart	1.7.36	Dowdallshill – Seasonal licence only – Suspended 14.8.41
Manorhamilton (Main Street)-Bundoran Railway Station	1.7.36	White Gates, Connolly's Store, Glenade Post Office Seasonal licence only
Dublin Eden Quay-Portmarnock (Strand)	14.9.36	Howth Road, Killester, Raheny, Baldoyle, Comerford's Cross
Rush Pier-Rush Church	11.11.36	Direct Road – Church bus Sunday only – Suspended 19.4.42 – Restored 26.11.45
Cavan Railway Station-Shercock Main Street	30.11.36	Bailieboro – Suspended 1941
Clones Diamond-Monaghan Diamond	13.12.36	Newbliss – Revoked 5.7.38
Ardee-Drumconrath	8.2.37	
Ardee-Duffy's Cross	8.2.37	
Ardee Railway Station-Aclint Cross	1.3.37	
Ardee Railway Station-Circular	1.3.37	Dromin, Rathesker
Ardee Railway Station-Mountain Lodge	1.3.37	Drumconrath
Dublin Aston's Quay-Cavan Railway Station	30.5.37	
Dublin Eden Quay-Rush (Markey's)	30.5.37	Seasonal licence only – Revoked 29.5.41
Dublin Eden Quay-Malahide (*Garda* Barracks)	31.5.37	Suspended 1941
Drogheda West Street-Circular Service	4.6.37	Cloughpatrick, Dowth Cross, Slane, Sallygardens Cross
Drumshanbo-Bundoran Railway Station	14.6.37	Manorhamilton Seasonal licence only
Gormanstown-Balbriggan (The Square)	1.6.38	Seasonal licence only
Monaghan (Diamond)-Smithborough (*Garda* Station)	6.7.38	Suspended 1941 – Restored 24.11.45 ran through to Clones September 1948 expired 31.10.57
Sligo (GN Office)-Mullaghmore (Pier)	1.6.39	Grange – Summer only June-September – Revoked 14.7.40
Bundoran Railway Station-Donegal Diamond	4.6.39	Finner Camp, Ballyshannon, Ballintra, Bridgetown Seasonal licence
Ballyshannon Market Yard-Ballintra Post Office	11.9.39	Tullymore Cross, Cavangarden Cross, Ballymagrorty National School
Dublin Eden Quay-Drogheda (Georges Square)	13.11.39	Skerries – Suspended 1941
Castleblaney Railway Station-Monaghan Diamond	5.2.40	Annyalla Church, Clontibret Cross, Castleshane Post Office
Portmarnock (Strand)-Sutton Cross	25.5.40	Suspended 1941
Newbliss Post Office-Monaghan Diamond	8.7.40	Greenans Cross, 3 Mile House, Drumclan Cross, Cornavarn Cross – Suspended 1941
Skerries (Monument)-Balbriggan Railway Station	28.10.40	Seasonal licence only – ran between 28th October and 30th April – Revoked on 9.12.40
Dublin Eden Quay-Rush (Markey's)	1.11.40	Suspended 1941
Carrick-Killybegs Railway Station	9.12.40	Kilcar – Suspended 10.10.44 – Restored 1946 – Revoked 4.6.53
Balbriggan Square-Gormanstown Cross	19.12.40	Suspended 1941
Dublin Eden Quay-Raheny	1.2.41	Nth. Strand, Howth Road, Clontarf, Killester
Sutton Cross-Eden Quay	31.3.41	Raheny, Castle Avenue, Vernon Avenue, Fairview – School service
Dublin Eden Quay-Malahide (*Garda* Barracks)	6.4.41	Fairview, Howth Road, Killester, Raheny, Baldoyle.
Dublin Eden Quay-Dundalk (Market Square)	3.7.41	Skerries – Seasonal licence only
Portrane (Mental Hosp)-Swords (Main Street Taylors PH)	4.5.42	Donabate, Hearse Road, Lissenhall Bridge
Dublin Eden Quay-Drogheda West Street	6.5.42	Skerries – Seasonal licence only
Sutton Railway Station-Baily Post Office	12.6.44	Hill of Howth Tram replacement service

Appendix D GNR Directory of Bus Routes		
Route	**Start Date**	**Route & Comments**
Howth Railway Station-Summit	16.6.44	Hill of Howth Tram replacement service
Drumshanbo (High Street)-Bundoran Railway Station	1.1.45	Cooney's Cross, Drumkeeran, Manorhamilton, Kinlough
Ballyshannon (Market Yard)-Portnoo (Main Street)	1.6.45	Seasonal licence only
Dundalk (Market Square)-Carlingford (Station Road)	26.11.45	Ravensdale Cross, Jenkinstown Cross, Gyles Quay Cross
Dundalk (Market Square)-Carlingford (Station Road)	26.11.45	Ravensdale expired 31.10.57
Dundalk (Market Square)-Circular Service	26.11.45	Carlingford Road Cross, Ballymascanlon Post Office, Bellurgan Station
Dundalk (Market Square)-Corcreaghy (Connolly's)	26.11.45	Workhouse Cross, Knockbridge, Louth, Drumgowna Cross
Dundalk (Market Square)-Carlingford (Station Road)	1.12.45	Ballymascanlon, Bellurgan Station, Gyles Quay Cross
Drogheda (Bull Ring)-Woodtown Cross	19.1.46	Slane – Revoked 4.6.53
Drogheda (Bull Ring)-Ardee	14.4.46	Baltray, Termonfeckin, Clougherhead, Dunleer
Malinmore (Hotel)-Glencolumbkille (RC Church)	14.4.46	Direct Road Church bus Sunday only
Drogheda (Bull Ring)-Usher's Mill	15.4.46	Direct Road
Glenties Railway Station-Dungloe (Sweeney's Hotel)	1.5.46	Maas, Gweebara Bridge, Lettermacaward School, Doochary
Sligo (Quay Street)-Ballintrillick Creamery	1.6.46	Tullyhill Cross, Drumcliffe Post Office, Muninane Cross, Kieran's Bridge Tuesday and Saturday only
Ballybofey (Garda Station)-Letterkenny (Market Square)	1.7.46	Drumkeen
Cliffoney (Garda Station)-Ballyshannon (Market Yard)	7.10.46	Revoked 4.6.53
Cavan (Casement Street)-Ballyconnell (Main Street)	8.10.46	Expired 31.10.50
Ballybay Market Square-Cootehill Main Street	10.10.46	Operated on Fair Days
Cootehill Main Street-Ballybay Market Square	10.10.46	Cummery Cross, Anney Cross, Coyles Cross, McCabes Cross
Dundalk (Market Square)-Gyles Quay Cross	21.1.47	Ballymascanlon Post Office, Bellurgan Station, Annaghloughan
Glenties Railway Station-Portnoo (Hotel)	3.2.47	Maas expired 31.10.47
Monaghan Diamond-Carrickmacross Railway Station	3.2.47	Castleshane Post Office, Clontibret Cross, Castleblaney, Lisdoonan Cross
Glenties Railway Station-Lettermacaward School	4.2.47	Maas
Drogheda (Bull Ring)-Ardee (Campbell's Hotel)	18.2.47	Collon, Woodtown Cross, Drumconrath, Mandlestown Cross
Dundalk (Market Square)-Ardee (Campbell's Hotel)	18.2.47	Dunleer, Stabannon
Carrickmacross-Inniskeen Railway Station	11.3.47	Essexford – expired 31.10.57
Carrick-on-Shannon Station-Drumshanbo (High Street)	28.7.47	Leitrim
Ardee (Campbell's Hotel)-Collon (Garda Station)	22.9.47	
Dundalk (Market Square)-Louth	22.9.47	Knockbridge
Ardee (Railway Station)-Aclint's Cross	4.11.47	Tallonstown Cross, Drumconrath Cross
Ardee (Railway Station)-Churchtown Cross	4.11.47	Sniper Hill Cross, Glack Cross
Drogheda (Bull Ring)-Dowth Post Office	22.11.47	Dowth Cross, Sheep Grange Cross, Ballinacrag Cross
Donegal (Diamond)-Glenties (Cannon's Hotel)	15.12.47	Mountcharles, Inver, Dunkineely, Bruckless, Killybegs
Drogheda (Bull Ring)-Garristown (O'Connell's Shop)	20.12.47	
Drogheda (Geo.Square)-Greenmount/Boyne Linen Mills	2.2.48	Patrick Street, Scarlet, Street, Bredin Street, Stoney Lane
Ardara-Glenties	1.5.48	Expired 31.10.50
Cavan (Casement Street)-Ballinagh	1.5.48	Clarebawn Bridge, Keshill Cross
Ardara-Portnoo	2.6.48	Direct Road – Seasonal licence only
Drogheda-Blackhall Cross	19.6.48	Newtown Cross, Cartown Cross, Sandpit Ch, Blackhall Church
Dundalk-Kilcurry	4.7.48	Direct Road
Dublin (North Wall)-Amiens Street Station	17.7.48	Beresford Place, Store Street – Saturday only service for B&I Boat
Ardee (Campbell's Hotel)-Blackrock	8.8.48	Churchtown Cross, Louth, Knockbridge, Dundalk – Seasonal licence only
Carlingford-Greenore	8.8.48	Seasonal licence only – expired 7.8.58
Butlins (Mosney)-Gormanstown Cross	23.8.48	Seasonal licence only
Dungloe-Gweebarra Bridge	28.9.48	Service started due to Gweebara Bridge restrictions – Revoked 1.2.54
Drogheda-Gormanlough (Ryan's Pub)	2.10.48	Slane – Seasonal licence only Revoked 4.6.53
Ballyshannon Market Yard-Bundoran Railway Station	1.11.48	Direct Road
Drogheda-Duleek	6.12.48	Platin Cross
Drogheda-Kentstown RC Church	5.3.49	Duleek – Church bus Sunday only
Dublin Eden Quay-Balbriggan Main Street	30.5.49	Swords, Rush, Lusk, Skerries – Seasonal licence only
Annagasson (The Cross)-Dundalk (Market Square)	4.6.49	Castlebellingham
Killybegs (Railway Station)-Largey Village	5.6.49	Seasonal licence only – expired 4.6.51
Dublin Eden Quay-Butlins Mosney	8.6.49	Seasonal licence only – expired 7.6.56
Dundalk (Market Square)-Butlins Mosney	9.6.49	Seasonal licence only – expired 8.6.53
Dublin Airport-Butlins Mosney	11.6.49	Swords, Balbriggan Seasonal licence only
Culloville (Railway Station)-Carrickmacross (Main Street)	1.12.49	Capragh, Nancy Keenan's Cross
Dundalk (Market Square)-Carrickmacross Main Street	1.12.49	Ballykelly Cross, Corcreaghy
Carrickmacross (Railway Station)-Corcreaghy	3.12.49	Expired 31.10.50

Appendix D GNR Directory of Bus Routes		
Route	**Start Date**	**Route & Comments**
Grangebellew Cross-Drogheda (South Quay)	3.12.49	Ballymakenny Church, Kellystown School
Drogheda-Duleek Street Mel Factory	12.12.49	Mary Street, James Street, Bull Ring, Shop Street, Trinity Street
Killybegs Railway Station-Glencolumbkille Post Office	12.12.49	Kilcar, Carrick
Dundalk (Market Square)-Ballykelly Cross	30.1.50	Rice's Bridge – Revoked 4.6.53
Monaghan-Castleblaney	1.2.50	Ardaghy, Kilnacran, Scotch Corner
Dublin Eden Quay-Howth (East Pier)	7.4.50	Fairview, Dollymount, New Coast Road, Sutton
Dundalk (Market Square)-Red Barn Road	4.6.50	Crowe Street, Jocelyn Street, St Gerard's Square
Dundalk (Hughes Pk)-Quay Street	5.6.50	Hill Street, Demense, Market Square, Seatown Place
Dundalk (Market Square)-Quay Street	5.6.50	Crowe Street, Jocelyn Street, St Gerard's Square
Dundalk (Race Course Road)-Hughes Park	5.6.50	Newry Road, Bridge Street, Church Street, Market Square, Hill Street
Dundalk (Race Course Road)-Quay Street	5.6.50	Newry Road, Crowe Street, Roden Place, Seatown Place
Tenure Church-Drogheda (South Quay)	10.6.50	Mullary Cross
Bundoran (Station Road)-Knock	1.7.50	Sligo, Ballysodare, Charlestown – Seasonal licence only
Dundalk (Quay Street)-Ardee Terrace	13.11.50	Seatown Place, Market Square, Park Street, The Crescent
Dundalk (Quay Street)-Moira Terrace	13.11.50	Expired 31.10.54
Monaghan-Clogher Border	4.12.50	Tydavnet Post Office
Drogheda-Kilmoon Cross	6.1.51	Duleek – Revoked 4.6.53
Drogheda (Pearse Park)-Marsh Road	8.1.51	Glenview, Bothar Brugha, West Street, Bull Ring, James Street
Bundoran-Mullaghmore	1.6.51	Castlegal – Seasonal licence only
Bundoran-Rossnowlagh Strand	1.6.51	Ballyshannon – Seasonal licence only
Drogheda (Corner John Street)-Rosnaree Cross	30.6.51	
Drogheda (Newfoundwell Cross)-Mornington Tower Cross	15.7.51	Seasonal licence only – Revoked 30.6.56
Ballybay (The Square)-Shercock (Main Street)	21.7.51	Lackin Bridge
Donegal (Railway Station)-Ballyshannon (Market Yard)	3.12.51	Direct Road – Seasonal licence only
Dundalk (Market Square)-Castletown Cross	3.12.51	Clanbrassil Street, Bridge Street, Castletown Road
Dundalk (Market Square)-Carrickmacross (McMahon Street)	1.1.52	Channonrock, Inniskeen, Essexford
Greenore (Railway Station)-Dundalk (Market Square)	1.1.52	Crossalaney, Grange NS, Bellurgan
Cavan (Casement Street)-Oldcastle Railway Station	8.1.52	Crosskeys, Ballyjamesduff, Mount Nugent
Drogheda (Mell Factory)-Newfoundwell Corner	3.3.52	Trinity Street, Georges Square, Hardman's Gardens, Pearse Park
Butlins (Mosney)-Balbriggan	31.5.52	Seasonal licence only – expired 30.5.53
Bailieboro Main Street-Cavan Farnham Street	5.1.53	Stradone
Cavan-Bailieborough	5.1.53	Direct Road
Dublin Aston's Quay-Navan	5.1.53	Blanchardstown, Dunboyne, Dunshaughlin
Dublin Eden Quay-Baldoyle	5.1.53	Killester, Raheny
Dundalk (Market Square)-Greenore	5.1.53	Ravensdale – expired 31.10.57
Glenties Railway Station-Gweebarra Bridge	5.1.53	Extended to Lettermacaward 1.2.54 – expired 31.10.57
St Johnston-Murlog Church	29.3.53	Lynch's Cross, McKean's Cross, Clarke's Cross Church bus Sunday only
Dundalk Market Square-Waterworks Cross	5.4.53	Main Road
Dundalk (Fatima Pk)-Ardee Terrace	20.4.53	Moira Terrace, Market Square
Dundalk (Fatima Pk)-Market Square	20.4.53	Moira Terrace
Dundalk (Fatima Pk)-Quay Street	20.4.53	Moira Terrace, Market Square
Dundalk (Market Square)-Ardee Terrace	20.4.53	Direct Road
Sligo (Quay Street)-Bundoran	1.6.53	Drumcliffe, Grange, Cliffoney – Seasonal licence only
Killybegs-Carrick	20.6.53	Kilcar – Seasonal licence only
Drogheda (Duleek Street)-Bull Ring	7.9.53	James Street, Mary Street, St Moran's Terrace
Drogheda (Newfoundwell Corner)-Bull Ring	7.9.53	George's Square
Dundalk (Fatima Pk)-Brig-a-Crin Church	13.9.53	Expired 3.11.55
St Johnston (Main Street)-Lifford (Diamond)	1.11.53	Porthall Station Road Church bus Sunday only
Carrick-on-Shannon Station-Manorhamilton	11.1.54	Seasonal licence only – Revoked 10.12.54
Drumshanbo (Main Street)-Drumkeeran	11.1.54	Seasonal licence only – Revoked 10.12.54
Kinlough-Bundoran	11.1.54	Seasonal licence only – Revoked 10.12.54
Dublin Eden Quay-Baldoyle (Willie Nolan Road)	22.3.54	Killester, Raheny
Drogheda (Bull Ring)-Kilmoon Cross	14.8.54	Duleek
Carrickmacross-Castleblaney	6.9.54	Revoked
Carrickmacross-Castleblaney	6.9.54	Direct Road
Killybegs-Kilcar	6.9.54	Largey – Seasonal licence only
Castleblaney-McQuaids Cross	1.11.54	Direct Road
Dundalk-Boyle's Cross (Uncle Tom's Garage)	21.11.54	Direct Road

Appendix D GNR Directory of Bus Routes		
Route	**Start Date**	**Route & Comments**
Drogheda-Mullingar	14.2.55	Navan, Kells, Delvin (via Trim, Athboy on Tuesday, Thursday, Saturday only)
Dublin Eden Quay-Raheny (St Annes Estate)	28.2.55	Raheny Village
Drogheda (Bull Ring)-Skerries	1.5.55	Seasonal licence only
Cavan-Virginia Town	1.11.55	Kilnaleck, Ballyjamesduff
Drogheda (Newfoundwell)-Laytown	1.6.56	Mornington Tower – Seasonal licence only
Carrickmacross-Cavan	1.11.56	Cootehill
Dundalk (Market Square)-Dunleer	4.3.57	Direct Road – expired 31.10.57
Dublin Eden Quay-Howth (St Mary's Place)	1.5.57	Killester, Raheny, Sutton
Castleblaney-Cremartin Cross	28.6.57	Direct Road
Carlingford-Greenore	1.10.57	Direct Road
Carrick-on-Shannon Railway Station-Sligo (Quay Street)	1.10.57	Drumshanbo, Dowra, Drumkeeran, Dromahair. Partial SLNCR replacement service Tuesday, Thursday, Friday only
Carrickmacross-Ballybay Market Square	14.10.57	Castleblaney
Carrickmacross-Clones	14.10.57	Castleblaney, Ballybay, Swan's Cross, Newbliss
Cliffoney-Ballyshannon	14.10.57	Bundoran – Seasonal licence only
Clones-Cavan	14.10.57	Scotshouse, Redhills, Ballyhaise – railway replacement service
Cootehill-Swan's Cross	14.10.57	Rockcorry
Dundalk-Blackstaff Cross	14.10.57	McShane's Cross
Dundalk-Culloville Station	14.10.57	McShane's Cross, Blackstaff Cross
Monaghan-Glaslough	14.10.57	Silverstream Post Office
Dundalk (Market Square)-Workhouse Cross	22.12.57	Direct Road
Clones-Cootehill	3.1.58	Newbliss, Bog Cross
Drogheda-Garristown	14.4.58	Duleek, Boolie's Cross, Ardcath
Drogheda-Navan	14.4.58	Duleek, O'Brien's Cross, Rathdrina Cross, McGruder's Cross, Slane
Drogheda-Oldcastle	14.4.58	Slane, Navan, Kells, Virginia
Oldcastle-Kells	14.4.58	Virginia
Oldcastle-Virginia	14.4.58	Direct Road
Drogheda-Navan	19.4.58	Slane
Section 2-Northern Ireland Routes		
Belfast Queens Street-Lurgan	20.3.29	Broomhedge, Flatfield, Damhead, Maze
Belfast Queens Street-Lurgan	20.3.29	Aghalee, Lisburn
Lurgan-Kilmore	28.3.29	Thursday only
Dungannon-Fintona	6.5.29	Donaghmore, Castlecaufield, Ballygawley, Omagh
Warrenpoint-Kilkeel	5.6.29	
Portadown-Maghery	16.9.29	Birches – Saturday only
Belfast-Omagh	16.9.29	Portadown, Dungannon, Castlecaufield, Ballygawley
Omagh-Fintona	2.12.29	Halfway House
Portadown-Armagh	23.12.29	Loughgall
Portadown-Newry	23.12.29	Laurelvale, Tanderagee, Poyntzpass, Jerretspass
Portadown-Ahorey	23.12.29	Saturday & Sunday only
Markethill-Keady	23.12.29	Friday only
Belfast Queens Street-Diamond	1.1.30	Bell's Corner, Dundrod, Nutts Corner, Crumlin
Kilkeel-Lisnacree	6.2.30	Thursday & Saturday only
Belfast-Keady	18.3.30	Tanderagee, Markethill extended to Keady Friday only
Belfast-Markethill	30.3.30	Lisburn, Lurgan, Gilford, Tanderagee, Clare.
Lurgan-Aghalee	4.5.30	Whitehall
Lurgan-Letter Box	4.5.30	Whitehall – Sunday only service
Lurgan-Gawley's Gate	4.5.30	Thursday & Saturday only
Victoria Bridge-Aghyaran	8.7.30	Castlederg
Strabane-Aghyaran	10.7.30	Victoria Bridge, Castlederg
Newtownstewart-Castlederg	10.7.30	Ardstraw, Magheracreggan
Dungannon-Cappagh	1.3.31	Donaghmore – Thursday only
Portadown Railway Station-Town	18.5.31	
Omagh-Londonderry	7.6.31	Newtownstewart, Strabane, Bready Post Office
Armagh City-Armagh Railway Station	1.9.31	City Hall, Market Square, Irish Street
Armagh-Keady	2.11.31	Milford, Tassagh Bridge
Keady-Armagh	2.11.31	Drumhillery – Tuesday & Saturday only
Keady-Moy	2.11.31	Armagh – operated on Moy Fair Days only

Appendix D GNR Directory of Bus Routes		
Route	**Start Date**	**Route & Comments**
Keady-Armagh	2.11.31	Madden – Tuesday only
Dungannon-Ballygawley	17.6.32	Donaghmore – 2nd Friday of each month (Ballygawley Fair Day)
Aughnacloy-Fintona	17.6.32	Augher
Omagh Railway Station-Omagh Town	1.7.32	Via Northern Bank and Swinging Bars Weekdays only
Belfast-Londonderry	1.9.32	Strabane, Omagh, Dungannon, Portadown
Belfast-Keady	25.10.32	Gilford, Tanderagee, Markethill
Castlederg-Victoria Bridge	17.5.33	
Armagh-Lislea	4.6.33	Sunday only
Armagh-Milford	4.6.33	Sunday only
Keady-Darkley	4.6.33	Sunday only
Keady-Carnagh	4.6.33	Sunday only
Goraghwood (Railway Station)-Banbridge (Railway Station)	11.9.33	Newcastle/Banbridge train bus link to G'Wood (for Dublin) ceased 14.10.34
Keady-Newtownhamilton	9.4.34	Operated Newtownhamilton Fair Day only last Saturday in month
Laurelvale-Banbridge	1.4.35	Via Scarva Sunday only
Section 3 – Cross Border Routes		
Dundalk Railway Station-Newry Imperial Hotel	1.7.29	Ravensdale, Feede Cross, Flurrybridge
Dublin Eden Quay-Belfast College Square	4.9.29	Dundalk, Newry, Banbridge, Dromore, Lisburn Sunday only – Revoked 31.10.35
Dundalk-Newtownhamilton	7.7.30	Silverbridge later curtailed to serve only as far as Drumbilla Border
Sligo-Londonderry (Lorne Street)	22.9.30	Bundoran, Ballyshannon, Donegal, Stranorlar, St Johnston, Carrigans
Keady-Ballybay	2.11.31	Craeghanroe, Castleblaney
Monaghan-Armagh	2.11.31	Middletown
Armagh-Ballybay	2.11.31	Keady, Castleblaney
Enniskillen-Cavan	23.4.32	Swanlinbar former Phair Brothers licence – acquired operator
Cavan Railway Station-Enniskillen Railway Station	1.5.32	Belturbet, Ballyconnell, Bawnboy, Swanlinbar, Drumcard, Five Points
Monaghan-Fintona	17.6.32	Emyvale, Aughnacloy, Greystone, Augher
Dungannon-Monaghan	11.7.32	Greystone, Aughnacloy, Emyvale
Dundalk Market Square-Castleblaney West Street	25.7.32	via Ballinacarry Bridge for Culloville expired 31.10.54
Ballybay-Keady Market Square	25.7.32	Doohamlet, Castleblaney – Replaced by occasional licence service
Castleblaney West Street-Keady Market Square	25.7.32	Carrickalane, Creaghanroe
Ballybay-Armagh Railway Station	25.7.32	Castleblaney, Carnagh, Keady, Tassagh Bridge, Milford
Sligo GSR Station-Londonderry Lorne Street	25.7.32	Drumcliffe, Grange, Ballyshannon, Convoy, Raphoe, St Johnston, Carrigans
Donegal Diamond-Londonderry Lorne Street	25.7.32	Stranorlar, Convoy, Raphoe, St Johnston, Carrigans
Monaghan (Market Square)-Dungannon	25.7.32	Emyvale, Aughnacloy, Greystone – seasonal licence only
Omeath (Chapel)-Newry	25.7.32	via Direct Road to Newry Sunday only – Suspended 27.4.42 – Restored August 1944
Stranorlar-Londonderry	1.10.32	Via Lifford and Strabane licence – Revoked 1.1.39
Carlingford (Square)-Newry	17.12.32	North Commons, Sloan Road, Calvary Hill, Omeath
Armagh-Cavan	1.1.33	Ballybay, Cootehill
Dundalk Market Square-Newry Imperial Hotel	14.11.34	Ravensdale Post Office, Feede Cross, Flurrybridge
Ballybofey Garda Station-Londonderry Foyle Road Station	15.11.34	Stranorlar, Convoy, Raphoe, St Johnston, Carrigans
Londonderry Foyle Road Station-St Johnston Post Office	2.1.39	Carrigans National School journey
Strabane Railway Station-Lifford	22.9.39	Occasional licence 1939/44
Raphoe (Diamond)-Londonderry	15.12.47	St Johnston, Carrigans
Greenore (Railway Station)-Newry	1.1.52	Carlingford, Omeath – DNGR bus substitution service

Note

In the above table the date of 25.7.32 appears frequently. This was the appointed day in terms of the Irish Free State Road Transport Act 1932 by which all bus services must have been registered in order to comply with the terms of the act. This is not necessarily the date of commencement of a service as the service may have already existed prior to that date.

It is a matter of regret that, at the time of the demise of the Great Northern Railway Company, colour photography, at least by enthusiasts, was relatively uncommon. This section therefore includes a number of GNR vehicles post October 1958 and therefore might well be regarded as a 'Requiem to GNR'.

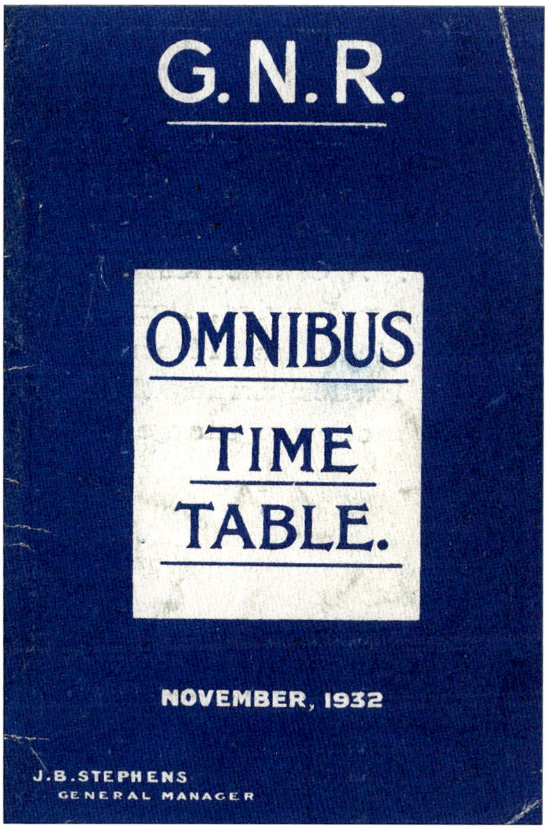

The four phases of GNR timetables; from top left February 1931 – July 1932, top right July 1932 – January 1933, bottom left January 1933 – September 1947 and bottom right, May 1948 – October 1958. *(SS)*

Original GNR livery

(Top) GNR Gardner No. 320 pulling out of Killybegs Station providing the onward bus connection for passengers and mails to Kilcar in July 1959. *(GL)*

(Centre) In August 1958 the very last GNR Gardner to be overhauled, No. 327 emerged from the works and this photograph records the moment. *(SS)*

(Lower) GNR Gardner No. 325 is seen, semi-retired parked adjacent to Donegal garage in July 1960 but still in full GNR livery. *(GL)*

Gardners in CIE livery

(Top) Three shades of GNR Gardners at Donegal – the front vehicle, No. 324 has just been overhauled prior to collection by the Transport Museum in Belfast and is resplendent in its freshly applied Oxford blue and cream livery, followed by a CIE two tone green and a red and cream liveried example. *(RP)*

(Centre) A red and cream GNR Gardner at Dundalk Station in July 1961. *(GL)*

(Lower) Twenty months after the CIE takeover Gardner No. 399 is seen at Stranorlar Station in the Donegal interpretation of the CIE livery, complete with 'Flying Snail' symbol. *(GL)*

(Top) Consecutively numbered Gardners 398 and 399 in two-tone green and primrose tours livery respectively at Donegal in 1961. *(AM)*

(Centre) A rear view of two Gardners, Nos. 386 and 387 which were converted to Ambulances, taken at Ballina Garage in 1965. Note the fitting of 'barn doors' to facilitate the loading and unloading of stretchers. *(GL)*

(Lower) The same two vehicles from the front. Ballina garage is to the left of the picture. *(GL)*

AEC Regal III

(Top) **AEC Regal III No. 423 at Drogheda Railway Station just days before the GNR takeover.** *(WM)*

(Centre) **Seen at CIE's Broadstone works on 19th July 1959 is AEC Regal No. 431, one of the half-dozen 'Southdown' type timber-framed 35-seat coach examples with full-width canopy.** *(GL)*

(Lower) **Front and rear profiles of two AEC Regals – No. 423 (left) and No. 430 (right) at Dundalk garage in 1965.** *(GL)*

Leyland Royal Tiger

Three views of Saunders-Roe Leyland Royal Tiger PSUC1/9 No. 225 as U225 with CIE. In this 1963 view (top) it is about to depart Busaras, Dublin for Carrickmoss and is still fitted with the roof mounted luggage rack. By 1970 the roof rack had gone (centre) in this view at Bray Station but the CIE 'broken wheel' logo had been applied. In the bottom view it is *en route* from Greystones to Bray. Conductors disliked these vehicles with their narrow gangways on the 7ft 6in wide bodies. *(GL – all)*

AEC Regal IV

(Top) AEC Regal IV No. 270 at Londonderry Foyle Road Station about to depart on a short working to St Johnson in 1957. *(SS)*

(Centre) Under CIE ownership these two AEC Regals became AU 334 and 338 and are seen inside Dundalk Garage in storage in July 1960, wearing the tours livery of primrose and lavender. Their use this year was confined to the months of August and September. *(GL)*

(Lower) Dundalk again and AEC Regal AU269 has just been painted into CIE red and cream in this 1961 view. The rear entrance has been retained. To the left side and rear of the bus is the former GNR stores. *(GL)*

(Top) By 1965 No. 344 (now CIE AU344) has gained a front entrance and has been converted for use by one person. It is sandwiched between a L&LSR Leyland PS2 and a Saunders-Roe bodied Leyland Royal Tiger outside the original County Donegal Railway Station at Letterkenny, which is still in use today as a Bus Éireann office. *(GL)*

(Centre) At Drogheda South Quay in 1963 AU 336 is parked next to another former GNR vehicle, AEC Regent No. 434. By now the Regal has lost its front bumper, revealing the cooling vents designed to improve airflow. *(GL)*

(Lower) This off-side view of No. 340, which is about to reverse into Dundalk Garage, clearly shows the engine cooling grills. *(GL)*

AEC Regent II & III

(Top) Still in GNR blue but without the coat of arms former No. 287, a 1947 AEC Regent II, is seen turning from O'Connell Street into Eden Quay in this 1959 Dublin view. *(GL)*

(Centre) The location is The Crescent, Dundalk, just across the road from the former GNR Dundalk Bus Office. Two AEC Regents may be seen; that in the foreground, No. 440 in the correct version of the CIE green livery, while in the background another Regent carries Dundalk's interpretation of the CIE livery of the time, with a light green roof. *(GL)*

(Lower) Former GNR AEC Regent III No. 438 carries the livery which began to be adopted in 1961 of monastral blue and cream in this view at Edward Street Railway Station, Newry. This location was also used by the UTA to garage buses as may be seen by the two Leyland PS1s behind the double-decker. *(GL)*

(Top) Another view of No. 438 in the blue CIE livery at Newry (note the different adverts) in the company of a former GNR AEC Regal. GNR regularly garaged buses in Northern Ireland to work cross-border services. *(GL)*

(Centre) Former AEC Regent III No. 440, one of the 1953 batch, carries its new CIE two-tone green livery at Dundalk. The intrusion of a side advertisement rather detracts from the lining out which has been applied. *(GL)*

(Lower) At CIE's works at Inchicore in 1970 former AEC Regent II No. 292 was in use in this livery as works transport. Alongside is the works fire engine. *(GL)*

1953 AEC Regent III

(Top) In 1953 GNR purchased its final batch of AEC Regents. Which were 8ft wide. Renumbered AR301 by CIE it is seen here in July 1959 at Eden Quay, Dublin in Dundalk's version of the CIE livery, the difference being the light green roof. This variation was interpreted by many as a final act of defiance by former GNR staff. *(GL)*

(Centre) Another 8ft wide AEC Regent was AR306, this time with the (correct) green roof. It is at South Quay, Drogheda. *(GL)*

(Lower) At Sutton Railway Station in 1959 is CIE R438, a 1949 Leyland PD2/3. It is operating on the tram replacement service No. 87 between Sutton and Baily Post Office. *(GL)*

CIE 'replacement' buses

Dundalk Bus Station in 1969, with examples of CIE Leyland Leopards classes C and E, which largely replaced the former GNR vehicles, flanking former AEC Regal 273 (by now AU273). *(GL)*

Also seen in 1969 is Cavan Garage with CIE C106 prominent and a rear view of former GNR AEC Regal 341. The building beyond it belonged to the local Ford dealer Jacksons, who for many years also ran buses. *(GL)*

GNR service vehicles

(Top) Garage tender No. 2 together with AEC Regal A430 at Dundalk in July 1965. *(GL)*

(Lower) Garage tender GT6 also in Dundalk, in 1969. It began its long career with GNR as a Leyland Lion bus in 1930 (as No. 110) and was converted to a lorry (No. 150) and eventually to a tender with de-mountable container which provided all manner of recovery equipment. *(GL)*

Railbuses

(Top) By the time this photograph was taken GNR railbus No. 8178 was now a Civil Engineer's departmental vehicle and is seen inside the Portadown engine shed of the GNR. The vehicle began life as an AEC 426, despite the Leyland Lion radiator now fitted. It was converted to railbus E, renumbered E2 in 1936 and again renumbered 1 in 1947. It is now preserved in the Ulster Folk and Transport Museum at Cultra. *(GL)*

(Centre) By 1959 former railbus No. 2, which had begun life as an AEC 416, becoming a railbus in 1944, having replaced an earlier model which had been destroyed in a collision that year, was being converted by CIE into a Civil Engineer's departmental vehicle. *(GL)*

(Lower) Another view of railbus 8178, this time at Goraghwood Station following the vehicle receiving a puncture to its front nearside rubber tyre, which occurred on 8th September 1963 and rendered it un-serviceable. It remained here for some time. *(GL)*

Sold out of service

(Top and centre) **Although the Hill of Howth tramway operated for the last time in May 1959, this was not to be the last time it would be possible to travel on No. 10, as following preservation and shipment to England it appeared in Blackpool's 75th anniversary celebrations. Note the longitudinal seating in the centre of the lower saloon, rather than being under the windows, thus allowing passengers to appreciate the spectacular views of Dublin Bay.** *(JAS both)*

After sale by the GNR, Gardner No. 208 (ZC 1576) passed to the SLNCR for a short period, before being sold again, this time to the Erne Bus Service of Carrigallen in whose livery it is seen. *(MC)*

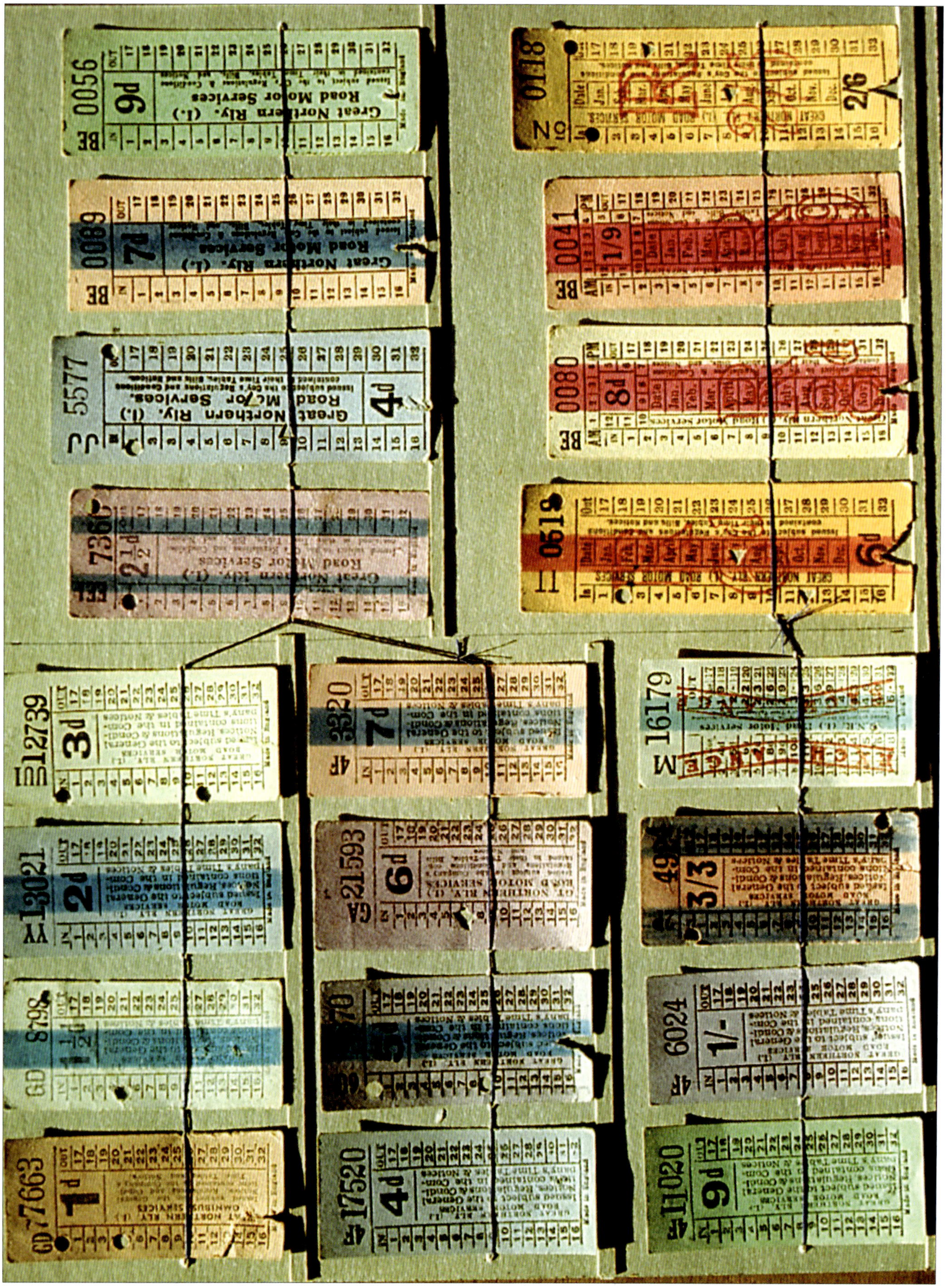

A selection of Road Motor Service Tickets. *(MC)*

GREAT NORTHERN RAILWAY

1953

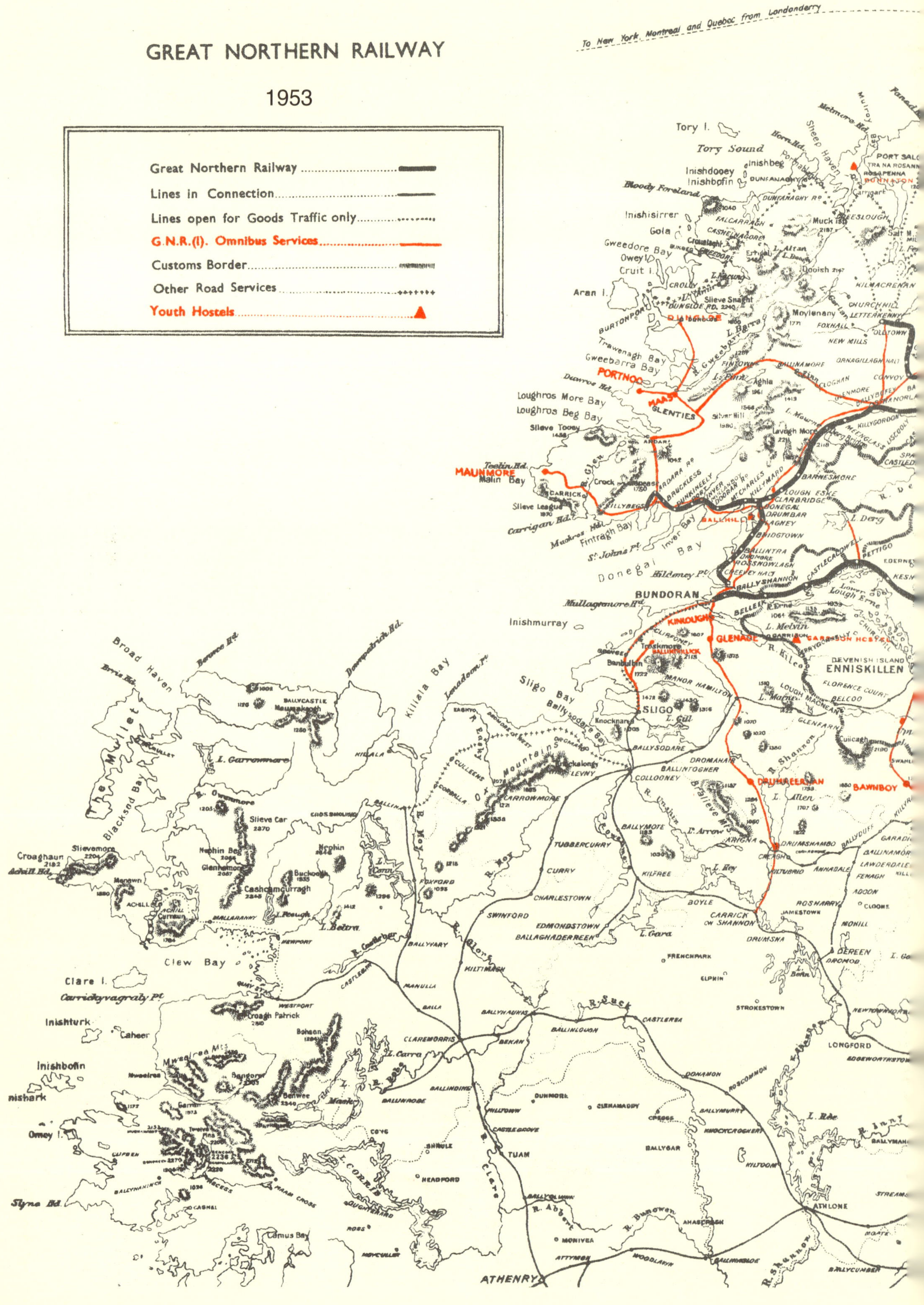